DISCARDED

Under the editorship of

WAYNE C. MINNICK

The Florida State University

Charlotte I. Lee
Northwestern University

ORAL INTERPRETATION

THIRD EDITION

HOUGHTON MIFFLIN COMPANY · BOSTON

CARL A. RUDISILL LIBRARY
LENOIR RHYNE COLLEGE

808.54
L510
82284
Feb. 1973

The letter to Mrs. Robert L. Stevenson is from *The Selected Letters of Henry James,* edited by Leon Edel. Copyright © 1955 by Leon Edel. Reprinted by permission of Paul R. Reynolds, Inc., 599 Fifth Avenue, New York, 17, New York.

"Hedda Gabler" by Henrik Ibsen, translated by William Archer (1904), is reprinted with the permission of Charles Scribner's Sons from *The Collected Works of Henrik Ibsen,* Volume X.

AUTHORS AND PUBLISHERS have permitted the inclusion of copyright material in this book with the understanding that these materials are for classroom and school use only. For other use, application should be made to the copyright holders as listed on the pages on which selections appear.

Copyright © 1965, 1959 by Charlotte I. Lee
Copyright 1952 by Charlotte I. Lee

All rights reserved, including the right to reproduce this book or parts thereof in any form.

PRINTED IN THE U.S.A.

PREFACE

This text on oral interpretation is based on the twofold conviction that the study of literature is a rewarding and challenging experience, and that sharing the results of such study with an audience gives motivation and focus to analysis, and pleasure and satisfaction in performance. Interpretation is built on scholarship, technical know-how, sensitivity, and the desire to share. It demands total synthesis.

Interpretation, as we shall use the term and as it has been accepted in academic circles, goes several steps beyond a more vocalization of silent reading. It requires an appreciation of one's material as a work of literary art, and the ability to communicate that work of art through voice and body. It demands both intellectual and emotional response from the interpreter, and a control and channeling of the understanding and emotion to elicit the appropriate response from the audience. It is with such completeness of understanding and skill in communication that this book is concerned.

The interpreter is an artist, revivifying one art through another. As a musician translates the written notes into sound and thus conveys the achievement of the composer to the listener, so the interpreter brings to life the printed symbols which have preserved the ideas and experiences of mankind for centuries. Interpretation is thus an art of *re-creation.* The instruments of communication are voice and body. But voice and body are *merely* instruments, and while they must be used with skill and ease, they must always be controlled by an alert and informed mind.

With a view to developing the necessary understanding and appreciation, this book lays considerable stress on analysis of organization, structure, style, and the various devices which writers use in non-fiction prose, the short story, drama, and poetry — from simile to cadence, from paragraph to rhyme. It attempts to teach the student how to evaluate material in terms of literary worth as well as audience appeal. It suggests ways to analyze pieces of literature and to examine similar selections comparatively. And it offers suggestions for preparing and presenting material to an audience.

The word "suggestions" must not be overlooked. There is great danger in being too specific or too dogmatic. Every piece of literature presents its own challenges and must be approached with an open, albeit informed, mind. There is no magic "how-to-do-it" formula. The basic principles of analysis and preparation presented in this book have proved useful, but they will vary in degree of usefulness from one work to another. If the interpreter prepares intelligently, applying what he has learned in careful analysis, he should be able to use his voice and body to serve the demands of the literature.

Part One is concerned largely with the analysis and interpretation of selections. Chapters One and Two establish broad fundamental principles common to all kinds of literature and thus serve as background for a more detailed examination of the various literary types in the sections which follow. Chapters Three and Four deal respectively with the aspects of body and voice which the interpreter must bring under control if he is to communicate effectively.

Part Two is devoted to the interpretation of prose. The first chapter examines the elements common to prose, with particular attention to non-dramatic writing, such as essays, biography, history, and letters. The second chapter deals with the function and dimensions of description. The third discusses the problems and advantages of narrative writing, and ends with a unit on Chamber Theatre.

Part Three is concerned with drama. The first chapter deals with the general characteristics of the genre. The second gives attention to character analysis and suggests ways of communicating motivation and individual traits. In these chapters, an attempt has been made to face squarely some of the technical problems which arise in the interpretation of drama: using (or not using) overt action, handling stage directions, picking up cues, and the like. In addition, Part Three reflects some of the current interest in "anti-plays," particularly the theatre of the absurd, as well as in the increasingly popular group interpretation of drama known as Readers Theatre.

Although numerous verse selections appear in earlier parts of the book, the interpretation of poetry *per se* is not discussed until Part Four. Experience shows that students are apt to distrust their ability to communicate poetry to others and to shy away from it until they have first "found" themselves in prose and drama. There is some justification for this feeling, since poetry carries structural discipline, rhythm, cadence, and condensation of emotion and idea to a higher degree than any other form of writing. Hence, in dealing with poetry the student encounters refinements of problems met in less complex form in prose and in drama. In Part Four, he learns how figures of speech function in a poem; how rhyme, tone color, and rhythm enhance meaning; how meter and cadence complement poetic language — in short, how the elements of poetry work together to produce a whole greater than the sum of its parts. Equally important, he learns that synthesis must follow analysis if the poem is to be re-created as a work of art.

The "Selections for Analysis and Oral Interpretation" at the end of each chapter were chosen with several considerations in mind: the interests of college students today; the challenge inherent in the selections — whether the interpreter would feel a sense of personal achievement in presenting them orally; a certain standard of literary excellence; the breadth and range of the selections — whether they would enlarge the student's understanding and introduce him to literature of many types and periods. The aim was to strike a balance between the well-known writers who are part of our literary heritage and the less well-known who are writing out of the experiences of our day. The humorous selections were included to demonstrate that neither the world nor the oral interpretation class need be a thoroughly solemn, sober place.

Suggestions for further reading are included at the ends of chapters where they seem relevant. They are selective rather than exhaustive and are intended to encourage the superior student to examine the ever-widening fields of literary criticism and aesthetics which are of particular interest to the interpreter. The books mentioned are easily available in most college libraries; in fact, the majority of them are now available in paperback editions as well.

The success or failure of this text depends in large measure on two elements which cannot be put down on the printed page. The first is the interest and enthusiasm of the individual student, without which any course is doomed from the beginning. The second is that invaluable and indefinable something which only an enthusiastic and dedicated teacher can give to any body of knowledge. If this text can serve as a guide and encouragement to student and teacher alike, it will have been well worth the hours spent in preparing it.

I am indebted to my colleagues throughout the country, and to their students, for sound criticism of previous editions of this text. The Third Edition reflects many of their opinions and critical judgments. My own students, too, made their contribution by asking intelligent questions which helped to clarify my thinking on theory and the practical application of that theory.

I am also indebted to the proprietors of copyright materials which are reprinted in this book, and to whom detailed acknowledgment is made elsewhere in these pages.

CHARLOTTE I. LEE

CONTENTS

PART 1

Basic Principles

1

A Beginning and An End

Interpretation is the art of communicating to an audience a work of literary art in its intellectual, emotional, and aesthetic entirety.

THE DEFINITION ANALYZED

Interpretation is the art of communicating . . . By its very definition, art implies skill in performance. It requires discipline and training in the use of the appropriate tools, intelligence, experience, and the ability to order both experience and response into meaningful form. The writer of a literary selection is the creative artist. He orders his ideas, words, sounds, and rhythms into a particular form. The interpreter, in turn, takes the symbols on the printed page and brings his own experience and insight to bear on the clues the author has given him. He then submits his experience and responses to the order imposed by the creative artist and assumes the responsibility of re-creating the total entity. This demands thorough analysis, painstaking rehearsal, and strict discipline in the use of voice and body. The oral interpreter's art, then, is comparable to that of a musician playing the work of an artist-composer.

The truest and finest art is disarming in its *seeming* simplicity. It makes its observers aware of the result, not of the means used to attain the result. Technical display is not art. Art implies the systematic application of knowledge and skill in effecting a desired result, and the desired result in interpretation is precisely the same as that of any other phase of speech — communication.

It is the perfect tribute when the members of the audience are so held by the material that they cannot immediately break the spell to applaud. When an audience says, "What a beautiful voice!" or "What graceful gestures!" the interpreter has failed. When the audience's attention is held by the effect of the material presented, the interpreter has succeeded. But this unobtrusiveness on the interpreter's part does not result from casual preparation, or from a feeling that, since the literature is the important thing, he need do no more than face his hearers, open the book, and open his mouth. On the contrary, it is the result of a preparation so thorough and a technique so perfectly coordinated that the audience cannot see the wheels go around.

. . . *communicating to an audience* . . . An audience may be one person or several thousand. No matter what the size or calibre of the audience, the interpreter's responsibilities are the same. As skillfully and subtly as he can, he must communicate what is on the printed page, making intelligent use of every detail to achieve the organic whole. The listeners' understanding, their mental and emotional response to the content and the form in which it is presented, depends to a large degree on the interpreter's ability to discover these elements himself and to project them satisfactorily.

How are these elements communicated to the audience? They are communicated by voice and body, working together and controlled by understanding of and concentration on the material. Consequently, the interpreter trains his voice and body so that they will respond unobtrusively to the requirements of the literature. He strives to eliminate mannerisms which may distract his audience. He is aware of the effect of posture, muscle tone, and general platform presence. He disciplines his physical action so that it aids his communication and in no way calls attention to itself. He works with his voice during practice periods so that he may be heard and understood. He is aware that he needs flexibility in range, force, stress, and volume if he is to do justice to the writing and bring out whatever strength and beauty the author has achieved through the sounds and relationships of the words.

The modern interpreter often chooses not to memorize his materials completely. The time that would be consumed in committing the words to memory can be better spent in study and in perfecting the techniques of communication. Technically speaking, it does not matter in the least whether the material is completely memorized or not. If it is, the interpreter must concentrate on communicating the total effect rather than on the act of remembering. If he has chosen not to memorize completely, he must be sufficiently free of the text to concentrate on communicating with the audience rather than on reading. By the time the material has been analyzed in detail, put back together again, and practiced conscientiously, it will be so firmly implanted in the interpreter's consciousness that an occasional glance at the page should suffice.

Whether he memorizes his selection or not, the modern interpreter has his book — or a typescript of it — with him during performance. Its presence serves two important purposes. First, it establishes the interpreter as the intermediary between the author and the audience. This is not to imply, however, that the interpreter has no more important part than to open his mouth and let the words from the printed page come out. His is the satisfaction of re-creation.

When we speak of the printed page, we are speaking of a tool, a medium. For neither the pages in a book nor the words on the page are the literary work of art. The printed page is merely a means of preserving word-symbols through which an author once set down as precisely as he could certain thoughts, emotions, and attitudes. The printed page is the record — what the interpreter works from; but it is not the thing itself. Through his voice and body the symbols on the page are revivified, and the ideas which they symbolize are re-created.

The second purpose which the presence of the book or manuscript serves is an aesthetic one. It alerts the members of the audience to the fact that the emotions presented are not in reality those of the person standing before them. Realizing this, they can respond without embarrassment. Moreover, it allows the audience to keep a degree of psychic and aesthetic distance, to respond to the literature out of their own experience without feeling that they are eavesdropping on a fellow human being. It enables them to respond to the literature instead of the performer. We have all, unfortunately, seen performers who are so emotionally involved that we are uncomfortable. The presence of the book or manuscript can *help* to avoid this, though the interpreter himself must keep his attention on *sharing* the author's response rather than demonstrating it.

. . . a work of literary art in its intellectual, emotional, and aesthetic entirety . . . The interpreter's concern is to communicate the total effect of the literary work of art. This does not mean that a work must be presented complete, or that excerpts cannot be used. It does mean that the various qualities which contribute to the total effect are to be seen in their proper relation to the whole. For purposes of analysis, it is convenient to break a work down into its parts, but it should always be kept in mind that such arbitrary division is only a device to facilitate understanding. We may conveniently speak of content and structure, of logical meaning and emotive quality. But this separation is useful only in the sense that it provides a way of getting at understanding. Content and structure do not in fact exist as separate entities; they form one organic whole. They must always be examined in relation to each

other in an attempt to arrive at the total achievement of the writer, which is undeniably more than the sum of its various parts. The interpreter must constantly put the material back together after each step in analysis.

Difficult as it is, then, to isolate and discuss separately certain aspects of a work of art, a full appreciation of the whole is enhanced by careful analysis of the particulars. In a general way, we may begin such an analysis by distinguishing the content from the structure of a piece of literature.

In the broadest sense, content has to do with what is being said; structure with the way it is said. Content has two aspects. The first is the *intellectual* or *logical aspect,* which is simply what the material "says." It is addressed to the mind, and involves understanding the meanings of the words and the relationships between words and groups of words. The other aspect of content is its *emotive quality,* the capacity of the meaning *and* sound to arouse pleasure or pain, to stimulate to activity or repose through association. But because words seldom have meaning independent of association, or emotion-arousing qualities without meaning, for all purposes except analysis the logical and emotional qualities of a work of art can never be completely divorced. Since understanding takes place on the intellectual and emotional levels simultaneously, the skilled interpreter must find out what the author is saying, experience emotionally what is said, and communicate his total response — mental and emotional — to the audience.

Structure is so closely interwoven with content that it is difficult to discuss either without doing violence to both. Structure embraces the organization and expression of the ideas, the choice of words, the relationship of the parts to each other and to the whole. It is concerned with the manner of expression, from simple lucidity to the most complex ornamentations of language. In prose, for instance, it includes the pattern of individual sentences as well as the effect created by several sentences in combination; in drama, the rhythm of the characters' speeches, the structure of the sentence or the poetic line, and the interrelationship of the speeches, scenes, and acts of the entire play; in poetry, all the contributions to the sound patterns, including stanzaic structure, scansion, rhyme, and length of line. These elements will be examined in more detail as each of these types of writing is discussed in later chapters.

. . . *aesthetic entirety* . . . embraces all the qualities which must be considered in appreciating a piece of writing as a successful work of literary art. These elements must always be evaluated in relation to each other and to the whole. "Aesthetic entirety" includes all the matters we have touched on above, plus many more which we shall talk about throughout this book. Aesthetics deals with the theory of the fine arts and the individual's response to them. Though it includes all areas of art, our concern will be, of course, primarily with literary art.

We are not ready to discuss the term "aesthetic" fully until we have used the tools of analysis to discover everything an author has put into a particular work and then performed the difficult but rewarding task of synthesis. At the moment, we need only be aware that there are aesthetic standards for the way the parts work together to create a literary whole, and that it is this *whole* which must be communicated to the audience with all its elements intact and correlated.

In short, it is the task of the interpreter to perceive and to communicate to his audience the intellectual, emotional, and aesthetic qualities of his material, not as separate entities but as a unified and coordinated whole. His aim is to present the material in its totality. His responsibility is to communicate the work of another, not to exhibit his own talents, sensitivity, or erudition. The writer is the creative artist; the interpreter, the re-creative artist.

SOURCES OF MATERIAL

The interpreter has an almost unlimited range of material from which to choose. He may use prose, poetry, or drama. He need only consider the literary worth of the selection, its suitability for his audience, and his own interests. From the experienced interpreter's point of view, this freedom of choice is a distinct advantage, but it may present the student with his first problem. From the wealth of available material, how is he to select something for his early assignments?

The first question, obviously, is where to look. Anthologies provide helpful short cuts in the search for material. The interpreter will find collections of prose — essays, short stories, humorous and satirical pieces, biographies, diaries, even novels, and so on through the entire range of prose writing. He will find poetry classified by kind, as lyric, narrative, humorous, didactic; by period or nation, as Elizabethan, Victorian, modern American, and the like; and by subject or spirit, as poems of nature, of Christmas, of patriotism. If he wishes to try drama, there are any number of volumes which include entire plays, both one-act and full-length, or selected scenes. There are also anthologies which cut across these classifications — chronological surveys of a literature, or anthologies of regional writing, for example; and of course there are volumes of selected works of individual authors. Several useful anthologies are listed at the end of this chapter; dozens more are available in inexpensive editions in any bookstore or in hardback editions in any library. They are especially valuable to the beginning student of interpretation because they offer a wide selection within a single volume. After the first few assignments, he will have a better idea of the kind of material that appeals to him and where to look for it.

The student interpreter should begin by asking himself what interests him most. Is it the city or the country? Some exotic part of the world or his own home state? Perhaps he is much more interested in people than in places. What kind of people? In what circumstances? Has he been excited about a book he has read recently? If so, he should go back and read it again. It may do nicely for his first assignment.

CHOOSING THE SELECTION: THREE TOUCHSTONES

The advice to choose material for the first assignment because of its interesting subject matter does not imply that no effort should be made to evaluate its literary worth. On the contrary, throughout this book there will be constant concern with evaluation and analysis of material. Though there are numerous ways to treat any subject, some are more effective than others.

Most of us are attracted first to a piece of writing because of what it says — by its content. As our sophistication increases, we appreciate more fully the complexities of meaning and structure.

Let us assume that the student has made a tentative choice of material, or that he has narrowed the possibilities down to two or three selections equally appealing as far as content is concerned. Before making a final decision, he wishes to evaluate his choice as a piece of literature. As his first touchstones, he will do well to consider three factors — *universality, individuality*, and *suggestion.*

Universality does not mean that the material will immediately appeal to all persons regardless of their intellectual or cultural backgrounds. It means, rather, that the idea expressed is potentially interesting to all people because it touches on a common experience. The emotional response it evokes is one most readers (or listeners) have felt at one time or another — love or hate, hope or fear, joy or despair.

Literature draws its material from life, but literature is not *exactly like* life. A writer selects and controls attitudes and motivations. He imposes order on the flux and change of human existence. And he gives us clues to direct us in relating our own experience to the order he has selected. Even deliberately distorted events can have relevance to our existence. When writing has universality, the interpreter will be able to call upon his own background and experience to help him respond to such writing. When he communicates all the levels of meaning to his audience, they in turn will have a basis for identification with their own experiences.

The second of these touchstones of good writing is individuality—the writer's fresh approach to a universal subject. It is revealed in his choice of words, his images, and his method of organization. In order to decide whether or not the author has handled his subject with individuality, the interpreter needs to have some acquaintance with a wide variety of literature. It takes time and experience to be able to recognize individuality. Gradually, however, the student will see that it results in large part from the author's selectivity and control and is reflected in both content and structure.

The subtlest and most rewarding writing is characterized by suggestion. It leaves the reader something to do: it does not tell him quite everything. This does not mean that the writing is obscure. It means, rather, that the author has chosen references and words which allow the reader to enrich the subject matter from his own background. There must, however, be a sufficiently clear set of suggestions for the imagination to follow. Frequently, considerable analysis will be necessary to find and properly use these directions; but once the possibilities for relevant association are realized, the writing continues to grow in meaning and in emotional impact for the interpreter and his audience.

It is obvious, of course, that these three touchstones — universality, individuality, and suggestion — are closely related and serve to enhance and balance each other in effective writing: the idea is drawn from an experience which all men are able to share; the method of expressing the idea is different from that used by other authors; and the suggestion of associated ideas and responses points the way for the imagination to follow and allows for continuing enrichment of the various levels of meaning. Sometimes these touchstones are not present in a selection in equal force, nor is it necessary that they should be. But if any one of them is totally absent or patently weak, the interpreter will do well to look elsewhere for material if he wishes to interest and move his audience.

By way of illustration, let us look at two brief poems, one by Helen Hoyt and one by Emily Dickinson. Each contains an intensely personal experience and is written in the first person.

The Sense of Death

Since I have felt the sense of death,
Since I have borne its dread, its fear —
Oh, how my life has grown more dear
Since I have felt the sense of death!
Sorrows are good, and cares are small,
Since I have known the loss of all.

Since I have felt the sense of death,
And death forever at my side —
Oh, how the world has opened wide
Since I have felt the sense of death!
My hours are jewels that I spend,
For I have seen the hours end.

Since I have felt the sense of death,
Since I have looked on that black night —
My inmost brain is fierce with light
Since I have felt the sense of death.
O dark, that made my eyes to see!
O death, that gave my life to me!

HELEN HOYT

Before we look at the second poem, a word of explanation may be in order. Miss Dickinson did not give her poems titles and indeed never readied them for publication. Consequently, there are several versions of some of the poems, each differing in punctuation and even in word choice. Furthermore, Miss Dickinson's use of capital letters and hyphens is thoroughly unique.

I felt a Funeral, in my Brain,
And Mourners to and fro
Kept treading — treading — till it seemed
That Sense was breaking through —

And when they all were seated,
A Service, like a Drum —
Kept beating — beating — till I thought
My Mind was going numb —

From *The Home Book of Modern Verse,* edited by Burton E. Stevenson. Copyright renewed in 1953 by Burton E. Stevenson. Reprinted by permission of Morgan Guaranty Trust Company of New York as Trustee of the Burton E. Stevenson Endowment for Children.

And then I heard them lift a Box
And creak across my Soul
With those same Boots of Lead, again,
Then Space — began to toll,

As all the Heavens were a Bell,
And Being, but an Ear,
And I, and Silence, some strange Race
Wrecked, solitary, here —

And then a Plank in Reason, broke,
And I dropped down, and down —
And hit a World, at every Crash,
And Got through knowing — then —

EMILY DICKINSON

The universality of the fact of death or the effect of death cannot be denied. However, these two poems present this universal experience in markedly different ways. In the first place, Miss Hoyt is talking about the aftermath of *having sensed* death — probably physical death. Miss Dickinson is talking about the period *of the sensing* — and probably about despair, a kind of spiritual death so numbing and soul-shattering that it became a "funeral" in her brain. Miss Hoyt uses straightforward language and sentences loosely linked together without a steady progression of thought. Miss Dickinson also uses straightforward language, but she introduces an extended metaphor which gives pace and progress to her writing. Finally, Miss Hoyt draws definite, even moralistic, conclusions. Miss Dickinson merely describes the experience and draws no conclusions.

Miss Hoyt obviously wishes to place death and a resultant acute appreciation of life in sharp contrast. A quick count reveals that half the lines are concerned with death and half with life — a very comfortable balance. And yet the distinct impression remains that this poem is more about death than life.

She asks us to take "Since" in the sense of "after" as well as in the sense of cause and effect. She repeats her title as six of the eighteen lines of the poem, and approximates it by parallel construction in three more. Such repetition could be most effective in creating a driving, insistent impact. However, the phrase "felt the sense of death" does not cut into our consciousness with much force. The word "sense" implies recognition or perception. It is quite possible to "feel" a "perception," of course, but let us look at the details which she has chosen to give us this perception of death. Death is characterized by "dread," "fear," "forever at my side," "the hours end," "black night" and "O dark." None of these references is fresh or individual. Each has been used in the same connection for so many centuries that it has become trite. Taken separately and skillfully developed, each could have a wealth of suggestion, but Miss Hoyt gives us no time or incentive to establish an individual identification with what the "sense" of death was for her, or indeed might be for us.

Admittedly, Miss Hoyt's insistent use of "Since" in nine of the eighteen lines clearly tells us that the experience of sensing death led her to a new awareness of the value of life. Unfortunately, her references to life are equally vague and familiar. Life is referred to in "grown more dear," "Sorrows are good," "cares are small," "world has opened wide," "hours are jewels that I spend," "inmost brain is fierce with light," "eyes to see" and "gave my life to me." "Sorrows" is so inclusive and allows for such a weight of personal association that we cannot fix on the paradox of sorrows being "good" before we are whisked on to "cares" which are "small." Presumably, this line is intended to set up a balance, but it does not quite come off, partly because of the inclusiveness and permissiveness of "sorrows" and "cares," and partly because even small cares are not "good" as she asks us to believe sorrows have become. The use of the singular "sorrow" and "care" would at least have allowed us to accept these terms in a more abstract sense, and hence to identify more easily with the emotional implication. There is, too, a disturbingly familiar ring in "hours are jewels" and in the verb "spend." Though it may be quibbling to say that one does not "spend" jewels unless one lives in a medieval economy, nevertheless the association here is strained. The phrase "inmost brain is fierce with light" is probably the strongest line of the poem, particularly since Miss Hoyt has carefully set it against "black night." But again, it goes nowhere — except back to the already quite familiar refrain.

Further study of this poem will reveal little individuality, either in the selection of details or the way they are expressed. The element of suggestion is also poorly established — beyond the basic premise that after one comes close to death, whether in the actual physical sense or in having been made aware of its omnipresence, life becomes more precious. The words and figures of speech chosen to develop this premise lack the force, freshness, sharpness of focus, and emotive quality to make us feel that the poet has said something important in a way we have never quite thought of before.

Miss Dickinson also begins her poem with "I felt," but the clear positioning in time past and the implied completion of the event put it firmly in perspective without the vague, continuing "Since I have . . . ." Moreover, we are at once drawn into strong suggestion with "funeral." A funeral carries such a complex weight of values and images that we are bombarded by an association of grief, dignity, ritual, the presence of the body, and a mixture of respect and grim, formal, finality. To *feel* a funeral goes beyond merely attending one. And to feel a funeral in the brain goes still further. We are immediately aware of a new and individual approach to the universal subject of death — of spiritual death which destroys the life of the senses, crushes hope, and even denies the power of the soul.

We are given time to develop the complexity suggested here, our focus sharpened by the mourners going to and fro and by the sound they make "treading — treading." We are then returned to sensation in the last line of the first stanza. Two suggested interpretations of this line, rather than being contradictory, provide a thin thread of suspense, strengthened by "till it seemed." On one level "Sense" may be taken to mean the mind bending under the strain of the "treading." This interpretation is strongly suggested by "Brain" in the opening line. But Miss Dickinson may also mean that awareness — "Sense" — had become so acute that the sensation was unbearable. These two interpretations are not mutually exclusive, and both can well operate here in a deliberate and disturbing ambiguity.

The balancing of the concrete elements of a funeral service with the sensation felt in the brain continues to the last line of the third stanza. It is held together and kept vivid by a strict chronological progression, as well as by constant references to sound, already prepared for in "treading — treading." Sound reaches an almost unbearable intensity as "Space — began to toll," and becomes overwhelming in the opening lines of the next stanza. Our attention is snatched from this climax of sound by "and Silence," which by its very contrast is equally deafening.

At the same time the mourners and the pallbearers disappear abruptly, leaving the senses "solitary." But the experience does not stop there. It continues in a swift downward pattern, suggesting the lowering into the grave and much more. The breaking "Plank in Reason" suggests a wealth of associations and adds still another dimension to the horror of the drop "down, and down — " which culminates in the highly graphic "hit" and "Crash" in the next to last line. The repeated use of "and" involves us in this swift and helpless dropping.

The last line, like several of the others, carries deliberate ambiguity and moves on more than one level. "Got through" may mean *finished* knowing in the human manner, as well as *broke through* into a superhuman or mystical knowledge possible only after death or a great spiritual crisis. The " — then — " functions on more than one level also. It completes the chronological progression; it terminates the immediate recorded experience; it teases us with a hint that there was more. A skilled interpreter can convey this multiplicity of meanings to his audience.

In our brief analysis of Miss Hoyt's poem, we criticized the lack of strength in her balancing of life and death. Miss Dickinson is not talking about life and death as contrasting states, but she manages very skillfully to keep us aware of the world of the living. The reference to those who are attending the "funeral" which she felt in her brain is strong through the first three stanzas, but held constantly within the framework of her point of view. Even in the sensation responses there is a quality of living awareness. "Sense," "Mind," "Soul," "Being," "Ear," "Race," and "Reason" all relate to but do not parallel "knowing" in the final line. There is also an alive, human quality in "hit a World," and "every Crash," because they are so essentially physical.

Thus from the opening line we are aware of a fresh, individual approach to the sensation Miss Dickinson is writing about. It catches and holds our interest because it is an unusual but certainly acceptable way of talking about a subject whose universality cannot be denied. It is a succinct, compressed statement which cuts into our awareness and increases our understanding.

During the discussion of Miss Dickinson's poem we mentioned the term "deliberate ambiguity." Ambiguity is sometimes confused with lack of clarity, but the term as it is used in modern literary criticism means "having more than one possible meaning, all of which are relevant and congruent within the organic whole of the piece of writing." Ambiguity may result in some obscurity, but it must not defy careful study or split the literary selection into incompatible segments. The kind of ambiguity we have been discussing is one of the richest sources of suggestion for the very reason that it does not narrowly circumscribe the experience of the poem.

Miss Hoyt used outworn and too-familiar references to suggest the terror of death and the glory of life. Miss Dickinson used images which stirred the senses and caused us to respond emotionally and physically. At the same time, she engaged our minds by juxtaposing unexpected and strongly suggestive words. Almost any line will serve as an example, but two of the most striking are the opening line and the reference to "a Plank in Reason." At its best, then, suggestion takes us beyond the poem without taking us out of the poem. Suggestion and individuality go hand in hand.

There are numerous matters which we have completely ignored in our evaluation of these two poems. We shall refer to them in succeeding chapters when we work with analysis. It was not our intention — although it was a temptation — to do more than illustrate how the three touchstones of universality, individuality, and suggestion can operate within a piece of literature.

✶ Bibliography

As we mentioned within the chapter, there are innumerable anthologies, many of them in inexpensive editions, where the interpreter will find a wealth of material to choose from. Also, most of the current textbooks listed at the end of the Appendix contain a wide variety of selections. One anthology in particular, however, is designed explicitly for the interpreter.

Bacon, Wallace A., and Robert S. Breen. *Literature for Interpretation.* New York: Holt, Rinehart and Winston, Inc., 1961.

Contains prose fiction, poetry, letters, diaries, and drama. Organized by type and chronology.

The student will find help in clarifying terms and in understanding the various approaches to criticism and analysis in the following books. Each contains an extensive bibliography.

Barnet, Sylvan, Morton Berman, and William Burto. *A Dictionary of Literary Terms.* New York: Little, Brown and Company, 1960.

A paperback of brief definitions and cross references.

Beckson, Karl, and Arthur Ganz. *A Reader's Guide to Literary Terms.* New York: Farrar, Straus and Company, 1960. The Noonday Press, N203.

Similar to the title above but somewhat more complete.

Butcher, Samuel Henry. *Aristotle's Theory of Poetry and Fine Art, with a Critical Text and Translation of the Poetics.* Fourth Edition. New York: Dover Publications, 1951.

Readable translation of Aristotle's classic study with an essay on Aristotelian criticism by John Gassner.

Crane, R. S. (ed.). *Critics and Criticism.* Chicago: University of Chicago Press, 1952. Phoenix Books Edition, abridged, P15, 1960.

A collection of essays by eminent critics of the "Chicago school" of criticism.

Frye, Northrop. *The Well-Tempered Critic.* Bloomington, Indiana: Indiana University Press, 1963.

A look at some of the diverse approaches to literary criticism currently in vogue. Contains sound and workable conclusions.

Gardner, Helen. *The Business of Criticism.* New York: Oxford University Press, 1963.

A defense of the historical method of criticism and a plea for the re-alliance of criticism with scholarship.

Gilbert, Allan H. (ed.). *Literary Criticism.* Vol. 1, Plato to Dryden; Vol. 2, Pope to Croce. Detroit: Wayne State University Press, 1962.

Brief, helpful comments on excerpts from the great critics. Extended bibliographies for each period plus a general bibliography. Carefully indexed for cross-reference.

Hall, Vernon, Jr. *A Short History of Literary Criticism.* New York: The Gotham Library, 1963.

A survey of the history of literary criticism from Plato to the New Critics. Separate chapters on the literary thought of Marx, Darwin, and Freud.

Hyman, Stanley Edgar. *The Critical Performance: An Anthology of American and British Literary Criticism of Our Century.* New York: Vintage Books, 1956.

Essays by outstanding contemporary critics.

Kaplan, Charles (ed.). *Criticism: Twenty Major Statements.* San Francisco, Chandler Publishing Company, 1964.

Representative essays on criticism from Plato to T. S. Eliot.

Shipley, Joseph T. (ed.). *Dictionary of World Literature: Criticism-Forms-Techniques.* Second Edition. New York: Philosophical Library, Inc., 1945.

A complete, scholarly sourcebook of terms and writers.

Smith, James Harry, and Edd Winfield Parks (eds.). *The Great Critics: An Anthology of Literary Criticism.* New York: W. W. Norton and Company, Inc., 1951.

Brief excerpts and comments on the theories of critics from Aristotle to the mid-twentieth century.

Wimsatt, W. K., Jr., and Cleanth Brooks. *Literary Criticism: A Short History.* New York: Alfred A. Knopf, Inc., 1957.

A clear, succinct account of the development of the field of literary criticism.

2

Analyzing the Selection

In the preceding chapter the three touchstones of universality, individuality, and suggestion were used in comparing two short poems. Even so brief an examination revealed some differences between the two and served as a starting point for the interpreter who needs to know how to choose a selection to which he can respond and which will satisfy his audience by providing a fresh, rich universal experience.

After making his selection, the interpreter must thoroughly investigate everything to be found within the particular piece of literature itself. He must know precisely what the author has given him to work with. Only when he fully understands the author's achievement can the interpreter decide how he will use his techniques to re-create that achievement for his audience.

The public speaker must be constantly concerned with the selection, arrangement, and expression of ideas in order to win a desired response. The interpreter, by contrast, is relieved of the problems of organization and style. The author has already taken care of those matters for him. He must, however, accept the responsibility for discovering and making proper use of the author's organization and method of presentation.

First, the interpreter must make every effort to find out precisely what the author is trying to say. He may easily understand the general meaning of a selection and yet find some specific lines or phrases that are not wholly clear. If so, he must look up the unfamiliar words and references; he cannot afford to gloss over them. The word or allusion is there because the author felt that it best expressed exactly what he wished to say. For the author, it was not *almost* the right word; it was *precisely* the word he wanted. Consequently, the interpreter cannot hope to achieve the author's full purpose if he has only a vague idea of the definitions or connotations of the words. In fact, he may even distort an idea if he mistakes the meaning of a word or phrase.

The dictionary is, of course, the first source the interpreter should consult when he is unsure of a word. The dictionary gives primarily *denotative* meanings — what the word *denotes explicitly.* For example, it *defines* "funeral" as "the ceremonies connected with the burial or cremation of the dead; obsequies."[1] And it defines "obsequies" as "a funeral rite or ceremony."[2] But of course we all know perfectly well what a funeral is.

Nevertheless, as we looked at the word in Emily Dickinson's poem in the preceding chapter, a cluster of associations began to grow out of our experience with "funeral." Gradually, the word began to mean more than the bare dictionary definition. The "more" was the *connotative* meaning. To connote means to "suggest or convey (associations, overtones, etc.) in addition to the explicit, or denoted, meaning. . . ."[3] Thus connotative meaning is an associated meaning and is often based on subjective values. The successful writer gives his reader enough clues to the way he wants the word taken so that the connotative meaning is *not* entirely subjective. We must remember that the definition says "suggest or convey . . . *in addition* to," not "instead of." We will have more to say about connotation when we examine the various ways it operates in the major types of literature. It is most important in a consideration of the emotive quality of content, but it must not be overlooked or misunderstood in getting at logical content as well. When a writer selects a particular word from several possible choices, he does so because that word conveys something over and above what it "means." What that something else is, what special flavor it adds to the whole, is for the interpreter to ferret out and convey to his audience.

Closely allied to connotative meaning is the function of allusions. Allusions are references to persons, places, or events, real or mythological, which call up relevant associations. They are useful because in a word or phrase they can establish an entire complex of connotations. Tennyson's "Ulysses" and Auden's "Musée des Beaux Arts," for example, (see pages 67 and 42) are both based on allusion.

ORGANIZATION OF IDEAS

After making sure of the meanings of the words, the interpreter must then examine the organization of ideas. Most material divides rather easily into three parts: the introduction or "lead-in" portion, the body

[1] *Webster's New World Dictionary of the American Language,* College Edition. Cleveland and New York: The World Publishing Company, p. 587.
[2] *Ibid.,* p. 1013.
[3] *Ibid.,* p. 311

of the material, and the conclusion or "tying-up" unit. Obviously, the body of the material contains the main point the author wishes to make. However, the selection and arrangement of details and ideas in the introductory unit is important as preparation for the audience as well as for the interpreter.

Authors use various means of catching and holding a reader's interest in the introductory sections. It is the interpreter's responsibility to discover what method the author has used and through his technique to make it work in performance. The writer may tell a story to introduce the situation. He may begin with a description, or use a purely explanatory or expository introduction. In any case, the interpreter must ask himself, "How does the author lead into the main point he wishes to make?" "Where does the lead-in end and the main point begin to emerge?"

The same questions need to be asked about the conclusion. Where has the author made his point, and to what use has he put the material which follows this focal point? He may conclude with a summary, or he may end with narrative or description. It is the interpreter's problem to discover the purpose of each unit of the material and use it effectively.

When the interpreter has discovered the divisions and progressions of thought within the material, he must then examine the details of organization within each separate unit. This is important if the listeners are to perceive each section in its proper relation to every other section.

Within each unit there are "key" sentences or phrases upon which the thought progression depends. They may contain a new idea or another aspect of an idea introduced previously. The interpreter must know the position and function of each "key" so that he can establish it clearly in the minds of his audience, in its proper relationship to all the other phrases and sentences and to the whole unit.

As the interpreter discovers the "key" details within the introduction, body, and conclusion of the selection and evaluates each one in its relationship to the whole, he will become aware that they vary in degree of importance. There are often several minor climaxes leading up to and/or following the major climax. A climax may be the culmination of the logical content, the high point of emotional impact, or a combination of both. Thus we may speak of *logical* climax and *emotional* climax, remembering again that this separation is only for convenience in analysis, and that ultimately we shall put them back together as they operate within the whole.

In a play or story, the logical climax is often called the crisis. It is that point at which the conflict becomes so intense that a resolution must occur, after which only one outcome is possible. In an essay, the logical climax occurs when the writer makes his main point with such clarity that his conclusion is inevitable. In a poem, it is the point at which he completes the logical development upon which the emotional progression is based.

The emotional climax is the moment of highest emotional impact and involvement for the reader. If this seems to be a completely subjective matter, we must not forget that the writer gives us clues to follow. If our analysis has been careful and we are letting the author have his way, we will seldom fail to be moved most strongly at the point of emotional climax. The important consideration here is to be sure that we are taking into account the *whole* of the selection in our response. As we noted in Chapter 1, there are many degrees of emotion. The emotional climax may be as gentle as those in the two Frost poems at the end of this chapter, or as dramatic as that found in the account of Mary's execution in "The New World" (see page 39). If only part of a long selection is to be used, locating the climax or climaxes within that unit is especially important if the audience is to feel that it has received a complete, unified experience which reached a point of fulfillment.

Often the highest emotional intensity will come at the logical climax. Occasionally, however, this is not the case. The logical climax may precede the emotional high point and prepare for it. This will be true, for instance, when the emotional climax depends upon a character's or writer's response to a completed cycle of events. On the other hand, if the outcome of events depends upon a character's emotional reaction, the emotional climax will precede the logical one, as it does in Miss Dickinson's poem where the impact of space, silence, and solitude precedes the completion of the fall. This dual aspect of climax may seem difficult to handle, but complete understanding reinforced by experience will enable the interpreter to cope with the problem. It is important to remember that literature moves on several levels and consequently may achieve its logical climax in one place and its emotional climax in another, although neither may be said to be independent of the other. The interpreter must always remember to put the material back together after each step in analysis, so that he may look again at the whole as a guide to the use of his own techniques.

The logical climax, for instance, will probably need a particularly high degree of mental directness. On the other hand, if the interpreter is driving too hard at the listeners' minds, the emotional climax may suffer. The audience will receive the full emotional impact only if the interpreter himself is responding as he reads. This does not mean that he pulls out all the stops and bursts into tears or shakes his fists in fury. He must, however, train himself to respond in such a way that his muscle tension is in harmony with what the words are saying. The interpreter who reads only with his voice and his mind may interest his listeners, but he will seldom move them.

THE AUTHOR'S ATTITUDE

The next consideration is the author's attitude toward what he is saying. Attitude reflects the author's relationship to his subject matter or to his audience, or both. All the elements which indicate attitude go to determine the *tone* of a piece of writing. Does the author intend the material to be taken literally, or is he appealing primarily to the imagination? Is he being humorous, serious, satiric, bitter, or completely objective in his comments? He gives his readers numerous clues. One of the most important is the title. Sometimes a writer will indicate quite clearly in his title where he wants the focus of attention, as does Clayton Long in "Deer in the Surf" (see page 37). Robert Frost gives us his conclusion in the title "For Once, Then, Something" (see page 35). W. H. Auden suggests a possible inspiration for his poem, as well as a symbolic level of meaning, in the title "Musée des Beaux Arts" (see page 42).

The author reveals his attitude in large part by his choice of words. Sometimes they are filled with connotative meaning, so that the reader's natural response to the situation is heightened and carefully channelled in a particular way. Sometimes they are incongruous for the subject matter itself, and the reader becomes aware that the author is making a comment or value judgment as he progresses. This is true of the selection from Bergen Evans' *The Natural History of Nonsense,* which we shall examine later (see page 138). James Thurber obtains much of his humor from his matter-of-fact treatment of preposterous events. Emily Dickinson chooses "cordial" social words to describe her encounter with death in "Because I Could Not Stop for Death" (see page 49). Robert Frost blends scientific words with informality as he addresses the star in "Choose Something Like a Star" (see page 34).

In short, when considered in relation to the universal implications of the subject matter, the author's style, which includes his choice of words and the way he puts them together helps to indicate whether his attitude is one of serious high purpose, deep emotional involvement, detachment, bitterness, gentle amusement, broad humor, or satire.

An author's attitude influences, and consequently is partially revealed by, his method of organizing ideas. The way he groups words into phrases, clauses, and sentences indicates what he considers their relationship to be. The sentences that are put together in paragraphs or in stanzas of poetry, as a means of explaining, expanding, or limiting a key sentence, also give us clues to attitude.

In addition to inferring the author's attitude from the "internal evidence" of the selection, it is usually helpful to learn something about him as a person — to see the individual selection in the light of his whole experience. Biographies and introductions to collected works are very useful in the case of established authors. With a young or relatively unknown author, conclusions must often be based on nothing more than assumptions made from reading as much of his work as possible. The interpreter must be very careful, however, not to become so involved in details of the author's life that he loses sight of the specific piece of literature he is examining. His sharpest focus must be on the literature itself, not on the footnotes gathered together from miscellaneous sources.

The important thing to remember is that the interpreter must be concerned with the attitude of the author as nearly as it can be discovered from his title, his style, his way of life, and his other writings. It is the author's attitude that must come through, not the interpreter's.

INTRINSIC FACTORS

So far we have been concerned largely with a general view of the material the interpreter chooses to use. Now we shall turn our attention to the details that work together to produce certain clearly discernible factors in a work of literary art. These factors, which we shall call the *intrinsic factors,*[4] will be found in varying degrees in all successful writing. But our interest here will go beyond illustration to an examination of how they function for the interpreter's more complete understanding, and how the matters we have discussed thus far relate to the effectiveness of intrinsic factors.

The intrinsic factors are unity and harmony, variety and contrast, balance and proportion, and rhythm. They have been termed the "intrinsic" factors because they are "in" any literary selection under consideration, and because they appear the same to all qualified judges inasmuch as appreciation of them does not depend on the uniqueness and range of personal experience but on judgment of the thing itself. Since they are evident in content and structure, and in the relationship between the two, the interpreter will need to know exactly how they function within his own selection. He will also come to appreciate the author's skill in handling

[4] For a fuller discussion of intrinsic factors, see C. C. Cunningham, *Literature as a Fine Art.* New York: The Ronald Press, 1941.

them, and thus acquire another standard by which to make critical judgments.

These intrinsic factors must not be thought of as separate entities; they must be considered in relation to all the other qualities of the selection if they are to make their true contribution to the total effect. They have bearing on, and are affected by, the arrangement and organization of the material, and on the logical meaning and emotive quality as well. After the material has been thoroughly analyzed in terms of these factors, it must, as always, be put back together again. The audience must never be aware of any one of these factors in itself, only of the total effect. As a matter of fact, analysis will show that none of them can be completely separated from the others: they overlap, correlate with, and affect each other. Each makes its subtle contribution to the whole. We shall discuss the intrinsic factors very briefly and then identify and analyze them in a piece of writing.

Unity and Harmony

Unity is the combining and ordering of all the parts that make up the whole. It consists of those elements of content and form which hold the writing together and keep the reader's and the listener's minds focused on a total effect.

Unity may be achieved in a number of ways. Sometimes it is accomplished through a character. This character may remain relatively unchanged while others develop around him and thus serve as a unifying core; or he may go through a clear and unmistakable process of development, which in itself holds the material together. Again, unity may be strengthened by singleness of setting. It may depend upon the limitation or progression of time. Many stories, for example, take the characters and incidents in chronological sequence, with an implied or explicit time progression in transitions like "and then," "next," "a few hours later," "after this," and so on. Miss Dickinson used this method most skillfully in the poem we examined in the preceding chapter. Of course, such transitions are closely related to method of organization. Within the larger framework of organization there are numerous details which contribute subtly to the unification of the over-all effect. It is impossible to list all the things to be found in this category. The interpreter must approach each piece of literature as a new problem and by careful analysis find everything the author has provided to hold the selection together.

Harmony is the appropriate adjustment of parts to one another to form a satisfying whole. In literature it is the concord between the idea and

the way that idea is expressed. Harmony is achieved in part through the author's choice of words, his sentence structure, and the relationship of phrases and clauses within the sentences. Obviously, then, it depends to a large extent on elements of style. An equally important source of harmony, however, is the selection of details to set up associations in the readers' minds. Thus harmony is paired with unity. Although they differ somewhat in definition, they are clearly interdependent and must function together if the writing is to achieve its intended effect.

Variety and Contrast

A picture which is all in one color or a musical composition which uses only one repeated melody is, except in rare cases where a special effect is achieved through monotony, dull and uninteresting. In the same way, a piece of literature which lacks variety and contrast is not likely to hold our attention for long.

Variety is provided when two things of the same general kind differ from each other in one or more details. For example, several characters of the same age, sex, and social background may agree essentially but express themselves differently. Or one character at two or more points of his development may retain his unifying qualities but demonstrate his reactions in varying ways.

Contrast implies a sharper differentiation. It is concerned with the opposition or unlikeness of associated things. One character may be set against another by his responses to a situation or by his actions and motivations. He may be contrasted in appearance, age, wisdom, emotion, or any number of other attributes. One place or time may be contrasted with another. Quiet may be set against noise, dark against light, hope against despair, positive elements against negative. This is the basic effect Miss Hoyt was trying for in "The Sense of Death."

Thus variety and contrast are closely related. They function together to provide a change of emphasis or to heighten an effect. They are extremely effective in holding attention. The interpreter will find them invaluable in the clues they give him for vocal and physical vividness. At no time, however, must either the author or the interpreter allow variety and/or contrast to become so strong that the over-all effect is destroyed. These two factors must always be held within the bounds of unity and harmony.

Balance and Proportion

Balance and proportion are less easy to evaluate than the other factors we have discussed. The test to be applied is the effectiveness with which

they implement the other factors and contribute to the effect of the whole.

Since proportion provides balance, the two must be considered together. A seesaw or teeter-totter balances when the middle brace is exactly the same distance from each end of the board. When equal weights are placed at each end, that balance is retained. But when a heavier weight is placed on one end of the board than on the other, the balance is destroyed. Balance can be restored by an adjustment of proportions — either by moving the brace toward the end on which the heavier weight rests or by moving the heavier weight closer to the point on which the board rests.

When equal weights or quantities lie at equal distances from a central point, the balance is said to be symmetrical. Identical candlesticks, for example, placed equidistant from the center of a mantelpiece provide symmetrical balance. Perfect balance is satisfying to the senses, but sometimes the asymmetrical or unequal balance achieved by an adjustment of distances, weights, and masses may be more interesting and effective. Instead of the candlesticks on the mantel, there may be a tall plant at one end and a low bright-colored bowl at the other. These two objects do not agree in size and shape, but the bulk or height of the one is somehow balanced by the intensity of the other.

Balance also exists within a piece of literature. It is brought about by the weight, intensity, or proportion of content on either side of the point at which the entire selection seems to pivot and change direction. This point of balance occurs at the crisis in a story or a play. In a poem we call it the *fulcrum* because a poem, especially a lyric poem, does not use conflict in the same way a play or a story does. This fulcrum or point of balance may or may not coincide with either the logical or the emotional climax.

The principle of point of balance is even more important in the consideration of brief, compact selections than in longer units, and the interpreter will find it particularly helpful in poetry. For example, in the twelfth line of "I Felt a Funeral" attention shifts from the funeral and the things of the earth to space. This, then, is the fulcrum of the poem.

Some selections seem to reach their balance point almost exactly in the middle — that is, there is about the same proportion of material leading up to and following the fulcrum. This is the case, for example, in Shelley's poem, "To ———" (see page 37). The first eight lines deal with love, hope, and pity in the abstract sense; the second eight lines turn directly to the poet's own personal concept of and capacity for love. Such symmetrical balance gives the interpreter a fairly easy problem. He need only be sure that he builds to the proper point and does not allow the interest to sag thereafter. If the author has arranged his material so that such handling is achieved without too much difficulty, he may be considered successful in his use of symmetrical balance.

Frequently, however, especially among modern writers, the balance will be off-center. In many cases, the greater proportion of the total material will precede the fulcrum. This is certainly true in "I Dreamed That I Was Old" (see page 39). Such asymmetrical balance is effective in producing sudden shock or a feeling of unrest. It is effective, however, only when the author has been careful to weight the smaller proportion of material with enough vividness and intensity to enable it to hold its own against the greater number of words it must balance. When this has been taken care of in the writing — as it should be — the interpreter need only make use of the clues the author has given him and add the proper amount of emotional intensity, emphasis, and stress to the smaller unit in order to achieve perfect balance in his performance.

Rhythm

Rhythm in literature is usually thought of as an element of poetic structure, such as the relationship between stressed and unstressed syllables. But it is an important aspect of content as well. Rhythm of content begins to emerge as the interpreter examines details of organization. The recurrent shift of attention from one character to another, or from one place or time to another, or the alternation of description and narration, dialogue and exposition can set up a rhythm of content. The rhythm of emotional quality can be measured by the increased and decreased intensity of the reader's response, and will become evident as the minor climaxes are discovered.

Rhythm of content is important to an interpreter because it is closely related to holding an audience's attention. Most people are able to concentrate fully and exclusively on an idea for only a brief span of time. The skillful writer allows for this fatigue or wavering of attention and permits the reader to relax from time to time. By understanding and conveying this rhythm of concentration, the interpreter can do the same for his audience.

Furthermore, listeners cannot be held at a high emotional pitch for very long at a time. In spite of themselves, and in spite of the interpreter's best efforts, they experience a sense of relaxation following the high points of emotional response. The wise writer and the informed interpreter will provide for this relaxation so that the emotional climaxes may be more effective, especially if they depend on accumulation of feeling.

The interpreter will receive a great deal of help from the intrinsic factors within a piece of literature. His problem is how to go about finding them and using the understanding gained from this analysis in his preparation and performance. Each selection will differ from every other in the degree of importance which must be attached to the various factors. The interpreter must let the author have his way, using what is actually *in* the writing rather than trying to fit it to a preconceived pattern. His first step should always be to look at his selection carefully and discover everything he can that the author has given him to work with. Then and *only then* should he concern himself specifically with unity and harmony, variety and contrast, balance and proportion, and rhythm. A careful consideration of these intrinsic factors will help him put the piece of literature back together so that all the elements operate within the organic whole.

A SAMPLE ANALYSIS

In the previous chapter we observed that Miss Dickinson's poem ranked somewhat higher than Miss Hoyt's when we measured them against the touchstones of universality, individuality, and suggestion. Let us look again at Miss Dickinson's "I Felt a Funeral" to discover how some of the details operate to insure the intrinsic factors as well. Since it is so brief, we will repeat it here and number the lines for easier reference.

I felt a Funeral, in my Brain,
And Mourners to and fro
Kept treading — treading — till it seemed
That Sense was breaking through —

And when they all were seated,
A Service, like a Drum —
Kept beating — beating — till I thought
My Mind was going numb —

And then I heard them lift a Box
And creak across my Soul
With those same Boots of Lead, again,
Then Space — began to toll,

As all the Heavens were a Bell,
And Being, but an Ear,
And I, and Silence, some strange Race
Wrecked, solitary, here —

And then a Plank in Reason, broke,
And I dropped down, and down —
And hit a World, at every Crash,
And Got through knowing — then —

There are probably no words in this poem that need to be looked up in the dictionary. In our earlier discussion, we touched briefly on the connotation of some of the words. We shall come back to this matter later — indeed it is impossible to avoid it in a selection so filled with suggestion — but for the moment we shall move on to organization.

The first line gives the complete opening situation. We know that she "felt" rather than saw a funeral and that she felt it in her brain. Immediately the possibility opens up that this poem is not about an actual funeral but about a sensation instead and, in a highly poetic way, an analogy. It may be the sense of death. It may be despair. It may be both. In any case, it is sensation within the rational part of one's body. That is a paradox in itself. Miss Dickinson takes two stanzas to establish this essential paradox, which we may consider as the introduction. The third and fourth stanzas take us from the tightly enclosed earthly "place" to space and the almost intolerable tolling followed by silence. On the opening line of the final stanza, we begin the descent and the conclusion of the experience. Thus the organization is really very simple and unified, and the logical climax is located in the last line, where the experience reaches its only possible outcome.

Though each stanza has its own emotional build, the major emotional climax coincides with the fulcrum, where heaviness is suddenly replaced by space and sound swells to sudden silence. The poem turns from earth, in a sense, to space in the final line of the middle stanza. After the weight of the box, the "creak across my Soul," which strongly suggests a creak across a floor, and the "Boots of Lead," we are suddenly confronted with the sharply contrasting vast and empty expanse of space. This is, as we have said, the fulcrum. It is approximately in the center of the poem and causes no trouble as far as balance and proportion of stanzas is concerned. Our next step will be to look closely at some details to see how they contribute to the intrinsic factors.

The poem gives us a sense of continuing development, and yet without real speed except for lines nineteen and twenty, where the drop occurs. This is achieved in part by the structure. The effect of steady continuation first suggested in "to and fro" is strengthened by the connectives "and," "till," "and when," "and then." It is interesting that the "and's" increase sharply in the last stanza so that the drop picks up speed and the experience is terminated with the final "then."

The verb forms also help to create this effect. Though the entire poem is in the past tense, there is a subtle variation within it. The repetition in "Kept treading — treading" and "Kept beating — beating" and "down and down" and the imperfect tense of "was breaking," "was going" give a feeling of action continuing over a period of time. It is interesting to notice, however, that at the fulcrum there is a shift into the infinitive with "began to toll," followed immediately by a subjunctive form throughout the entire fourth stanza ("As" in line thirteen certainly implies "as if"). The subjunctive is used when we speak of an hypothesis or a condition contrary to fact. The final stanza returns to the simple past with "broke," "dropped," "hit," and "Got through," which is about as completed a past as one can have!

We have already mentioned the use of "I felt" in the opening line. Taking the first person singular "I," we find that we move from "I felt" to "I thought," "I heard," "And I, and Silence" to "I dropped," "[I] hit," and "[I] Got through." Though the first four are evenly spaced one to a stanza, the last three occur in quick succession in the last three lines. Our attention is focused on the "I" at the opening of the poem, and then we are quickly introduced to the mourners. The rhythm of attention alternates, although not with perfect regularity, until the twelfth line, when space is introduced. We have no references to the mourners or to the funeral after that, and the next reference to "I" is "I, and Silence." A look at the funeral references will reveal that they continue at least by implication through line thirteen, with "toll" and "Bell," but it is really space that begins to toll and the heavens that are a bell.

When a writer returns often to a specific set of references, that set of references is called a *motif.* A motif in music, design, or literature is any detail repeated often enough to become significant. In music, it may be a phrase of melody or a set of chords. In design, it may be a leaf, a flower, a *fleur de lys,* for example. In literature, the repeated reference need not be an exact repetition. It may be recurring references to the elements, such as storms, clouds, or sunshine, or to things related to each other, such as colors, nature, or trades.

The first line refers to "my Brain," and this reference is strengthened, and at the same time delimited, three lines later by "Sense" which we discussed in Chapter 1 as we talked about suggestion. Thus we go from "my Brain" to "it seemed," "Sense," "I thought," and "My Mind." This mental motif is not present again until the final stanza, which opens with a reference to "Reason" and closes with "knowing." We are very carefully returned to the poet with "I" in line fifteen, and "Reason" and "knowing" are in identical positions with "Brain" and "Sense" in the opening stanza. Though psychologists might quibble, "heard" in line nine is more physical than mental. The next reference is to "Soul," then to "Being," and then to "Race," a large general category rather than a specific personal reference. Moreover, the race is "strange," "Wrecked," and most important, "solitary." Even more subtle is the use of "Ear" with "Being." Thus lines nine through sixteen form a unit which differs from the rest of the poem in motif. As we have remarked, there is also a shift in verb form, and it is the only place where the sentence continues past the stanza break without being broken by a dash.

A simple listing by line (see facing page) will make this dicussion more graphic. We must remember, however, that a list is not a poem. It is useful only as a step in analysis. In the interest of clarity we shall omit the capitals.

Remembering that the intrinsic factors are closely related and that a detail may contribute to more than one of them, let us see how what we have found relates to unity and harmony, variety and contrast, balance and proportion, and rhythm.

The use of "I" and "my" is a strong unifying factor. It is clearly established in the first ten lines and returned to in line fifteen and throughout the final stanza. The connectives and the simple progression of events also help to hold the poem together. The mental motif opens and closes the poem and is constant throughout, except for the middle portion where it is weaker but still operating in "heard" and "as [if]." The sound motif with the contrasting silence is heavy in the beginning, reaches a high level at the fulcrum, is somehow strengthened by the sudden silence, and returns with force in the final stanza. A feeling of weight and heaviness begins in the first stanza, reaches its peak in "lift a Box" and "Boots of Lead," and recurs in "Plank . . . broke" in lines eighteen and nineteen.

Harmony cannot be fully appreciated until we have examined poetic structure, but certainly the heaviness just referred to and the continuing, unbroken downward progression are harmonious with such a sensation as is here described. "Drum" suggests funeral drums; and a tolling bell, also associated with funerals, prolongs the mood. "Wrecked," "broke," and "Crash" help to suggest the destruction following the tolling of space. Careful examination will reveal a remarkable harmony between what is being said and the connotation and sound of the words with which it is said.

Within the unity of this brief poem, we find sufficient variety and contrast to hold our interest. A look at the funeral motif and the sound motif indicates that Miss Dickinson used very subtle variety indeed. Too much variety within so brief a poem would seriously threaten unity,

Line	Persons	*Mental, Physical, and Spiritual Motifs*	*Connectives*	*Verb Forms*	*Funeral Motifs*	*Sound and Silence*
1	I my	I felt my brain		I felt	funeral	
2	mourners		and		mourners	
3	they (implied)	it seemed	till	kept treading treading it seemed		treading treading
4	my (implied)	sense		was breaking		
5	they (mourners)		and when	were seated		
6					service drum	drum
7	I	I thought	till	kept beating beating I thought		beating beating
8	my	my mind		was going		
9	I them (mourners)	I heard	and then	I heard lift	box	heard them
10	them (implied) my	my soul	and	creak		creak across
11	their (implied)				lead	boots of lead
12		space	then	began to toll	toll	toll **FULCRUM**
13		heavens		as [if] . . . were	bell	bell
14		Being ear	and	as [if] . . . were (implied)		ear
15	I and silence	race	and . . . and	as [if] . . were (implied)		silence
16				as [if] . . . were (implied)		solitary
17		reason	and then	broke		plank broke
18	I		and . . . and	dropped		
19	I (implied)		and	hit		crash
20	I (implied)	knowing	and then	got through		

especially since contrast is so sharp. The poet's isolation is contrasted with the multiplicity of people in "Mourners" and "they all," until the isolation reaches its culmination in "I, and Silence . . . solitary." Their actions are contrasted with her immobility and numbing sensations. Space and the heavens are set off against weight and the tangible things of earth. Silence is set against a crescendo of sound. It is, in fact, because of contrast that the fulcrum operates so successfully.

Balance and proportion offer no real problem here since there is almost an equal number of lines and amount of emotional weight on either side of the fulcrum. The build to the fulcrum is steady. Immediately after the point of balance is reached, the action ceases momentarily so that even though the emotional and logical climaxes fall in the second portion of the poem, they do not overbalance the heaviness and familiarity of the funeral motif in the first section. Moreover, the emotional climax is controlled by the abstractions ("the Heavens," "Being," and "strange Race"). After the emotional climax, the speed picks up, and the repeated use of "and" tightens the progression to the conclusion.

Rhythm of content is strongest in the shift from the poet to the mourners which we mentioned earlier, and in the focus on their actions and then on her responses. Again, there is not enough time for a very elaborate pattern of rhythm of content in twenty short lines. As we continue to look at the poem, however, we are aware that both the variety and the contrast make a rhythmic contribution, as do some of the elements in unity.

There are innumerable small details which also contribute to the intrinsic factors. We cannot resist calling attention to the remarkable spacing of "treading," "creak across," and "Plank," all of which suggest floor boards, and to the positioning of "heard" and "Ear" and "Silence." The use of the already familiar "I" with "heard" controls the unity, and "heard" prepares us for "toll," "Bell," "Ear," "Silence," "Plank . . . broke," and finally "Crash."

Now the question arises of what the interpreter does with all this discovery. The answer is that he uses it fully and with complete confidence in his author. Whether or not the writer was conscious of using all these elements, or indeed of the intrinsic and extrinsic factors as such, is beside the point. It is the interpreter's responsibility to find everything the writer has given him to work with. Such an analysis as we have just completed usually results in increased respect for and confidence in the author. If he has not been completely successful, the interpreter will realize where the writing is weak and thus have additional criteria for literary judgment.

The approach used for this brief poem may also be used for longer poems and for prose. Of course, in a longer poem or a piece of prose the writer has more time to develop his material; therefore the fulcrum or crisis may not be as compact as it is in Miss Dickinson's poem. Furthermore, every selection, whether it be prose or poetry, will differ from every other selection in the relative importance of the extrinsic and intrinsic factors. Sometimes unity and harmony will be less important than variety. As we have seen in "I Felt a Funeral in My Brain," variety is less significant than contrast. In any case, the interpreter cannot begin to evaluate the intrinsic factors until he has found out what is in the material he has chosen.

As the interpreter begins to work on the material aloud in preparation for sharing it with his audience, he will find that the things he discovered in analysis serve as a guide to the use of his own techniques of voice and body. He knows what unifies the material. He knows where the variety is and can use it to hold attention without letting it violate the essential unity and harmony. His awareness of rhythm of content, and of the location of the fulcrum, becomes a guide for climaxes as well as for progression. In other words, he knows where the selection is going and exactly how it gets there.

Frequently, as the interpreter works on the literature aloud, he gains new insights and hears new melodies. Thus it is wise for him to begin oral preparation well in advance of performance. He needs to let the writing work on him as he works on it. He should start with the whole selection each time he begins a rehearsal session. After two or three readings of the whole, he should turn his attention to details and how they operate for unity and harmony. Then he should put the material back together. Finally, he should consider the other intrinsic factors, returning each time to the total achievement.

The interpreter must remember that his audience does not want a reading of his analysis; it wants to share the experience of the literature. If the analysis has been thorough and the preparation sound, the interpreter may trust his author and himself. But unless he knows exactly what the author has done, he cannot possibly re-create his work.

SELECTIONS FOR ANALYSIS AND ORAL INTERPRETATION

Each of these selections must be analyzed thoroughly. Do not try to make them follow the pattern of the Dickinson poem, however, because every piece of writing differs from every other one. Look at all the details we have discussed and *then* decide which ones contribute to unity and harmony, where variety and contrast exist within the unity and harmony. Find the fulcrum and climaxes, and consider balance and proportion. Look carefully for rhythm of content. Remember that details may contribute to more than one of the intrinsic factors. Start with the whole poem and let it work on you until you feel comfortable with it. Then move into objective analysis. After each step, go back to the complete poem and see how the pieces fit together. Remember that your audience wants the whole poem, not the separate pieces.

THE WORD CHOICE in this Frost poem was mentioned within the chapter. Notice how the address to the star works with the poet's comment to us to set up a rhythm of content. Watch for the shift from "you" to "us."

Choose Something Like a Star . . .

O Star (the fairest one in sight),
We grant your loftiness the right
To some obscurity of cloud —
It will not do to say of night,
Since dark is what brings out your light.
Some mystery becomes the proud.
But to be wholly taciturn
In your reserve is not allowed.
Say something to us we can learn
By heart and when alone repeat.
Say something! And it says, 'I burn.'
But say with what degree of heat.
Talk Fahrenheit, talk Centigrade.
Use language we can comprehend.
Tell us what elements you blend.
It gives us strangely little aid,
But does tell something in the end.
And steadfast as Keats' Eremite,
Not even stooping from its sphere,
It asks a little of us here.
It asks of us a certain height,
So when at times the mob is swayed
To carry praise or blame too far,
We may choose something like a star
To stay our minds on and be staid.

ROBERT FROST

From *Complete Poems of Robert Frost.* Copyright 1923, 1949 by Holt, Rinehart and Winston, Inc. Copyright renewed 1951 by Robert Frost. Reprinted by permission of Holt, Rinehart and Winston, Inc.

FROST DISPLAYS quite a different attitude in this poem. Compare the sentence lengths with those in the poem above. The final questions will take careful handling.

For Once, Then, Something

Others taunt me with having knelt at well-curbs
Always wrong to the light, so never seeing
Deeper down in the well than where the water
Gives me back in a shining surface picture
Me myself in the summer heaven godlike
Looking out of a wreath of fern and cloud puffs.
Once, when trying with chin against a well-curb,
I discerned, as I thought, beyond the picture,
Through the picture, a something white, uncertain,
Something more of the depths — and then I lost it.
Water came to rebuke the too clear water.
One drop fell from a fern, and lo, a ripple
Shook whatever it was lay there at bottom,
Blurred it, blotted it out. What was that whiteness?
Truth? A pebble of quartz? For once, then, something.

ROBERT FROST

THE NEXT TWO *Fables For Our Times* present similar problems in balance and proportion. Watch carefully for clues to attitude in the word choice and grammatical structure.

The Little Girl and the Wolf

One afternoon a big wolf waited in a dark forest for a little girl to come along carrying a basket of food to her grandmother. Finally a little girl did come along and she was carrying a basket of food. "Are you carrying that basket to your grandmother?" asked the wolf. The little girl said yes, she was. So the wolf asked her where her grandmother lived and the little girl told him and he disappeared into the wood.

When the little girl opened the door of her grandmother's house she saw that there was somebody in bed with a nightcap and nightgown on. She had approached no nearer than twenty-five feet from the bed when she saw that it was not her grandmother but the wolf, for even in a nightcap a wolf does not look any more like your grandmother than the Metro-Goldwyn lion looks like Calvin Cool-

From *Complete Poems of Robert Frost.* Copyright 1923, 1949 by Holt, Rinehart and Winston, Inc. Copyright renewed 1951 by Robert Frost. Reprinted by permission of Holt, Rinehart and Winston, Inc.

From *The New Yorker.* Copyright 1939 by The New Yorker Magazine, Inc. Reprinted by permission of Mrs. Helen Thurber and The New Yorker Magazine, Inc.

idge. So the little girl took an automatic out of her basket and shot the wolf dead.

Moral: It is not so easy to fool little girls nowadays as it used to be.

James Thurber

The Unicorn in the Garden

Once upon a sunny morning a man who sat in a breakfast nook looked up from his scrambled eggs to see a white unicorn with a gold horn quietly cropping the roses in the garden. The man went up to the bedroom where his wife was still asleep and woke her. "There's a unicorn in the garden," he said. "Eating roses." She opened one unfriendly eye and looked at him. "The unicorn is a mythical beast," she said, and turned her back on him. The man walked slowly downstairs and out into the garden. The unicorn was still there; he was now browsing among the tulips. "Here, unicorn," said the man, and he pulled up a lily and gave it to him. The unicorn ate it gravely. With a high heart, because there was a unicorn in his garden, the man went upstairs and roused his wife again. "The unicorn," he said, "ate a lily." His wife sat up in bed and looked at him, coldly. "You are a booby," she said, "and I am going to have you put in the booby-hatch." The man, who had never liked the words "booby" and "booby-hatch," and who liked them even less on a shining morning when there was a unicorn in the garden, thought for a moment. "We'll see about that," he said. He walked over to the door. "He has a golden horn in the middle of his forehead," he told her. Then he went back to the garden to watch the unicorn; but the unicorn had gone away. The man sat down among the roses and went to sleep.

As soon as the husband had gone out of the house, the wife got up and dressed as fast as she could. She was very excited and there was a gloat in her eye. She telephoned the police and she telephoned a psychiatrist; she told them to hurry to her house and bring a strait-jacket. When the police and the psychiatrist arrived they sat down in chairs and looked at her, with great interest. "My husband," she said, "saw a unicorn this morning." The police looked at the psychiatrist and the psychiatrist looked at the police. "He told me it ate a lily," she said. The psychiatrist looked at the police and the police looked at the psychiatrist. "He told me it had a golden horn in the middle of its forehead," she said. At a solemn signal from the psychiatrist, the police leaped from their chairs and seized the wife. They had a hard time subduing her, for she put up a terrific struggle, but they finally subdued her. Just as they got her into the strait-jacket, the husband came back into the house.

From *The New Yorker*. Copyright 1939 by The New Yorker Magazine, Inc. Reprinted by permission of Mrs. Helen Thurber and The New Yorker Magazine, Inc.

"Did you tell your wife you saw a unicorn?" asked the police. "Of course not," said the husband. "The unicorn is a mythical beast." "That's all I wanted to know," said the psychiatrist. "Take her away. I'm sorry, sir, but your wife is as crazy as a jay bird." So they took her away, cursing and screaming, and shut her up in an institution. The husband lived happily ever after.

Moral: Don't count your boobies until they are hatched.

JAMES THURBER

THE BALANCE and proportion in this poem were referred to within the chapter. Notice the use of the long sentences. Does this aspect of style reinforce or weaken the total effect? Pay particular attention to unity and variety.

To ——

One word is too often profan'd
  For me to profane it;
One feeling too falsely disdain'd
  For thee to disdain it;
One hope is too like despair
  For prudence to smother;
And pity from thee more dear
  Than that from another.

I can give not what men call love:
  But wilt thou accept not
The worship the heart lifts above
  And the heavens reject not,
The desire of the moth for the star,
  Of the night for the morrow,
The devotion to something afar
  From the sphere of our sorrow?

PERCY BYSSHE SHELLEY

THERE IS AN ANALOGY operating in this poem which establishes its unity and harmony as well as its rhythm of content.

Deer in the Surf

(Olympic Peninsula: 1957)

Her tracks were what astonished us at first.
Down by the surf, looking toward the sea,

Copyright © 1963, The Commonweal Publishing Corporation. Reprinted by permission of Clayton Long and The Commonweal Publishing Corporation.

What was that deer about? What did she see?
From green of trees, rushing to be immersed
In paler green, we'd come with turn of dawn.
So she, with other purpose, and otherwise,
Found the shore where twisted driftwood lies.
We thought, but got no good conclusions drawn.

The hounds she knew were of a fiercer kind
Than grumbled in our chastened blood. Some chance
Encounter, a forest shadow out of place,
Loosed the flashing hounds within her mind,
Spread those great eyes wide with frightened grace,
And struck the forest to her maddened dance.

CLAYTON LONG

THERE ARE MINOR climaxes here that will help avoid monotony within the simple progression.

from *Jean-Christophe*

When it was very hot, old Krafft used to sit under a tree, and was not long in dozing off. Then Jean-Christophe used to sit near him on a heap of loose stones or a milestone, or some high seat, uncomfortable and peculiar; and he used to wag his little legs, and hum to himself, and dream. Or sometimes he used to lie on his back and watch the clouds go by; they looked like oxen, and giants, and hats, and old ladies, and immense landscapes. He used to talk to them in a low voice, or be absorbed in a little cloud which a great one was on the point of devouring. He was afraid of those which were very black, almost blue, and of those which went very fast. It seemed to him that they played an enormous part in life, and he was surprised that neither his grandfather nor his mother paid any attention to them. They were terrible beings if they wished to do harm. Fortunately, they used to go by, kindly enough, a little grotesque, and they did not stop. The boy used in the end to turn giddy with watching them too long, and he used to fidget with his legs and arms, as though he were on the point of falling from the sky. His eyelids then would wink, and sleep would overcome him. Silence . . . The leaves murmur gently and tremble in the sun; a faint mist passes through the air; the uncertain flies hover, booming like an organ; the grasshoppers, drunk with the summer, chirp eag-

From *Jean-Christophe* by Romain Rolland. Translated by Gilbert Cannan. Copyright 1910, copyright renewed 1938 by Holt, Rinehart and Winston, Inc. Reprinted by permission of Holt, Rinehart and Winston, Inc. Also reprinted by permission of William Heinemann, Ltd.

erly and hurriedly; all is silent. . . . Under the vault of the trees the cry of the green woodpecker has magic sounds. Far away on the plain a peasant's voice harangues his oxen; the shoes of a horse ring out on the white road. Jean-Christophe's eyes close. Near him an ant passes along a dead branch across a furrow. He loses consciousness. . . . Ages have passed. He wakes. The ant has not yet crossed the twig.

ROMAIN ROLLAND

BALANCE IS OF great importance here as we mentioned within the chapter. Be sure you understand the allusions.

I Dreamed That I Was Old

I dreamed that I was old: in stale declension
Fallen from my prime, when company
Was mine, cat-nimbleness, and green invention,
Before time took my leafy hours away.

My wisdom, ripe with body's ruin, found
Itself tart recompense for what was lost
In false exchange: since wisdom in the ground
Has no apocalypse or pentecost.

I wept for my youth, sweet passionate young thought,
And cozy women dead that by my side
Once lay: I wept with bitter longing, not
Remembering how in my youth I cried.

STANLEY KUNITZ

THE TONE OF the introduction differs sharply from that of the rest of this excerpt. Keep a careful check on unity and harmony.

from *The New World*

A voluntary association of Protestant gentry was formed in 1585 for the defence of Elizabeth's life. In the following year evidence

Copyright © 1958 by Stanley Kunitz, from *Selected Poems 1928–1958* by Stanley Kunitz. Reprinted by permission of Little, Brown and Company–Atlantic Monthly Press.

Reprinted by permission of Dodd, Mead & Company from *The New World* by Winston S. Churchill. Copyright © 1956 by Dodd, Mead & Company, Inc. Distributed in Canada by courtesy of McClelland & Stewart, Ltd.

of a conspiracy, engineered by one Anthony Babington, an English Catholic, was laid before the Council of Walsingham. One of his agents had mingled with the conspirators for over a year. Mary's connivance was undeniable. Elizabeth was at last persuaded that her death was a political necessity. After a formal trial Mary was pronounced guilty of treason. Parliament petitioned for her execution, and Elizabeth at last signed the death warrant. Within twenty-four hours she regretted it and tried, too late, to stop the execution. She had a natural horror of being responsible for the judicial murder of a fellow sovereign, although she knew it was essential for the safety of her country. She was anxious that the supreme and final decision should not rest upon her.

The scene of Mary's death has caught the imagination of history. In the early morning of February 8, 1587, she was summoned to the great hall of Fotheringay Castle. Accompanied by six of her attendants, she awaited the servants of the English Queen. From the neighbouring countryside the gentry gathered to witness the sentence. Mary appeared at the appointed hour soberly clad in black satin. In the quietness of the hall she walked with stately movements to the cloth-covered scaffold erected by the fireplace. The solemn formalities were smoothly completed. But the zealous Dean of Peterborough attempted to force upon the Queen a last-minute conversion. With splendid dignity she brushed aside his loud exhortations. "Mr. Dean," she said, "I am a Catholic, and must die a Catholic. It is useless to attempt to move me, and your prayers will avail me but little."

Mary had arrayed herself superbly for the final scene. As she disrobed for the headsman's act, her garments of black satin, removed by the weeping handmaids, revealed a bodice and petticoat of crimson velvet. One of her ladies handed her a pair of crimson sleeves, which she put on. Thus the unhappy Queen halted, for one last moment, standing blood-red from head to foot against the black background of the scaffold. There was a deathly hush throughout the hall. She knelt, and at the second stroke the final blow was delivered. The awed assembly had fulfilled its task. In death the majestic illusion was shattered. The head of an ageing woman with false hair was held up by the executioner. A lapdog crept out from beneath the clothes of the bleeding trunk.

As the news reached London bonfires were lit in the streets. Elizabeth sat alone in her room, weeping more for the fate of a Queen than a woman. The responsibility for this deed she shifted with an effort on to the shoulders of her masculine advisers.

Winston S. Churchill

LOCATING THE fulcrum and climax depends upon a careful analysis of attitude here.

Dover Beach

The sea is calm tonight.
The tide is full, the moon lies fair
Upon the straits; — on the French coast the light
Gleams and is gone; the cliffs of England stand
Glimmering and vast, out in the tranquil bay.
Come to the window, sweet is the night-air!
Only, from the long line of spray
Where the sea meets the moon-blanched land,
Listen! you hear the grating roar
Of pebbles which the waves draw back, and fling,
At their return, up the high strand,
Begin, and cease, and then again begin,
With tremulous cadence slow, and bring
The eternal note of sadness in.

Sophocles long ago
Heard it on the Aegean, and it brought
Into his mind the turbid ebb and flow
Of human misery; we
Find also in the sound a thought,
Hearing it by this distant northern sea.

The Sea of Faith
Was once, too, at the full, and round earth's shore
Lay like the folds of a bright girdle furled.
But now I only hear
Its melancholy, long, withdrawing roar,
Retreating, to the breath
Of the night-wind, down the vast edges drear
And naked shingles of the world.

Ah, love, let us be true
To one another! for the world, which seems
To lie before us like a land of dreams,
So various, so beautiful, so new,
Hath really neither joy, nor love, nor light,
Nor certitude, nor peace, nor help for pain;
And we are here as on a darkling plain
Swept with confused alarms of struggle and flight,
Where ignorant armies clash by night.

MATTHEW ARNOLD

Be sure you know the allusion upon which the last eight lines depend. The length and structure of the sentences is interesting.

Musée des Beaux Arts

About suffering they were never wrong,
The Old Masters: how well they understood
Its human position; how it takes place
While someone else is eating or opening a window or just
  walking dully along;
How, when the aged are reverently, passionately waiting
For the miraculous birth, there always must be
Children who did not specially want it to happen, skating
On a pond at the edge of the wood:
They never forgot
That even the dreadful martyrdom must run its course
Anyhow in a corner, some untidy spot
Where the dogs go on with their doggy life and the torturer's horse
Scratches its innocent behind on a tree.

In Brueghel's *Icarus*, for instance: how everything turns away
Quite leisurely from the disaster; the ploughman may
Have heard the splash, the forsaken cry,
But for him it was not an important failure; the sun shone
As it had to on the white legs disappearing into the green
Water; and the expensive delicate ship that must have seen
Something amazing, a boy falling out of the sky,
Had somewhere to get to and sailed calmly on.

W. H. Auden

Style underscores this satire on the sentimental novel of the early eighteenth century. Several sections within this excerpt may be used as units in themselves.

from *Tom Jones*

Mr. Western grew every day fonder and fonder of Sophia, insomuch that his beloved dogs themselves almost gave place to her in his affections; but as he could not prevail on himself to abandon these, he contrived very cunningly to enjoy their company together with that of his daughter by insisting on her riding a-hunting with him.

Sophia, to whom her father's word was a law, readily complied with his desires, though she had not the least delight in a sport which was of too rough and masculine a nature to suit with her disposition. She had, however, another motive besides her obedience to accompany the old gentleman in the chase; for by her presence

Copyright 1940 by W. H. Auden. Reprinted from *The Collected Poetry of W. H. Auden,* by permission of Random House, Inc. Also reprinted by permission of Faber and Faber, Ltd.

she hoped in some measure to restrain his impetuosity, and to prevent him from so frequently exposing his neck to the utmost hazard.

The strongest objection was that which would have formerly been an inducement to her, namely, the frequent meeting with young Jones, whom she had determined to avoid; but as the end of the hunting season now approached, she hoped by a short absence with her aunt to reason herself entirely out of her unfortunate passion, and had not any doubt of being able to meet him in the field the subsequent season without the least danger.

On the second day of her hunting, as she was returning from the chase and was arrived within a little distance from Mr. Western's house, her horse, whose mettlesome spirit required a better rider, fell suddenly to prancing and capering in such a manner that she was in the most imminent peril of falling. Tom Jones, who was at a little distance behind, saw this, and immediately galloped up to her assistance. As soon as he came up, he immediately leapt from his own horse and caught hold of hers by the bridle. The unruly beast presently reared himself on end on his hind legs and threw his lovely burden from his back, and Jones caught her in his arms.

She was so affected with the fright that she was not immediately able to satisfy Jones, who was very solicitous to know whether she had received any hurt. She soon after, however, recovered her spirits, assured him she was safe, and thanked him for the care he had taken of her. Jones answered, "If I have preserved you, madam, I am sufficiently repaid; for I promise you I would have secured you from the least harm, at the expense of a much greater misfortune to myself than I have suffered on this occasion."

"What misfortune?" replied Sophia, eagerly. "I hope you have come to no mischief."

"Be not concerned, madam," answered Jones. "Heaven be praised you have escaped so well, considering the danger you was in. If I have broke my arm, I consider it as a trifle in comparison of what I feared upon your account."

Sophia then screamed out, "Broke your arm! Heaven forbid."

"I am afraid I have, madam," says Jones, "but I beg you will suffer me first to take care of you. I have a right hand yet at your service to help you into the next field, where we have but a very little walk to your father's house."

Sophia, seeing his left arm dangling by his side while he was using the other to lead her, no longer doubted of the truth. She now grew much paler than her fears for herself had made her before. All her limbs were seized with a trembling, insomuch that Jones could scarce support her; and as her thoughts were in no less agitation, she could not refrain from giving Jones a look so full of tenderness that it almost argued a stronger sensation in her mind than even gratitude and pity united can raise in the gentlest female bosom without the assistance of a third more powerful passion.

Mr. Western, who was advanced at some distance when this accident happened, was now returned, as were the rest of the horsemen. Sophia immediately acquainted them with what had befallen Jones and begged them to take care of him. Upon which Western, who had been much alarmed by meeting his daughter's horse without its rider, and was now overjoyed to find her unhurt, cried out, "I am glad it is no worse; if Tom hath broken his arm, we will get a joiner to mend un again."

The squire alighted from his horse, and proceeded to his house on foot with his daughter and Jones. An impartial spectator who had met them on the way would, on viewing their several countenances, have concluded Sophia alone to have been the object of compassion; for as to Jones, he exulted in having probably saved the life of the young lady at the price only of a broken bone; and Mr. Western, though he was not unconcerned at the accident which had befallen Jones, was, however, delighted in a much higher degree with the fortunate escape of his daughter.

The generosity of Sophia's temper construed this behaviour of Jones into great bravery, and it made a deep impression on her heart; for certain it is, that there is no one quality which so generally recommends men to women as this, proceeding, if we believe the common opinion, from that natural timidity of the sex, which is, says Mr. Osborne, so great that a woman is "the most cowardly of all the creatures God ever made"—a sentiment more remarkable for its bluntness than for its truth. Aristotle in his *Politics* doth them, I believe, more justice when he says, "The modesty and fortitude of men differ from those virtues in women; for the fortitude which becomes a woman would be cowardice in a man, and the modesty which becomes a man would be pertness in a woman." Nor is there, perhaps, more of truth in the opinion of those who derive the partiality which women are inclined to show to the brave from this excess of their fear. Mr. Bayle (I think in his article of Helen) imputes this, and with greater probability, to their violent love of glory; for the truth of which we have the authority of him who of all others saw farthest into human nature, and who introduces the heroine of his *Odyssey,* the great pattern of matrimonial love and constancy, assigning the glory of her husband as the only source of her affection towards him.

However this be, certain it is that the accident operated very strongly on Sophia; and indeed after much inquiry into the matter I am inclined to believe that at this very time the charming Sophia made no less impression on the heart of Jones; to say truth, he had for some time become sensible of the irresistible power of her charms.

HENRY FIELDING

MAKE FULL USE of the direct discourse without breaking the unity. Notice how carefully the stanzas are balanced.

When I Was One-and-Twenty

When I was one-and-twenty
  I heard a wise man say,
"Give crowns and pounds and guineas
  But not your heart away;
Give pearls away and rubies
  But keep your fancy free."
But I was one-and-twenty,
  No use to talk to me.

When I was one-and-twenty
  I heard him say again,
"The heart out of the bosom
  Was never given in vain;
'Tis paid with sighs a plenty
  And sold for endless rue."
And I am two-and-twenty,
  And oh, 'tis true, 'tis true.

A. E. Housman

Alexander Pope uses numerous figures of speech and two expanded analogies in this famous poem.

from *The Essay On Criticism*

  A little learning is a dang'rous thing;
Drink deep, or taste not the Pierian spring.
There shallow draughts intoxicate the brain,
And drinking largely sobers us again.
Fir'd at first sight with what the Muse imparts,
In fearless youth we tempt the heights of Arts,
While from the bounded level of our mind,
Short views we take, nor see the lengths behind;
But more advanc'd, behold with strange surprise
New distant scenes of endless science rise!

  So pleas'd at first the tow'ring Alps we try,
Mount o'er the vales, and seem to tread the sky,
Th' eternal snows appear already past,
And the first clouds and mountains seem the last;
But, those attain'd, we tremble to survey
The growing labours of the lengthen'd way,
Th' increasing prospect tires our wand'ring eyes,
Hills peep o'er, and Alps on Alps arise!

From "A Shropshire Lad"—Authorized Edition—from *Complete Poems* by A. E. Housman. Copyright © 1959 by Holt, Rinehart and Winston, Inc. Reprinted by permission of Holt, Rinehart and Winston, Inc. Also reprinted by permission of The Society of Authors and Messrs. Jonathan Cape, Ltd.

A perfect Judge will read each work of Wit
With the same spirit that its author writ:
Survey the Whole, nor seek slight faults to find
Where nature moves, and rapture warms the mind;
Nor lose, for that malignant dull delight,
The gen'rous pleasure to be charm'd with wit.
But in such lays as neither ebb, nor flow,
Correctly cold, and regularly low,
That shunning faults, one quiet tenour keep;
We cannot blame indeed — but we may sleep.
In Wit, as Nature, what affects our hearts
Is not th' exactness of peculiar parts;
'Tis not a lip, or eye, we beauty call,
But the joint force and full result of all.
Thus when we view some well-proportion'd dome,
(The world's just wonder, and ev'n thine, O Rome!)
No single parts unequally surprise,
All comes united to th' admiring eyes;
No monstrous height, or breadth, or length appear;
The Whole at once is bold, and regular.

ALEXANDER POPE

THIS MODERN TRANSLATION of a myth provides an excellent opportunity for variety. The author's attitude is also important.

from *Paris and Helen*

Now, just before the birth of Paris, Hecabe had dreamed that she brought forth a faggot from which wriggled countless fiery serpents. She awoke screaming that the city of Troy and the forests of Mount Ida were ablaze. Priam at once consulted his son Aesacus, the seer, who announced: 'The child about to be born will be the ruin of our country! I beg you to do away with him.'

A few days later, Aesacus made a further announcement: 'The royal Trojan who brings forth a child today must be destroyed, and so must her offspring!' Priam thereupon killed his sister Cilla, and infant son Munippus, born that morning from a secret union with Thymoetes, and buried them in the sacred precinct of Tros. But Hecabe was delivered of a son before nightfall, and Priam spared both their lives, although Herophile, priestess of Apollo, and other seers, urged Hecabe at least to kill the child. She could not bring herself to do so; and in the end Priam was prevailed upon to send for his chief herdsman, one Agelaus, and entrust him with the task.

From *The Greek Myths* (Baltimore: Penguin Books, Inc., 1955), II, 269–272, by Robert Graves. Copyright © 1955 by Robert Graves. Reprinted by permission of International Authors N.V., Penguin Books, Inc., Penguin Books, Ltd., and A. P. Watt & Son.

Agelaus, being too soft-hearted to use a rope or a sword, exposed the infant on Mount Ida, where he was suckled by a she-bear. Returning after five days, Agelaus was amazed at the portent, and brought the waif home in a wallet — hence the name 'Paris' — to rear with his own new-born son; and took a dog's tongue to Priam as evidence that his command had been obeyed. But some say that Hecabe bribed Agelaus to spare Paris and keep the secret from Priam.

Paris's noble birth was soon disclosed by his outstanding beauty, intelligence, and strength: when little more than a child, he routed a band of cattle-thieves and recovered the cows they had stolen, thus winning the surname Alexander. Though ranking no higher than a slave at this time, Paris became the chosen lover of Oenone, daughter of the river Oeneus, a fountain-nymph. She had been taught the art of prophecy by Rhea, and that of medicine by Apollo while he was acting as Laomedon's herdsman. Paris and Oenone used to herd their flocks and hunt together; he carved her name in the bark of beech-trees and poplars. His chief amusement was setting Agelaus's bulls to fight one another; he would crown the victor with flowers, and the loser with straw. When one bull began to win consistently, Paris pitted it against the champions of his neighbours' herds, all of which were defeated. At last he offered to set a golden crown upon the horns of any bull that could overcome his own; so, for a jest, Ares turned himself into a bull, and won the prize. Paris's unhesitating award of this crown to Ares surprised and pleased the gods as they watched from Olympus; which is why Zeus chose him to arbitrate between the three goddesses.

He was herding his cattle on Mount Gargarus, the highest peak of Ida, when Hermes, accompanied by Hera, Athene, and Aphrodite, delivered the golden apple and Zeus's message: 'Paris, since you are as handsome as you are wise in affairs of the heart, Zeus commands you to judge which of these goddesses is the fairest.'

Paris accepted the apple doubtfully. 'How can a simple cattleman like myself become an arbiter of divine beauty?' he cried. 'I shall divide this apple between all three.'

'No, no, you cannot disobey Almighty Zeus!' Hermes replied hurriedly. 'Nor am I authorized to give you advice. Use your native intelligence!'

'So be it,' sighed Paris. 'But first I beg the losers not to be vexed with me. I am only a human being, liable to make the stupidest mistakes.'

The goddesses all agreed to abide by his decision.

'Will it be enough to judge them as they are?' Paris asked Hermes, 'or should they be naked?'

'The rules of the contest are for you to decide,' Hermes answered with a discreet smile.

'In that case, will they kindly disrobe?'

Hermes told the goddesses to do so, and politely turned his back.

Aphrodite was soon ready, but Athene insisted that she should remove the famous magic girdle, which gave her an unfair advantage by making everyone fall in love with the wearer. 'Very well,' said Aphrodite spitefully. 'I will, on condition that you remove your helmet — you look hideous without it.'

'Now, if you please, I must judge you one at a time,' announced Paris, 'to avoid distractive arguments. Come here, Divine Hera! Will you other two goddesses be good enough to leave us for awhile?'

'Examine me conscientiously,' said Hera, turning slowly around, and displaying her magnificent figure, 'and remember that if you judge me the fairest, I will make you lord of all Asia, and the richest man alive.'

'I am not to be bribed, my Lady . . . Very well, thank you. Now I have seen all that I need to see. Come, Divine Athene!'

'Here I am,' said Athene, striding purposefully forward. 'Listen, Paris, if you have enough common sense to award me the prize, I will make you victorious in all your battles, as well as the handsomest and wisest man in the world.'

'I am a humble herdsman, not a soldier,' said Paris. 'You can see for yourself that peace reigns throughout Lydia and Phrygia, and that King Priam's sovereignty is uncontested. But I promise to consider fairly your claim to the apple. Now you are at liberty to put on your clothes and helmet again. Is Aphrodite ready?'

Aphrodite sidled up to him, and Paris blushed because she came so close that they were almost touching.

'Look carefully, please, pass nothing over. . . . By the way, as soon as I saw you, I said to myself: "Upon my word, there goes the handsomest young man in Phrygia! Why does he waste himself here in the wilderness herding stupid cattle?" Well, why do you, Paris? Why not move into a city and lead a civilized life? What have you to lose by marrying someone like Helen of Sparta, who is as beautiful as I am, and no less passionate? I am convinced that, once you two have met, she will abandon her home, her family, everything, to become your mistress. Surely you have heard of Helen?'

'Never until now, my Lady. I should be most grateful if you would describe her.'

'Helen is of fair and delicate complexion, having been hatched from a swan's egg. She can claim Zeus for a father, loves hunting and wrestling, caused one war while she was still a child — and, when she came of age, all the princes of Greece were her suitors. At present she is married to Menelaus, brother of the High King Agamemnon; but that makes no odds — you can have her if you like.'

'How is that possible, if she is already married?'

'Heaven! How innocent you are! Have you never heard that it is my divine duty to arrange affairs of this sort? I suggest now that you tour Greece with my son Eros as your guide. Once you reach Sparta, he and I will see that Helen falls head over heels in love with you.'

'Would you swear to that?' Paris asked excitedly.

Aphrodite uttered a solemn oath, and Paris, without a second thought, awarded her the golden apple.

By this judgment he incurred the smothered hatred of both Hera and Athene, who went off arm-in-arm to plot the destruction of Troy; while Aphrodite, with a naughty smile, stood wondering how best to keep her promise.

ROBERT GRAVES

WORD CHOICE IN this poem was mentioned within the chapter. It provides an interesting contrast to the Dickinson poem analyzed earlier.

Because I Could Not Stop for Death

Because I could not stop for Death,
He kindly stopped for me;
The carriage held but just ourselves
And Immortality.

We slowly drove, he knew no haste,
And I had put away
My labor, and my leisure too,
For his civility.

We passed the school where children played
At wrestling in a ring;
We passed the fields of gazing grain,
We passed the setting sun.

We paused before a house that seemed
A swelling of the ground;
The roof was scarcely visible,
The cornice but a mound.

Since then 'tis centuries; but each
Feels shorter than the day
I first surmised the horses' heads
Were toward eternity.

EMILY DICKINSON

The allusions are vital in the understanding of this poem.

Bavarian Gentians

Not every man has gentians in his house
In soft September, at slow, sad Michaelmas.

Bavarian gentians, tall and dark, but dark
Darkening the day-time torch-like with the smoking blueness of Pluto's
gloom,
Ribbed hellish flowers erect, with their blaze of darkness spread blue
Blown into points, by the heavy white draught of the day.

Torch-flowers of the blue-smoking darkness, Pluto's dark blue blaze
Black lamps from the hall of Dio, smoking dark blue
Giving off darkness, blue darkness, upon Demeter's yellow-pale day,
Lead me then, lead me the way.

Reach me a gentian, give me a torch!
Let me guide myself with the blue, forked torch of a flower
Down the darker and darker stairs, where blue is darkened on blueness
Down the way Persephone goes, just now, in first-frosted September
To the sightless realm where darkness is married to dark
And Persephone herself is but a voice, as a bride
A gloom invisible enfolded in the deeper dark
Of the arms of Pluto as he ravishes her once again
And pierces her once more with his passion of the utter dark.

Among the splendour of black-blue torches, shedding fathomless darkness
on the nuptials.

Give me a flower on a tall stem, and three dark flames,
For I will go to the wedding, and be wedding-guest
At the marriage of the living dark.

D. H. Lawrence

This excerpt gives the interpreter numerous opportunities for variety.

from *The New Snobbism*

Somewhere between the Emotional Snobs and the Intellectual Snobs are the Sensitivity or Taste Snobs — those who are scorn-

From *The Complete Poems of D. H. Lawrence,* edited by Vivian de Sola Pinto and F. Warren Roberts. Copyright 1933 by Frieda Lawrence. Reprinted by permission of The Viking Press, Inc.

Pp. 34–39, p. 54 from *The Snobs* by Russell Lynes. Copyright 1950 by Harper & Brothers. Reprinted by permission of Harper & Row, Publishers, Incorporated.

ful of any whose aesthetic antennae they consider less receptive than their own. It is customary, I believe, to classify the Art Snobs, the Literary Snobs, and the Musical Snobs with the Intellectual Snobs, but it seems to me that they belong in a limbo between the Emotional and the Intellectual categories, with plenty of latitude to permit them to jump either way. Furthermore the matter of taste comprehends more than just the arts (and, as we shall see, includes certain other vagaries of man's predilection for lording it over man). But let us take the arts first.

To categorize the Art Snobs into all of their many subdivisions would be an intricate and, I am afraid, tiresome business. We would, for example, have to consider the various shadings that range all the way from the Traditionalist or Permanent Value Snobs to the Modern or *I always keep an open mind* group. There are, however, a few basic behavior patterns that betray the Art Snob at any level. In a gallery he can be observed to stand back from a picture at some distance, his head cocked slightly to one side, and then after a rather long period of gazing (during which he may occasionally squint his eyes) he will approach to within a few inches of the picture and examine the brushwork; he will then return to his former distant position, give the picture another glance, and walk away. The Art Snob can be recognized in the home (*i.e.* your home) by the quick look he gives the pictures on your walls, quick but penetrating, as though he were undressing them. This is followed either by complete and obviously pained silence or by a comment such as, "That's really a very pleasant little water color you have there." In his own house his manner is also slightly deprecating. If you admire a print on his wall, he is likely to say, "I'm glad you like it. It's really not bad considering it is such a late impression." Or if he is in the uppermost reaches of Art Snobs and owns an "old master" which you admire, he will say, "Of course Berenson lists it as a Barna da Sienna, but I've never satisfied myself that it isn't from the hand of one of his pupils."

The literary Snob has not only read the book you are reading but takes pleasure in telling you the names of all the earlier and more obscure books by the same author, and why each one was superior to the better known one that has come to your attention.

Musical Snobs are in general of two sorts — Classical Snobs and Jazz Snobs. The former can sometimes be identified at concerts because they keep their eyes closed. This can for obvious reasons be misleading, but if closed eyes are accompanied by a regular movement of the hands in time with the music, it is clear that the listener is beating time to himself. This is characteristic of the lowest orders of Classical Snob. If he has a score of the music which he follows while it is being played, he may be a professional musician looking for subtleties of interpretation; he may, on the other hand, merely be a higher order of Classical Snob. The surest way to identify the Classical Snob is to see whether he comes back after the intermission or not; if he stays only for the more difficult or abstruse part of the program and ignores the more popular portion, he is either a snob or a professional critic, or possibly both.

Musical Snobs, Jazz Division, beat time not with their hands but with their feet. They do not talk about records or recordings but about specific choruses, solo passages, or "breaks." They know the dates and numbers of original pressings and occasionally they collect never-played records much the same way some book collectors prefer rare copies with uncut pages. They are well grounded in the brand of jazz they refer to as "authentic" (New Orleans, Memphis, Chicago) and they are extremely partisan about what they consider to be "advanced" (Progressive Jazz, Bebop, or even Dixieland). There are some overtones of social and racial snobbery in the way Jazz Snobs identify themselves with jazz musicians.

. . . . . .

It will not have escaped the reader (and so I might as well admit it) that this cursory attempt to classify and define snobs is an example not only of Intellectual Snobbism but of Moral, Sensual, Occupational, Political, Emotional, and above all of Reverse or Antisnob Snobbism. I am sure there is no greater snob than a snob who thinks he can define a snob.

RUSSELL LYNES

BE SURE YOU understand all the unusual words in this poem. Take particular care in handling the grammatical structure so that all the long, involved sentences are clear.

The Snow-Storm

Announced by all the trumpets of the sky,
Arrives the snow, and, driving o'er the fields,
Seems nowhere to alight: the whited air
Hides hills and woods, the river, and the heaven,
And veils the farm-house at the garden's end.
The sled and traveller stopped, the courier's feet
Delayed, all friends shut out, the housemates sit
Around the radiant fireplace, enclosed
In a tumultuous privacy of storm.

Come see the north wind's masonry.
Out of an unseen quarry evermore
Furnished with tile, the fierce artificer
Curves his white bastions with projected roof
Round every windward stake, or tree, or door.
Speeding, the myriad-handed, his wild work
So fanciful, so savage, nought cares he

For number or proportion. Mockingly,
On coop or kennel he hangs Parian wreaths;
A swan-like form invests the hidden thorn;
Fills up the farmer's lane from wall to wall,
Maugre the farmer's sighs; and at the gate
A tapering turret overtops the work.
And when his hours are numbered, and the world
Is all his own, retiring, as he were not,
Leaves, when the sun appears, astonished Art
To mimic in slow structures, stone by stone,
Built in an age, the mad wind's nightwork,
The frolic architecture of the snow.

RALPH WALDO EMERSON

✶ Bibliography

Many of the following books deal with the evaluation of art in various forms, but they are applicable to the art of literature as well.

Beardsley, Monroe, Robert Daniel, and Glenn Leggett. *Theme and Form.* Englewood Cliffs, New Jersey: Prentice-Hall, Inc., 1956.

Brief essays on the structure of the various modes of literature combined with an anthology arranged according to themes.

Geiger, Don. *The Sound, Sense, and Performance of Literature.* Chicago: Scott, Foresman and Company, 1963.

The interpreter of literature is the special interest of this book, built on the premise that oral interpretation is in itself an act of criticism.

Langer, Susanne K. *Philosophy in a New Key.* Cambridge, Massachusetts: Harvard University Press, 1942.

Discussion of art as cognitive discourse.

Pepper, Stephen. *The Work of Art.* Bloomington, Indiana: Indiana University Press, 1955.

Propounds his theory of funding and fusion in response and contains a clarification of object and vehicle.

Richards, I. A. *Principles of Literary Criticism.* New York: Harcourt, Brace and Company, 1925.

One of the classics of modern literary criticism.

Vivas, Eliseo, and Murray Krieger. *The Problems of Aesthetics.* New York: Holt, Rinehart and Winston, Inc., 1935.

Essays on the nature and problems of aesthetics as a discipline and criteria for judgment.

Wellek, René, and Austin Warren. *Theory of Literature.* New York: Harcourt, Brace and Company, 1956.

Discussion of the nature and function of literature with helpful notes and good bibliography.

The fields of linguistics and semantics also have bearing on the interpreter's study of literature. The following books are good introductions to the two fields.

Hayakawa, S. I. *Language in Thought and Action.* New York: Harcourt, Brace and Company, 1949.

The basic principles of semantics as they relate to speech and literature.

Sapir, Edward. *Language: An Introduction to the Study of Speech.* New York: Harcourt, Brace and Company, 1921. Harvest Books edition, HB7, 1949.

A clear exposition of the principles of linguistics and their application to literary study.

3

The Use of the Body in Oral Interpretation

The interpreter's first problem, as we have seen, is to find suitable material which will be worth the time and effort he must spend in preparing it for performance. After he has chosen his selection, his next responsibility is to gain as complete an understanding as possible of all its elements — its logical meaning, its emotional overtones, and its qualities of literary craftsmanship. Finally, when he feels that he thoroughly understands the material, he must turn his attention to the most effective way of communicating it to the audience. It is at this point that control of the twofold instrument of body and voice becomes important. Just as a musician cannot give a satisfactory performance without having first perfected the handling of his instrument, so an interpreter, who is both instrument and instrumentalist, cannot do justice to the selection he has chosen unless he devotes some attention to technique.

The term "technique" does not imply artificiality in the use of voice and body. In fact, the finer the technique, the less apparent it is to the audience. Technique may be defined as style of performance. The style of performance in the art of interpretation must be unobtrusive if the interpreter is not to call attention to what he is doing and thus distract the audience from the material. Display of vocal or physical virtuosity as an end in itself has been outmoded since the decline of the "mechanical" school of elocution in the nineteenth century. Such display is considered in poor taste today, and is interesting only to the degree that an exhibition of calisthenics or a recital of scales and arpeggios would be interesting. It is the material that is important, and the interpreter uses technique as a means of communicating the material, not the material as a vehicle for displaying technique.

The modern interpreter develops vocal and bodily technique as a pianist practices scales, so that his muscles may respond without apparent prompting or effort to the demands he makes on them. Only then can he hope to achieve a total response from his audience. Conscious attention to technique belongs to the practice period and has no place in performance. During a performance the interpreter's attention should be concentrated on his material and on the response of his audience to that material. If his preparation has been adequate, the muscles of the vocal mechanism and of the entire body will respond according to the habits set up in practice. As skill increases through experience, this habitual response will become more dependable.

Since oral interpretation obviously implies the use of the voice, it would seem that the vocal mechanism should be considered first. It is a mistake, however, to overlook or underestimate the subtle but very significant role of the body in oral interpretation. As a matter of fact, the body begins the process of communication even before the voice is heard. From the moment the audience is aware of the physical presence of the interpreter, he is arousing a response, establishing in them what the psychologists call a "set," or condition of mental readiness, toward the reading they are about to hear. It is true that he does not begin to communicate the *specific* material until he starts to speak, but by his bodily action he gives intimations of his mental attitude toward himself, his audience, and his material. His state of physical tension or relaxation reflects his emotional state, which in turn is often indicative of his confidence in himself and in his chosen selection.

An audience is quick to resent an overbearing or cocky attitude, and is equally quick to question the authority of a speaker who seems unsure of his ability. The interpreter will strike a happy medium when he is confident that he is adequately prepared, that his material is satisfactory, and that his audience is capable of understanding and responding to that material. When he has doubts on any of these points, his uncertainty will be reflected in his physical bearing, and the audience will sense his insecurity and unconsciously share his discomfort. It is important, then, for the reader to avoid any mannerisms that may give an unfavorable impression, whether of virtuosity, arrogance, or lack of self-confidence.

Thus through bodily carriage and physical actions the interpreter sets up definite attitudes in the audience toward himself and his material, quite apart from the specific content of that material. But the body performs an even more important function in relation to the specific content. The physical reaction of the interpreter to his material, accompanying and indeed springing out of his mental response, is a vital factor in drawing a complete response from the audience.

Bodily action may be defined as any movement of the muscles of the body. This movement may be a full gesture, or it may be merely a relaxation or tension of the small muscles around the eyes or mouth, across the shoulders and back, in the legs, or a combination of any or all of these. It includes the approach to and departure from the platform, movements of the head, arms, shoulders, hands, torso, and legs, change of posture, facial expression, and the muscle tone of the entire body. The modern interpreter has no desire to establish or call upon a set of rules for posture and gesture. He knows that the test of bodily action is its effectiveness in the communication of the material at hand, rather than its conformity to technical rules. Bodily action is effective only when it is completely suited to the material and thus helps to elicit the desired response; when it is so unobtrusive as to go unnoticed except in so far as it contributes to that response; and when it is free of personal mannerisms which would distract the audience.

POSTURE

The basis of effective bodily action is good *posture,* which is primarily a matter of proper positional relations between the parts of the body. Good posture is that arrangement of the bones and muscles which puts the body in its perfect natural alignment so that each unit does its proper job of supporting and controlling the bodily structure without undue tension or strain. When this is accomplished, the entire body is balanced, flexible, responsive, and coordinated. Barring physical defects, good posture requires nothing more complicated than standing straight and easy from the ankle bone to the crown of the head so that the various parts of the skeletal structure fall naturally into place. This is not as easy as it sounds, however, if bad posture has been allowed to develop.

Because the muscles of the body are easily trained and adjust themselves rather quickly, tensions and strains may not be apparent after bad posture is firmly established, even though they continue to exist. For example, one of the most prevalent errors in posture is to allow the spine to sway in at the center of the back. This causes the neck to be thrust forward and the pelvis to be tipped out of natural alignment in order to preserve the balance of the skeletal structure. Such posture, which produces tight muscles in the throat and across the base of the ribs, interferes with natural voice placement and inhibits proper breath control. At the opposite extreme, when the spine is allowed to curve out so that the shoulders droop, the chest sags and the pelvis tips forward, causing the stomach to protrude. Such posture crowds the important diaphragm muscle and cuts down on the breath capacity.

Every adolescent is familiar with the admonition, repeated with annoying frequency, to stand up straight, hold the shoulders back, and pull the stomach in. Small wonder that he finds this posture not only difficult but uncomfortable to maintain, for this well-meant bit of parental advice contains a basic contradiction. Holding the shoulders back throws the body out of line, causing a degree of tension through the lower part of the torso as well as an almost irresistible desire to thrust the head forward in order to retain the feeling of balance. The secret of standing up straight is not to hold the shoulders back but to let them rest easily and naturally on top of the rest of the body. If the spine is straight and the entire body is in perfect natural alignment, from the ankle bone up through the knees and pelvis, the shoulders will assume their proper position and the chest will lift slightly, causing the large muscles which control the abdominal wall to be drawn in, so that, when the abdominal muscles are contracted, inches seem to disappear below the waist. The head should be held tall, in easy balance, neither poked forward nor tilted back out of alignment with the other parts of the skeletal frame.

If bad posture has placed the responsibility for balance on improper muscles, and the body has become accustomed to the strain thus imposed, the correct alignment may at first tire some of the neglected muscles. Gradually, however, they will resume their normal function and will be strengthened by proper use. Then the speaker will look and feel at ease, alert, and poised. Moreover, the muscles which control breathing and vocal projection will be released to do their job effectively.

MUSCLE TONE

Muscle tone refers to the degree of tension or relaxation present in the entire body. It is an extremely important consideration in projecting material to an audience, because an audience responds to what it sees as strongly as to what it hears. Muscle tone can reinforce or detract from the total impression the interpreter wishes to convey.

When the posture is good, the body is in a state of controlled relaxation, with no undue muscular strain or tension. The properly poised body is flexible and responsive, and moves with coordination and fluidity. It is "all of a piece." Controlled relaxation is not to be confused with apathy or lack of physical energy. The interpreter who looks as if he is too tired, depressed, or bored to stand up straight communicates an unfortunate impression to his audience — and draws an undesirable empathic response from them. For they reflect in their own muscle tone his sense of weariness, depression, or boredom. Relaxation is an easing of tension; it is not total disintegration. The degree of relaxation is controlled in the interest of dignity and poise, and is partly determined by the requirements of the material to be presented.

Muscle tone is affected by the mental attitude of the speaker as well as by his control of the physical aspects of posture. It will vary from obvious tension to assured, controlled relaxation in direct proportion to the interpreter's confidence in himself, his material, and his audience. Any performance will carry with it a degree of excitement which is translated into physical tension. The secret is to be able to channel that tension so that it becomes an asset instead of a hazard. The "butterflies" in the stomach are not a sign of fear but of excitement, which, properly understood and controlled, communicates itself to the audience in terms of a vital, stimulating performance. Too frequently, however, the inexperienced performer attributes this tension to stage fright — and immediately sets up a fear-pattern. If the material is acceptable and preparation has been adequate, then the "butterflies" are a good sign. They are the result of excitement and involvement without which no performance can possibly succeed. Of course, if the interpreter has prepared inadequately and is really unsure of his ability, or at least is not sure that he has done the best he could, then there is no help or sympathy for him. He cannot hope to solve his problem until he is willing to put more time and effort into careful and complete preparation.

GESTURE

A *gesture* may be defined as any clearly discernible movement which helps express or emphasize an idea. In the usual sense, gestures are overt actions limited to the hands and arms — and occasionally the head and shoulders. These parts of the body do not function as separate entities, however, but involve a "follow-through" which both affects and is affected by the degree of muscular tension of every other part of the body. Thus it is impossible to treat gesture apart from an awareness of posture and of muscle tone in general.

Unlike the oral interpreter trained in the theories and practices of the last century, when books on "elocution" and "expression" devoted several chapters to detailed study of gesture, the modern reader is little concerned with gesture as a separate, specific part of his training. Rather, he believes that gesture is an integral part of bodily action, that it grows out of his response to his material, and that it must aid in complete communication. If an action does not help communicate the material, it is not a gesture; it is only a distracting and extraneous movement which violates the basic principle that nothing an interpreter does should call attention to itself. This is not to say that gestures are not to be used. It *is* to say that their use must be dictated by the needs of the material being presented.

The interpreter's use of gestures normally depends upon two considerations. The first, as we have said, is his material. The interpreter will use whatever bodily action is necessary to make the meaning clear to his audience and to convey the emotional quality effectively. He is attempting to create a total impression in the minds of his listeners and thus help them re-create what the author has experienced. Too many or too specific gestures are likely to call attention to the person of the interpreter and hence distract from the material. This particular problem will be treated in more detail in the unit on drama, where it is brought into sharper focus.

The second consideration in the use of gestures is the personality of the speaker. Some interpreters respond physically to their material with greater ease than others. If gesturing is difficult for the interpreter and makes him self-conscious, he should forget about it and concentrate on empathic response and muscle tone. He should use whatever gestures he wishes in practice until he can handle them effectively when he needs them, but he should never let gestures as such become an issue when he is before an audience. When the interpreter's concentration shifts from his material to the problem of gestures, his audience will be quick to sense his preoccupation. If, on the other hand, the interpreter has a tendency to "talk with his whole body," he should use whatever gestures make him feel at ease and help him communicate his material. It is important, however, to keep in mind both facets of this advice — "make him feel at ease" and "help him communicate." There is the danger that what makes the interpreter feel at ease may distract his audience and thus actually block communication.

Perhaps the interpreter has developed certain habitual physical actions which are not gestures at all, in the sense that they do not help express the idea. He may be using a repetitious movement, such as a constant raising and lowering of one hand, a tilt of the head, or a shrug of the shoulders. Such personal mannerisms, called autistic gestures because they grow out of the interpreter's own personality, direct attention to the interpreter himself and prevent the audience from concentrating on his material.

Under ordinary circumstances, it is inadvisable for the interpreter to work before a mirror because by doing so he is likely to divorce bodily action from its proper function of communication. If, however, he suspects that he has a too-regular pattern of movement, an occasional check-up before a large mirror will help call this fault to his attention.

As we have noted, the modern interpreter does not plan specific gestures. Though he sometimes follows an explicit pattern of physical movement in the middle stage of preparation, in performance he abandons the large, explicit movements and goes forward into the realm of suggested action. He never marks passages as a reminder to execute a carefully worked out movement at a particular place. Rather, he strives for such complete understanding of the material that he will be able to respond to it fully — his gestures an integral part of that response.

A good gesture conforms to no rules except the rule of effectiveness. It is effective when it helps to communicate, is unobtrusive, and does not result in distracting mannerisms. It depends upon and grows out of the reader's total response to the material. Like every other aspect of technique, gesturing must be the result of the interpreter's mental and emotional response to what is on the printed page. As such, it will be a powerful force in engendering the desired response in the listeners.

EMPATHY

One of the interpreter's most powerful tools is his control and use of empathy. Although its roots are in the classic Greek, *empathy* is a term borrowed from modern psychology. Meaning literally a "feeling into," it is defined as both "the imaginal or mental projection of oneself into the elements of a work of art" and "a mental state in which one identifies or feels himself in the same state of mind as another person or a group."[1] This "mental projection of oneself" into a piece of literature implies, of course, emotional response to the writing in addition to logical comprehension.

Every writer who deals with emotions, no matter to what degree, uses words and phrases in such relationship that they cause some mental disturbance, which may take the form of pleasure or pain, activity or repose. The interpreter responds mentally to these words and phrases as he prepares the material. If he has not experienced precisely what the author is describing or creating, he can usually recall some parallel or approximate situation which once called up in him a comparable response. As he responds emotionally to the written material, his muscles

[1] H. C. Warren, ed., *Dictionary of Psychology.* Boston: Houghton Mifflin Company, 1934.

tighten or relax, usually without his conscious effort. This tightening or relaxing of the muscles affects the tone of the entire body.

The interaction of emotional and physical response, then, is the basis of empathy as it concerns the interpreter. The following experiment will clarify this interaction and show how it works:

1. Shut your mind to your immediate surroundings and recall some occasion or experience which made you feel happy and exhilarated. It does not matter in the least what the experience was, as long as it made you feel particularly pleased with yourself and with your world. Spend as long as you wish in recapturing the circumstances and the accompanying emotion.

2. Next, turn your thoughts to a set of circumstances which made you violently angry. Concentrate on every detail and allow yourself to become thoroughly resentful. This is the chance to say all the things you thought of after it was too late. Work yourself up into a state of complete irritation.

3. Now go back to the pleasant situation. Allow plenty of time for your anger to subside and for the feeling of pleasure to reinstate itself.

4. Having restored your good humor, recall a situation about which you were fearful — perhaps a notice to see the dean, or an appointment with someone from whom you have been expecting a stern and deserved reprimand. Let the feeling of dread and apprehension take hold of you for a few minutes. You go to the appointment and find to your extreme relief that you were wrong in assuming that the interview would be an unpleasant one. Take time for the feeling of relief to flow through you and relax you.

5. Now return once more to the pleasant situation, and try to recapture the feeling of exhilaration.

In the course of this experiment you will have experienced by recall and association a number of basic emotions. Each emotion, if you allowed it to be recalled and re-experienced completely, caused a change in the muscles of various parts of your body. This change was subtle, and perhaps you were unaware that it had taken place. Review the series of emotions, and become conscious of what happened to your facial muscles, the muscles in your back and neck, and even those in your legs and feet.

A word of warning is advisable at this point. The muscular response is in itself a result of inner or mental activity. The outward or physical signs are an indication of that inner activity, never a substitute for it. The mental and emotional response must come first; the muscular response must follow. Thus the first and basic step in empathy is the interpreter's full mental, emotional, and physical response to the piece of literature he has selected to read. Without this total response, the second step is impossible.

The second step in empathy has to do with the audience's response to the interpreter's material. This usually takes the form of an unconscious imitation of the speaker's muscle tone. When the interpreter is responding empathically to his material, he gives physical cues to his hearers, who in turn respond by muscular imitation. This muscular imitation helps intensify their emotional response. It is the same phenomenon which causes us to frown and feel depressed or irritated, to smile and feel happy, to yawn and feel tired or bored because someone else is frowning, smiling, or yawning. Understanding the principle of empathic response is vitally important to the interpreter. By a bare reading aloud, without preparation and without projecting himself into the material, he may manage to transfer the essential logical content from the printed page to the minds of his audience, but he cannot lay claim to the name of *interpreter* unless he makes use of empathic response.

The true interpreter will be aware of the value of empathy even in the way he approaches the platform. During his introduction he will use it to help establish an emotional readiness in his audience. If his selection is brief and intense, like the Dickinson poem in Chapter 2, he will find that his audience moves with him much more surely if he makes proper use of empathy. His own mental and emotional state of readiness will affect the tone of all his muscles. And the audience, by unconscious imitation of what it sees, will adopt the physical tone which reflects the emotional response the poet and the interpreter are communicating.

Psychologists have a complex scientific framework within which they study empathy, with varying theories to explain its source and effects. We as interpreters, however, are primarily concerned with how it works in the delicate but basic problem of inter-action among the literary selection, the interpreter who presents that selection, and the members of the audience. In its simplest physical terms, empathy involves a sympathetic or imitative tension or relaxation of the muscles. As it immediately concerns the interpreter, it is at once his own muscular response to the sense and spirit of what he is reading and a means of eliciting physical response from the audience. Hence he needs sufficient control over the muscle tone of his body to enable him to react appropriately to his mental and emotional responses. The interpreter must work conscientiously to develop a flexible, responsive body so that he may make full use of all his muscles to achieve complete communication from the printed page to his audience.

Finally, it should be noted that the current of empathy runs in both directions, for the reader in turn receives a stimulus from his audience. Thus, generated by the material on the printed page, the circuit of response is complete: from the material to the interpreter, out to the audience, and back again to the interpreter.

SELECTIONS FOR ANALYSIS AND ORAL INTERPRETATION

ALL THE FOLLOWING selections have a strong suggestion of physical action. In preparing them for oral interpretation, let your muscles respond completely, taking time in some cases to work out specific action, which you may or may not use in performance, to help you achieve the proper muscle tone and posture.

Remember that each selection must be analyzed for organization, attitude, and factors of art, as well as for suggested bodily action.

BE SURE YOU UNDERSTAND all the allusions in this first selection.

The Second Coming

Turning and turning in the widening gyre
The falcon cannot hear the falconer;
Things fall apart; the centre cannot hold;
Mere anarchy is loosed upon the world,
The blood-dimmed tide is loosed, and everywhere
The ceremony of innocence is drowned;
The best lack all conviction, while the worst
Are full of passionate intensity.

Surely some revelation is at hand;
Surely the Second Coming is at hand.
The Second Coming! Hardly are those words out
When a vast image out of *Spiritus Mundi*
Troubles my sight: somewhere in sands of the desert
A shape with lion body and the head of a man,
A gaze blank and pitiless as the sun,
Is moving its slow thighs, while all about it
Reel shadows of the indignant desert birds.
The darkness drops again; but now I know
That twenty centuries of stony sleep
Were vexed to nightmare by a rocking cradle,
And what rough beast, its hour come round at last,
Slouches towards Bethlehem to be born?

WILLIAM BUTLER YEATS

Reprinted with permission of the publisher from *The Collected Poems of W. B. Yeats* by William Butler Yeats. Copyright 1924 by The Macmillan Company, renewed 1952 by Bertha Georgie Yeats. Also reprinted with permission of Mrs. W. B. Yeats, A. P. Watt & Son, and The Macmillan Company of Canada.

This selection will profit from the use of some carefully timed gestures. The timing will be dictated by the author's attitude, which in turn is enforced by his style.

from *The Complete Book of Absolutely Perfect Housekeeping*

The first step in proper bed-making is to strip the bed completely and air out the room. This is easily done by opening a window, or, if it should be too cold outside, blowing a few times. Next the mattress is turned. This is correctly done by grasping the mattress firmly at the side by the loops provided and flipping it lightly over. If, as you do this, you hear something snap and find that you can't straighten up again, you haven't got the knack. Keep practicing. As soon as the mattress is turned, get out a file and smooth off your broken nails before going on to the next step. You don't want to snag the sheets, do you? You may also, if you wish, apply some liniment to your right shoulder.*

The next step is to put on the mattress pad or mattress cover, and this should be done now as it will be very hard to do it later.

The bottom sheet is put on next. This is important. If you mix up the sheets and accidentally put the top sheet on the bottom and the bottom sheet on top, no one will get any sleep at all that night since they will all be suffering from vertigo. The bottom sheet must not only be put on the bottom, but also it is urgent that it be put on upside down and inside out to insure even wear. You see, the top sheet, which is *always* put on top (this is an absolute *rule*) is put on right side out and upside up. Then, when the sheets are changed, the top sheet is put on the bottom (this is an exception to the rule above) it is then put on inside out and upside down and the new sheet is put right side out and upside up. You must understand, however, that right side out for a top sheet is actually inside out, while inside out on the bottom sheet really means right side out. The reason for this is obvious — when you turn the top of the top sheet down, you want the turned-down part to be right side out, not inside out. (However, don't ever turn the bottom of the bottom sheet up as this would result in utter confusion.) If this is not clear, the simplest thing to do is to change both sheets at once, or, better still, provide a nice clean pile of sweet-smelling hay or straw which can be thrown out from time to time and replaced as needed.

We are now going to place the bottom sheet on the mattress. Some women throw the sheet over the mattress any old way, and then walk around and around the bed, tugging the sheet this way and that and smoothing it out and pulling it up and down till all the life has gone out of it. This is highly imperfect bedmaking.

* You may now find it necessary to apply liniment to the mattress, too.

From *The Complete Book of Absolutely Perfect Housekeeping*, copyright © 1956, by Elinor Goulding Smith. Reprinted by permission of Harcourt, Brace & World, Inc.

The proper way is as follows. Take up the sheet in the hands. Grasp the sheet by the selvage at the side. Make sure the top of the sheet is toward the bottom of the bed and that the sheet is inside out (that is of course actually right side up). Also be sure the sheet is more or less centrally located, lengthwise. Now stand by the side of the bed, with your feet parallel and toes pointing straight ahead. Hold your back straight, head up, chin in, etc. Now, with one small flick of the wrists the sheet should place itself on the bed, straight, centered and smooth. If it didn't, you didn't get the flick right. Try again tomorrow. But above all, don't touch it again now. If you start tugging it about, you will never learn the right flick.

The bottom sheet must be tucked in all around before even considering the top sheet. Some women do the head and foot first and then the sides. This is inefficient. The correct way is to start at the nearest corner, *miter it firmly no matter how it struggles,* and continue once around the bed, tucking in the sides and mitering corners as you go. When you have reached the starting place, DON'T LOOK BACK.

The placing of the top sheet is exactly like the placing of the bottom sheet (except that it is now right side up, which means inside out, and with its top facing the head of the bed). The top sheet is tucked in only at the bottom. Isn't that lucky? Do not tuck it too far in, as you may then pull out the whole business, bottom sheet and all, when you withdraw your hands. If you tuck it *too* far in, you may be trapped there and never get your hands out at all. Keep your enthusiasm in check at all times.

You may now place the blankets on the bed, using the same flick of the wrist. This is a very tricky business, because it sometimes happens that at this exact moment the cat suddenly decides to take a nap on that very bed and lands in the middle just as the blankets are settling down nicely into place. In this case it is best to remain calm. Continue to make the bed *around* the animal. This may leave an unsightly bump in the center of the bed, but eventually she is certain to get hungry and will leave of her own accord. Should she fail to do this, *call a veterinarian at once* as a healthy animal is always hungry, and she may be coming down with some obscure type of cat ailment. On the other hand, she may not be suffering from cat enteritis at all, but is simply having a litter of kittens. In this case, your best bet is to sleep in a semi-circular position so as not to disturb the kittens until they are six weeks old and strong enough to make their way to somebody else's bed.

Once the blankets are on, you may fold down the top of the top sheet nicely over the blankets, and then proceed to tuck in the sides and miter the bottom corners. Some authorities believe that a fold should be made at the bottom of the bed to allow room for feet. I don't go along with this theory at all. There is no necessity for people to sleep on their backs with their feet sticking straight up. It is conducive to snoring. They should learn to sleep on their sides, with their feet nice and flat or folded well up toward the middle of the bed where there is more room. Or, better still, they can sleep on their stomachs with their toes curled down over the end of the mattress. There's *plenty* of room for their feet if they lie in the proper positions.

Many women, after making up the bed, cover it all up with a bedspread. In certain cases, this may well be the wisest maneuver. Do not forget to place the pillow (having first shaken it well) neatly at the head of the bed as placing it at the foot will only confuse things further.

During the period in which you are acquiring the flick of the wrist and using the proper self-control in regard to straightening and tugging, there may be a certain amount of complaining on the part of your family. Don't let them get away with this. Explain to them that you have made the beds in strict accord with the finest authorities (that's me) and that if the sheets are wrinkled it is no doubt due to *improper entering of the bed* on their part. If they're just going to climb in any old way, you can't be blamed for wrinkles.

In time you will acquire the knack of absolutely perfect bed-making. Or they will become accustomed to wrinkles. (Tell them to think of their bed as a little nest.) Either way.

ELINOR GOULDING SMITH

MUSCLE TONE AND posture will help suggest the power and strength of this Greek hero.

Ulysses

It little profits that an idle king,
By this still hearth, among these barren crags,
Matched with an agèd wife, I mete and dole
Unequal laws unto a savage race,
That hoard, and sleep, and feed, and know not me.
I cannot rest from travel; I will drink
Life to the lees. All times I have enjoyed
Greatly, have suffered greatly, both with those
That loved me, and alone; on shore, and when
Through scudding drifts the rainy Hyades
Vexed the dim sea. I am become a name;
For always roaming with a hungry heart
Much have I seen and known — cities of men,
And manners, climates, councils, governments,
Myself not least, but honored of them all, —
And drunk delight of battle with my peers,
Far on the ringing plains of windy Troy.
I am a part of all that I have met;

Yet all experience is an arch wherethrough
Gleams that untraveled world, whose margin fades
Forever and forever when I move.
How dull it is to pause, to make an end,
To rust unburnished, not to shine in use!
As though to breathe were life! Life piled on life
Were all too little, and of one to me
Little remains: but every hour is saved
From that eternal silence, something more,
A bringer of new things; and vile it were
For some three suns to store and hoard myself,
And this gray spirit yearning in desire
To follow knowledge, like a sinking star,
Beyond the utmost bound of human thought.
This is my son, my own Telemachus,
To whom I leave the sceptre and the isle, —
Well-loved of me, discerning to fulfil
This labor, by slow prudence to make mild
A rugged people, and through soft degrees
Subdue them to the useful and the good.
Most blameless is he, centred in the sphere
Of common duties, decent not to fail
In offices of tenderness, and pay
Meet adoration to my household gods,
When I am gone. He works his work, I mine.
There lies the port; the vessel puffs her sail;
There gloom the dark broad seas. My mariners,
Souls that have toiled, and wrought, and thought with me, —
That ever with a frolic welcome took
The thunder and the sunshine, and opposed
Free hearts, free foreheads, — you and I are old;
Old age hath yet his honor and his toil.
Death closes all; but something ere the end,
Some work of noble note, may yet be done,
Not unbecoming men that strove with Gods.
The lights begin to twinkle from the rocks;
The long day wanes; the slow moon climbs; the deep
Moans round with many voices. Come, my friends,
'Tis not too late to seek a newer world.
Push off, and sitting well in order smite
The sounding furrows; for my purpose holds
To sail beyond the sunset, and the baths
Of all the western stars, until I die.
It may be that the gulfs will wash us down;
It may be we shall touch the Happy Isles,
And see the great Achilles, whom we knew.
Though much is taken, much abides; and though
We are not now that strength which in old days
Moved earth and heaven, that which we are, we are;

One equal temper of heroic hearts,
Made weak by time and fate, but strong in will
To strive, to seek, to find, and not to yield.

ALFRED, LORD TENNYSON

RHYTHM OF CONTENT and empathy work together to build climaxes in this Negro "sermon." The juxtaposition of folk phrases and Biblical style is interesting. Notice that the poet has *not* used dialect. Let him have his way.

The Creation

And God stepped out on space,
And he looked around and said:
I'm lonely —
I'll make me a world.

And far as the eye of God could see
Darkness covered everything,
Blacker than a hundred midnights
Down in a cypress swamp.
Then God smiled,
And the light broke,
And the darkness rolled up on one side,
And the light stood shining on the other,
And God said: That's good!

Then God reached out and took the light in his hands
And God rolled the light around in his hands
Until he made the sun;
And he set that sun a-blazing in the heavens.
And the light that was left from making the sun
God gathered it up in a shining ball
And flung it against the darkness,
Spangling the night with the moon and stars.
Then down between
The darkness and the light
He hurled the world;
And God said: That's good!

Then God himself stepped down —
And the sun was on his right hand,
And the moon was on his left;
The stars were clustered about his head,
And the earth was under his feet.
And God walked, and where he trod

From *God's Trombones* by James Weldon Johnson. Copyright 1927 by The Viking Press, Inc., 1954 by Grace Nail Johnson. Reprinted by permission of The Viking Press, Inc.

His footsteps hollowed the valleys out
And bulged the mountains up.

Then he stopped and looked and saw
That the earth was hot and barren.
So God stepped over to the edge of the world
And he spat out the seven seas —
He batted his eyes, and the lightnings flashed —
He clapped his hands, and the thunders rolled —
And the waters above the earth came down,
The cooling waters came down.

Then the green grass sprouted,
And the little red flowers blossomed,
The pine-tree pointed his finger to the sky,
And the oak spread out his arms,
The lakes cuddled down in the hollows of the ground,
And the rivers ran down to the sea;
And God smiled again,
And the rainbow appeared,
And curled itself around his shoulder.

Then God raised his arm and he waved his hand
Over the sea and over the land,
And he said: Bring forth! Bring forth!
And quicker than God could drop his hand,
Fishes and fowls
And beasts and birds
Swam the rivers and the seas,
Roamed the forests and the woods,
And split the air with their wings.
And God said: That's good!

Then God walked around,
And God looked around
On all that he had made.
He looked at his sun,
And he looked at his moon,
And he looked at his little stars;
He looked on his world
With all its living things,
And God said: I'm lonely still.

Then God sat down —
On the side of a hill where he could think;
By a deep, wide river he sat down;
With his head in his hands,
God thought and thought,
Till he thought: I'll make me a man!

Up from the bed of the river
God scooped the clay;
And by the bank of the river
He kneeled him down;
And there the great God Almighty
Who lit the sun and fixed it in the sky,
Who flung the stars to the most far corner of the night,
Who rounded the earth in the middle of his hand;
This Great God,
Like a mammy bending over her baby,
Kneeled down in the dust
Toiling over a lump of clay
Till he shaped it in his own image;

Then into it he blew the breath of life,
And man became a living soul.
Amen. Amen.

James Weldon Johnson

Gerard Manley Hopkins uses words in unusual but highly suggestive combinations. He presents obstacles to literal meanings, but there is a sweep and magnificence of sound in these two poems that is rewarding in itself. Given full sway, the sounds and the images will help the interpreter understand the ecstasy with which Hopkins regarded all the manifestations of Christ in nature.

The Starlight Night

Look at the stars! look, look up at the skies!
O look at all the fire-folk sitting in the air!
The bright boroughs, the circle-citadels there!
Down in dim woods the diamond delves! the elves'-eyes!
The grey lawns cold where gold, where quickgold lies!
Wind-beat whitebeam! airy abeles set on a flare!
Flake-doves sent floating forth at a farmyard scare! —
Ah well! it is all a purchase, all is a prize.

Buy then! bid then! — What? — Prayer, patience, alms, vows.
Look, look: a May-mess, like on orchard boughs!
Look! March-bloom, like on mealed-with-yellow sallows!
These are indeed the barn; within doors house
The shocks. This piece-bright paling shuts the spouse
Christ home, Christ and his mother and all his hallows.

Gerard Manley Hopkins

From *Poems of Gerard Manley Hopkins*, Third Edition, edited by W. H. Gardner. Copyright 1948 by Oxford University Press, Inc. Reprinted by permission.

God's Grandeur

The world is charged with the grandeur of God.
It will flame out, like shining from shook foil;
It gathers to a greatness, like the ooze of oil
Crushed. Why do men then now not reck his rod?
Generations have trod, have trod, have trod;
And all is seared with trade; bleared, smeared with toil;
And wears man's smudge and shares man's smell: the soil
Is bare now, nor can foot feel, being shod.

And for all this, nature is never spent;
There lives the dearest freshness deep down things;
And though the last lights off the black West went
Oh, morning, at the brown brink eastward, springs —
Because the Holy Ghost over the bent
World broods with warm breast and with ah! bright wings.

GERARD MANLEY HOPKINS

SEVERAL UNITS within this excerpt offer excellent opportunities for subtle use of the body.

from *The Little Prince*

Beside the well there was the ruin of an old stone wall. When I came back from my work, the next evening, I saw from some distance away my little prince sitting on top of this wall, with his feet dangling. And I heard him say:

"Then you don't remember. This is not the exact spot."

Another voice must have answered him, for he replied to it:

"Yes, yes! It is the right day, but this is not the place."

I continued my walk toward the wall. At no time did I see or hear anyone. The little prince, however, replied once again:

"— Exactly. You will see where my track begins, in the sand. You have nothing to do but wait for me there. I shall be there to-night."

I was only twenty meters from the wall, and I still saw nothing.

After a silence the little prince spoke again:

"You have good poison? You are sure that it will not make me suffer too long?"

I stopped in my tracks, my heart torn asunder; but still I did not understand.

From *Poems of Gerard Manley Hopkins,* Third Edition, edited by W. H. Gardner. Copyright 1948 by Oxford University Press, Inc. Reprinted by permission.

From *The Little Prince* by Antoine de Saint-Exupéry, copyright, 1943, by Reynal and Hitchcock, Inc. Reprinted by permission of Harcourt, Brace & World, Inc.

"Now go away," said the little prince. "I want to get down from the wall."

I dropped my eyes, then, to the foot of the wall — and I leaped into the air. There before me, facing the little prince, was one of those yellow snakes that take just thirty seconds to bring your life to an end. Even as I was digging into my pocket to get out my revolver I made a running step back. But, at the noise I made, the snake let himself flow easily across the sand like the dying spray of a fountain, and, in no apparent hurry, disappeared, with a light metallic sound, among the stones.

I reached the wall just in time to catch my little man in my arms; his face was white as snow.

"What does this mean?" I demanded. "Why are you talking with snakes?"

I loosened the golden muffler that he always wore. I had moistened his temples, and had given him some water to drink. And now I did not dare ask him any more questions. He looked at me very gravely, and put his arms around my neck. I felt his heart beating like the heart of a dying bird, shot with someone's rifle . . .

"I am glad that you have found what was the matter with your engine," he said. "Now you can go back home —"

"How do you know about that?"

I was just coming to tell him that my work had been successful, beyond anything that I had dared to hope.

He made no answer to my question, but he added:

"I, too, am going back home today . . ."

Then, sadly —

"It is much farther . . . It is much more difficult . . ."

I realized clearly that something extraordinary was happening. I was holding him close in my arms as if he were a little child; and yet it seemed to me that he was rushing headlong toward an abyss from which I could do nothing to restrain him . . .

His look was very serious, like someone lost far away.

"I have your sheep. And I have the sheep's box. And I have the muzzle . . ."

And he gave me a sad smile.

I waited a long time. I could see that he was reviving little by little.

"Dear little man," I said to him, "You are afraid . . ."

He was afraid, there was no doubt about that. But he laughed lightly.

"I shall be much more afraid this evening . . ."

Once again I felt myself frozen by the sense of something irreparable. And I knew that I could not bear the thought of never hearing that laughter any more. For me, it was like a spring of fresh water in the desert.

"Little man," I said, "I want to hear you laugh again."

But he said to me:

"Tonight, it will be a year . . . My star, then, can be found right above the place where I came to the Earth, a year ago . . ."

"Little man," I said, "tell me that it is only a bad dream — this affair of the snake, and the meeting-place, and the star . . ."

But he did not answer my plea. He said to me, instead:

"The thing that is important is the thing that is not seen . . ."

"Yes, I know . . ."

"It is just as it is with the flower. If you love a flower that lives on a star, it is sweet to look at the sky at night. All the stars are a-bloom with flowers . . ."

"Yes, I know . . ."

"It is just as it is with the water. Because of the pulley, and the rope, what you gave me to drink was like music. You remember — how good it was."

"Yes, I know . . ."

"And at night you will look up at the stars. Where I live everything is so small that I cannot show you where my star is to be found. It is better, like that. My star will be just one of the stars, for you. And so you will love to watch all the stars in the heavens . . . They will all be your friends. And, besides, I am going to make you a present . . ."

He laughed again.

"Ah, little prince, dear little prince! I love to hear that laughter!"

"That is my present. Just that. It will be as it was when we drank the water . . ."

"What are you trying to say?"

"All men have the stars," he answered, "but they are not the same things for different people. For some, who are travelers, the stars are guides. For others they are no more than little lights in the sky. For others, who are scholars, they are problems. For my businessman they were wealth. But all these stars are silent. You — you alone — will have the stars as no one else has them —"

"What are you trying to say?"

"In one of the stars I shall be living. In one of them I shall be laughing. And so it will be as if all the stars were laughing, when you look at the sky at night . . . You — only you — will have stars that can laugh!"

And he laughed again.

"And when your sorrow is comforted (time soothes all sorrows) you will be content that you have known me. You will always be my friend. You will want to laugh with me. And you will sometimes open your window, so, for that pleasure . . . And your friends will be properly astonished to see you laughing as you look up at the sky! Then you will say to them, 'Yes, the stars always make me laugh!' And they will think you are crazy. It will be a very shabby trick that I shall have played on you . . ."

And he laughed again.

"It will be as if, in place of the stars, I had given you a great number of little bells that knew how to laugh . . ."

And he laughed again. Then he quickly became serious:

"Tonight — you know . . . Do not come."

"I shall not leave you," I said.

"I shall look as if I were suffering. I shall look a little as if I were dying. It is like that. Do not come to see that. It is not worth the trouble . . ."

"I shall not leave you."

But he was worried.

"I tell you — it is also because of the snake. He must not bite you. Snakes — they are malicious creatures. This one might bite you just for fun . . ."

"I shall not leave you."

But a thought came to reassure him:

"It is true that they have no more poison for a second bite."

That night I did not see him set out on his way. He got away from me without making a sound. When I succeeded in catching up with him he was walking along with a quick and resolute step. He said to me merely:

"Ah! You are there . . ."

And he took me by the hand. But he was still worrying.

"It was wrong of you to come. You will suffer. I shall look as if I were dead; and that will not be true . . ."

I said nothing.

"You understand . . . It is too far. I cannot carry this body with me. It is too heavy."

I said nothing.

"But it will be like an old abandoned shell. There is nothing sad about old shells . . ."

I said nothing.

He was a little discouraged. But he made one more effort:

"You know, it will be very nice. I, too, shall look at the stars. All the stars will be wells with a rusty pulley. All the stars will pour out fresh water for me to drink . . ."

I said nothing.

"That will be so amusing! You will have five hundred million little bells, and I shall have five hundred million springs of fresh water . . ."

And he too said nothing more, because he was crying . . .

"Here it is. Let me go on by myself."

And he sat down, because he was afraid. Then he said, again:

"You know — my flower . . . I am responsible for her. And she is so weak! She is so naïve! She has four thorns, of no use at all, to protect herself against all the world . . ."

I too sat down, because I was not able to stand up any longer.

"There now — that is all . . ."

He still hesitated a little; then he got up. He took one step. I could not move.

There was nothing there but a flash of yellow close to his ankle.

He remained motionless for an instant. He did not cry out. He fell as gently as a tree falls. There was not even any sound, because of the sand.

And now six years have already gone by . . . I have never told this story. The companions who met me on my return were well content to see me alive. I was sad, but I told them: "I am tired."

Now my sorrow is comforted a little. That is to say — not entirely. But I know that he did go back to his planet, because I did not find his body at daybreak. It was not such a heavy body . . . And at night I love to listen to the stars. It is like five hundred million little bells . . .

But there is one extraordinary thing . . . When I drew the muzzle for the little prince, I forgot to add the leather strap to it. He will never have been able to fasten it on his sheep. So now I keep wondering: what is happening on his planet? Perhaps the sheep has eaten the flower . . .

At one time I say to myself: "Surely not! The little prince shuts his flower under her glass globe every night, and he watches over his sheep very carefully . . ." Then I am happy. And there is sweetness in the laughter of all the stars.

But at another time I say to myself: "At some moment or other one is absent-minded, and that is enough! On some one evening he forgot the glass globe, or the sheep got out, without making any noise, in the night . . ." And then the little bells are changed to tears . . .

Here, then, is a great mystery. For you who also love the little prince, and for me, nothing in the universe can be the same if somewhere, we do not know where, a sheep that we never saw has — yes or no? — eaten a rose . . .

Look up at the sky. Ask yourselves: Is it yes or no? Has the sheep eaten the flower? And you will see how everything changes . . .

And no grown-up will ever understand that this is a matter of so much importance!

ANTOINE DE SAINT-EXUPÉRY

THERE IS AN INTERESTING shift in empathy at the fulcrum of this poem. The allusions help prepare for the shift.

Swans

Fraudulent perhaps in that they gave
No sense of muscle but a swollen languor
Though moved by webs: yet idly, idly

From *Collected Poems* by Lawrence Durrell. Copyright © 1956, 1960 by Lawrence Durrell. Dutton Paperback Edition. Reprinted by permission of E. P. Dutton & Co., Inc. Also reprinted by permission of Faber and Faber, Ltd.

As soap-bubbles drift from a clay-pipe
They mowed the lake in tapestry,

Passing in regal exhaustion by us,
King, queen and cygnets, one by one.
Did one dare to remember other swans
In anecdotes of Gauguin or of Rabelais?
Some became bolsters for the Greeks,
Some rubber Lohengrins provided comedy.
The flapping of the wings excited Leda.
The procession is over and what is now
Alarming is more the mirror split
From end to end by the harsh clap
Of the wooden beaks, than the empty space
Which follows them about,
Stained by their whiteness when they pass.

We sit like drunkards and inhale the swans.

LAWRENCE DURRELL

THESE TWO POEMS by the same poet offer sharply contrasting physical responses. The first is held at a fairly steady level. The second has quick, demanding contrasts.

Child on Top of a Greenhouse

The wind billowing out the seat of my britches,
My feet crackling splinters of glass and dried putty,
The half-grown chrysanthemums staring up like accusers,
Up through the streaked glass, flashing with sunlight,
A few white clouds all rushing eastward,
A line of elms plunging and tossing like horses,
And everyone, everyone pointing up and shouting.

THEODORE ROETHKE

Old Lady's Winter Words

To seize, to seize, —
I know that dream.
Now my ardors sleep in a sleeve.

"Child on Top of a Greenhouse," copyright 1946 by Editorial Publications, Inc., from *Words For The Wind* by Theodore Roethke. Reprinted by permission of Doubleday & Company, Inc.

"Old Lady's Winter Words," copyright 1952 by Theodore Roethke, from *Words For The Wind* by Theodore Roethke. Reprinted by permission of Doubleday & Company, Inc.

My eyes have forgotten.
Like the half-dead, I hug my last secrets.
O for some minstrel of what's to be,
A bird singing into the beyond,
The marrow of God, talking,
Full merry, a gleam
Gracious and bland,
On a bright stone.
Somewhere, among the ferns and birds,
The great swamps flash.
I would hold high converse
Where the winds gather,
And leap over my eye,
An old woman
Jumping in her shoes.
If only I could remember
The white grass bending away,
The doors swinging open,
The smells, the moment of hay, —
When I went to sea in a sigh,
In a boat of beautiful things.
The good day has gone:
The fair house, the high
Elm swinging around
With its deep shade, and birds.
I have listened close
For the thin sound in the windy chimney,
The fall of the last ash
From the dying ember.
I've become a sentry of small seeds,
Poking alone in my garden.
The stone walks, where are they?
Gone to bolster a road.
The shrunken soil
Has scampered away in a dry wind.
Once I was sweet with the light of myself,
A self-delighting creature,
Leaning over a rock,
My hair between me and the sun,
The waves rippling near me.
My feet remembered the earth,
The loam heaved me
That way and this.
My looks had a voice;
I was careless in growing.

If I were a young man,
I could roll in the dust of a fine rage.

The shadows are empty, the sliding externals.
The wind wanders around the house
On its way to the back pasture.
The cindery snow ticks over stubble.
My dust longs for the invisible.
I'm reminded to stay alive
By the dry rasp of the recurring inane,
The fine soot sifting through my south windows.
It is hard to care about corners,
And the sound of paper tearing.
I fall, more and more,
Into my own silences.
In the cold air,
The spirit
Hardens.

THEODORE ROETHKE

SANDBURG HAS CAUGHT an experience of tension in this autobiographical sketch.

from *Theme in Shadow and Gold*

I had my "puppy love." Day and night her face would be floating in my mind. I liked to practice at calling up her face as I had last seen it. Her folks lived in the Sixth Ward on Academy Street next to the Burlington tracks of the Q. They usually left a crock on the porch with a quart ticket in it. I took the ticket out of the crock, tilted my can and poured milk into my quart measure, and then poured it into the crock, well aware she was sometimes at the kitchen window watching my performance, ducking away if I looked toward the window. Two or three times a week, however, the crock wasn't there and I would call "Milk!" in my best boy-baritone and she would come out with the crock in her hands and a smile on her face. At first she would merely say "Quart" and I would pour the quart, take my can, and walk away. But I learned that if I spoke as smooth and pleasant a "Good morning" as I could, then she would speak me a "Good morning" that was like a blessing to be remembered. I learned too that if I could stumble out the words, "It's a nice day" or "It's a cold wind blowing" she would say a pert "Yes, it is" and I would go away wondering how I would ever get around to a one- or two-minute conversation with her.

I was more bashful than she. If she had been in the slightest as smitten as I was, she would have "talked an arm off me." But she didn't. It was a lost love from the start. I was smitten and she

From *Always The Young Strangers,* copyright, 1952, 1953, by Carl Sandburg. Reprinted by permission of Harcourt, Brace & World, Inc.

wasn't. And her face went on haunting me. Today I can call up her girl face and say it's as fine as any you'd like to rest your eyes on, classic as Mona Lisa and a better-rounded rosy mouth. I had no regrets she had smitten me and haunted me. I asked for nothing and she promised the same. I could say I had known my first love. It was a lost love but I had had it. It began to glimmer away after my first and only walk with her.

I dropped in with another boy one summer night to revival services at the Knox Street Congregational Church. There I saw her with another girl. After the services a chum of mine took the other girl and I found myself walking with the girl of my dreams. I had said, "See you home?" and she had said, "Certainly." And there we were walking in a moonlight summer night and it was fourteen blocks to her home. I knew it was my first or last chance with her. I said it was a mighty fine moonlight night. She said "Yes" and we walked a block saying nothing. I said it was quite a spell of hot weather we had been having. She said "Yes" and we walked another block. I said one of the solo singers at the church did pretty good. And again she agreed and we walked on without a word. I spoke of loose boards in the wooden sidewalk of the next block and how we would watch our step, which we did.

I had my right hand holding her left arm just above the elbow, which I had heard and seen was the proper way to take a girl home. And my arm got bashful. For blocks I believed maybe she didn't like my arm there and the way I was holding it. After a few blocks it was like I had a sore wooden arm that I ought to take off and have some peace about it. Yet I held on. If I let go I would have to explain and I couldn't think of an explanation. Not for a flickering second did it dawn on me to say, "You know I'm crazy about you and crazy is the right word." I could have broken one of the two blocks we walked without a word by saying, "Would you believe it, your face keeps coming back to me when I'm away from you — all the time it keeps coming back as the most wonderful face my eyes ever met." Instead I asked her how her father, who was a freight-train conductor on the Q., liked being a conductor and did he find it nice work.

We made the grade at last. The fourteen blocks came to an end. I could no more have kissed her at the gate of her house than a man could spit against Niagara Falls and stop the water coming down. Instead of trying to kiss her I let go her arm and said "Good night" and walked away fast as if I had an errand somewhere. I didn't even stand still to see if she made it to the front door. I had made the decision I wasn't for her nor she for me. We were not good company for each other. If we were, at least one of us would have said something about what good company we were. I still adored her face and its genuine loveliness, but it had come clear to me that we were not "cut out for each other." I had one satisfaction as I walked home. My bashful right arm gradually became less wooden. The blood began circulating in it and my fingers were loose instead of tight and I could wiggle them.

CARL SANDBURG

LET YOUR MUSCLES respond to this famous speech on the seven ages of man. Keep the progression firm and unified.

from *As You Like It*

ACT II, SCENE 7

JAQUES: All the world's a stage,
And all the men and women merely players.
They have their exits and their entrances,
And one man in his time plays many parts,
His acts being seven ages. At first the infant,
Mewling and puking in the nurse's arms.
Then the whining school-boy, with his satchel
And shining morning face, creeping like snail
Unwillingly to school. And then the lover,
Sighing like furnace, with a woeful ballad
Made to his mistress' eyebrow. Then a soldier,
Full of strange oaths, and bearded like the pard,
Jealous in honor, sudden, and quick in quarrel,
Seeking the bubble reputation
Even in the cannon's mouth. And then the justice,
In fair round belly with good capon lin'd,
With eyes severe and beard of formal cut,
Full of wise saws and modern instances;
And so he plays his part. The sixth age shifts
Into the lean and slipper'd pantaloon,
With spectacles on nose and pouch on side,
His youthful hose, well sav'd, a world too wide
For his shrunk shank, and his big manly voice,
Turning again toward childish treble, pipes
And whistles in his sound. Last scene of all,
That ends this strange eventful history,
Is second childishness and mere oblivion,
Sans teeth, sans eyes, sans taste, sans everything.

WILLIAM SHAKESPEARE

IT WILL BE NECESSARY to keep in mind both the situation in England in 1802 and the kind of writing which Milton left as a heritage. An aware-

From *The Complete Plays and Poems of William Shakespeare*, eds. William Allan Neilson and Charles Jarvis Hill. Boston: Houghton Mifflin Company, 1942.

ness of Milton as a unifying force throughout the sonnet will help in handling the parallel grammatical structures and will indicate the degree of strength and dignity of muscle tone.

London, 1802

Milton! thou shouldst be living at this hour:
England hath need of thee: she is a fen
Of stagnant waters: altar, sword, and pen,
Fireside, the heroic wealth of hall and bower,
Have forfeited their ancient English dower
Of inward happiness. We are selfish men;
Oh! raise us up, return to us again;
And give us manners, virtue, freedom, power.
Thy soul was like a Star, and dwelt apart;
Thou hadst a voice whose sound was like the sea:
Pure as the naked heavens, majestic, free,
So didst thou travel on life's common way,
In cheerful godliness; and yet thy heart
The lowliest duties on herself did lay.

William Wordsworth

James Agee has caught the combination of shy pride, bewilderment, and sense of isolation of a small boy whose father has been killed in an automobile accident. Let your muscles respond fully to help project the builds and drops of tension. This fairly long excerpt contains several shorter units which can be used separately.

from *A Death in the Family*

Chapter Sixteen

The air was cool and gray and here and there along the street, shapeless and watery sunlight strayed and vanished. Now that he was in this outdoor air he felt even more listless and powerful; he was alone, and the silent, invisible energy was everywhere. He stood on the porch and supposed that everyone he saw passing knew of an event so famous. A man was walking quickly up the street and as Rufus watched him, and waited for the man to meet his eyes, he felt a great quiet lifting within him of pride and of shyness, and he felt his face break into a smile, and then an uncontrollable grin, which he knew he must try to make sober again; but the man walked past without looking at him, and so did the next

Copyright © 1957 by The James Agee Trust. From *A Death in the Family* by permission of Ivan Obolensky, Inc., New York, New York.

man who walked past in the other direction. Two schoolboys passed whose faces he knew, so he knew they must know his, but they did not even seem to see him. Arthur and Alvin Tripp came down their front steps and along the far sidewalk and now he was sure, and came down his own front steps and halfway out to the sidewalk, but then he stopped, for now, although both of them looked across into his eyes, and he into theirs, they did not cross the street to him or even say hello, but kept on their way, still looking into his eyes with a kind of shy curiosity, even when their heads were turned almost backwards on their necks, and he turned his own head slowly, watching them go by, but when he saw that they were not going to speak he took care not to speak either.

What's the matter with them, he wondered, and still watched them; and even now, far down the street, Arthur kept turning his head, and for several steps Alvin walked backwards.

What are they mad about?

Now they no longer looked around, and now he watched them vanish under the hill.

Maybe they don't know, he thought. Maybe the others don't know, either.

He came out to the sidewalk.

Maybe everybody knew. Or maybe he knew something of great importance which nobody else knew. The alternatives were not at all distinct in his mind; he was puzzled, but no less proud and expectant than before. My daddy's dead, he said to himself slowly, and then, shyly, he said it aloud: "My daddy's dead." Nobody in sight seemed to have heard it; he had said it to nobody in particular. "My daddy's dead," he said again, chiefly for his own benefit. It sounded powerful, solid, and entirely creditable, and he knew that if need be he would tell people. He watched a large, slow man come towards him and waited for the man to look at him and acknowledge the fact first, but when the man was just ahead of him, and still did not appear even to have seen him, he told him, "My daddy's dead," but the man did not seem to hear him, he just swung on by. He took care to tell the next man sooner and the man's face looked almost as if he were dodging a blow but he went on by, looking back a few steps later with a worried face; and after a few steps more he turned and came slowly back.

"What was that you said, sonny?" he asked; he was frowning slightly.

"My daddy's dead," Rufus said, expectantly.

"You mean that sure enough?" the man asked.

"He died last night when I was asleep and now he can't come home ever any more."

The man looked at him as if something hurt him.

"Where do you live, sonny?"

"Right here"; he showed with his eyes.

"Do your folks know you out here wandern round?"

He felt his stomach go empty. He looked frankly into his eyes and nodded quickly.

The man just looked at him and Rufus realized: He doesn't believe me. How do they always know?

"You better just go on back in the house, son," he said. "They won't like you being out here on the street." He kept looking at him, hard.

Rufus looked into his eyes with reproach and apprehension, and turned in at his walk. The man still stood there. Rufus went on slowly up his steps, and looked around. The man was on his way again but at the moment Rufus looked around, he did too, and now he stopped again.

He shook his head and said, in a friendly voice which made Rufus feel ashamed, "How would your daddy like it, you out here telling strangers how he's dead?"

Rufus opened the door, taking care not to make a sound, and stepped in and silently closed it, and hurried into the sitting room. Through the curtains he watched the man. He still stood there, lighting a cigarette, but now he started walking again. He looked back once and Rufus felt, with a quailing of shame and fear, he sees me; but the man immediately looked away again and Rufus watched him until he was out of sight.

How would your daddy like it?

He thought of the way they teased him and did things to him, and how mad his father got when he just came home. He thought how different it would be today if he only didn't have to stay home from school.

He let himself out again and stole back between the houses to the alley, and walked along the alley, listening to the cinders cracking under each step, until he came near the sidewalk. He was not in front of his own home now, or even on Highland Avenue; he was coming into the side street down from his home, and he felt that here nobody would identify him with his home and send him back to it. What he could see from the mouth of the alley was much less familiar to him, and he took the last few steps which brought him out onto the sidewalk with deliberation and shyness. He was doing something he had been told not to do.

He looked up the street and he could see the corner he knew so well, where he always met the others so unhappily, and, farther away, the corner around which his father always disappeared on the way to work, and first appeared on his way home from work. He felt it would be good luck that he would not be meeting them at that corner. Slowly, uneasily, he turned his head, and looked down the side street in the other direction; and there they were: three together, and two along the far side of the street, and one alone, farther off, and another alone, farther off, and, without importance to him, some girls here and there, as well. He knew the faces of all these boys well, though he was not sure of any of their names. The moment he saw them all he was sure they saw him, and sure that they knew. He stood still and waited for them, looking from one to another of them, into their eyes, and step by step at their several distances, each of them at all times looking into his eyes and knowing, they came silently nearer. Waiting, in silence, during those many seconds before the first of them came really near him, he felt that it was so long to wait, and be watched so closely and silently, and to watch back, that he wanted to go back into the alley and not be seen by them or by anybody else, and yet at the same time he knew that they were all approaching him with the realization that something had happened to him that had not happened to any other boy in town, and that now at last they were bound to think well of him; and the nearer they came but were yet at a distance, the more the gray, sober air was charged with the great energy and with a sense of glory and of danger, and the deeper and more exciting the silence became, and the more tall, proud, shy and exposed he felt; so that as they came still nearer he once again felt his face break into a wide smile, with which he had nothing to do, and, feeling that there was something deeply wrong in such a smile, tried his best to quieten his face and told them, shyly and proudly, "My daddy's dead."

JAMES AGEE

✶ Bibliography

The current textbooks all contain some discussion of the use of the body in oral communication. The books listed below are more technical and specialized in their treatment but contain much that will be of interest to the serious student of interpretation.

Birdwhistell, Ray L. *Introduction to Kinesics: An Annotation System for Analysis of Body Motion and Gesture*. Louisville, Kentucky: University of Louisville Press, n.d.

One of the early basic studies in the relationship between kinesics and oral communication.

Blackmur, R. P. *Language As Gesture*. New York: Harcourt, Brace and Company, 1952.

Detailed analysis of specific poems to illustrate the theory of poetry as language of gesture.

Burke, Kenneth. *The Philosophy of Literary Form: Studies in Symbolic Action*. Revised Edition. New York: Vintage Books, Inc., 1957.

Essays on rhetoric and poetics but basically a discussion of the theory of symbolic action.

Katz, Robert L. *Empathy: Its Nature and Uses.* New York: The Macmillan Company, 1963.

Emphasis on the dynamics of empathy and its social and aesthetic uses.

Ruesch, Jurgen, and Weldon Kees. *Non-verbal Communication.* Berkeley, California: University of California Press, 1956.

The relationship between digital and analogical communication with a strong recommendation for the development of the latter.

Stewart, David A. *A Preface to Empathy.* New York: Philosophical Library, 1956.

Empathy examined as identification and as a creative process.

4

Voice Development for Oral Interpretation

In the preceding chapter we gave most of our attention to the development of a flexible, responsive body. From time to time, however, we touched upon the effect of bodily action on vocal technique. Body and voice are a twofold instrument, and the modern interpreter learns to control them both so that they work together in perfect combination to communicate whatever the literature demands. The body makes its own special contribution; but it is the voice, of course, which is basic to oral interpretation. Unless the interpreter can be heard and understood, muscle response and appropriate gestures will be of little value.

Most people speak adequately for general conversation and informal communication. But the oral interpretation of literature requires additional flexibility and special control. The fact that the interpreter uses his speaking voice every day, and has done so since he was a child, is no guarantee that it is an adequate instrument for artistic re-creation. The interpreter needs to know first of all just how his voice functions, and how it can be controlled and developed in order to provide wider range in pitch, greater flexibility in volume and stress, richer variations in quality, and finer degrees of subtlety in duration and rate. Once he understands how these factors can be controlled, he must work to develop his voice no less consciously than does the singer. As his voice control improves, he should be increasingly able to meet the demands of the various types of literary material with intelligence and sensitivity.

Perhaps it should be pointed out that the discussion in this chapter has to do with the normal speaking voice, not with any type of speech defect. Speech defects are in the province of the speech therapist and as such do not come into consideration here. This discussion and the suggested exercises that accompany it are entirely concerned with improving and enriching the normal voice, which may need some attention to make it sufficiently flexible, strong, and responsive to play its part in the artistic communication of literature to an audience.

BREATH CONTROL

The first concern of anyone interested in voice improvement should be breath control, because without adequate breath properly controlled the production of good vocal tone is impossible. Proper use of the normal breathing mechanism is simple. Any difficulties are due to bad habits which may be the result of physical or psychological tensions. An understanding of the muscles involved in the breathing process and of the functions they perform may help locate and release some of these tensions.

In inhalation — intake of air — the major concern is with the amount; in exhalation — outgo — it is with varied control. The whole process of breathing rests on two basic physiological and physical principles: the balance of tension and relaxation in opposing sets of muscles which serve to control the creation of a vacuum.

When the diaphragm, the large dome-shaped muscle at the floor of the chest, *contracts,* it lowers and pushes downward against the *relaxed* abdominal muscles; thus the lengthwise expansion of the chest is increased. As this action is taking place, the muscles between the outer surfaces of the ribs contract, the rib cage is thus lifted and extended, and the side-to-side and front-to-back expansion of the chest is accomplished. This increase in size creates a vacuum inside the chest cavity. Atmospheric pressure forces air into the vacuum so that the pressure inside and outside the body is equalized. The air is forced down through the windpipe (trachea), on through the bronchial tubes, and finally comes to rest in the flexible air sacs in the lungs in which the bronchioli terminate. The air sacs in the lungs inflate as the air enters, and when the lungs are thus extended the process of inhalation is complete. Obviously, then, breathing is an active muscle process.

When the mechanism is ready for the process of exhalation to take place (following the exchange of oxygen and carbon dioxide in the blood), the muscle fibres in the diaphragm relax and the diaphragm rises into the dome-shaped position high in the chest. The muscles on the outside of the rib cage relax as the ones between the ribs on the inside contract. This action pulls the extended rib cage inward. All this pressure upward and inward acts upon the elastic lung tissue containing the air forced in during inhalation; the elastic tissue begins to collapse, and the air is forced out of the lungs, up through the bronchial tubes, through the windpipe, and finally out of the nose or mouth. Thus one cycle of respiration is completed.

In exhaling for speech, however, there is frequently another action in addition to the relaxing of the diaphragm in the lower chest area. This action is the firm contraction of the abdominal muscles which are relaxed for inhalation. As they contract for exhalation, they support the action accomplished by the relaxing of the diaphragm, and in this way help to control the outgo of air. This process is known as "forced exhalation" — a term somewhat misleading, perhaps, because the contraction of the abdominal muscles should be an easy and natural process, particularly for a trained speaker who wishes "support" of a tone projected by sustained exhalation. It is simply an additional action, or rather a continuation of action, in the process of exhalation during silent breathing.

Now, where should the student of voice begin his exercises so that he will have greater breath capacity and better control over exhalation? He will want these muscle processes to function effectively so that he may give smooth interpretation to long flowing lines of poetry, for instance, or force a swift exhalation for command or expression of emotion in dramatic dialogue.

The first thing to remember is that proper breathing is possible only when the posture is good. If each muscle is to perform its assigned function, the body must be in a state of controlled relaxation — that is, in a state of nicely balanced relaxation and essential tension. Wrongly induced tension inhibits the flexibility of muscles that control the intake and the outward flow of air. One of the most frequent errors in breathing practice is forcing the muscles of the rib cage and the abdomen into a rigid position. These muscles must be firm, but they cannot function if they are locked. If the muscles below the ribs are "tucked in" after a full inhalation, they will be ready to help in the important function of control.

In exercises for improved breathing habits it is particularly important, when standing, to have the weight easily and comfortably supported by the feet and legs, to have the spinal column erect but not forced into position, the shoulders level, and the muscles that support them free from tension. Strong lifting of the shoulders in inhalation serves only to put tension in the wrong area, with consequent effect on the vocal tone if phonation is to take place with the exhaled breath. Furthermore, exercise is easier and more effective if done in a comfortable place, with a good supply of fresh air.

A simple exercise to demonstrate the proper balance between tension and relaxation in the special muscles of respiration will be profitable.

This exercise also tends to show *where* concentration of energy should be — at the "beltline" rather than in the throat.

1. Contract the abdominal muscles *sharply* and force the air out of the chest on a single vocalization such as "Ah — h — h," much as if sighing. Hold the contraction of these muscles an appreciable instant, then *suddenly* release the tension. Notice that the air rushes into the chest and fills the lower portion (perhaps more) of the lungs upon the release of the tension. Exhale by forcing air out of the chest with the gradual contraction of the abdominal muscles as the diaphragm relaxes and returns to its dome-shaped position.

2. Repeat the process described in Exercise 1, and as the air rushes in on the release of tension in the abdominal muscles, make a conscious effort to lift the upper rib cage slightly (Careful — *not* the shoulders!) so that more space is created in the upper chest, and the whole chest is well extended and can accommodate a large intake of air. The upper portion of the lungs should be filled now, as well as the lower. Exhale, pushing the air out with the relaxing of the diaphragm and the gradual contracting of abdominal muscles and lowering of the rib cage. (Don't collapse and let the shoulders sag!)

3. Repeat the process described in Exercise 2 as far as the sudden exhalation followed by the easy full inhalation. Now, as you start to exhale the full breath, begin to vocalize by counting aloud. As you begin to run out of breath for vocalizing, begin gradually to contract the abdominal muscles (*not* the upper chest ones) as you continue counting. You are now utilizing "forced exhalation." When you can no longer force air out of the chest by the strong but comfortable contraction of the abdominal muscles, stop the vocalized counting. Don't sacrifice a good quality of tone in the effort to "squeeze out" more sound. This will only result in undue tension in the upper chest and throat muscles — the very thing you want to avoid.

This exercise is basic to the development of good breath control and should be used as a starter for any period of exercise. Most instructions say: "Breathe in," *then* "breathe out." This one suggests breathing out first, in order to empty the chest of the air in it at the moment of beginning the exercise. In this way, a "stuffing" of the chest is avoided. Then comes the breathing in, followed by the controlled breathing out — the inevitable order whether "exercising" or not, for no one can go on holding his breath forever.

The student should not work steadily at this or any other exercise when he begins to feel tired. Until he grows used to a changed method of control or a marked effort to increase capacity, he should go back for a "rest" to his usual manner of breathing. It should become increasingly clear, however, as he follows this type of exercise that the sooner he can make this method automatic, the easier will be his whole breathing process.

As he is able to take in larger amounts of air with ease and to continue forced exhalation to support the tone, he should be able to count more numbers on one breath. He should try with each exercise period to say a few more, being careful always that there is no strain in the throat, no forcing of the tone or sacrifice of good quality. He should count at what seems an easy volume (loudness) for him, and at a pleasing level of pitch.

The student interpreter should try his breath control on the following passage, keeping an unbroken flow of sound to the end of each sentence, without, of course, doing violence to the meaning and connotation of the words.

from *The Pied Piper of Hamelin*

And out of the houses the rats came tumbling.
Great rats, small rats, lean rats, brawny rats,
Brown rats, black rats, gray rats, tawny rats,
Grave old plodders, gay young friskers,
   Fathers, mothers, uncles, cousins,
Cocking tails and pricking whiskers,
   Families by tens and dozens,
Brothers, sisters, husbands, wives —
Followed the Piper for their lives.

ROBERT BROWNING

It is obviously impractical to attempt to complete the long sentence on a single breath, except as an exercise. Such a procedure would threaten the clarity of the thought and the relationship of the phrases to one another. Some of the phrasal units will need to be separated by pauses of varying lengths when the material is read aloud. During these pauses the speaker has an opportunity to replenish his supply of breath. He must take care not to let the pauses break the continuity of thought. The position and duration of the pauses must always grow out of the relationship of the phrases to each other and to the complete thought being expressed. The interpreter will learn to breathe where he must pause, not pause in order to breathe. It will usually be impossible to get a capacity breath except in the major pauses which complete the units of thought. Therefore, the final step in control of breathing is to learn to inhale quickly and unobtrusively, while still using the proper muscles.

Frequently a speaker will be inhaling properly and using his full capacity for breath but still not be able to sustain a long flow of sound.

Here the problem is not one of an insufficient supply of air but of inadequate control of exhalation. This is one of the major causes of "dropping" final words or syllables so that they do not carry to the last row of the audience. A simple exercise will help determine whether or not the control muscles collapse instead of exerting steady pressure as they relax:

Inhale a full, comfortable breath. Hold a lighted match directly in front of your lips as close as your profile will allow. Start to count aloud in full voice. You should be able to continue until the match burns down. If you blow the flame out, check the state of control of the muscles in and around the rib cage. Most of us exhale more than we need to on certain sounds, such as "*t*wo" or "*th*ree" or "*f*our." Light another match, take another deep breath and try the exercise again, speaking very softly with conscious control of the rate of relaxation of the muscles involved. You will feel as if you may explode, but you won't, and you will be made aware of where the control must be exercised. As you gradually increase your volume to normal, you will find that the match flickers but that you will not extinguish it by a sudden spurt of air.

VOLUME AND PROJECTION

These two inseparable factors in communication are so important that they must always be of utmost concern to the reader, actor, or speaker. Anyone who has been in an audience of any size and found to his distress that he could not hear the speaker knows the immense importance of sufficient volume and good projection. The interpreter's main purpose is, after all, to communicate his material to his audience. If he cannot be heard, he has obviously failed in his primary objective.

Actually, "volume" and "projection" are sometimes used interchangeably, and indeed they are both part of the interpreter's ability to be heard and understood. For greater clarity in this discussion, however, let us consider *volume* as degree of loudness and *projection* as the act of directing the voice to a specific target.

Of course, the interpreter must be able to make his voice fill the room in which his audience is gathered. He must learn to control his volume in order to fill the space easily without distorting his voice, or blasting down the back wall if his space is limited. He must know how much volume is required and how to achieve the greatest possible flexibility within that requirement. His understanding of the entire breathing process is basic to his control of volume.

Mere loudness, however, is not always enough. It is, unfortunately, not unusual to encounter an amateur speaker who can be heard but cannot be understood. Obviously, this touches on the problems of pronunciation and articulation, which will be considered later in this chapter. Being understood, however, depends to a degree on the speaker's control of projection.

The first requirement of adequate projection is sufficient volume so that the tone will carry as far as the material and situation demand. The second requirement is the right mental attitude. This applies to the speaker with good control of volume as well as to the one who is less expert. For good communication, and hence projection, is a product not only of breath control but also of the speaker's constant awareness of the listener. Such awareness is often spoken of in the theater as "audience sense." Though this sense is a difficult thing to explain, it has its base in the speaker's attitude of reaching out toward an audience with every line he wants to communicate. These lines may be a robust and sturdy utterance, such as Ulysses' address to his fellow mariners. They may be as delicate, subjective, and personal as those that shape Maxwell Bodenheim's "Death" (see page 119). Regardless of the energy of idea or feeling, the reader or actor with a fine sense of "audience participation" will have a psychological "set" that will help him reach toward the audience with his voice. The interpreter as well as the actor should keep in mind the old adage of show business and "play to the balcony." In other words, he should keep the back row of his listeners in mind and be sure that his words reach them. This advice is sound whether his audience is composed of a few people grouped around a fireplace or hundreds gathered in an auditorium or theater.

This mental attitude toward communication has an indirect but observable effect on the physiological control of projection. Thinking of his listeners, wanting to be sure that they hear and share the full effect of the literature, the speaker will tend to keep his posture erect and his head lifted slightly so that his throat is free from tension.

Focus of Projection

It is sometimes helpful to think of the voice as a tangible thing — a thing to be aimed and thrown at a target. This trick of "throwing the voice" may smack of ventriloquism, yet it is a practice everyone uses at times. The child calling to attract the attention of his playmate down the street sends his voice down to him; the football fan shouting advice to the players on the field directs his voice without conscious thought to the exact spot where his attention is focused. When the adult is carrying on a conversation in a room full of people, he may project across the room to answer a remark or add his bit to a conversation. When he wishes to be confidential, he lets his voice drop and his circle of mental directness narrow so that he fills only the desired area.

These exercises for focus of projection can be most effectively practiced in a large room. They are conceived primarily in terms of an imagined concrete situation, so that by thinking specifically of *what* to do, and using any words that come to mind, the interpreter can concentrate on the volume and focus suggested.

1. You are seated at a desk in the center front of the room. You see a friend at the door; you call an easy greeting. He waves and goes on. You think of something that you ought to tell him. You call his name quickly, but he apparently doesn't hear, for he keeps on going. Without leaving your place, call again; have a good full breath as you start to call and direct the sound at his fast-disappearing back. Do the same thing again with more volume and longer sounds supported by forced exhalation. Be sure you catch him this time.

2. You are giving directions to a group of people about to work out a diagram. The room is large, and everyone must hear. Direct your remarks to various places, thinking of certain people who might be there. After you have given instructions and the group starts to work, there is a question down front. You shift your focus of projection, reduce your volume, and answer the person who asked the question. You then decide that others might need that special information, too. You raise your volume and expand your area of projection to call quite loudly in order to attract everyone's attention, then repeat to the group what you have said to the individual. As you do this, take care to direct your voice to the various parts of the room so that all will hear.

When you have made some progress in projection through such exercises as these just described, move on to practice with literary material.

An interesting problem in projection is to be found in Shakespeare's *Julius Caesar*. As Brutus goes up into the pulpit to make his famous speech to the crowd, he addresses a single remark to those near him. On the opening line try to get the feeling of speaking to those who stand beside you and then of including the several hundred citizens who are milling around the Forum. It is necessary to quiet them during the early part of the speech.

BRUTUS: Be patient till the last. Romans, countrymen, and lovers! hear me for my cause, and be silent, that you may hear; believe me for mine honor, and have respect to mine honor, that you may believe; censure me in your wisdom, and awake your senses, that you may the better judge. If there be any in this assembly, any dear friend of Caesar's, to him I say, that Brutus' love to Caesar was no less than his. If then that friend demand why Brutus rose against Caesar, this is my answer: Not that I lov'd Caesar less, but that I lov'd Rome more.

In the following lines from the famous trial scene of *The Merchant of Venice,* two characters are speaking. Our concern at the moment is not primarily with the difference in their voices or mental attitudes, but rather with the changes in focus and consequent projection in their speeches. (The parenthetical stage directions are inserted for this specific exercise. They do not appear in the text of the play.) The Duke speaks to Portia at close range on his greeting and first question and on the opening line of his second speech. After "take your place" it is assumed that she moves away from him so that his question,

> Are you acquainted with the difference
> That holds this present question in the court?

must carry over a greater distance than his first remarks but still be addressed directly to Portia. His order to Antonio and Shylock to "stand forth" may be thought of as carrying even farther, since they are probably among a group of people outside the judges' area. Practice the Duke's speeches until you can place them where you want them, and then follow the same procedure in Portia's speeches.

DUKE: Give me your hand. Come you from old Bellario?
PORTIA: (*To Duke as she gives him her hand*) I did, my lord.
DUKE: You are welcome; take your place.
Are you acquainted with the difference
That holds this present question in the court?
PORTIA: (*From her place a few feet away from the Duke*) I am informed throughly of the cause.
(*To the assemblage*) Which is the merchant here, and which the Jew?
DUKE: Antonio and old Shylock, both stand forth.
PORTIA: (*To Shylock after he has stepped forward from the crowd*) Is your name Shylock?

In working to develop volume and projection, the interpreter is concentrating on one of the basic requirements of all speech: that it reach its audience. Volume depends largely on adequate breath supply and proper support in exhalation. Projection combines these physical aspects with the psychological aspect of mental directness.

PITCH AND QUALITY

Although pitch and quality are different attributes of sound, they are so closely related in origin and control in the human voice that they may be considered together. The way the vocal bands vibrate determines basically both the pitch and the quality of the vocal tone — the pitch by the rate, the quality by the complexity of the vibration.

The *pitch* of a sound is its place on the musical scale. It is located very generally in terms of the scale range, as high, medium, or low pitch. Skill in using pitch is of considerable importance to the interpreter in suggesting shades of meaning and in reflecting attitude. Changes in pitch give variety and richness to the material being read and help to hold the attention of the audience. Since a change of pitch produces *inflection,* a speaker's *inflection range* is the entire pitch span between the highest and lowest tone of which he is capable.

Any pattern in the variation of levels of pitch results in melody. When there are no discernible changes of pitch, the result is a monotone. Melody is an asset to the interpreter, but it can also become a problem. Most individuals have in their daily speech a characteristic pattern of inflections which is a part of their own personalities. This is highly commendable, and certainly it is to be expected that some of that pattern will be carried over into their work before an audience. It often happens, however, that the reader's pattern is so marked as to call attention to itself and thus get in the way of re-creation of the material. For example, in the reading of poetry, which tends to be patterned by design, one of the most common and annoying vocal patterns is that which permits each line or each new thought to start on a high pitch and drift to a low tone at the close. The following lines are an example of poetic structure in which this problem must be controlled.

Fair flower, that dost so comely grow,
Hid in this silent, dull retreat,
Untouched thy honied blossoms blow,
Unseen thy little branches greet:
  No roving foot shall crush thee here,
  No busy hand provoke a tear.

PHILIP FRENEAU, *The Wild Honeysuckle*

And again, in less conventional poetry:

I hear America singing, the varied carols I hear,
Those of mechanics, each one singing his as it should be blithe and strong,
The carpenter singing his as he measures his plank or beam,
The mason singing his as he makes ready for work, or leaves off work . . .

WALT WHITMAN, *I Hear America Singing*

Occasionally an interpreter will use too much melody or too frequent changes of pitch for the type of material being read. This results in a suggestion of sentimentality, in what one might call a "woman's club flavor," that robs the material of much of its innate dignity and strength. The requirements of the material, its purpose and over-all effect — these must be the deciding factors in determining the extent of pitch variation.

Quality, more difficult to define distinctively, can best be described as that characteristic of a tone which distinguishes it from all other tones of the same pitch and intensity. It is sometimes called timbre, or to use the German word, *Klang*, meaning the "ring" of the tone. In describing quality, one frequently uses words that suggest *color* — a "golden" tone, a "silver-voiced" orator, a "blue" note. It is the distinctive, individual quality of his voice that makes it possible to recognize the friend one hears but does not see.

Quality of tone is perhaps most closely associated with mood and feeling. Vocal quality will be influenced by the interpreter's empathic response to whatever elements of emotion, strength, and beauty are inherent in the material. Whether he exclaims with Hecuba, "Ah woe! . . . For what woe lacketh here?" or shouts with an early celebrator, "It's gonna be a great day!" his sensitive response to the mood, together with his understanding of the connotation of the words used, should help him to communicate fully the feeling in the material. The interpreter who is true to his art will never adopt a certain quality and impose it on the selection. A display of "rich" quality or of a variety of qualitative effects, like every other display of technique for its own sake, is in poor taste and violates the fundamental rule of unobtrusiveness.

We may conclude this discussion of quality by presenting a portion of a famous example of harmony between sound and feeling — that is, between quality and emotion. In the lines from *King Lear* in which Lear, old, enraged, and embittered, defies the storm on the heath, the interpreter will appreciate the contribution to the mood of angry defiance made by the actual sound of the words, in addition to their connotation:

> LEAR: Blow, winds, and crack your cheeks! rage! blow!
> You cataracts and hurricanes, spout
> Till you have drench'd our steeples, drown'd the cocks!
> You sulph'rous and thought-executing fires,
> Vaunt-couriers of oak-cleaving thunderbolts,
> Singe my white head! And thou, all-shaking thunder,
> Smite flat the thick rotundity o' the world!
> Crack nature's moulds, all germens spill at once
> That make ingrateful man.

Pitch and quality working together, then, are invaluable in helping the interpreter bring out the universality and suggestion in a piece of literature. He must pay particular attention to the control of these two aspects of vocal technique because they contribute so much to the communication of the emotional content.

RATE AND PAUSE

The *rate* at which a person speaks is often habitual, a part of his personality and his entire background. It probably serves him very well for ordinary conversation, but he may need to adjust his habitual rate to do justice to an author's style and purpose. As with the other elements of vocal technique, the interpreter must train his ear to hear himself in practice and in conversation. There is no magic formula for slowing a too-rapid pace. It requires constant attention. The selection of material which by its style and connotation encourages a slower pace will be helpful. Very frequently the mere physical process of forming a sequence of sounds will affect the rate at which a sentence can be read intelligibly and effectively. Thus, the interpreter will do well to make certain that he is forming every sound accurately and controlling his rate so that this is possible.

Within the over-all rate there will be opportunities for subtle variety. Emotion, connotation, suggestion, and the combination of vowels and consonants will all provide the clues.

Rate is not only the speed with which sounds are uttered in sequence, but also the length and frequency of pauses separating the sequences of sounds. Of course, the interpreter will long since have recognized the *phrasal pause* which clarifies the relationships of words in phrases to convey units of thoughts. The pause may also become one of the most effective tools for building suspense and climaxes and for reinforcing emotional content.

The beginner is usually afraid to hold the pause long enough for its dramatic effect to register with his listener. If a pause is motivated by real understanding, by identification with the feeling suggested, it may be sustained for a much longer time and with greater effect than the beginner realizes. He need only be sure that something relevant to the material is going on during the pause, first in his own mind and consequently in the minds of his listeners. The pause must stay within the total concept of the selection and supply whatever transition or suspense is needed. He should work not only to use pauses in the most effective places, but to vary and sustain the lengths of the pauses as the material demands. Punctuation, of course, may serve the reader as a guide to the feeling — but it is only a guide. Punctuation is used on the printed page to signal the eye. It guides the reader in establishing the relationship of words and phrases and their division into sentences. The interpreter can sometimes use change of pitch, quality, or emphasis, or a combination of these, to signal the ear of his listeners. He need not always use a pause. Moreover, it must be remembered that rules and fashions change in punctuation as in everything else. Thus the interpreter's full understanding and response, together with his sense of responsibility to his audience, are the final determinants in the use of pauses.

In the following scene from *Cyrano de Bergerac,* Cyrano is speaking of his monstrous nose, and of its effect on his entire being. The interpreter must make exquisite use of pause here. As he works on the interpretation, he will realize also that the tempo of the scene begins to change with "Oh, not that ever!" He will see how this change to a faster, more smoothly flowing rate is effected, and will realize that it goes hand in hand with Cyrano's struggle to turn from his romantic, self-revelatory mood to his customary half-comic acceptance of his nose.

CYRANO: My old friend — look at me,
And tell me how much hope remains for me
With this protuberance! Oh I have no more
Illusions! Now and then — bah! I may grow
Tender, walking alone in the blue cool
Of evening, through some garden fresh with flowers
After the benediction of the rain;
My poor big devil of a nose inhales
April . . . and so I follow with my eyes
Where some boy, with a girl upon his arm,
Passes a patch of silver . . . and I feel
Somehow, I wish I had a woman too,
Walking with little steps under the moon,
And holding my arm so, and smiling. Then
I dream — and I forget. . . .
And then I see
The shadow of my profile on the wall!
LEBRET: My friend! . . .
CYRANO: My friend, I have my bitter days,
Knowing myself so ugly, so alone.
Sometimes —
LEBRET: You weep?
CYRANO: (*Quickly*) Oh, not that ever! No,
That would be too grotesque — the tears trickling down
All the long way along this nose of mine?
I will not so profane the dignity
Of sorrow. Never any tears for me!

From *Cyrano de Bergerac* by Edmond Rostand. Translated by Brian Hooker. Copyright 1923 by Holt, Rinehart and Winston, Inc. Copyright 1951 by Doris C. Hooker. Reprinted by permission of Holt, Rinehart and Winston, Inc.

To develop additional skill in the use of rate, the interpreter should work on selections demanding basically different rate patterns. As he reads the material aloud with feeling, he will realize that the "quantity" or length of the individual sound, whether vowel or consonant, must be effectively observed, as well as the length of pauses between sounds. He will probably conclude that often, in a prevailing rapid rate, the sounds as well as the pauses are short, and that the converse relation is true in a slower rate. Many of the lyrics of the Gilbert and Sullivan productions are wonderful examples of the way sound suggests rate, particularly the fast-moving "Nightmare Song" from *Iolanthe:*

When you're lying awake with a dismal headache,
And repose is taboo'd by anxiety —
I conceive you may use any language you choose
To indulge in, without impropriety . . .

INTELLIGIBILITY OF SPEECH

We have already had occasion to note that speech, to fulfill its basic function of communication, must be understandable or intelligible, and hence that it must be heard. But to be fully intelligible, speech must be not only audible but also distinct and accurate. The listener cannot keep his attention on the material if he is constantly called upon to "translate" slovenly speech sounds or mispronunciations. Therefore the interpreter will want his speech sounds to be correct as well as distinct and pleasing. It is true that nothing is more irritating to the listener than a speaker's self-conscious, overly careful mouthing of vowels and consonants. It smacks of affectation and insincerity. Moreover, it violates the cardinal rule of interpretation because it draws attention to the reader and his technique and away from the material. On the other hand, if the reader cannot be understood, he certainly cannot communicate. Consequently, he must learn to pronounce and articulate with such clarity and accuracy that any audience will be able to understand him.

A distinction between pronunciation and articulation may be helpful. *Pronunciation* refers to *the correctness of sounds and accents* in spoken words; it is not immediately concerned with shaping the sounds. *Articulation,* on the other hand, refers to *the shaping of the sounds* by the speaker's lips, teeth, tongue, and hard and soft palates. Sometimes it is hard to decide whether a fault is a matter of pronunciation or of articulation. When someone says "He kep' it" for "He kept it," is it faulty pronunciation or slovenly articulation? The listener will probably decide in this instance that the trouble is, by definition, faulty pronunciation. On the other hand, when he hears a lisping sound, as "thithter Thuthy" for "sister Susy," he has no hesitation in deciding that the difficulty is faulty articulation.

Pronunciation is considered acceptable when all the sounds of a word are uttered correctly in their proper order and with accent (stress) on the proper syllable. Current good usage is the guide to correct pronunciation, with a standard dictionary the final authority. It is not always the unfamiliar polysyllables that trip up the reader. Since he will be likely to distrust himself on them, he will probably look them up in the dictionary. The real pitfalls are the common, everyday words which he may have fallen into the habit of pronouncing incorrectly. Hence the interpreter will want to check his pronunciation of ordinary words to avoid this type of error. A mispronunciation can ruin a fine oral line. In addition, it may so distract a listener that he momentarily loses the thought. When this happens, communication suffers.

If the reader knows what correct pronunciation is, and has checked his own everyday speech, he may profitably turn his attention to improving the formation of sounds and to strengthening their projection. Faulty projection of distinct sounds is closely related to the position of the sound in the word or phrase. The end of the word or phrase may often be slighted or left off, even though the preceding sounds are distinct enough. In the exercises for control of sustained exhalation, it was pointed out that adequate control is needed to complete fully the ends of lines or sentences. This control and the accurate shaping of end sounds are of course closely allied. The failure to finish words is one of the faults that interfere most with good communication. Particularly is this so if the interpreter or actor is performing in a large auditorium or theater.

The consonant sounds that help most in achieving distinctness are the plosives, *p, b, t, d, k, g*. These sounds are called plosives because the release which completes their formation is a sudden, sharp "explosion" in the air. It is this plosive element that promotes their carrying power. The interpreter should practice common words, alone and in combinations, until he is sure that his sounds, especially the final ones, are distinct. Words like *drop, cab, eight, good, kick, gig, slept, cribbed, asked,* and *sixths* are examples. "Tongue twisters" using these and many other sounds are too numerous to mention, and are the property of all who know Peter Piper and his ilk. Such jingles provide excellent practice in accuracy and flexibility.

CARL A. RUDISILL LIBRARY
LENOIR RHYNE COLLEGE

The fricative sounds, *f, v, s, z*, etc., so called because they escape the speech mechanism with a slight "hiss" of friction, also demand accurate formation. Sometimes, as was suggested in the brief exercise for control of exhalation, the vigor of the escaping sound needs to be toned down. The sound that gives the most trouble in this respect is the ever-present *s* and *z* pair of sibilants. Actually, *s* and *z* are among the most frequently used consonants in the English language. No wonder that the noise made by a large group of people talking has been called the "hissing of geese"! (Nor need the company be entirely feminine to create this effect.) The interpreter should check the sound of *s* as he articulates it in lines like these:

Choric Song

There is sweet music here that softer falls
Than petals from blown roses on the grass,
Or night-dews on still waters between walls
Of shadowy granite, in a gleaming pass;
Music that gentlier on the spirit lies,
Than tired eyelids upon tired eyes;
Music that brings sweet sleep down from the blissful skies.
Here are cool mosses deep,
And thro' the moss the ivies creep,
And in the stream the long-leaved flowers weep,
And from the craggy ledge the poppy hangs in sleep.

ALFRED, LORD TENNYSON

If the sound is too prominent or sharp, a "whistled" *s*, a slight relaxing of the groove in the tongue, which directs the sound against the teeth, should help. Or perhaps what is needed is a definite shortening or cutting off of the sound by stopping the outgo of air more quickly. If the sound of *s* seems "slushy" or unclear, increased effort should be made to direct the stream of air sharply over the center of the tongue, to expel it centrally between the closely aligned edges of upper and lower teeth. If there is a marked deficiency in the *s*, or in any other sound for that matter, a speech therapist should be consulted.

After he has checked on individual sounds and words, the interpreter should turn to pieces of material that involve difficult combinations of sounds. The following lines are examples of some particularly difficult combinations.

Set each sharp-edged, fire-bitten brick
Straight by the plumb-line's shivering length . . . .

ELINOR WYLIE, *Sanctuary*

Eyes that are cobwebbed windows in a house,
Deserted, bleak, where a soul once lived, and fled,
Behind whose drawn green shutters slippered ghosts
Conjure among the diffident dead . . . .

LEW SARETT, *The World Has a Way with Eyes*

SELECTIONS FOR ANALYSIS AND ORAL INTERPRETATION

IN ANALYZING THESE selections, pay particular attention to the vocal problems each presents. Almost without exception they require more than the normal supply of breath, either because of long, flowing sentences or unusual demands of volume or force. Some have interesting problems in projection. They all require maximum flexibility of range to communicate the richness of sounds which help them achieve their full effectiveness when they are read aloud.

PROBABLY THE CLASSIC example of the value of sound combinations is to be found in this familiar nonsense poem.

Jabberwocky

'Twas brillig, and the slithy toves
  Did gyre and gimble in the wabe:
All mimsy were the borogoves,
  And the mome raths outgrabe.

"Beware the Jabberwock, my son!
  The jaws that bite, the claws that catch!
Beware the Jubjub bird, and shun
  The frumious Bandersnatch!"

He took his vorpal sword in hand;
  Long time the manxome foe he sought —
So rested he by the Tumtum tree,
  And stood awhile in thought.

And, as in uffish thought he stood,
  The Jabberwock, with eyes of flame,
Came whiffling through the tulgey wood,
  And burbled as it came!

One, two! One, two! And through and through
  The vorpal blade went snicker-snack!
He left it dead, and with its head
  He went galumphing back.

"And hast thou slain the Jabberwock?
  Come to my arms, my beamish boy!
O frabjous day! Callooh, Callay!"
  He chortled in his joy.

'Twas brillig, and the slithy toves
  Did gyre and gimble in the wabe:
All mimsy were the borogoves,
  And the mome raths outgrabe.

LEWIS CARROLL

THIS RELATIVELY LONG selection will divide into smaller units for purposes of attention to vocal techniques. There are opportunities for vocal variety in the opening dialogue as well as in the quarrel. Moreover, the separate memory units require some consideration of rate and pitch.

from *91 Revere Street*

"A penny for your thoughts, Schopenhauer," my mother would say.

"I am thinking about pennies," I'd answer.

"When I was a child I used to love telling Mamá everything I had done," Mother would say.

"But you're not a child," I would answer.

I used to enjoy dawdling and humming "Anchors Aweigh" up Revere Street after a day at school. "Anchors Aweigh," the official Navy song, had originally been the song composed for my father's class. And yet my mind always blanked and seemed to fill with a clammy hollowness when Mother asked prying questions. Like other tongue-tied, difficult children, I dreamed I was a master of cool, stoical repartee. "What have you been doing, Bobby?" Mother would ask. "I haven't," I'd answer. At home I thus saved myself from emotional exhaustion.

At school, however, I was extreme only in my conventional mediocrity, my colorless, distracted manner, which came from restless dreams of being admired. My closest friend was Eric Burckhard, the son of a professor of architecture at Harvard. The Burckhards came from Zurich and were very German, not like Ludendorff, but in the kindly, comical, nineteenth-century manner of Jo's German husband in *Little Men,* or in the manner of the crusading *sturm und drang* liberal scholars in second year German novels. "Eric's mother and father are *both* called Dr. Burckhard," my mother once said, and indeed there was something endearingly repellent about Mrs. Burckhard with her doctor's degree, her

Reprinted from *Life Studies* by Robert Lowell, by permission of Farrar, Straus & Company, Inc. Copyright © 1956, 1959 by Robert Lowell.

long, unstylish skirts, and her dramatic, dulling blond braids. Strangely the Burckhards' sober continental bourgeois house was without golden mean — everything was either hilariously old Swiss or madly modern. The Frau Doctor Burckhard used to serve mid-morning hot chocolate with rosettes of whipped cream, and receive her friends in a long, uncarpeted hall-drawing room with lethal ferns and a yellow beeswaxed hardwood floor shining under a central skylight. On the wall there were large expert photographs of what at a distance appeared to be Mont Blanc — they were in reality views of Frank Lloyd Wright's Japanese hotel.

I admired the Burckhards and felt at home in their house, and these feelings were only intensified when I discovered that my mother was always ill at ease with them. The heartiness, the enlightenment, and the bright, ferny greenhouse atmosphere were too much for her.

Eric and I were too young to care for books or athletics. Neither of our houses had absorbing toys or an elevator to go up and down in. We were inseparable, but I cannot imagine what we talked about. I loved Eric because he was more popular than I and yet absolutely *sui generis* at the Brimmer School. He had a chalk-white face and limp, fine, white-blond hair. He was frail, elbowy, started talking with an enthusiastic Mont Blanc chirp and would flush with bewilderment if interrupted. All the other boys at Brimmer wore little tweed golf suits with knickerbockers, but Eric always arrived in a black suit coat, a Byronic collar, and cuffless gray flannel trousers that almost hid his shoes. The long trousers were replaced on warm days by gray flannel shorts, such as were worn by children still in kindergarten. Eric's unenviable and freakish costumes were too old or too young. He accepted the whims of his parents with a buoyant tranquillity that I found unnatural.

My first and terminating quarrel with Eric was my fault. Eventually almost our whole class at Brimmer had whooping cough, but Eric's seizure was like his long trousers — untimely: he was sick a month too early. For a whole month he was in quarantine and forced to play by himself in a removed corner of the Public Garden. He was certainly conspicuous as he skiproped with his Swiss nurse under the out-of-the-way Ether Memorial Fountain far from the pond and the swan boats. His parents had decided that this was an excellent opportunity for Eric to brush up on his German, and so the absoluteness of his quarantine was monstrously exaggerated by the fact that child and nurse spoke no English but only a guttural, British-sounding, Swiss German. Round and round and round the Fountain, he played intensely, frailly, obediently, until I began to tease him. Though motioned away by him, I came close. I had attracted some of the most popular Brimmer School boys. For the first time I had gotten favorable attention from several little girls. I came close. I shouted. Was Eric afraid of girls? I imitated his German. *Ein, swei, drei,* BEER. I imitated Eric's coughing. "He is afraid he will give you whooping cough if he talks or lets you come nearer," the nurse said in her musical Swiss-English voice. I came nearer. Eric flushed, grew white, bent double with coughing. He began to cry, and had to be led away from the Public Garden. For a whole week I routed Eric from the Garden daily, and for two or three days I was a center of interest. "Come see the Lake Geneva spider monkey!" I would shout. I don't know why I couldn't stop. Eric never told his father, I think, but when he recovered we no longer spoke. The breach was so unspoken and intense that our classmates were actually horrified. They even devised a solemn ritual for our reconciliation. We crossed our hearts, mixed spit, mixed blood. The reconciliation was hollow.

ROBERT LOWELL

THIS POEM WILL REQUIRE particular attention to control of inflection and emphasis to make it clear and meaningful.

A Hymn To God The Father

1623

Wilt thou forgive that sin where I begun,
    Which is my sin though it were done before?
Wilt thou forgive those sins through which I run,
    And do them still, though still I do deplore?
When thou hast done, thou hast not done,
        For I have more.

Wilt thou forgive that sin by which I've won
    Others to sin, and made my sin their door?
Wilt thou forgive that sin which I did shun
    A year or two, but wallow'd in a score?
When thou hast done, thou hast not done,
        For I have more.

I have a sin of fear, that when I've spun
    My last thread, I shall perish on the shore;
Swear by thyself that at my death thy Sun
    Shall shine as it shines now, and heretofore;
And having done that, thou hast Donne.
        I have no more.

JOHN DONNE

"WILD GRAPES" CALLS for considerable variety of projection and volume. The narrative lines, of course, must be directed to the audience. The brother's first instructions are delivered as he stands beside the little girl; his "loud cries" are directed to her as she hangs suspended in the air.

Wild Grapes

What tree may not the fig be gathered from?
The grape may not be gathered from the birch?
It's all you know the grape, or know the birch.
As a girl gathered from the birch myself
Equally with my weight in grapes, one autumn,
I ought to know what tree the grape is fruit of.
I was born, I suppose, like anyone,
And grew to be a little boyish girl
My brother could not always leave at home.
But that beginning was wiped out in fear
The day I swung suspended with the grapes,
And was come after like Eurydice
And brought down safely from the upper regions;
And the life I live now's an extra life
I can waste as I please on whom I please.
So if you see me celebrate two birthdays,
And give myself out as two different ages,
One of them five years younger than I look—
One day my brother led me to a glade
Where a white birch he knew of stood alone,
Wearing a thin head-dress of pointed leaves,
And heavy on her heavy hair behind,
Against her neck, an ornament of grapes.
Grapes, I knew grapes from having seen them last year.
One bunch of them, and there began to be
Bunches all round me growing in white birches,
The way they grew round Leif the Lucky's German;
Mostly as much beyond my lifted hands, though,
As the moon used to seem when I was younger,
And only freely to be had for climbing.

My brother did the climbing; and at first
Threw me down grapes to miss and scatter
And have to hunt for in sweet fern and hardhack;
Which gave him some time to himself to eat,
But not so much, perhaps, as a boy needed.
So then, to make me wholly self-supporting,
He climbed still higher and bent the tree to earth

From *Complete Poems of Robert Frost.* Copyright 1923 by Holt, Rinehart and Winston, Inc. Copyright renewed 1951 by Robert Frost. Reprinted by permission of Holt, Rinehart and Winston, Inc.

And put it in my hands to pick my own grapes.
"Here, take a tree-top, I'll get down another.
Hold on with all your might when I let go."
I said I had the tree. It wasn't true.
The opposite was true. The tree had me.
The minute it was left with me alone
It caught me up as if I were the fish
And it the fishpole. So I was translated
To loud cries from my brother of "Let go!
Don't you know anything, you girl? Let go!"

But I, with something of the baby grip
Acquired ancestrally in just such trees
When wilder mothers than our wildest now
Hung babies out on branches by the hands
To dry or wash or tan, I don't know which,
(You'll have to ask an evolutionist) —
I held on uncomplainingly for life.
My brother tried to make me laugh to help me.
"What are you doing up there in those grapes?
Don't be afraid. A few of them won't hurt you.
I mean, they won't pick you if you don't them."
Much danger of my picking anything!
By that time I was pretty well reduced
To a philosophy of hang-and-let-hang.

"Now you know how it feels," my brother said,
"To be a bunch of fox-grapes, as they call them,
That when it thinks it has escaped the fox
By growing where it shouldn't — on a birch,
Where a fox wouldn't think to look for it —
And if he looked and found it, couldn't reach it —
Just then come you and I to gather it.
Only you have the advantage of the grapes
In one way: you have one more stem to cling by,
And promise more resistance to the picker."

One by one I lost off my hat and shoes,
And still I clung. I let my head fall back
And shut my eyes against the sun, my ears
Against my brother's nonsense; "Drop," he said,
"I'll catch you in my arms. It isn't far."
(Stated in lengths of him it might not be.)
"Drop or I'll shake the tree and shake you down."
Grim silence on my part as I sank lower,
My small wrists stretching till they showed the banjo strings.
"Why, if she isn't serious about it!
Hold tight awhile till I think what to do.

I'll bend the tree down and let you down by it."
I don't know much about the letting down;
But once I felt ground with my stocking feet
And the world came revolving back to me,
I know I looked long at my curled-up fingers,
Before I straightened them and brushed the bark off.
My brother said: "Don't you weigh anything?
Try to weigh something next time, so you won't
Be run off with by birch trees into space."

It wasn't my not weighing anything
So much as my not knowing anything —
My brother had been nearer right before.
I had not taken the first step in knowledge;
I had not learned to let go with the hands,
As still I have not learned to with the heart,
And have no wish to with the heart — nor need,
That I can see. The mind — is not the heart.
I may yet live, as I know others live,
To wish in vain to let go with the mind —
Of cares, at night, to sleep; but nothing tells me
That I need to learn to let go with the heart.

ROBERT FROST

WALTER DE LA MARE's familiar poem calls for considerable attention to volume and projection. Be careful not to let the projected calls become so strong that they overbalance the quiet contrast.

The Listeners

"Is there anybody there?" said the Traveler,
  Knocking on the moonlit door;
And his horse in the silence champed the grasses
  Of the forest's ferny floor.
And a bird flew up out of the turret,
  Above the Traveler's head:
And he smote upon the door again a second time;
  "Is there anybody there?" he said.
But no one descended to the Traveler;
  No head from the leaf-fringed sill
Leaned over and looked into his gray eyes,
  Where he stood perplexed and still.
But only a host of phantom listeners

From *Collected Poems* by Walter de la Mare. Copyright 1941 by Walter de la Mare. Reprinted by permission of The Literary Trustees of Walter de la Mare and the Society of Authors.

That dwelt in the lone house then
Stood listening in the quiet of the moonlight
To that voice from the world of men:
Stood thronging the faint moonbeams on the dark stair,
That goes down to the empty hall,
Hearkening in an air stirred and shaken
By the lonely Traveler's call.
And he felt in his heart their strangeness,
Their stillness answering his cry,
While his horse moved, cropping the dark turf,
'Neath the starred and leafy sky;
For he suddenly smote on the door, even
Louder, and lifted his head: —
"Tell them I came, and no one answered,
That I kept my word," he said.
Never the least stir made the listeners,
Though every word he spake
Fell echoing through the shadowiness of the still house
From the one man left awake:
Aye, they heard his foot upon the stirrup,
And the sound of iron on stone,
And how the silence surged softly backward,
When the plunging hoofs were gone.

WALTER DE LA MARE

THERE IS GREAT subtlety in the repeated sounds in these companion poems. Your diction must be accurate to make use of all the complex tone color. Do not underestimate their simplicity of sound pattern.

Love Note I: Surely

Surely you stay my certain own, you stay
My you. All honest, lofty as a cloud.
Surely I could come now and find you high,
As mine as you ever were; should not be awed.
Surely your word would pop as insolent
As always: "Why, of course I love you, dear."
Your gaze, surely, ungauzed as I could want.
Your touches, that never were careful, what they were.
Surely — But I am very off from that.
From surely. From indeed. From decent arrow
That was my clean naïveté and my faith.
This morning men deliver wounds and death.
They will deliver death and wounds tomorrow.
And I doubt all. You. Or a violet.

Love Note II: Flags

Still, it is dear defiance now to carry
Fair flags of you above my indignation,
Top, with a pretty glory and a merry
Softness, the scattered pound of my cold passion.
I pull you down in my foxhole. Do you mind?
You burn in bits of saucy color then.
I let you flutter out against the pained
Volleys. Against my power crumpled and wan.
You, and the yellow pert exuberance
Of dandelion days, unmocking sun:
The blowing of clear wind in your gay hair;
Love changeful in you (like a music, or
Like a sweet mournfulness, or like a dance,
Or like the tender struggle of a fan).

GWENDOLYN BROOKS

THIS EXCERPT FROM *A Death in the Family* follows immediately after the unit used in Chapter 3. For better continuity we have repeated a few sentences, which you may wish to put into your own words as an introduction or merely use to remind yourself of the situation. The appropriateness of the excerpt for this chapter really begins with "My daddy's dead."

from *A Death in the Family*

He knew the faces of all these boys well, though he was not sure of any of their names. The moment he saw them all he was sure they saw him, and sure that they knew. He stood still and waited for them, looking from one to another of them, into their eyes, and step by step at their several distances, each of them at all times looking into his eyes and knowing, they came silently nearer. Waiting, in silence, during those many seconds before the first of them came really near him, he felt that it was so long to wait, and be watched so closely and silently, and to watch back, that he wanted to go back into the alley and not be seen by them or by anybody else, and yet at the same time he knew that they were all approaching him with the realization that something had happened to him that had not happened to any other boy in town, and that now at last they were bound to think well of him; and the nearer

"Love Note I: Surely" and "Love Note II: Flags" from *Selected Poems* by Gwendolyn Brooks. Copyright 1945 by Gwendolyn Brooks Blakely. Reprinted with the permission of Harper & Row, Publishers, Incorporated.

Copyright © 1957 by The James Agee Trust. From *A Death in the Family* by permission of Ivan Obolensky, Inc., New York, New York.

they came but were yet at a distance, the more the gray, sober air was charged with the great energy and with a sense of glory and of danger, and the deeper and more exciting the silence became, and the more tall, proud, shy and exposed he felt; so that as they came still nearer he once again felt his face break into a wide smile, with which he had nothing to do, and, feeling that there was something deeply wrong in such a smile, tried his best to quieten his face and told them, shyly and proudly, "My daddy's dead."

Of the first three who came up, two merely looked at him and the third said, "Huh! Betcha he ain't"; and Rufus, astounded that they did not know and that they should disbelieve him, said, "Why he is so!"

"Where's your satchel at?" said the boy who had spoken. "You're just making up a lie so you can lay out of school."

"I am not laying out," Rufus replied. "I was going to school and my Aunt Hannah told me I didn't have to go to school today or tomorrow or not till — not for a few days. She said I mustn't. So I am not laying out. I'm just staying out."

And another of the boys said, "That's right. If his daddy is dead he don't have to go back to school till after the funerl."

While Rufus had been speaking two other boys had crossed over to join them and now one of them said, "He don't have to. He can lay out cause his daddy got killed," and Rufus looked at the boy gratefully and the boy looked back at him, it seemed to Rufus, with deference.

But the first boy who had spoken said, resentfully, "How do *you* know?"

And the second boy, while his companion nodded, said, "Cause my daddy seen it in the paper. Can't your daddy read the paper?"

The paper, Rufus thought; it's even in the paper! And he looked wisely at the first boy. And the first boy, interested enough to ignore the remark against his father, said, "Well how did he get killed, then?" And Rufus, realizing with respect that it was even more creditable to get killed than just to die, took a deep breath and said, "Why, he was . . ."; but the boy whose father had seen it in the paper was already talking, so he listened, instead, feeling as if all this were being spoken for him, and on his behalf, and in his praise, and feeling it all the more as he looked from one silent boy to the next and saw that their eyes were constantly on him. And Rufus listened, too, with as much interest as they did, while the boy said with relish, "In his ole Tin Lizzie, that's how. He was driving along in his ole Tin Lizzie and it hit a rock and throwed him out in the ditch and run up a eight-foot bank and then fell back and turned over and over and landed right on top of him *whomph* and mashed every bone in his body, that's all. And somebody come and found him and he was dead already time they got there, that's how."

"He was instantly killed," Rufus began, and expected to go ahead and correct some of the details of the account, but nobody seemed to hear him, for two other boys had come up and just as he began to speak one of them said, "Your daddy got his name in the paper didn' he, and you too," and he saw that now all the boys looked at him with new respect.

"He's dead," he told them. "He got killed."

"That's what my daddy says," one of them said, and the other said, "What you get for driving a auto when you're drunk, that's what my dad says," and the two of them looked gravely at the other boys, nodding, and at Rufus.

"What's drunk?" Rufus asked.

"What's drunk?" one of the boys mocked incredulously: "Drunk is fulla good ole whiskey"; and he began to stagger about in circles with his knees weak and his head lolling. "At's what drunk is."

"Then he wasn't," Rufus said.

"How do *you* know?"

"He wasn't drunk because that wasn't how he died. The wheel hit a rock and the other wheel, the one you steer with, just hit him on the chin, but it hit him so hard it killed him. He was instantly killed."

"What's instantly killed?" one of them asked.

"What do *you* care?" another said.

"Right off like that," an older boy explained, snapping his fingers. Another boy joined the group. Thinking of what instantly meant, and how his father's name was in the paper and his own too, and how he had got killed, not just died, he was not listening to them very clearly for a few moments, and then, all of a sudden, he began to realize that he was the center of everything and that they all knew it and that they waited to hear him tell the true account of it.

"I don't know nothing about no chin," the boy whose father saw it in the paper was saying. "Way I heard it he was a-drivin along in his ole Tin Lizzie and he hit a rock and ole Tin Lizzie run off the road and throwed him out and run up a eight-foot bank and turned over and over and fell back down on top of him *whomp*."

"How do *you* know?" an older boy was saying. "*You* wasn't there. Anybody here knows it's *him*." And he pointed at Rufus and Rufus was startled from his revery.

"Why?" asked the boy who had just come up.

"Cause it's his daddy," one of them explained.

"It's my daddy," Rufus said.

"What happened?" asked still another boy, at the fringe of the group.

"My daddy got killed," Rufus said.

"His daddy got killed," several of the others explained.

"My daddy says he bets he was drunk."

"Good ole whiskey!"

"Shut up, what's *your* daddy know about it."

"Was he drunk?"
"No," Rufus said.
"No," two others said.
"Let *him* tell it."
"Yeah, *you* tell it."
"Anybody here ought to know, it's him."
"Come on and tell us."
"Good ole whiskey."
"Shut your mouth."
"Well come on and tell us, then."

They became silent and all of them looked at him. Rufus looked back into their eyes in the sudden deep stillness. A man walked by stepping into the gutter to skirt them.

JAMES AGEE

BE CAREFUL THAT you understand all the allusions and "theatre jargon" in this poem. When a poet as sophisticated as T. S. Eliot pays such careful attention to obvious rhyme, we must certainly take our cue from him and enjoy it fully.

Gus: The Theatre Cat

Gus is the Cat at the Theatre Door.
His name, as I ought to have told you before,
Is really Asparagus. That's such a fuss
To pronounce, that we usually call him just Gus.
His coat's very shabby, he's thin as a rake,
And he suffers from palsy that makes his paws shake.
Yet he was, in his youth, quite the smartest of Cats —
But no longer a terror to mice and to rats.
For he isn't the Cat that he was in his prime;
Though his name was quite famous, he says, in its time.
And whenever he joins his friends at their club
(Which takes place at the back of the neighbouring pub)
He loves to regale them, if someone else pays,
With anecdotes drawn from his palmier days.
For he once was a Star of the highest degree —
He has acted with Irving, he's acted with Tree.
And he likes to relate his success on the Halls,
Where the Gallery once gave him seven cat-calls.
But his grandest creation, as he loves to tell,
Was Firefrorefiddle, the Fiend of the Fell.

"I have played," so he says, "every possible part,
And I used to know seventy speeches by heart.

From *Old Possum's Book of Practical Cats,* copyright, 1939, by T. S. Eliot. Reprinted by permission of Harcourt, Brace & World, Inc. Also reprinted by permission of Faber and Faber, Ltd.

I'd extemporize back-chat, I knew how to gag,
And I knew how to let the cat out of the bag.
I knew how to act with my back and my tail;
With an hour of rehearsal, I never could fail.
I'd a voice that would soften the hardest of hearts,
Whether I took the lead, or in character parts.
I have sat by the bedside of poor Little Nell;
When the Curfew was rung, then I swung on the bell.
In the Pantomime season I never fell flat,
And I once understudied Dick Whittington's Cat.
But my grandest creation, as history will tell,
Was Firefrorefiddle, the Fiend of the Fell."

Then, if someone will give him a toothful of gin,
He will tell how he once played a part in *East Lynne.*
At a Shakespeare performance he once walked on pat,
When some actor suggested the need for a cat.
He once played a Tiger — could do it again —
Which an Indian Colonel pursued down a drain.
And he thinks that he still can, much better than most,
Produce blood-curdling noises to bring on the Ghost.
And he once crossed the stage on a telegraph wire,
To rescue a child when a house was on fire.
And he says: "Now, these kittens, they do not get trained
As we did in the days when Victoria reigned.
They never get drilled in a regular troupe,
And they think they are smart, just to jump through a hoop."
And he'll say, as he scratches himself with his claws,
"Well, the Theatre's certainly not what it was.
These modern productions are all very well,
But there's nothing to equal, from what I hear tell,
        That moment of mystery
        When I made history
As Firefrorefiddle, the Fiend of the Fell."

T. S. ELIOT

MUCH OF THE HUMOR in this memory of a traumatic experience results from "stage directions" for the use of vocal variety.

from *Ring Out, Wild Bells*

When I finally got around to seeing Max Reinhardt's cinema version of "A Midsummer-Night's Dream," and saw a child named

Reprinted by permission of Dodd, Mead & Company from *Bed of Neuroses* by Wolcott Gibbs. Copyright, 1936, by Wolcott Gibbs.

Mickey Rooney playing Puck, I remembered suddenly that long ago I had taken the same part.

Our production was given on the open-air stage at the Riverdale Country School, shortly before the war. The scenery was only the natural scenery of that suburban dell, and the cast was exclusively male, ranging in age from eleven to perhaps seventeen. While we had thus preserved the pure, Elizabethan note of the original, it must be admitted that our version had its drawbacks. The costumes were probably the worst things we had to bear, and even Penrod, tragically arrayed as Launcelot in his sister's stockings and his father's drawers, might have been embarrassed for us. Like Penrod, we were costumed by our parents, and like the Schofields, they seemed on the whole a little weak historically. Half of the ladies were inclined to favor the Elizabethan, and they had constructed rather bunchy ruffs and farthingales for their offspring; others, who had read as far as the stage directions and learned that the action took place in an Athenian wood, had produced something vaguely Athenian, usually beginning with a sheet. Only the fairies had a certain uniformity. For some reason their parents had all decided on cheesecloth, with here and there a little ill-advised trimming with tinsel.

My own costume was mysterious, but spectacular. As nearly as I have ever been able to figure things out, my mother found her inspiration for it in a Maxfield Parrish picture of a court jester. Beginning at the top, there was a cap with three stuffed horns; then, for the main part, a pair of tights that covered me to my wrists and ankles; and finally slippers with stuffed toes that curled up at the ends. The whole thing was made out of silk in alternate green and red stripes, and (unquestionably my poor mother's most demented stroke) it was covered from head to foot with a thousand tiny bells. Because all our costumes were obviously perishable, we never wore them in rehearsal, and naturally nobody knew that I was invested with these peculiar sound effects until I made my entrance at the beginning of the second act.

Our director was a man who had strong opinions about how Shakespeare should be played, and Puck was one of his favorite characters. It was his theory that Puck, being "the incarnation of mischief," never ought to be still a minute, so I had been coached to bound onto the stage, and once there to dance up and down, cocking my head and waving my arms.

"I want you to be a little whirlwind," this man said.

Even as I prepared to bound onto the stage, I had my own misgivings about those dangerously abundant gestures, and their probable effect on my bells. It was too late, however, to invent another technique for playing Puck, even if there had been room for anything but horror in my mind. I bounded out onto the stage.

The effect, in its way, must have been superb. With every leap I rang like a thousand children's sleighs, my melodies foretelling

God knows what worlds of merriment to the enchanted spectators. It was even worse when I came to the middle of the stage and went into my gestures. The other ringing had been loud but sporadic. This was persistent, varying only slightly in volume and pitch with the vehemence of my gestures. To a blind man, it must have sounded as though I had recklessly decided to accompany myself on a xylophone. A maturer actor would probably have made up his mind that an emergency existed, and abandoned his gestures as impractical under the circumstances. I was thirteen, and incapable of innovations. I had been told by responsible authorities that gestures went with this part, and I continued to make them. I also continued to ring — a silvery music, festive and horrible.

If the bells were hard on my nerves, they were even worse for the rest of the cast, who were totally unprepared for my new interpretation. Puck's first remark is addressed to one of the fairies, and it is mercifully brief.

I said, "How now, spirit! Whither wander you?"

This unhappy child, already embarrassed by a public appearance in cheesecloth and tinsel, was also burdened with an opening speech of sixteen lines in verse. He began bravely:

> "Over hill, over dale,
> Thorough brush, thorough brier,
> Over park, over pale,
> Thorough flood, thorough fire . . ."

At the word "fire," my instructions were to bring my hands up from the ground in a long, wavery sweep, intended to represent fire. The bells pealed. To my startled ears, it sounded more as if they exploded. The fairy stopped in his lines and looked at me sharply. The jingling, however, had diminished; it was no more than if a faint wind stirred my bells, and he went on:

> "I do wander every where,
> Swifter than the moone's sphere . . ."

Here again I had another cue, for a sort of swoop and dip indicating the swiftness of the moone's sphere. Again the bells rang out, and again the performance stopped in its tracks. The fairy was clearly troubled by these interruptions. He had, however, a child's strange acceptance of the inscrutable, and was even able to regard my bells as a last-minute adult addition to the program, nerve-racking but not to be questioned. I am sure it was only this that got him through that first speech.

My turn, when it came, was even worse. By this time the audience had succumbed to a helpless gaiety. Every time my bells rang, laughter swept the spectators, and this mounted and mingled with the bells until everything else was practically inaudible. I began my speech, another long one, and full of incomprehensible references to Titania's changeling.

"Louder," said somebody in the wings. "You'll have to talk louder."

It was the director, and he seemed to be in a dangerous state. "And for heaven's sake, stop that jingling!" he said.

I talked louder, and I tried to stop the jingling, but it was no use. By the time I got to the end of my speech, I was shouting and so was the audience. It appeared that I had very little control over the bells, which continued to jingle in spite of my passionate efforts to keep them quiet.

All this had a very bad effect on the fairy, who by this time had many symptoms of a complete nervous collapse. However, he began his next speech:

> "Either I mistake your shape and making quite,
> Or else you are that shrewd and knavish sprite
> Call'd Robin Goodfellow: are you not he
> That . . ."

At this point I forgot that the rules had been changed and I was supposed to leave out the gestures. There was a furious jingling, and the fairy gulped.

"Are you not he that, that . . ."

He looked miserably at the wings, and the director supplied the next line, but the tumult was too much for him. The unhappy child simply shook his head.

"Say anything!" shouted the director desperately. "Anything at all!"

The fairy only shut his eyes and shuddered.

"All right!" shouted the director. "All right, Puck. *You* begin *your* next speech."

By some miracle, I actually did remember my next lines, and had opened my mouth to begin on them when suddenly the fairy spoke. His voice was a high, thin monotone, and there seemed to be madness in it, but it was perfectly clear.

"Fourscore and seven years ago," he began, "our fathers brought forth on this continent a new nation, conceived . . ."

He said it right through to the end, and it was certainly the most successful speech ever made on that stage, and probably one of the most successful speeches ever made on any stage. I don't remember, if I ever knew, how the rest of us ever picked up the dull, normal thread of the play after that extraordinary performance, but we must have, because I know it went on. I only remember that in the next intermission the director cut off my bells with his penknife, and after that things quieted down and got dull.

WOLCOTT GIBBS

THE DELICACY OF SOUND and action in this poem will require considerable vocal control.

Death

I SHALL walk down the road.
I shall turn and feel upon my feet
The kisses of Death, like scented rain.
For Death is a black slave with little silver birds
Perched in a sleeping wreath upon his head.
He will tell me, his voice like jewels
Dropped into a satin bag,
How he has tip-toed after me down the road,
His heart made a dark whirlpool with longing for me.
Then he will graze me with his hands
And I shall be one of the sleeping silver birds
Between the cold waves of his hair, as he tip-toes on.

MAXWELL BODENHEIM

THERE ARE SEVERAL "stage directions" for vocal changes in this selection. Make use of them for the climaxes and the variety and contrast. The text is from the Confraternity-Douay Bible.

from *The Old Testament*

DANIEL, CHAPTER FIVE

Belshazzar the king made a great feast to a thousand of his lords, and drank wine before the thousand. Belshazzar, while he tasted the wine, commanded to bring the golden and silver vessels which Nebuchadnezzar his father had taken out of the temple which was in Jerusalem; that the king and his lords, his wives and his concubines, might drink therefrom. Then they brought the golden vessels that were taken out of the temple of the house of God which was at Jerusalem; and the king and his lords, his wives and his concubines, drank from them. They drank wine, and praised the gods of gold, and of silver, of brass, of iron, of wood, and of stone.

In the same hour came forth the fingers of a man's hand, and wrote over against the candlestick upon the plaster of the wall of the king's palace; and the king saw the part of the hand that wrote. Then the king's countenance was changed in him, and his thoughts troubled him; and the joints of his loins were loosed, and his knees smote one against another. The king cried aloud to bring in the enchanters, the Chaldeans, and the soothsayers. The king spake and said to the wise men of Babylon, Whosoever shall read this

From *Minna and Myself* by Maxwell Bodenheim. New York: Pagan Publishing Company, 1918.

writing, and show me the interpretation thereof, shall be clothed with purple, and have a chain of gold about his neck, and shall be the third ruler in the kingdom. Then came in all the king's wise men; but they could not read the writing; nor make known to the king the interpretation. Then was the king Belshazzar greatly changed in him, and his lords were perplexed.

Now the queen by reason of the words of the king and his lords came into the banquet house: the queen spake and said, O king, live for ever; let not thy thoughts trouble thee, nor let thy countenance be changed. There is a man in thy kingdom, in whom is the spirit of the holy gods; and in the days of thy father light and understanding and wisdom, like the wisdom of the gods, were found in him; and the king Nebuchadnezzar thy father, the king, *I say,* thy father, made him master of the magicians, enchanters, Chaldeans, and soothsayers; forasmuch as an excellent spirit, and knowledge, and understanding, interpreting of dreams, and showing of dark sentences, and dissolving of doubts, were found in the same Daniel, whom the king named Belteshazzar. Now let Daniel be called, and he will show the interpretation.

Then was Daniel brought in before the king. The king spake and said unto Daniel, Art thou that Daniel, who are of the children of the captivity of Judah, whom the king my father brought out of Judah? I have heard of thee, that the spirit of the gods is in thee, and that light and understanding and excellent wisdom are found in thee. And now the wise men, the enchanters, have been brought in before me, that they should read this writing, and make known unto me the interpretation thereof; but they could not show the interpretation of the king. But I have heard of thee, that thou canst give interpretations, and dissolve doubts: now if thou canst read the writing, and make known to me the interpretation thereof, thou shalt be clothed with purple, and have a chain of gold about thy neck, and shalt be the third ruler in the kingdom.

Then Daniel answered and said before the king, Let thy gifts be to thyself, and give thy reward to another; nevertheless I will read the writing unto the king, and make known to him the interpretation. O thou king, the Most High God gave Nebuchadnezzar thy father the kingdom, and greatness, and glory, and majesty: and because of the greatness that he gave him, all the peoples, nations, and languages trembled and feared before him: whom he would he slew, and whom he would he kept alive; and whom he would he raised up, and whom he would be put down. But when his heart was lifted up, and his spirit was hardened so that he dealt proudly, he was deposed from his kingly throne, and they took his glory from him: and he was driven from the sons of men, and his heart was made like the beasts', and his dwelling was with the wild asses; he was fed with grass like oxen, and his body was wet with the dew of heaven; until he knew that the Most High God ruleth in the kingdom of men, and that he setteth up over it whomsoever he will. And thou his son, O Belshazzar, hast not humbled thy heart, though thou knewest all this, but hast lifted up thyself against the Lord of heaven; and they have brought the vessels of his house before thee, and thou and thy lords, thy wives and thy concubines, have drunk wine from them; and thou hast praised the gods of silver and gold, of brass, iron, wood, and stone, which see not, nor hear, nor know; and the God in whose hand thy breath is, and whose are all thy ways, hast thou not glorified. Then was the part of the hand sent from before him, and this writing was inscribed.

And this is the writing that was inscribed: ME-NE, ME-NE, TE-KEL, U-PHAR-SIN. This is the interpretation of the thing: ME-NE; God hath numbered thy kingdom, and brought it to an end. TE-KEL; thou art weighed in the balances, and art found wanting. PE-RES; thy kingdom is divided, and given to the Medes and Persians.

Then commanded Belshazzar, and they clothed Daniel with purple, and put a chain of gold about his neck, and made proclamation concerning him, that he should be the third ruler in the kingdom.

In that night Belshazzar the Chaldean king was slain. And Darius the Mede received the kingdom, being about threescore and two years old.

✶ Bibliography

The following books have specific exercises on voice and diction. The interpreter will wish to consult them for any minor problems which may need attention.

Akin, Johnnye. *And So We Speak: Voice and Articulation.* Englewood Cliffs, New Jersey: Prentice-Hall, Inc., 1958.

Anderson, Virgil A. *Training the Speaking Voice.* Second Edition. New York: Oxford University Press, 1961.

Fairbanks, Grant. *Practical Voice Practice.* New York: Harper and Row, 1964.

Aimed specifically at audibility, intelligibility, and flexibility. A book designed for the normal voice with minor problems in the above areas.

Hanley, Theodore D., and Wayne L. Thurman. *Developing Vocal Skills.* New York: Holt, Rinehart and Winston, Inc., 1962.

Heinberg, Paul. *Voice Training — For Speaking and Reading Aloud.* New York: The Ronald Press Company, 1964.

Especially designed to provide an application of current scientific knowledge for the student of speech and drama.

Hicks, Helen Gertrude. *Voice and Speech for Effective Communication.* Vol. 1, Voice Production and Articulation; Vol. 2, Work Book for Listening and Vocal Improvement; Vol. 3, Passages for Reading Aloud. Dubuque, Iowa: William C. Brown Company, 1963.

Recordings are very useful to help train your ear. The following book has a complete annotated list of recordings of prose, poetry, and drama.

Roach, Helen. *Spoken Records.* New York: The Scarecrow Press, Inc., 1963.

PART 2

The Interpretation of Prose

5

Some Aspects of Prose

Up to this point we have discussed matters of analysis common to all types of writing, and the way the interpreter uses his voice and body to serve the demands of the literature. In this section we shall be concerned specifically with prose, and in the two sections which follow with drama and poetry respectively. We have seen that all literature has certain elements in common and that the basic principles of analysis and interpretation apply to all types. But it is equally true that each form imposes special problems of analysis and demands varying degrees of emphasis on one or more aspects of technique in preparation and presentation.

For example, the oral interpreter uses the same basic approach to poetry as to any other type of material, but he must also give special attention to condensation, sound patterns, and whatever strictures of stanzaic form, meter, and rhyme the poet has imposed. Drama requires special emphasis on character suggestion, on setting, and on the relationships between the characters, in addition to awareness of the form, which may be either prose or poetry. On the other hand, prose which is primarily non-dramatic may nevertheless contain passages which call for attention to character and setting, and thus present problems similar to those found in drama. Or it may be highly suggestive and come very close to poetry in its use of imagery. Therefore, this division of material into prose, drama, and poetry, and the further subdivisions made under these headings, must be regarded only as a convenience. For the concern of the modern interpreter is not with literary labels, except as they help him to analyze his material. His interest is, rather, in the selection of suitable material and in the complete understanding of the piece of writing which he wishes to communicate to his listeners. Classification can serve only as a starting point for a detailed analysis. It is the interpreter's responsibility to discover the problems and advantages in each type, and then to go beyond this generalization to the specific, individual variations within the particular selection he has chosen. For always, regardless of its form or type, each selection must be approached as an individual example. Before we consider examples illustrating the various kinds of prose writing, it would be well to review some aspects of literary style found in all prose writing.

Style is the channel through which the author relates his outlook on life to what he has to say in a given instance. It is the concrete, physical mode of written expression, and embodies such technical considerations as the organization of ideas, the choice of words, the relationships between words, the sentence structure, and the structure of paragraphs. Thus, in considering style the interpreter is concerned not only with understanding the writer's general outlook and its relation to the particular selection, but also with handling the physical, written expression. As Arnold Bennett says, "When a writer conceives an idea he conceives it in a form of words. That form of words is his style. . . ." It is shaped by the kind of person he is, by his general philosophy of life, and also by the culture and age in which he lives. It is dictated by his attitude toward his subject matter and toward his intended audience, his readers. Style is at the heart of the intrinsic factor of harmony and is basic in establishing the tone of any selection.

PARAGRAPHS

The first step in examining style might well be to discover how the elements which make up the whole are organized and arranged. This involves a consideration of the major thought units, the paragraphs.

Paragraph structure is important to the interpreter because each paragraph is a unit in the thought progression. The length and complexity of the unit, and of the sentences which make it up, reflect the author's approach to the thought and the pace at which he is moving. Short, simple sentences and paragraphs indicate a direct, perhaps relatively uncritical, approach and suggest immediacy of experience; long, complicated sentences and paragraphs suggest a more sophisticated and evaluative approach, perhaps an intellectualization of experience. The interpreter needs to be sensitive to these nuances of style and to reflect his awareness of them in his oral reading.

Moreover, the writer has indicated degrees of relationship and importance by what he has put together in the paragraphs. For instance, he may have included several relevant examples of a key idea in one unit, or he may have given each a separate paragraph, thus adding to their individual importance by setting them off from each other. A paragraph is a distinct subdivision of the main thought, dealing with a particular point and terminating only when that point has been developed.

SENTENCES

The way the author handles the sentences within the paragraphs is of practical concern to the interpreter, whose responsibility it is to make the total meaning clear to his audience. He must pay attention to length and grammatical construction as clues to attitude and tone in his analysis and as a guide to the use of his techniques in performance.

The way a writer combines words into sentences is an important element of his style. The simple sentence (a single independent clause) and the compound sentence (two or more independent clauses) are most characteristic of a simple, direct style. The complex sentence (one independent clause and one or more dependent clauses) and the compound-complex sentence (two or more independent clauses, and one or more dependent clauses), on the other hand, are the mark of a more involved and complex style. The interpreter must, both in evaluating style and in interpreting orally, not only note these elementary grammatical distinctions; he must also consider sentence length, position of subordinate elements, order of words, and use of parallelism and balanced constructions. The syntax of a sentence is a way of grouping the words to show their relationship and to point up degrees of importance. For example, contrast the syntax in these two phrases: ". . . all the marigolds and pinks in the bungalow gardens were bowed to earth with wetness" and "Drenched were the cold fuchsias. . . ." In the first example, the order is normal and leads easily to the completed thought. In the second phrase, however, "Drenched" is given strong emphasis by its position at the beginning of the sentence.

The writer in the following excerpt is describing his sensations on landing his plane after a dangerous flight. He feels unable to reflect on the experience he has been through and to translate it through his intellect into an ordered pattern, and the succession of short sentences gives an almost breathless sense of his emotional exhaustion, the impossibility he feels of putting his experiences into words.

> Had I been afraid? I couldn't say. I had witnessed a strange sight. What strange sight? I couldn't say. The sky was blue and the sea was white. I felt I ought to tell someone about it since I was back from so far away! But I had no grip on what I had been through.
>
> ANTOINE DE SAINT EXUPÉRY, *Wind, Sand, and Stars*

In the same way, numerous exclamatory or interrogative sentences or incomplete sentence fragments will affect the handling of a piece of prose for oral interpretation. Notice, for example, the vivacity and good humor suggested in this:

> God bless my soul! When do we find these contemptuous gentlemen lost to the world in the reading of Homer in his Greek or even of the bawdy Petronius in his Latin?
>
> Not at all! We find them amusing themselves with bagatelles compared with which . . .
>
> JOHN COWPER POWYS, *Enjoyment of Literature*

The exclamations give the writing speed and informality, while the question gives it intimacy and directness. The incomplete sentence, which is followed by a return to an earlier thought, leaves the reader to furnish the implied evaluation and again creates an atmosphere of conversation rather than of formal writing.

Longer sentences have more formality and must be broken down into speech phrases when read aloud. Long modifying phrases and clauses (italicized in the examples below) make a sentence undulate, and present the interpreter with a special challenge. At the beginning of the sentence, modifiers prepare the reader for the main idea and orient him toward it; and the interpreter has the problem of building up to the key words of the thought:

> *Wandering through clear chambers where the general effect made preferences almost as impossible as if they had been shocks, pausing at open doors where vistas were long and bland,* she would, *even if she had not already known,* have discovered for herself that Poynton was the record of a life.
>
> HENRY JAMES, *The Spoils of Poynton*

Modifiers in the middle of the sentence interrupt the main flow of the thought, even while explaining some elements within it. Here the interpreter must sustain the meaning, carrying the thread of the principal idea from one key word to another over the intervening material, without nullifying the contribution of those subordinate elements to the whole:

> The book in question, *which is at once a lasting contribution to English literature and a mere farrago of pretentious mediocrity,* was published about two months ago.
>
> VIRGINIA WOOLF, *The Common Reader*

Modifiers at the end of the sentence continue the idea, expanding or qualifying it, although the skeletal frame of the thought is already complete without them:

> I was at incredible pains in cutting down some of the largest trees for oars and masts, *wherein I was, however, much assisted by his Majesty's ship-carpenters, who helped me in smoothing them after I had done the rough work.*
>
> JONATHAN SWIFT, *Gulliver's Travels*

When any of the elements occur out of the normal order in such a way that the meaning is held up until almost the very end of the sentence, we have a periodic construction. Because the periodic sentence defers the completion of meaning, it creates suspense; and because it breaks the usual sentence pattern and alters the normal stresses, it is especially emphatic. Although the inversion of normal word order is perhaps most effective in longer sentences where there is greater opportunity to arouse suspense by deferring completion of meaning, it is a device that can give special emphasis to a short sentence as well. Skillfully and judiciously used, inversions and periodic effects are powerful stylistic devices, and the interpreter will want to take full advantage of unusual sentence patterns and use the element of suspense in such a way that the audience's interest is held through to the climactic completion of meaning at the end of the sentence.

Sentences with parallelisms and balanced constructions provide another challenge for the oral interpreter, since he must at once keep the parallel or coordinate elements equal in value and point the connection or contrast between them. A compound sentence, consisting of two independent clauses connected by a conjunction, is a very elementary example of syntactical parallelism; the clauses are so related in grammatical construction because the ideas are connected and have equal value. The connective "and," a usual signpost pointing out coordinations, as between parts of a compound subject or predicate, enables the interpreter to achieve a simple balance between parallel elements. The parallelism may be cast as a balanced construction, in which the parts are quite evenly set off against each other:

> No man is an island, entire of itself; every man is a piece of the continent, a part of the main.
>
> DONNE, *Devotions, XVII*

The parallelism here is easily and graphically shown by lining up the parts:

No man	is an island,	entire of itself;
every man	is a piece of the continent,	a part of the main.

Or it may be a series of elaborately wrought analogies and antitheses, reflected in the form in which the sentence is cast:

Harry, I do not only marvel where thou spendest thy time, but also how thou art accompanied; for though the camomile, the more it is trodden on the faster it grows, yet youth the more it is wasted the sooner it wears.

SHAKESPEARE, *Henry IV, Part I*

This sentence might be represented as follows:

Harry, I do	not only	marvel	where thou spendest thy time,
	but also		how thou art accompanied;
		for though	the camomile,
			the more it is trodden on
			the faster it grows,
		yet	youth
			the more it is wasted
			the sooner it wears.

The important thing for the interpreter to remember is that at the syntactical level parallelisms indicate parts of a sentence that are equal in value; at the stylistic level, ideas that are balanced against each other and mutually contribute to one another.

Too many sentences of similar construction or similar length result in a dead-level style that fails to hold the attention of the reader. Especially when read aloud, prose that repeats the same patterns and rhythms over and over falls monotonously on the ear. The skillful writer varies both the length and the structure of his sentences and lays claim to the reader's sustained attention by subtle shifts of emphasis and pattern. For instance, an uphill climb through three or four rather lengthy and difficult sentences may be broken by a short sentence which serves as a plateau on which one can catch one's breath and re-orient oneself to the view. The problems of variety and rhythm in style must, of course, be solved first by the writer, but the interpreter must keep them in mind in selecting his material, make himself aware of stylistic changes in pace, and in turn consciously use them to hold the attention of his audience and to point up shifts in tone.

SPEECH PHRASES

Another factor, which for the oral interpreter is closely related to prose style, is the speech phrase. The speech phrase is made up of the words which an interpreter groups together as he reads. The length of the speech phrases is often dictated by the punctuation the author has used, by the rhythm and meaning of the sentences, and by the practical considerations of ease and clarity in reading aloud.

Punctuation is the first guide, although it is meant for the eye whereas the interpreter is addressing the ear. A comma, for example, prevents the eye from running ahead and mistaking the sense of the sentence, but in oral reading it need not always mean a pause, for a change of the pitch, tempo, or volume of the voice can often serve the same purpose. For instance, in ". . . a condition to be seen, in a lesser degree, in a turkey cock," it is unnecessary to pause before and after "in a lesser degree"; a slight drop of the voice and change in rate of speech, or a combination of both, will achieve the effect less obtrusively than a pause.

While commas are more frequently guides to possible speech phrases than any other marks of punctuation, important clues are given also by semicolons, colons, parentheses, and dashes. A semicolon marks a turn of the thought, or a definite separation between two aspects of the same thought, and usually requires a slight pause to make the relationship clear to the listeners. Parentheses and dashes, in pairs, also mark off distinct speech phrases, often interpolative matter across which the main thought must be carried. (Long interpolations, of course, will need to be further subdivided for convenience and clarity in reading aloud.) A single dash, like the colon, often marks the pause that occurs just before a summing-up and implies a reference to some previous portion of the sentence.

But since punctuation is inserted as a visual aid in silent reading, it does not — unfortunately — prove an infallible or a complete guide to the oral interpreter in establishing his speech phrases. In fact, there are numerous occasions when the punctuation is inadequate for aural comprehension, and the interpreter may need to insert slight pauses for clarity. Pauses are often necessary, likewise, to point up similar or contrasting ideas, as in

> The same cartoon humor that shows goats munching tin cans depicts ostriches swallowing alarm clocks, monkey wrenches, and cylinder heads.

Although the punctuation is correct in this sentence, a pause between "cans" and "depicts" helps to balance the parallel ideas when the sentence is read aloud.

There is also the practical consideration of the number of words that can be satisfactorily uttered on one breath. In reading long, relatively complicated sentences, the interpreter will have some leeway in grouping his speech phrases. He will be guided by the need to simplify the long modifiers so that his audience will understand the meaning of the sentence at a single hearing. The speech phrases will tend to be longer because of the large number of phrases and clauses which must be kept in close relationship to the ideas they modify, and because of the need to bridge suspended thought across these modifiers. This single-sentence paragraph is an excellent example of the problem:

> There is an amusing belief among many country boys, for instance, that an owl has to turn his head to watch you and must watch you if you are near him, so that if you will only walk completely around him he will wring his own neck.

Read aloud without a pause, or any attention to the punctuation the author has inserted, this involved sentence would quickly lose an audience in a maze of clauses and convey little of the idea intended. Read aloud a second time, with full attention to each mark of punctuation, as reflected in a change of pitch, pace, or volume, the sentence becomes much clearer. The punctuation, however, does not take care of the parallel values in "that an owl has to turn his head to watch you and must watch you if you are near him," or of the suspension of thought from "so that" to "he will wring his own neck." The interpreter, therefore, will need to break these long units down into shorter speech phrases, though he will not shatter them into fragmentary units of two or three words, for this would destroy the relationship between the parts and the whole.

CHOICE OF WORDS

Any discussion of words as an aspect of style will obviously overlap, to some extent, our earlier discussion of words as an aspect of content, for style and content are actually inseparable. Nevertheless, the writer's choice of words is a vital part of his style and deserves special attention from that point of view.

We have already made a distinction between the denotations (dictionary meanings) and the connotations (suggestions, implications) of words. Now we should mention another important aspect of literary style — the writer's use of allusions, similes, and metaphors. These three figures of speech are all means of comparing one thing to another; thus they are instruments of connotative meaning. They will contribute primarily to harmony by intensifying theme or underscoring attitude. This is certainly the function of the simile in "June Recital" (the studio "decorated like the inside of a candy box"), which sets the tone for the excerpt (see page 192). Sometimes there is deliberate incongruity, such as we find in "Birds in Their Little Nests," which we shall examine in detail later in this chapter. Here Bergen Evans uses numerous literary and mythological allusions in juxtaposition with scientific facts.

Another point to note is whether the words are abstract or concrete — whether they convey primarily an idea, like "sweetness," or an image, like "honeysuckle." Whereas concrete terms have sense appeal and predominate in descriptive and narrative prose, abstractions appeal more directly to the intellect, without the mediation of the senses, and occur more often in expository prose, whose primary appeal is to the mind. But just as the appeal to the mind can be reinforced by appeals to the emotions and senses, so can concrete terms be used to flesh-out abstract ideas and give them form and meaning.

The length of words is a practical concern for one who is to read aloud, but from the stylistic point of view the important thing is whether words are formal or informal or even colloquial in tone, whether they are unusual words or words common in everyday speech — though long words are ordinarily more formal and unusual, short words less formal and more common. In any case, the words should be evaluated in the light of the prevailing tone of the selection. An unusual word, for example, might reflect the highly intellectual tone of the selection, convey a deliberately romantic or archaic tone, or be used incongruously for the sake of humor or irony. The stylistic study of words may even reach back into the field of linguistics. Although it will not often be necessary for the oral interpreter to delve into the origins and derivations of words, he must be prepared to do so if it seems helpful in bringing out complete meaning.

Finally, the repetition of words is an aspect of style that peculiarly concerns the oral interpreter. If words are repeated, the interpreter should decide why — and whether to play them up or down in reading aloud. If the writer repeated simply because repetition was unavoidable in communicating his idea lucidly, the interpreter might decide that a noticeable reiteration of the same sounds would distract his listeners and that the repeated words should not be given special stress in an oral reading. On the other hand, if the writer consciously repeated for emphasis or effectiveness, the rhetorical pattern will tell the interpreter so — and will enable him to decide that the repeated words should be read with marked emphasis. Powys uses an interesting repetition to describe the multiple personality of a bookseller:

> He is an ascetic hermit, he is an erotic immoralist, he is a papist, he is a Quaker, he is a communist, he is an anarchist, he is a savage iconoclast, he is a passionate worshipper of idols.

The parallel construction breaks this sentence into eight separate ideas, all of equal value. But perhaps more important to the interpreter is the fact that the repetition of the "he is" construction sets up a rhythm which allows the audience to complete each characteristic before moving on to the next, and at the same time alerts them for the one to come. In this way each quality is sharply pointed and the incongruity among them heightened.

The interpreter will not need to subject *all* words to such detailed scrutiny as that outlined above, but he will have to be constantly aware of all these possibilities for meaning and suggestion if he is to respond to his material at the deepest level of his consciousness.

PROSE RHYTHM

Another important guide for the interpreter is the rhythm of the prose selection. All well-written prose has rhythm — not the formal, patterned rhythm of poetry, but a control of the flow of words that makes relationships clear and causes emphasis to fall on the important words.

We are already acquainted with rhythm of content, which is established by the organization of the thought progression and the emotional progression. It depends upon the placement of key words and phrases, and of the major and minor climaxes, both logical and emotional, throughout the entire selection.

There is also a rhythm in prose *structure* which becomes evident when it is read aloud. This prose rhythm is established by the length and grammatical construction of the sentences and speech phrases, and by the position of the stresses. As the interpreter groups words into thought units and speech phrases, separating them by pauses of varying duration, he is creating *cadences.* A cadence is a flow of sound. Obviously, then, words which are grouped form a flow of sound. A pause interrupts this flow, whether it be a terminal pause at the end of a sentence or a very brief pause to set off a speech phrase. Thus length and frequency of pauses also become a part of prose rhythm.

Both the rate at which the cadences are uttered and the number of syllables within them affect the rhythm pattern. A mechanical measurement of the cadences in prose is usually not necessary. The interpreter whose ear is trained will be aware of their existence and contribution.

Stress in prose is, of course, the result of a number of elements. It can result from the need for clarity, from contrast, or from a particular combination of sounds. The use of numerous one-syllable words in sequence, for instance, may very well produce a sharp staccato rhythm, especially if the content is forceful. The distance between key words in a sentence or paragraph will also affect the number and placement of stresses.

In the following sentence from *The Natural History of Nonsense,* for example, "vital" and "ostrich" are words that should be pointed or emphasized in the interest of clarity. They are key words.

> The most vital of all the mythical birds, though, is the ostrich that hides its head in the sand at the approach of danger.

When the sentence is read aloud, its natural rhythm brings the emphasis on these words and also beats out an accent on the error to be refuted: "hides its head in the sand." Here rhythm reinforces meaning. It can also reinforce attitude or mood. In any event, the interpreter should make himself aware of it and be sure that he is swimming with, not against, its current. There may be times, however, when prose rhythm becomes so pronounced and regular that it actually hinders aural comprehension by drowning sense in sound. In such cases, the interpreter will have to work to keep the pattern from becoming too dominant.

Most of the accents or stresses, then, will stem from the reader's awareness of meaning and from the peculiar qualities of the author's style. It is seldom necessary to go through a piece of prose and mark each stress, though the interpreter may find it interesting or even helpful to do so.

Only by being sensitive to the natural rhythms in the writing, as well as to the formal structure of the sentences and the various requisites of content and indications of attitude, can the interpreter group speech phrases intelligently and place emphasis where it should fall, thus permitting the rhythm of prose structure to reinforce the content for total effect.

FACTUAL PROSE

The interpreter is not likely to be working extensively with strictly factual prose. Obviously, he would seldom choose to do a performance from an encyclopedia or a scientific work. Nevertheless, he may encounter passages or entire units in an essay which are technically factual and out of which the personal reflections of the author develop.

Factual prose, in the strictest definition of the term, is that in which the author gives verifiable information. It states that something is so. The writer's personal comment is kept at a minimum. Unadulterated examples of this type of writing are probably to be found only in books on science and mathematics, where one is told, for instance, that "in an isosceles triangle the angles opposite the equal sides are themselves equal," or in an encyclopedia which states on good authority that John Milton was born in England in 1608 and died in 1674. Objective journalistic reporting may also be considered factual when it limits itself to the simple formula of "who, where, when, what" and possibly "why."

In strictly factual material, the informative content and the logical development are of first importance. There is no emotional content, since the author is concerned with fact, not response to fact. It is, of course, possible for a fact to be so startling or shocking that even the unadorned statement will arouse emotional response in the reader, yet any arousal of emotion is due to subjective conclusions and associations on the part of the reader; it does not lie in the fact or in the writer's purpose. The content of factual writing depends for effectiveness upon authoritative statements, logical progression of proofs, and exact denotation of the words. In short, factual prose informs, defines, explains. Facts need not be "sold" — only established; for anything that is demonstrated as true (and by definition a fact is something that is true) is accepted by the rational mind.

The interpreter is most likely to have occasion to deal with prose which is factual in the sense that it makes use of facts to support a thesis — that is, prose in which the author is concerned with the implication or interpretation of the facts. In some cases, the facts will provide a touch of humor or satire, while in others the implied comment of the author is the desired end, and the factual content merely a means of achieving that end. In other words, the presentation of the facts themselves may be the basic purpose of the writing, or the facts may be merely the framework for an expression of attitude. It is the interpreter's responsibility to discover how the author uses the information he gives, and to make sure that he achieves the same purpose as he communicates the essay to his audience.

THE PERSONAL ESSAY

We have seen that, in general, the writer of factual prose is primarily concerned with things outside himself — that even when his personal reaction to the facts comes through, his chief interest remains the communication of the factual information. However, the writer of an essay is less concerned with presenting facts than with developing ideas and sharing his personal opinions. He may use facts to support his conclusions, but what he thinks and how he feels, and why, are the pivots on which his writing turns. He may be olympian and instructive in setting forth his ideas, or detached and ironical, or warmly personal; but whatever the tone of his remarks, he is speaking in his own person, and his attitude toward his subject is of primary importance.

As self-expression or self-revelation becomes the dominant motive for writing, the author puts more of himself as an individual into what he writes, the informative and instructional elements taper in importance, and attitude and mood become increasingly the handles by which the interpreter gets hold of the material. The writer's personality and his personal set of values are reflected in the facts and concrete objects which he selects to set up associations. This is especially true in accounts of travel and in autobiographical sketches. The associations or connotations lead the reader, and of course the listener, beyond the facts and the denotation of the words and phrases. For example, Jacques Barzun describes a certain mathematics teacher very sharply when he says that ". . . he would put the chalk to his lips, make a noise like a straining gear box, and write out the correct result." We have no idea what the man looked like, nor do we need to. The selection of the characteristic gesture of putting chalk to lips calls up in almost everyone a complete mental picture of bemused, pedantic concentration. The "noise like a straining gear box" suggests that he is more a machine than a man, and when the gears start to move — out comes the answer!

The references the writer uses will grow out of his awareness of their probable universal appeal and also out of his own background and experiences. For the understanding of purely factual material, an examination of the author's life and background is useful only as it establishes his authority to write on his subject. The facts exist apart from the author, and it is the facts that are important, not the author's personal philosophy as it may relate to the facts, or his emotional response to them. But when facts are the framework for a theme, the author's principle of selection becomes very important. Only by careful scrutiny of all expressions and references that seem to carry a comment, an evaluation, or a judgment, by understanding what all words mean and what they suggest, not merely in themselves but in the context, can the interpreter come to a complete understanding of what the author is saying about his subject, explicitly or by implication, and be able to convey that attitude to an audience.

The personal essay gives us an excellent opportunity to examine the aspects of style in detail and see how they can be of use to the interpreter. For a sample analysis we shall select a piece of writing which is basically factual and in which the facts are used expertly to support a thesis. *The Natural History of Nonsense* by Bergen Evans is such a book. Perhaps by analyzing an excerpt we may see in concrete terms how the oral interpreter prepares for a presentation of this modified kind of factual prose that, both because of its content and qualities of expression, will have interest for an audience.

In his book Mr. Evans is dealing on one level with facts, and on another, through the use of these facts, with the refutation of established errors. At a casual glance, it may appear that personal comment is minimal. On closer examination, however, one finds that the author, without violating the facts, has achieved a sophisticated humor and has managed to make his own attitude unmistakably apparent. The thesis which Mr. Evans tries to establish is that "we may be through with the past, but the past is not through with us." He also points out that our beliefs have not kept pace with our knowledge and that nothing is more vital than error. He expresses these thoughts in quick succession in his introductory chapters. The rest of the book is devoted to specific examples of error, to evidence of their common acceptance, and to the author's scientific disproval of these errors.

It is a tribute to Mr. Evans' ability as a writer that one finds it difficult to cut his material and still keep intact the progression from general to particular which he follows in most of his chapters. In the chapter from which the following excerpt is taken, the author is dealing with some common misconceptions about birds. He opens with a discussion of our sentimental acceptance of the power of mother-love in the nesting female, a belief which he proceeds to demolish completely. Next, he gives the same treatment to the mystic powers attributed to certain birds, such as ability to foretell the weather and to find their way back to a given spot by instinct. He then goes to the discussion which follows. (For convenience in analysis, we have numbered the paragraphs.)

Birds in Their Little Nests

[1] Another mystic link between birds and the Great Beyond is forged by those who insist that cocks crow with chronometric regularity. Some say they crow only on the hour; others maintain that they crow every twenty minutes. Formerly they were thought to observe sidereal time, each cock being an instinctive astronomer and knowing (as Chaucer says with a smile) the exact time for his own town. Today, when most people are unaware that the actual time differs with every town, the roosters are apparently assumed to have even greater powers. For if they crow by the clock, as they are said to, they must first reckon sidereal time for that locality and then

Copyright, 1946 by Bergen Evans. Reprinted from *The Natural History of Nonsense* by Bergen Evans, by permission of Alfred A. Knopf, Inc.

make an adjustment to suit the local conformity to the national time zone. Of course railway time and wartime and daylight-saving time wouldn't bother them, because they wouldn't have to care what hour it was so long as they crowed *on* the hour.

[2] Most vulgar errors about birds are confined to such general delusions as the foregoing. Save for a few domesticated species, birds are too swift and shy for any but highly observant persons to know anything at all about them. Yet there are a few specific errors, based on false analogies or just pure myth.

[3] There is an amusing belief among many country boys, for instance, that an owl has to turn his head to watch you and must watch you if you are near him, so that if you will only walk completely around him he will wring his own neck.

[4] The peacock is thought to be so ashamed of his ugly feet that, if he chances to see them while displaying, he will let his gorgeous tail fall out of sheer humiliation and chagrin. The fact is true, but the interpretation is definitely colored by the old desire to find a moral lesson in animal behavior. A peacock must keep his head erect in order to advance his train, so that when his head is lowered his train, of necessity, falls — a condition to be seen, in a lesser degree, in a turkey cock. But the ascription of this unavoidable sequence of events to wounded vanity is pure fantasy.

[5] The most vital of all the mythical birds, though, is the ostrich that hides its head in the sand at the approach of danger. It has outlived the roc and the phoenix, and will probably be with us long after Keats's nightingale, Shelley's skylark, and Poe's raven have been forgotten. Immortal bird, indeed! It is too precious to die. Women can get on without the plumes of the ordinary, living ostrich, but what would politicians, preachers, and prophets do without the convenient metaphor of this ornithological fiction?

[6] Next to the fact that it hides its head in the sand, the best-known thing about the ostrich is that it can digest iron. The same cartoon humor that shows goats munching tin cans depicts ostriches swallowing alarm clocks, monkey wrenches, and cylinder heads. The belief is time-honored. Three hundred years ago the ostrich was always represented with a horseshoe in its mouth; without this, it would have been thought to be some other species of bird.

[7] The extent of this belief and the harm that it causes is almost incredible. There is probably not a menagerie in existence that has not lost several birds in consequence of their being fed nail files and other lethal tidbits by zoo-haunting zanies. Mr. E. G. Boulenger, for many years a director of the London Zoological Society, lists the post-mortem findings in an ostrich that had died a few days after a holiday had burdened the zoo with an unusually large number of curious clodpolls. From the organs of the unhappy bird were extracted "two handkerchiefs, three gloves, a Kodak film spool, three feet of thick string, a pencil, a part of a celluloid comb, a bicycle tire valve, an alarm clock winding key, a glove fastener, a piece

of wood five inches long, part of a rolled gold necklace, two collar studs, a penny, four halfpennies, two farthings and a Belgian franc piece — a collection which is now on exhibition in the museum of the Tropical School of Medicine."

[8] How rarely does it occur to *Homo sapiens,* gloating at the zoo, that one of the purposes of the bars, moats, walls, and fences is to protect the animals from *him!*

BERGEN EVANS

The first step, as always, is to examine the material as a whole before turning to the specific aspects of style. What is the author saying? A single reading of the excerpt makes it clear that he is talking about birds and common misconceptions of their instinctive and physical abilities.

He has said in an earlier chapter that the avowed purpose of *The Natural History of Nonsense* is to point out popular misconceptions and refute them by facts. But if it were strictly a book of factual prose, it would contain no comment or expression of attitude by the author. And if that were the case, it would make much less delightful reading than it does. The added flavor comes from the author's attitude, which builds up an implied thesis throughout.

Consequently, it may be helpful to know something about the author in order to understand more completely his attitude toward his subject. Bergen Evans is a college professor. Urbane and cosmopolitan, widely traveled, he is interested in people and in what they think. He is old enough to have developed some special interests and some eccentricities, young enough to pursue his special interests with enthusiasm. But the biographical approach gives only a very general framework for the discovery of the author's attitude; the material itself gives more explicit clues.

The title may provide the first clue. In this case, *The Natural History of Nonsense* links incongruous terms and suggests a mind and wit that can hold unlike things in balance and see them in relation to one another.

But attitude is most clearly revealed by the terms in which the subject is discussed — particularly by the choice of words. There is not a paragraph within the excerpt under discussion which does not contain Mr. Evans' particular brand of sophisticated sarcasm — a sarcasm so delicately turned that it might be taken "straight" by the naïve, although the intellectual and the cosmopolitan cannot miss it and will be flattered and amused by it. For this author is attacking nonsense not only with facts but with ridicule, and one of his chief weapons is the use of incongruities — the cock reckoning sidereal time and then adjusting to the national time zone, or *Homo sapiens* feeding a bicycle tire valve to the ostrich. The absurdity of the scientifically untenable ideas is further heightened by their elaborate scientific exposition. Moreover, certain words and phrases are loaded with author's comment, as "the ascription of this unavoidable sequence of events," "the convenient metaphor of this ornithological fiction," "lethal tidbits by zoo-haunting zanies." Finally, the point of paragraph 5 would be lost if the interpreter took the exclamation "Immortal bird, indeed!" as a sincere tribute of reverential awe and failed to catch its ironic tone.

Even a cursory analysis of the Evans selection will reveal the precision with which the thought is organized and developed. Because of the brevity of the excerpt, the relative lengths of the paragraphs will have less significance than in a longer selection.

Each paragraph deals with a unit of the main thought. Except for the third and the last (which consist of a single sentence apiece), each of them opens with a topic sentence — that is, the author makes a statement and then goes on to amplify it. The thought progresses logically, paragraph by paragraph, from one lead or topic sentence to another. The first paragraph catches the reader's attention by humor, with its references to the cock and to the "Great Beyond." Considering the excerpt as a complete unit, the reader will be aware of this paragraph as an introduction designed to catch interest. It is relatively long by comparison, thus giving the author time to move easily into his thesis.

The second paragraph at once summarizes what has gone before and serves as a lead-in to the specific examples cited in the paragraphs that follow. It is brief and concise. The third paragraph touches lightly on an "amusing belief" about owls — a belief which the author assumes will not be taken seriously; consequently he does not dwell on it or bother to develop or deny this "amusing belief among many country boys."

The fourth deals with another misconception, this time about peacocks, and the author takes a few more lines to refute this one by a simple statement of scientific fact. The fifth, sixth, and seventh paragraphs are devoted to the ostrich: the fifth sets forth a misconception about this bird and notes its common acceptance; the sixth presents another erroneous belief, and the seventh, almost exactly the same length as the introductory paragraph, shows the results of acting on this belief. Thus, error after error is brought up and then refuted by facts. By a process of induction we have arrived at the point, in the eighth and clinching paragraph, of contrasting man's actual stupidity with his complacent assumption of superiority. This is the shortest unit of all, and has added power by contrast to the longer paragraph immediately before it.

An examination of the sentence structure of Bergen Evans' writing will reveal some interesting aspects of style. Mention has already been made of the importance of the topic sentence in each paragraph. Within these sentences, and to a lesser degree within those that follow, are key words or phrases upon which the other words and phrases depend and which they echo or amplify. In the interests of condensation, we shall confine our detailed analysis to the last four paragraphs, beginning with the discussion of the ostrich. The interpreter must, of course, analyze through a similar process the entire selection he intends to read.

The opening sentence of paragraph 5 introduces the most "vital" of mythical birds — a characterization which implies both "important" and "long-lived." This vital bird is the "ostrich," not of ornithology but of myth, that "hides its head in the sand at the approach of danger." Thus the first sentence has three important aspects: it establishes the notion of vitality, identifies the bird in question, and states the chief popular belief connected with it. This sentence contains the seeds from which the rest of the paragraph sprouts. The second sentence reinforces the idea of vitality and culminates in the exclamation, "Immortal bird, indeed!" It is immortal, we are told, because it is too precious to die. The final sentence points out why it is too precious to die, and refers in "convenient metaphor of this ornithological fiction" to the erroneous belief about the ostrich's reaction to danger. The interpreter must be fully aware of the way the sentences contribute to the progression of idea, and of the implied reference in the last sentence, if he is to preserve the unity of the paragraph for his listeners and at the same time give them a sense of its place in the development of the whole selection.

Paragraph 6 opens with a connective, "Next to the fact . . . ," which indicates that a new but related idea is to follow. Here the word "fact" is intentionally ironic, for the author has already said in the previous paragraph that this accepted belief is not fact but "fiction." Thus, as "fiction" was a key word indicating the direction of the thought, so the word "fact" will require a subtle pointing in oral delivery to bring out its connotation of error as opposed to its denotation of truth. After the transitional clause, the second popular belief about the ostrich is cited — that it can digest iron. In the second sentence this belief is coupled with a similar popular delusion about the digestive system of the goat. The ostrich and the iron are of course more important than the goat and the tin, since the author is here chiefly concerned with birds. The paragraph concludes with a reference to the long persistence of this particular misconception.

In paragraph 7 the author begins to set up his conclusion. The "extent of this belief" and "the harm that it causes" are the keynotes. The second sentence gives a general example, and in the third sentence the author, in his characteristic manner, proceeds to a specific example. This third sentence is a complicated one to read aloud because it contains a number of important elements. First, the authority is quoted and his authority established. Next, attention must be given to the word "post-mortem," which gives the initial clue to the degree of harm done. Of course, this is almost immediately made explicit by "that had died," but the full meaning of this clause hangs upon "a few days after a holiday," which in turn gains its force from "an unusually large number of curious clodpolls." The sentence that follows is longer and at first glance appears to be more difficult to read aloud; actually, it is simpler. The third sentence has already prepared us for "from the organs of the unhappy bird" and even for "were extracted." The list of articles offers no great problem, since no item is important in itself but is part of a cumulative effect which builds up through the list of curiously assorted articles and reaches its conclusion with the incongruous "Belgian franc piece." The words following the dash serve to sum up the list and re-establish the factual authenticity of the example. They also carry the implication that "you can go and see for yourself if you still are not convinced."

The final paragraph presents an interesting example of balance, and also of contrast, despite the fact that Mr. Evans has already prepared his readers subtly for the turn of attention to man's stupidity through such expressions as "zoo-haunting zanies" and "curious clodpolls." The single exclamatory sentence, which carries its stinger in the last five words, must be pointed with a strong implication of the irony it contains. The listeners must not be allowed to miss the implied contrast between the expected "protect *him* from the animals" and the actual statement, "protect the animals from *him*." This will require subtle control of rate and pause, as well as stress and inflection.

The next step in analyzing the excerpt, then, is to study the words within the sentences. This will already have been done to some extent in the course of sentence analysis. In addition to the key words and phrases, however, there will be a number of other words which, while not incomprehensible to the person of average background, nevertheless require some detailed attention. Special relations between words are important. Classical, literary, and historical allusions must be understood.

In paragraph 5 of the excerpt from *The Natural History of Nonsense*, for example, there are several terms that are rich in literary and mythological meaning. Obviously, from the context, the "roc" and the "phoenix" are birds, yet it adds considerably to the flavor of the sentence to recall that the roc was a fabulous Arabian bird so huge that it was reputedly able to carry off an elephant; that the phoenix has become a symbol of immortality since, according to Egyptian mythology, it had a life-span of five centuries, and was then consumed in fire, to rise again in youthful freshness from its own ashes. Keats' nightingale is of course to be found in his "Ode to a Nightingale," where it is hailed as "immortal Bird," an exclamation which Mr. Evans borrows and applies to the ostrich. Shelley's "To a Skylark" and Poe's "The Raven" are equally famous poems. Thus, Mr. Evans has skillfully used familiar literary references to establish, by implication and association, the place of the ostrich in popular mythology.

Even words which are wholly familiar may carry a special charge of meaning. We have already noted, for example, the importance of the words "metaphor" and "fiction" in the last sentence of paragraph 5, and the ironic tone of "fact" in the opening sentence of paragraph 6. No other words would have accomplished quite the same purpose. The interpreter cannot explain to his audience what the words mean or connote, but he can, by his own complete understanding of nuances of meaning and by his intelligent use of the technique of interpretation, make himself a crystalline medium through which that meaning may pass undistorted, perhaps even clarified. However, he must, as always, keep the principle of unity clearly in mind so that his attention to details does not obscure the effect of the whole.

The next step in preparation for a performance of this essay involves practicing it aloud to clarify the speech phrases and rhythm. Then, as always, it is necessary to put the selection back together so that each aspect of style makes its proper contribution to the total achievement.

DIDACTIC PROSE

When the writer not only sets forth his opinions, but becomes preceptor and directly exhorts the reader to accept certain principles or ideas as guides to thought or conduct, we say that the writing is *didactic*.[1] In didactic writing the subject is, of course, important, but as in all prose of opinion, it is the author's attitude — the complex of ideas he has about the subject and his feelings toward it — that actually motivates the writing.

Because didactic prose is directive — that is, it instructs with the aim of persuading — the organization is dictated by the author's concept of

1 While much of literature is "didactic" in the sense of conveying certain ethical values, the term is most commonly applied to writing which is directly instructional or preceptual.

what will best convert the reader to the way of thought or action which he himself considers good. Emotional connotations add their weight of persuasion and set up an interesting rhythm between the logical and emotional content, for a skilled writer knows that while man likes to think he is directed by his mind, his actions are in fact strongly influenced by his emotional response. This knowledge will be reflected also in the harmony between the idea and the way it is expressed. A writer of didactic literature has a specific audience in mind, and he selects his details for their associational value to that potential audience.

For example, in his essay "Of Revenge" Bacon wishes to instruct the reader on nobility of conduct and in so doing to dissuade him from vindictive action.

from *Of Revenge*

> Revenge is a kind of wild justice, which the more man's nature runs to, the more ought law to weed it out; for as for the first wrong, it doth but offend the law; but the revenge of that wrong putteth the law out of office. Certainly, in taking revenge a man is but even with his enemy, but in passing it over he is superior; for it is a prince's part to pardon: and Solomon, I am sure, saith, *It is the glory of a man to pass by an offence.* That which is past is gone and irrevocable, and wise men have enough to do with things present and to come; therefore they do but trifle with themselves, that labor in past matters. . . . This is certain, that a man that studieth revenge keeps his own wounds green, which otherwise would heal and do well. Public revenges are for the most part fortunate; as that for the death of Caesar; for the death of Pertinax; for the death of Henry the Third of France; and many more. But in private revenges it is not so. Nay rather, vindictive persons live the life of witches; who, as they are mischievous, so end they infortunate.
>
> FRANCIS BACON

Here Bacon appeals first to the logic of the law and to the unequivocal statement that revenge makes one "but even with his enemy." Immediately he transfers the appeal to the emotions by saying that it is a "prince's part to pardon," and by citing Solomon on the "glory" of overlooking an offense. His references to emperors and wise men, to princes and to Solomon, are appeals to the educated man who would like to think of himself as having something in common with such men. The next appeal is again directed to the mind; there can be no question of the logic of the statement that what "is past is gone." In the complete essay from which this excerpt is taken, the middle section continues this alternation of appeals to the mind and to the emotions, and the closing statement is clearly emotional. Didactic writing will probably have its climax where the emotional and logical appeals come together at their highest point. In the excerpt from Bacon this point comes in the sentence beginning, "This is certain . . ." Here the certainty is obviously based on logic, while the reference to green wounds has a powerful empathic and connotative appeal.

Didactic prose confronts the interpreter with relatively few problems because it presents an easily discernible thesis and frankly attempts to persuade. The context makes the author's attitude abundantly clear, and all facts, specific examples, anecdotes, and emotional appeals are pointed toward one end — persuasion that this thesis should be accepted by right-thinking persons. For obvious reasons, the interpreter will normally choose for presentation a piece of didactic writing expressing a view with which he himself can sympathize, and to which his audience may be presumed to be at least not actively hostile. First, as interpreter it is his role to communicate to the audience exactly what the author intended to communicate to his readers. If he is out of sympathy with the material and shows it by intonation or gesture (in short, by tongue-in-cheek reading), he is not interpreting but commenting, even though he follows the printed page word for word. Second, if the writer has visualized an audience open to persuasion and the interpreter begins to battle his listeners, he may be going beyond the author's intent. This is oral delivery of a sort, but it is not interpretation.

JOURNALS, DIARIES, AND LETTERS

Journals and diaries often make excellent selections for performance, because they provide an intimate glimpse into special moments in the lives of interesting personalities. Ostensibly at least, most diaries were written for the private pleasure of the writer. They are likely to be less formal in style than the essay, which is intended for public consumption, and their organization is often dictated by highly subjective associations. A careful examination of the elements of style, however, will help the interpreter get at facets of the writer's personality and reveal attitudes and degrees of emotional involvement. In working with so personal a revelation as a diary or journal, it is also important to find out as much as possible about the writer and his times, since his motivation for recording certain details probably grew directly out of his relationship to his environment and the people in it.

The diarist may be said to be speaking as himself to himself. There is an element of danger in this idea, however. The interpreter who chooses to communicate such a record to an audience must not let his performance become so private that the audience feels it is intruding. Moreover, there must be sufficient projection, both mental and vocal, to hold their attention and interest. One of the ways of achieving this delicate balance between private and public thoughts is to allow the writer to "think aloud" as he puts his thoughts in order or as he re-reads them aloud. This will help the interpreter keep his mind actively engaged in organizing and expressing the total entry.

It is not necessary or indeed desirable to try to re-create visually in performance the act of writing or the physical details of the writer or his immediate surroundings. Any strong suggestion of "pen-in-hand" action would slow the selection down unduly or strain the audience's willingness to believe. The interpreter's real concern is not how fast the diarist wrote or with which hand or what type of pen, but rather in what he finally put down for readers to share.

In recent years there has been a wealth of published correspondence. Much of the appeal of letters is undoubtedly the same as that of diaries and journals. Letters, however, present an added problem for the interpreter. First, he will need to make a distinction between public and private letters. Public letters may be handled very much as one would approach an oration or a public address. They are usually designed to persuade a large group of hearers or readers to a course of action or to the acceptance of an idea. The writer will have selected details which have strong universal appeal and refer to matters with which his intended audience is easily familiar. The letters of St. Paul are excellent examples of public letters and are particularly interesting to examine for word choice and organization. Since the writer of a public letter is speaking to a specific audience, the interpreter may find it helpful to imagine that the specific audience and his own are identical. This will help achieve directness. He may address them in the person of the writer or, more probably, in the person of another selected to present the letter to the intended audience.

Because private letters involve a more complex relationship between writer and recipient, the interpreter will need to find out all he can about both parties concerned. Often the letter he has selected to read is a reply to one received earlier by the writer; consequently, a chain of references may have to be investigated. The method of organization and the style of writing will reflect the purpose of the letter and the relationship between the writer and the addressee. The Browning letters at the end of this chapter, for example, are by two poets who have never met but who know each other's work. Dylan Thomas is writing to a very close friend when he sends his apology and explanation to Vernon Watkins. Leonardo da Vinci's letter, on the other hand, is addressed to a nobleman with whom he is not on intimate terms . . . indeed to a prospective employer! Again, as with diaries and journals, the interpreter may insure mental directness by assuming the attitude of the writer as he composes the letter or as he re-reads it.

In some cases, of course, the interpreter is more interested in the reaction of the addressee than in the writer and will choose to handle the letter as if being read by the addressee. If this seems the more desirable approach, he must cope with the two-fold problem of using the writer's style effectively and at the same time suggesting the reaction of another person. Obviously, such an approach is most useful when the relationship between the two people is clearly drawn or so well-known that the response is predictable. Letters are often used in this way within plays and narratives where the characters have already been established. In such situations the letter becomes virtually a part of the plot and motivation.

In all the forms of prose examined in this chapter the writer is addressing his audience in his own person. Biographical material may help the interpreter get at some of the aspects of his personality, but a close examination of all the elements of style will be his surest clue.

SELECTIONS FOR ANALYSIS AND INTERPRETATION

Stephen Spender, himself a poet, biographer, and critic, uses style most effectively for humor within a basically serious essay. It is interesting to contrast his own style with that used in the academic satire in the dialogue.

from *How Much Should a Biographer Tell?*

. . . .

The duty of the nineteenth-century biographer was to conceal, just as much as to reveal, things about his subject. Biographers such as John Morley, when he wrote the life of Gladstone, and Forster, when he wrote that of Dickens, considered it their duty to suppress what was private to the subject in ways that might be considered irrelevant to his public achievement, painful to his family, discreditable to a "life" that was held up to the public as an example, a model, supposedly consistent with the hero's greatness. Private behavior had to be interpreted into public achievement, not — as is often now the case — public achievement reconciled with irregular private behavior.

The biographer regarded himself as a kind of filter. Having been

From "How Much Should a Biographer Tell?" by Stephen Spender. Reprinted by permission of The Saturday Review and Mr. Stephen Spender.

entrusted by members of the family with letters, diaries, private papers, and other such material, he would then separate what was private from what was of public interest and produce, in the interests of his hero, his hero's family, and his readers alike, an edited and censored version of the whole sum of public and private events that goes to make a life. Sometimes, of course, awkward facts were already in the public's possession, in which case the biographer had to explain them away, defending the hero from the charge that he went in for sharp practice or had syphilis. . . .

There are a good many reasons why today we take a different view. . . . We are inclined to think that everything, however private, is relevant to the work, the man, and the vocation. We are moving toward a state of affairs in which the work of a writer and his biography will merge, as it were, into a single consciousness. When we know all about the work and all about the life, both work and life will contribute meanings to a sum. And if we knew everything about a Keats, a D. H. Lawrence or a James Joyce, we feel sure that we would understand more about his writing.

Whether we are right in thinking this way, I do not know. But in our age it is scarcely possible for us to think otherwise. We cannot draw that boundary between the relevant public material and the irrelevant private that seemed so obvious to people before the era of psychoanalysis. To us, everything about an artist is relevant to his vocation. So we are haunted by the ideal of knowing not only the work of a Shakespeare, a Milton, a Keats, or a D. H. Lawrence, but also the whole man.

Hence to discover, to analyze, to state everything has become the biographer's crusade, as though he were writing his subject's autobiography — the confessions of the "I" — as well as his biography — the acts of the "he." . . .

The surprising thing is that the famous, or even the near-famous, do not go around with research workers attached to them, disguised perhaps as drinking companions or secretaries. If this has not happened already, it will certainly happen tomorrow. One can well imagine the discussion that might take place at a meeting of the Trustees of X Foundation at which such a project were being adopted:

Director-General: We are all agreed, then, to give Miss Vera Higgins a further extension of her grant so she may continue for another seven years researching into the life of the eighteenth-century poet William Draper, are we not?

Professor Arthur J. Henson (acidly): Agreed, yes, though perhaps we should write in the minutes that the poet's name is Diaper, William Diaper, 1685 to 1717.

D.-J. (*sic*): Diaper, you're quite right. It's a name I seem to have a block about. Somehow I can't quite connect it with poetry. The fact that we're supporting research into William Diaper (1685–1717), does rather underline the fact that we're scraping the bottom of the barrel with regard to research into the past. This brings me to the very interesting project of Dr. Tommy Liberwitz of Missoula that we now have to consider. Dr. Liberwitz writes pointing out that it's high time research caught up with the living, with the present hour. Why always research into obscure dead writers, when there are obscure living ones all around us? Dr. Liberwitz mentions in his application that he appreciates the risk endemic to the living, that posterity may not share the degree of interest that we attach to them. But he also points out that it is safe to assume that no living poet could be of less interest to the future than some of those past poets we already research into. He makes the additional point that in a sense no writer can be obscure enough to be an object for research. What could be more exciting than to discover a great body of information, written by a scholar living at that time, about a poet living 200 years ago, whom no one had ever heard of! It would be the equivalent of discovering, at one blow, an eighteenth-century lesser Dylan Thomas inseparable from an eighteenth-century lesser John Malcolm Brinnin. Gentlemen, I think you will agree that we should support Dr. Liberwitz in his project. Now Dr. Liberwitz points out that there is living in the island of Majorca a British poet, in fact a very famous one, by the name of Mr. Random Greaves.

PROFESSOR HENSON: Graves, Robert Graves.

D.-J. (*sic*): Ah yes, Graves. Somehow I have a block about associating the idea of graves with poetry . . . etc.

Who can doubt that Dr. Liberwitz and his six children are at this moment bound for Majorca, where Dr. Liberwitz will offer his services as Mr. Graves's secretary and Mrs. Liberwitz will assist Mrs. Graves with the housekeeping?

It is not certain, however, that Mr. Graves would welcome such a visitation. Already one sees signs among writers of their taking measures to evade or even to mislead the sleuths. T. S. Eliot, I have heard, very characteristically directs all his paid bills, invitation cards, odd scraps of notes, to a single source, where they are assiduously collected and annotated. Ever since he wrote those notes to *The Waste Land* he has been a strong believer in putting off the watchdog by throwing him a big hunk of meat.

Another poet has left instructions in his will calling on his friends to destroy his letters to them.

It seems very unlikely that these precautions will have much effect; indeed, they are more likely to provoke research than to put it off.

My own view is that I do not think that the dead have very much claim to be protected from research workers. I respect the feelings of relatives who try to protect their forebears' reputations (like those descendants of W. E. Gladstone who took an action against someone who in his memoirs said that Gladstone picked up London prostitutes), but I think that on the whole such protection is misguided. It may even not be entirely disinterested, since in defending an ancestor one is also asserting the respectability of one's own genes. Nor do I think that the living should be greatly concerned with what is written about them after they are dead. There is a certain point in mortality when, if one is of any interest at all, everything about one legitimately does become public property. (I exclude opening Shakespeare's grave.)

But it is, I think, important that the living should have their privacy protected. There are several reasons. One is that the capital out of which the creative draw on for their work is private experience, personal living. The right hand that paints or writes is largely dependent on the left hand that knows and cares nothing for the public and should not be known by it.

Statesmen and politicians are expected to preserve in their private affairs standards and ways of behaving that are consistent with their public attitudes. That is why those who do not manage to evade this demand are such two-dimensional figures, the billboard into which an amplifier is fitted. It is very important that no such demands be made on novelists, poets, artists.

The penalty of making private affairs public is that the private then becomes answerable to public standards. That there is a tendency today for this to happen even among artists is shown, I think, by some of the current dichotomies — beats and squares, for example. The beat is a person who, in answer to the demand that he should conform to public standards, publicizes outrageously private ones — strips in front of an audience, for example. The square is a person who sacrifices his own private life and makes himself conform to public standards in his private behavior and eventually, alas, in his work.

Shakespeare circulated among a small number of friends the sonnets that have been a scandal ever since he wrote them, and they were not published till after his death. If he had been living in the twentieth century, they would have been sold privately by these friends to American libraries. Research workers would long ago have discovered who the friend and the Dark Lady were and what Shakespeare did with each. All this would be, of course, immensely interesting. Dr. A. L. Rowse would not have to claim that he was the only person who could provide all the answers to what, despite his claims, remain mysteries.

The only trouble is that Shakespeare would not have written the sonnets. And if the research workers continue their good work, it may happen that before long, anyone who is not a blatant exhibitionist and who has any reputation at stake will not dare write a private letter. Too late, we may find that confidence — which is all — has been destroyed, and that the well-meaning, up-to-the-moment research worker has killed the goose that lays the golden egg.

STEPHEN SPENDER

This famous essay is an excellent example of the skillful inter-weaving of long, complex sentences with short, direct statements. Use the style to help emphasize the key sentences.

from *The American Scholar*

In self-trust all the virtues are comprehended. Free should the scholar be — free and brave. Free even to the definition of freedom, "without any hindrance that does not arise out of his own constitution." Brave; for fear is a thing which a scholar by his very function puts behind him. Fear always springs from ignorance. It is a shame to him if his tranquility, amid dangerous times, arise from the presumption that like children and women, his is a protected class; or if he seek a temporary peace by the diversion of his thoughts from politics or vexed questions, hiding his head like an ostrich in the flowering bushes, peeping into microscopes, and turning rhymes, as a boy whistles to keep his courage up. So is the danger a danger still; so is the fear worse. Manlike let him turn and face it. Let him look into its eye and search its nature, inspect its origin — see the whelping of this lion — which lies no great way back; he will then find in himself a perfect comprehension of its nature and extent; he will have made his hands meet on the other side, and can henceforth defy it and pass on superior. The world is his who can see through its pretension. What deafness, what stone-blind custom, what overgrown error you behold is there only by sufferance — by your sufferance. See it to be a lie, and you have already dealt it its mortal blow.

Yes, we are the cowed — we the trustless. It is a mischievous notion that we are come late into nature; that the world was finished a long time ago. As the world was plastic and fluid in the hands of God, so it is ever to so much of his attributes as we bring to it. To ignorance and sin, it is flint. They adapt themselves to it as they may; but in proportion as a man has any thing in him divine, the firmament flows before him and takes his signet and form. Not he is great who can alter matter, but he who can alter my state of mind. They are the kings of the world who give the color of their present thought to all nature and all art, and persuade men by the cheerful serenity of their carrying the matter, that this thing which they do is the apple which the ages have desired to pluck, now at last ripe, and inviting nations to the harvest. The great man makes the great thing. Wherever Macdonald sits, there is the head of the table. Linnaeus makes botany the most alluring of studies, and wins it from the farmer and the herbwoman; Davy, chemistry; and Cuvier, fossils. The day is always his who works in it with serenity and great aims. The unstable estimates of men crowd to him whose mind is filled with a truth, as the heaped waves of the Atlantic follow the moon.

For this self-trust, the reason is deeper than can be fathomed —

darker than can be enlightened. I might not carry with me the feeling of my audience in stating my own belief. But I have already shown the ground of my hope, in adverting to the doctrine that man is one. I believe man has been wronged; he has wronged himself. He has almost lost the light that can lead him back to his prerogatives. Men are become of no account. Men in history, men in the world of today, are bugs, are spawn, and are called "the mass" and "the herd." In a century, in a millennium, one or two men; that is to say, one or two approximations to the right state of every man. All the rest behold in the hero or the poet their own green and crude being — ripened; yes, and are content to be less, so *that* may attain to its full stature. What a testimony, full of grandeur, full of pity, is borne to the demands of his own nature, by the poor clansman, the poor partisan, who rejoices in the glory of his chief. The poor and the low find some amends to their immense moral capacity, for their acquiescence in a political and social inferiority. They are content to be brushed like flies from the path of a great person, so that justice shall be done by him to that common nature which it is the dearest desire of all to see enlarged and glorified. They sun themselves in the great man's light, and feel it to be their own element. They cast the dignity of man from their downtrod selves upon the shoulders of a hero, and will perish to add one drop of blood to make that great heart beat, those giant sinews combat and conquer. He lives for us, and we live in him.

RALPH WALDO EMERSON

THE FREQUENT USE of the imperative "Let him" will not cause the interpreter undue difficulty if he allows the sentence lengths to make their contribution to variety and contrast.

Of Travel

Travel, in the younger sort, is a part of education; in the elder, a part of experience. He that travelleth into a country before he hath some entrance into the language, goeth to school, and not to travel. That young men travel under some tutor, or grave servant, I allow well; so that he be such a one that hath the language, and hath been in the country before; whereby he may be able to tell them what things are worthy to be seen in the country where they go; what acquaintances they are to seek; what exercises or discipline the place yieldeth. For else young men shall go hooded, and look abroad little. It is a strange thing, that in sea voyages, where there is nothing to be seen but sky and sea, men should make diaries; but in land-travel, wherein so much is to be observed, for the most part they omit it; as if chance were fitter to be registered than observation. Let diaries therefore be brought in use. The things to be seen and observed are, the courts of princes, specially when they give audience to ambassadors; the courts of justice, while they sit and hear causes; and so of consistories ecclesiastic; the churches and monasteries, with the monuments which are therein extant; the walls and fortifications of cities and towns, and so the havens and harbours; antiquities and ruins; libraries; colleges, disputations, and lectures, where any are; shipping and navies; houses and gardens of state and pleasure, near great cities; armories; arsenals; magazines; exchanges, burses; warehouses; exercises of horsemanship, fencing, training of soldiers, and the like; comedies, such whereunto the better sort of persons do resort; treasuries of jewels and robes; cabinets and rarities; and, to conclude, whatsoever is memorable in the places where they go. After all which the tutors or servant ought to make diligent inquiry. As for triumphs, masks, feasts, weddings, funerals, capital executions, and such shows, men need not to be put in mind of them; yet are they not to be neglected. If you will have a young man to put his travel into a little room, and in short time to gather much, this you must do. First as was said, he must have some entrance into the language before he goeth. Then he must have such a servant or tutor as knoweth the country, as was likewise said. Let him carry with him also some card or book describing the country where he travelleth; which will be a good key to his inquiry. Let him keep also a diary. Let him not stay long in one city or town; more or less as the place deserveth, but not long; nay, when he stayeth in one city or town, let him change his lodging from one end and part of the town to another; which is a great adamant of acquaintance. Let him sequester himself from the company of his countrymen, and diet in such places where there is good company of the nation where he travelleth. Let him upon his removes from one place to another, procure recommendation to some person of quality residing in the place whither he removeth; that he may use his favour in those things he desireth to see or know. Thus he may abridge his travel with much profit. As for the acquaintance which is to be sought in travel; that which is most of all profitable, is acquaintance with the secretaries and employed man of ambassadors: for so in travelling in one country he shall suck the experience of many. Let him also see and visit eminent persons in all kinds, which are of great name abroad; so that he may be able to tell how the life agreeth with the fame. For quarrels, they are with care and discretion to be avoided. They are commonly for mistresses, healths, place, and words. And let a man beware how he keepeth company with choleric and quarrelsome persons; for they will engage him into their own quarrels. When a traveller returneth home, let him not leave the countries where he hath travelled altogether behind him; but maintain a correspondence by letters with those of his acquaintance which are of most worth. And let his travel appear rather in his discourse than in his apparel or gesture; and in his discourse let him be rather advised in his answers, than forward to tell stories; and let it appear that he doth not change his country manners for those of foreign parts; but only prick in some flowers of that he hath learned abroad into the customs of his own country.

FRANCIS BACON

THE EXPANDED METAPHORS operating within this famous meditation help govern its organization and reveal the mind and attitude of its author. Be sure you understand the reference to the bell.

from *Devotions Upon Emergent Occasions*

XVII

Perchance he for whom this bell tolls, may be so ill, as that he knows not it tolls for him; and perchance I may think myself so much better than I am, as that they who are about me, and see my state, may have caused it to toll for me, and I know not that. The Church is Catholic, universal, so are all her actions; all that she does belongs to all. When she baptizes a child, that action concerns me; for that child is thereby connected to that Head which is my Head too, engrafted into that body, whereof I am a member. And when she buries a man, that action concerns me: all mankind is of one Author, and is one volume; when one man dies, one chapter is not torn out of the book, but translated into a better language; and every chapter must be so translated; God employs several translators; some pieces are translated by age, some by sickness, some by war, some by justice; but God's hand is in every translation; and his hand shall bind up all our scattered leaves again, for that Library where every book shall lie open to one another: As therefore the bell that rings to a sermon, calls not upon the preacher only, but upon the congregation to come; so this bell calls us all: but how much more me, who am brought so near the door by this sickness. There was a contention as far as a suit (in which both piety and dignity, religion and estimation, were mingled), which of the religious orders should ring to prayers first in the morning; and it was determined, that they should ring first that rose earliest. If we understand aright the dignity of this bell that tolls for our evening prayer, we would be glad to make it ours, by rising early, in that application, that it might be ours, as well as his, whose indeed it is. The bell doth toll for him that thinks it doth; and though it intermit again, yet from that minute, that that occasion wrought upon him, he is united to God. Who casts not up his eye to the sun when it rises? but who takes off his eye from a comet when that breaks out? Who bends not his ear to any bell, which upon any occasion rings? but who can remove it from that bell, which is passing a piece of himself out of this world? No man is an island, entire of itself; every man is a piece of the continent, a part of the main; if a clod be washed away by the sea, Europe is the less, as well as if a promontory were, as well as if a manor of thy friends or of thine own were; any man's death diminishes me, because I am involved in mankind; and therefore never send to know for whom the bell tolls; it tolls for thee. Neither can we call this a begging of misery or a borrowing of misery, as though we were not miserable enough of ourselves, but must fetch in more from the next house, in taking upon us the misery of our neighbors. Truly it were an excusable covetousness if we did; for affliction is a treasure, and scarce any man hath enough of it. No man hath affliction enough that is not matured, and ripened by it, and made fit for God by that affliction. If a man carry treasure in bullion, or in a wedge of gold, and have none coined into current monies, his treasure will not defray him as he travels. Tribulation is treasure in the nature of it, but it is not current money in the use of it, except we get nearer and nearer our home, Heaven, by it. Another man may be sick too, and sick to death, and this affliction may lie in his bowels, as gold in a mine, and be of no use to him; but this bell, that tells me of his affliction, digs out, and applies that gold to me; if by this consideration of another's danger I take mine own into contemplation, and so secure myself by making my recourse to my God, who is our only security.

John Donne

The travel accounts of these three writers vary as widely as the areas and events with which they deal. The style each uses is dictated in part, indeed, by the atmosphere of the location as well as by his personal response to concrete objects. Notice the change in style as the narrator gives way to the speaker in the first excerpt.

from *Heart of Darkness*

The reaches opened before us and closed behind, as if the forest had stepped leisurely across the water to bar the way for our return. We penetrated deeper and deeper into the heart of darkness. It was very quiet there. At night sometimes the roll of drums behind the curtain of trees would run up the river and remain sustained faintly, as if hovering in the air high over our heads, till the first break of day. Whether it meant war, peace, or prayer we could not tell. The dawns were heralded by the descent of chill stillness; the wood-cutters slept, their fires burned low; the snapping of a twig would make you start. We were wanderers on a prehistoric earth, on an earth that wore the aspect of an unknown planet. We could have fancied ourselves the first of men taking possession of an accursed inheritance, to be subdued at the cost of profound

From *Heart of Darkness* by Joseph Conrad. Reprinted by permission of J. M. Dent & Sons, Ltd., and the Trustees of the Joseph Conrad Estate.

anguish and of excessive toil. But suddenly, as we struggled round a bend, there would be a glimpse of rush walls, of peaked grass-roofs, a burst of yells, a whirl of black limbs, a mass of hands clapping, of feet stamping, of bodies swaying, of eyes rolling, under the droop of heavy and motionless foliage. The steamer toiled along slowly on the edge of a black and incomprehensible frenzy. The prehistoric man was cursing us, praying to us, welcoming us — who could tell? We were cut off from the comprehension of our surroundings; we glided past like phantoms, wondering and secretly appalled, as sane men would be before an enthusiastic outbreak in a madhouse. We could not understand because we were too far and could not remember, because we were traveling in the night of first ages, of those ages that are gone, leaving hardly a sign — and no memories.

"The earth seemed unearthly. We are accustomed to look upon the shackled form of a conquered monster, but there — there you could look at a thing monstrous and free. It was unearthly, and the men were — No, they were not inhuman. Well, you know, that was the worst of it — this suspicion of their not being inhuman. It would come slowly to one. They howled and leaped, and spun, and made horrid faces; but what thrilled you was just the thought of their humanity — like yours — the thought of your remote kinship with this wild and passionate uproar. Ugly. Yes, it was ugly enough; but if you were man enough you would admit to yourself that there was in you just the faintest trace of a response to the terrible frankness of that noise, a dim suspicion of there being a meaning in it which you — you so remote from the night of first ages — could comprehend. And why not? The mind of man is capable of anything — because everything is in it, all the past as well as all the future. What were there after all? Joy, fear, sorrow, devotion, valour, rage — who can tell? — but truth — truth stripped of its cloak of time. Let the fool gape and shudder — the man knows, and can look on without a wink. But he must at least be as much of a man as these on the shore. He must meet that truth with his own true stuff — with his own inborn strength. Principles won't do. Acquisitions, clothes, pretty rags — rags that would fly off at the first good shake. No; you want a deliberate belief. An appeal to me in this fiendish row — is there? Very well; I hear; I admit, but I have a voice, too, and for good or evil mine is the speech that cannot be silenced. Of course, a fool, what with sheer fright and fine sentiments, is always safe. Who's that grunting? You wonder I didn't go ashore for a howl and a dance? Well, no — I didn't. Fine sentiments, you say? Fine sentiments, be hanged! I had no time. I had to mess about with white-lead and strips of woollen blanket helping to put bandages on those leaky steam-pipes — I tell you. I had to watch the steering, and circumvent those snags, and get the tin-pot along by hook or by crook. There was surface-truth enough in these things to save a wiser man. And between whiles I had to look after the savage who was fireman. He was an improved specimen; he could fire up a vertical boiler. He was there below me, and, upon my word, to look at him was as edifying as seeing a dog in a parody of breeches and a feather hat, walking on his hind-legs. A few months of training had done for that really fine chap. He squinted at the steam-gauge and at the water-gauge with an evident effort of intrepidity — and he had filed teeth, too, the poor devil, and the wool of his pate shaved into queer patterns, and three ornamental scars on each of his cheeks. He ought to have been clapping his hands and stamping his feet on the bank, instead of which he was hard at work, a thrall to strange witchcraft, full of improving knowledge. He was useful because he had been instructed; and what he knew was this — that should the water in that transparent thing disappear, the evil spirit inside the boiler would get angry through the greatness of his thirst, and take a terrible vengeance. So he sweated and fired up and watched the glass fearfully (with an impromptu charm, made of rags, tied to his arm, and a piece of polished bone, as big as a watch, stuck flat-ways through his lower lip), while the wooded banks slipped past us slowly, the short noise was left behind, the interminable miles of silence — and we crept on, towards Kurtz. But the snags were thick, the water was treacherous and shallow, the boiler seemed indeed to have a sulky devil in it, and thus neither that fireman nor I had any time to peer into our creepy thoughts."

JOSEPH CONRAD

USE ALL THE RICHNESS of sound in this selection. Be sure to see and hear the various details as they are encountered. The final paragraph must be handled carefully so that it does not break the unity.

from *Prospero's Cell*

Somewhere between Calabria and Corfu the blue really begins. All the way across Italy you find yourself moving through a landscape severely domesticated — each valley laid out after the architect's pattern, brilliantly lighted, human. But once you strike out from the flat and desolate Calabrian mainland towards the sea, you are aware of a change in the heart of things: aware of the horizon beginning to stain at the rim of the world: aware of *islands* coming out of the darkness to meet you.

In the morning you wake to the taste of snow on the air, and climbing the companion-ladder, suddenly enter the penumbra of shadow cast by the Albanian mountains — each wearing its cracked crown of snow — desolate and repudiating stone.

From *Prospero's Cell* by Lawrence Durrell. Reprinted by permission of E. P. Dutton & Co., Inc., and Faber and Faber, Ltd.

A peninsula nipped off while red hot and allowed to cool into an antarctica of lava. You are aware not so much of a landscape coming to meet you invisibly over those blue miles of water as of a climate. You enter Greece as one might enter a dark crystal; the form of things becomes irregular, refracted. Mirages suddenly swallow islands, and wherever you look the trembling curtain of the atmosphere deceives.

Other countries may offer you discoveries in manners or lore or landscape; Greece offers you something harder — the discovery of yourself.

LAWRENCE DURRELL

THERE ARE ACTUALLY several episodes within this excerpt, and the style varies with the mood.

from *Travels With Charley*

My plan was clear, concise, and reasonable, I think. For many years I have traveled in many parts of the world. In America I live in New York, or dip into Chicago or San Francisco. But New York is no more America than Paris is France or London is England. Thus I discovered that I did not know my own country. I, an American writer, writing about America, was working from memory, and the memory is at best a faulty, warpy reservoir. I had not heard the speech of America, smelled the grass and trees and sewage, seen its hills and water, its color and quality of light. I knew the changes only from books and newspapers. But more than this, I had not felt the country for twenty-five years. In short, I was writing of something I did not know about, and it seems to me that in a so-called writer this is criminal. My memories were distorted by twenty-five intervening years.

Once I traveled about in an old bakery wagon, double-doored rattler with a mattress on its floor. I stopped where people stopped or gathered, I listened and looked and felt, and in the process had a picture of my country the accuracy of which was impaired only by my own shortcomings.

So it was that I determined to look again, to try to rediscover this monster land. Otherwise, in writing, I could not tell the small diagnostic truths which are the foundations of the larger truth. One sharp difficulty presented itself. In the intervening twenty-five years my name had become reasonably well known. And it has been my experience that when people have heard of you, favorably or not, they change; they become, through shyness or the other qualities that publicity inspires, something they are not

From *Travels With Charley* by John Steinbeck. Copyright © 1961, 1962 by The Curtis Publishing Company, Inc. Copyright © 1962 by John Steinbeck. Reprinted by permission of The Viking Press, Inc.

under ordinary circumstances. This being so, my trip demanded that I leave my name and my identity at home. I had to be peripatetic eyes and ears, a kind of moving gelatin plate. I could not sign hotel registers, meet people I knew, interview others, or even ask searching questions. Furthermore, two or more people disturb the ecologic complex of an area. I had to go alone and I had to be self-contained, a kind of casual turtle carrying his house on his back.

With all this in mind I wrote to the head office of a great corporation which manufactures trucks. I specified my purpose and my needs. I wanted a three-quarter-ton pick-up truck, capable of going anywhere under possibly rigorous conditions, and on this truck I wanted a little house built like the cabin of a small boat. . . . Although I didn't want to start before Labor Day, when the nation settles back to normal living, I did want to get used to my turtle shell, to equip it and learn it. It arrived in August, a beautiful thing, powerful and yet lithe. It was almost as easy to handle as a passenger car. And because my planned trip had aroused some satiric remarks among my friends, I named it Rocinante, which you will remember was the name of Don Quixote's horse. . . .

There was some genuine worry about my traveling alone, open to attack, robbery, assault. It is well known that our roads are dangerous. And here I admit I had senseless qualms. It is some years since I have been alone, nameless, friendless, without any of the safety one gets from family, friends, and accomplices. There is no reality in the danger. It's just a very lonely, helpless feeling at first — a kind of desolate feeling. For this reason I took one companion on my journey — an old French gentleman poodle known as Charley. Actually his name is Charles le Chien. He was born in Bercy on the outskirts of Paris and trained in France, and while he knows a little poodle-English, he responds quickly only to commands in French. Otherwise he has to translate, and that slows him down. He is a very big poodle, of a color called *bleu*, and he is blue when he is clean. Charley is a born diplomat. He prefers negotiation to fighting, and properly so, since he is very bad at fighting. Only once in his ten years has he been in trouble — when he met a dog who refused to negotiate. Charley lost a piece of his right ear that time. But he is a good watch dog — has a roar like a lion, designed to conceal from night-wandering strangers the fact that he couldn't bite his way out of a *cornet de papier*. He is a good friend and traveling companion, and would rather travel about than anything he can imagine. . . .

Equipping Rocinante was a long and pleasant process. I took far too many things, but I didn't know what I would find. Tools for emergency, tow lines, a small block and tackle, a trenching tool and crowbar, tools for making and fixing and improvising. Then there were emergency foods. I would be late in the northwest and caught by snow. I prepared for at least a week of emergency. Water was easy; Rocinante carried a thirty-gallon tank.

I thought I might do some writing along the way, perhaps essays, surely notes, certainly letters. I took paper, carbon, typewriter, pencils, notebooks, and not only those but dictionaries, a compact encyclopedia, and a dozen other reference books, heavy ones. I suppose our capacity for self-delusion is boundless. I knew very well that I rarely make notes, and if I do I either lose them or can't read them. I also knew from thirty years of my profession that I cannot write hot on an event. It has to ferment. I must do what a friend calls "mule it over" for a time before it goes down. And in spite of this self-knowledge I equipped Rocinante with enough writing material to take care of ten volumes. Also I laid in a hundred and fifty pounds of those books one hasn't got around to reading — and of course those are the books one isn't ever going to get around to reading. Canned goods, shotgun shells, rifle cartridges, tool boxes, and far too many clothes, blankets and pillows, and many too many shoes and boots, padded nylon sub-zero underwear, plastic dishes and cups and a plastic dishpan, a spare tank of bottled gas. The overloaded springs sighed and settled lower and lower. I judge now that I carried about four times too much of everything. . . .

I crossed into New York State at Rouses Point and stayed as near to Lake Ontario as I could because it was my intention to look at Niagara Falls, which I had never seen, and then to slip into Canada, from Hamilton to Windsor, keeping Lake Erie on the south, and to emerge at Detroit — a kind of end run, a small triumph over geography. . . .

It rained in New York State, the Empire State, rained cold and pitiless, as the highway-sign writers would put it. Indeed the dismal downpour made my intended visit to Niagara Falls seem redundant. I was then hopelessly lost in the streets of a small but endless town in the neighborhood of Medina, I think. I pulled to the side of the street and got out my book of road maps. But to find where you are going, you must know where you are, and I didn't. The windows of the cab were tightly closed and opaque with steaming rain. My car radio played softly. Suddenly there was a knock on the window, the door was wrenched open, and a man slipped into the seat beside me. The man was quite red of face, quite whiskey of breath. His trousers were held up by red braces over the long gray underwear that covered his chest.

"Turn that damn thing off," he said, and then turned off my radio himself. "My daughter saw you out the window," he continued. "Thought you was in trouble." He looked at my maps. "Throw those things away. Now, where is it you want to go?"

I don't know why it is a man can't answer such a question with the truth. The truth was that I had turned off the big highway 104 and into the smaller roads because the traffic was heavy and passing vehicles threw sheets of water on my windshield. I wanted to go to Niagara Falls. Why couldn't I have admitted it? I looked down at my map and said, "I'm trying to get to Erie, Pennsylvania."

"Good," he said. "Now, throw those maps away. Now you turn around, go two traffic lights, that'll bring you to Egg Street. Turn left there and about two hundred yards on Egg turn right at an angle. That's a twisty kind of street and you'll come to an overpass, but don't take it. You turn left there and it will curve around like this—see? Like this." His hand made a curving motion. "Now, when the curve straightens out you'll come to three branching roads. There's a big red house on the left-hand branch so you don't take that, you take the right-hand branch. Now, have you got that so far?"

"Sure," I said. "That's easy."

"Well repeat it back so I'll know you're going right."

I had stopped listening at the curving road. I said, "Maybe you better tell me again."

"I thought so. Turn around and go two traffic lights to Egg Street, turn left for two hundred yards and turn right at an angle on a twisty street till you come to an overpass but don't take it."

"That clears it up for me," I said quickly. "I sure do thank you for helping me out."

"Hell," he said, "I ain't even got you out of town yet."

Well, he got me out of town by a route which, if I could have remembered it, let alone followed it, would have made the path into the Labyrinth at Knossos seem like a throughway. When he was finally satisfied and thanked, he got out and slammed the door, but such is my social cowardice that I actually did turn around, knowing he would be watching out the window. I drove around two blocks and blundered my way back to 104, traffic or not.

Niagara Falls is very nice. It's like a large version of the old Bond sign on Times Square. I'm very glad I saw it, because from now on if I am asked whether I have seen Niagara Falls I can say yes, and be telling the truth for once.

When I told my adviser that I was going to Erie, Pennsylvania, I had no idea of going there, but as it turned out, I was. My intention was to creep across the neck of Ontario, bypassing not only Erie but Cleveland and Toledo.

I find out of long experience that I admire all nations and hate all governments, and nowhere is my natural anarchism more aroused than at national borders where patient and efficient public servants carry out their duties in matters of immigration and customs. I have never smuggled anything in my life. Why, then, do I feel an uneasy sense of guilt on approaching a customs barrier? I crossed a high toll bridge and negotiated a no man's land and came to the place where the Stars and Stripes stood shoulder to shoulder with the Union Jack. The Canadians were very kind. They asked where I was going and for how long, gave Rocinante a cursory inspection, and came at last to Charley.

"Do you have a certificate of rabies vaccination on the dog?"

"No, I haven't. You see he's an old dog. He was vaccinated long ago."

Another official came out. "We advise you not to cross the border with him, then."

"But I'm just crossing a small part of Canada and re-entering the U.S."

"We understand," they said kindly. "You can take him into Canada but the U.S. won't let him back."

"But technically I am still in the U.S. and there's no complaint."

"There will be if he crosses the line and tries to get back."

"Well, where can I get him vaccinated?"

They didn't know. I would have to retrace my way at least twenty miles, find a vet, have Charley vaccinated, and then return. I was crossing only to save a little time, and this would wipe out the time saved and much more.

"Please understand, it is your government, not ours. We are simply advising you. It's the rule."

I guess this is why I hate governments, all governments. It is always the rule, the fine print, carried out by fine-print men. There's nothing to fight, no wall to hammer with frustrated fists. I highly approve of vaccination, feel it should be compulsory; rabies is a dreadful thing. And yet I found myself hating the rule and all governments that made rules. It was not the shots but the certificate that was important. And it is usually so with governments — not a fact but a small slip of paper. These were such nice men, friendly and helpful. It was a slow time at the border. They gave me a cup of tea and Charley half a dozen cookies. And they seemed genuinely sorry that I had to go to Erie, Pennsylvania, for the lack of a paper. And so I turned about and proceeded toward the Stars and Stripes and another government. Exiting I had not been required to stop, but now the barrier was down.

"Are you an American citizen?"

"Yes, sir, here's my passport."

"Do you have anything to declare?"

"I haven't been away."

"Have you a rabies vaccination certificate for your dog?"

"He hasn't been away either."

"But you are coming from Canada."

"I have not been in Canada."

I saw the steel come into eyes, the brows lower to a level of suspicion. Far from saving time, it looked as though I might lose much more than even Erie, Pennsylvania.

"Will you step into the office?"

This request had the effect on me a Gestapo knock on the door might have. It raises panic, anger, and guilty feelings whether or not I have done wrong. My voice took on the strident tone of virtuous outrage which automatically arouses suspicion.

"Please step into the office."

"I tell you I have not been in Canada. If you were watching, you would have seen that I turned back."

"Step this way, please, sir."

Then into the telephone: "New York license so-and-so. Yes. Pick-up truck with camper top. Yes — a dog." And to me: "What kind of dog is it?"

"Poodle."

"Poodle — I said poodle. Light brown."

"Blue," I said.

"Light brown. Okay. Thanks."

I do hope I did not sense a certain sadness at my innocence.

"They say you didn't cross the line."

"That's what I told you."

"May I see your passport?"

"Why? I haven't left the country. I'm not about to leave the country." But I handed over my passport just the same. He leafed through it, pausing at the entry-and-exit stamps of other journeys. He inspected my photograph, opened the yellow smallpox vaccination certificate stapled to the back cover. At the bottom of the last page he saw pencilled in a faint set of letters and figures. "What is this?"

"I don't know. Let me see. Oh, that! Why, it's a telephone number."

"What's it doing in your passport?"

"I guess I didn't have a slip of paper. I don't even remember whose number it is."

By now he had me on the run and he knew it. "Don't you know it is against the law to deface a passport?"

"I'll erase it."

"You should not write anything in your passport. That's the regulation."

"I won't ever do it again. I promise." And I wanted to promise him I wouldn't lie or steal or associate with persons of loose morals, or covet my neighbor's wife, or anything. He closed my passport firmly and handed it back to me. I'm sure he felt better having found that telephone number. Suppose after all his trouble he hadn't found me guilty of anything, and on a slow day.

"Thank you, sir," I said. "May I proceed now?"

He waved his hand kindly. "Go ahead," he said.

And that's why I went toward Erie, Pennsylvania, and it was Charley's fault. I crossed the high iron bridge and stopped to pay toll. The man leaned out the window. "Go on," he said, "it's on the house."

"How do you mean?"

"I seen you go through the other way a little while ago. I seen the dog. I knew you'd be back."

"Why didn't you tell me?"

"Nobody believes it. Go ahead. You get a free ride one way."

He wasn't government, you see. But government can make you feel so small and mean that it takes some doing to build back a sense of self-importance. Charley and I stayed at the grandest auto court we could find that night, a place only the rich could afford, a pleasure dome of ivory and apes and peacocks and moreover with a restaurant, and room service. I ordered ice and soda and made a scotch and soda and then another. Then I had a waiter in and bespoke soup and a steak and a pound of raw hamburger for Charley, and I overtipped mercilessly. Before I went to sleep I went over all the things I wished I had said to that immigration man, and some of them were incredibly clever and cutting.

JOHN STEINBECK

THIS JOURNAL ENTRY is a glimpse of a famous person seen through the eyes of a great American poet who was also a newspaper man. Look for indications of Whitman's attitude toward Lincoln. Decide how you will handle his peculiar prose style so that it does not obscure this portrait.

Abraham Lincoln

August 12th — I see the President almost every day, as I happen to live where he passes to or from his lodgings out of town. He never sleeps at the White House during the hot season, but has quarters at a healthy location some three miles north of the city, the Soldiers' home, a United States military establishment. I saw him this morning at about 8½ coming in to business, riding on Vermont avenue, near L street. He always has a company of twenty-five or thirty cavalry, with sabres drawn and held upright over their shoulders. They say this guard was against his personal wish, but he let his counselors have their way. The party makes no great show in uniform or horses. Mr. Lincoln on the saddle generally rides a good-sized, easy-going gray horse, is dress'd in plain black, somewhat rusty and dusty, wears a black stiff hat, and looks about as ordinary in attire, &c., as the commonest man. A lieutenant, with yellow straps, rides at his left, and following behind, two by two, come the cavalry men, in their yellow-striped jackets. They are generally going at a slow trot, as that is the pace set them by the one they wait upon. The sabres and accoutrements clank, and the entirely unornamental *cortège* as it trots toward Lafayette square arouses no sensation, only some curious stranger stops and gazes. I see very plainly ABRAHAM LINCOLN'S dark brown face, with the deep-cut lines, the eyes, always to me with a deep latent sadness in the expression. We have got so that we exchange bows, and very cordial ones. Sometimes the President goes and comes in an open barouche. The cavalry always accompany him, with drawn sabres. Often I notice as he goes out evenings — and sometimes in the morning, when he returns early — he turns off and halts at the large and handsome residence of the Secretary of War, on K street, and holds conference there. If in his barouche, I can see from my window he does not alight, but sits in his vehicle, and Mr. Stanton comes out to attend him. Sometimes one of his sons, a boy of ten or twelve, accompanies him, riding at his right on a pony. Earlier in the summer I occasionally saw the President and his wife, toward the latter part of the afternoon, out in a barouche, on a pleasure ride through the city. Mrs. Lincoln was dress'd in complete black, with a long crape veil. The equipage is of the plainest kind, only two horses, and they nothing extra. They pass'd me once very closely, and I saw the President in the face fully, as they were moving slowly, and his look, though abstracted, happen'd to be directed steadily in my eye. He bow'd and smiled, but far beneath his smile I noticed well the expression I have alluded to. None of the artists or pictures has caught the deep, though subtle and indirect expression of this man's face. There is something else there. One of the great portrait painters of two or three centuries ago is needed.

WALT WHITMAN

CHESTERTON RELIES almost entirely on references to universal experiences. Note the progression from general to particular to personal. The details must not overshadow the over-all purpose.

How to Be a Dunce

Boyhood is a most complex and incomprehensible thing. Even when one has been through it, one does not understand what it was. A man can never quite understand a boy, even when he has been the boy. There grows all over what was once the child a sort of prickly protection like hair; a callousness, a carelessness, a curious combination of random and quite objectless energy with a readiness to accept conventions. I have blindly begun a lark which involved carrying on literally like a lunatic; and known all the time that I did not know why I was doing it. When I first met my best friend in the playground, I fought with him wildly for three-quarters of an hour; not scientifically and certainly not vindictively (I had never seen him before and I have been very fond of him ever since) but by a sort of inexhaustible and insatiable impulse, rushing hither and thither about the field and rolling over and over in the mud. . . . There is no explaining these things; if those who have done them cannot explain them. But since then I have seen boys in many

From *Autobiography* by G. K. Chesterton. Copyright 1936. Reprinted by permission of Miss D. E. Collins and Sheed & Ward, Inc., New York. Also reprinted by permission of A. P. Watt & Son and Hutchinson & Company, Ltd.

countries and even of many colours; Egyptian boys in the bazaars of Cairo or mulatto boys in the slums of New York. And I have found that by some primordial law they all tend to three things; to going about in threes; to having no apparent object in going about at all; and, almost invariably speaking, to suddenly attacking each other and equally suddenly desisting from the attack.

Some may still question my calling this conduct conventional; from a general impression that two bankers or business partners do not commonly roll each other head-over-heels for fun, or in a spirit of pure friendship. It might be retorted that two business partners are not always by any means such pure friends. But in any case, it is true to call the thing a convention in more than the verbal sense of a collusion. And it is exactly this convention that really separates the schoolboy from the child. When I went to St. Paul's School, in Hammersmith, there really was a sort of convention of independence; which was in a certain degree a false independence, because it was a false maturity. Here we must remember once more the fallacy about "pretending" in childhood. The child does not really *pretend* to be a Red Indian; any more than Shelley pretended to be a cloud or Tennyson to be a brook. The point can be tested by offering a political pamphlet to the cloud, a peerage to the brook, or a penny for sweets to the Red Bull of the Prairies. But the boy really is pretending to be a man; or even a man of the world; which would seem a far more horrific metamorphosis. Schoolboys in my time could be blasted with the horrible revelation of having a sister, or even a Christian name. And the deadly nature of this blow really consisted in the fact that it cracked the whole convention of our lives; the convention that each of us was on his own; an independent gentleman living on private means. The secret that each of us did in fact possess a family, and parents who paid for our support, was conventionally ignored and only revealed in moments of maddened revenge. But the point is that there was already a faint touch of corruption in this convention; precisely because it was more serious and less frank than the tarradiddles of infancy. We had begun to be what no children are — snobs. Children disinfect all their dramatic impersonations by saying "Let us pretend." We schoolboys never said "Let us pretend"; we only pretended. . . .

The idea that I had come to school to work was too grotesque to cloud my mind for an instant. It was also in too obvious a contrast with the facts and the result. I was very fond of my friends; though, as is common at such an age, I was much too fond of them to be openly emotional about it. But I do remember coming, almost seriously, to the conclusion that a boy must go to school to study the characters of his schoolmasters. And I still think that there was something in it. After all, the schoolmaster is the first educated grown-up person that the boy comes to see constantly, after having been introduced at an early age to his father and mother. . . .

For the rest, I think the chief impression I produced, on most of the masters and many of the boys, was a pretty well-founded conviction that I was asleep. Perhaps what nobody knew, not even myself, was that I was asleep and dreaming. The dreams were not much more sensible or valuable than they commonly are in persons in such profound slumber; but they already had this obscure effect on my existence; that my mind was already occupied, though I myself was idle. . . . I was somewhat solitary; not sharply unpopular or in any sense persecuted, but solitary. But though I was solitary, I was not sorry; and I think I can claim that I was not sulky. One effect of this was that my first acquaintances, as distinct from my ultimate friends, were odd and scrappy sort of people like myself. These individuals were accidents; one or two of them I fear were disasters. I remember one youth who made one appearance in my daily life, that puzzled me like a detective story. I cannot imagine how I came to cultivate his society; still less how he came to cultivate mine. For he was a brilliant mathematician, and must presumably have worked hard at mathematics; whereas I worked less at mathematics, if possible, than at anything else. Moreover, I was very untidy and he was very tidy, with a large clean collar and an Eton jacket, also a large head very neatly brushed but something odd and perhaps too mature about his froglike face. One day he asked me whether I could lend him a Hall & Knight's Algebra. So far as enthusiasm for that study was concerned I could answer, "Thy need is greater than mine," with all the gesture of Sir Philip Sidney; but I had to observe some minimum of attention to the mathematical class; so in lending him the book, I told him I should want it back some time next week. As the time approached, I was much mystified by the fact that I found it quite difficult to get it back. He gave evasive replies; he interposed postponements and hazy promises; till at last I quarrelled with him, using the words of action which are really commoner among schoolboys as words than as actions; but anyhow indicating that I should make an earnest effort to punch his head. To this threat he ultimately capitulated; and eventually led me to his locker, which he reluctantly opened. And his locker was stuffed from top to bottom with about twenty-five identical copies of Hall & Knight's Algebra, which he had presumably collected by similar arts from similar acquaintances. I believe he left the school later, without any particular scandal; and I hope the poor fellow recovered his mental balance somewhere else. I write in no superior spirit; I was quite capable myself at many early stages of going mad in a quiet way; but not by an exaggerated appetite for Hall & Knight's Algebra.

G. K. Chesterton

It is very important to keep in mind occasion and recipient in analyzing these letters. This letter and Miss Barrett's reply, which follows, were mentioned within the chapter.

[*A Letter to Miss Barrett*]

New Cross, Hatcham, Surrey
[January 10th, 1845]

I love your verses with all my heart, dear Miss Barrett, — and this is no off-hand complimentary letter that I shall write, — whatever else, no prompt matter-of-course recognition of your genius, and there a graceful and natural end of the thing.

Since the day last week when I first read your poems, I quite laugh to remember how I have been turning and turning again in my mind what I should be able to tell you of their effect upon me, for in the first flush of delight I thought I would this once get out of my habit of purely passive enjoyment, when I do really enjoy, and thoroughly justify my admiration — perhaps even, as a loyal fellow-craftsman should, try and find fault and do you some little good to be proud of hereafter! — but nothing comes of it all — so into me has it gone, and part of me has it become, this great living poetry of yours, not a flower of which but took root and grew — Oh, how different that is from lying to be dried and pressed flat, and prized highly, and put in a book with a proper account at top and bottom, and shut up and put away . . . and the book called a 'Flora,' besides!

After all, I need not give up the thought of doing that, too, in time; because even now, talking with whoever is worthy, I can give a reason for my faith in one and another excellence, the fresh strange music, the affluent language, the exquisite pathos and true new brave thought; but in this addressing myself to you — your own self, and for the first time, my feeling rises altogether.

I do, as I say, love these books with all my heart — and I love you too. Do you know I was once not very far from seeing — really seeing you? Mr. Kenyon said to me one morning 'Would you like to see Miss Barrett?' then he went to announce me, — then he returned . . . you were too unwell, and now it is years ago, and I feel as at some untoward passage in my travels, as if I had been close, so close, to some world's-wonder in chapel or crypt, only a screen to push and I might have entered, but there was some slight, so it now seems, slight and just sufficient bar to admission, and the half-opened door shut, and I went home my thousands of miles, and the sight was never to be?

Well, these Poems were to be, and this true thankful joy and pride with which I feel myself,

Yours ever faithfully,

Robert Browning

It is interesting to compare Miss Barrett's Victorian, lady-like restraint with Mr. Browning's exuberance.

[*A Letter to Mr. Browning*]

50 Wimpole Street
Jan. 11, 1845

I thank you, dear Mr. Browning, from the bottom of my heart. You meant to give me pleasure by your letter — and even if the object had not been answered, I ought still to thank you. But it is thoroughly answered. Such a letter from such a hand! Sympathy is dear — very dear to me: but the sympathy of a poet, and of such a poet, is the quintessence of sympathy for me! Will you take back my gratitude for it? — agreeing, too, that of all the commerce done in the world, from Tyre to Carthage, the exchange of sympathy for gratitude is the most princely thing!

For the rest you draw me on with your kindness. It is difficult to get rid of people when you once have given them too much pleasure — *that* is a fact, and we shall not stop for the moral of it. What I was going to say — after a little natural hesitation — is, that if ever you emerge without inconvenient effort from your 'passive state,' and will *tell* me of such faults as rise to the surface and strike you as important in my poems, (for of course, I do not think of troubling you with criticism in detail) you will confer a lasting obligation on me, and one which I shall value so much, that I covet it at a distance.

I do not pretend to any extraordinary meekness under criticism and it is possible enough that I might not be altogether obedient to yours. But with my high respect for your power in your Art and for your experience as an artist, it would be quite impossible for me to hear a general observation of yours on what appear to you my master-faults, without being the better for it hereafter in some way. I ask for only a sentence or two of general observation — and I do not ask even for *that,* so as to tease you — but in the humble, low voice, which is so excellent a thing in women — particularly when they go a-begging!

The most frequent general criticism I receive, is, I think, upon the style, — 'if I *would* but change my style'! But *that* is an objection (isn't it?) to the writer bodily? Buffon says, and every sincere writer must feel, that '*Le style c'est l'homme;*' a fact, however, scarcely calculated to lessen the objection with certain critics.

Is it indeed true that I was so near to the pleasure and honour of making your acquaintance? and can it be true that you look back upon the lost opportunity with any regret? But — you know — if you had entered the 'crypt,' you might have caught cold, or been tired to death, and *wished* yourself 'a thousand miles off;' which would have been worse than travelling them. It is not my interest, however, to put such thoughts in your head about its being 'all for the best;' and I would rather hope (as I do) that what I lost by one chance I may recover by some future one. Winters shut me up as they do dormouse's eyes; in the spring, *we shall see:* and I am so much better that I seem turning round to the outward world again. And in the meantime I have learnt to know your voice, not merely from the poetry but from the kindness in it. Mr. Kenyon often speaks of you — dear Mr. Kenyon! — who most unspeakably, or only speakably with tears in my eyes, — has been my friend and helper, and my book's friend and helper! critic and sympathiser, true friend of all hours! You know him well enough, I think, to understand that I must be grateful to him.

I am writing too much, — and notwithstanding that I am writing too much, I will write of one thing more. I will say that I am your debtor, not only for this cordial letter and for all the pleasure which came with it, but in other ways, and those the highest: and I will say that while I live to follow this divine art of poetry, in proportion to my love for it and my devotion to it, I must be a devout admirer and student of your works. This is in my heart to say to you — and I say it.

And for the rest, I am proud to remain,

Your obliged and faithful

ELIZABETH B. BARRETT

DYLAN THOMAS WRITES intimately and informally in this second letter of apology, which he instructed Vernon Watkins to read first. Compare the organization and word choice in the two letters as clues to his increased penitence.

GRYPHON FILMS,
2–6 West Street, London, W.C. 2

TO BE READ FIRST

as from Majoda, New Quay, Cardiganshire
28 Oct. 1944

My dear Gwen and Vernon,

What on earth can you think of me? It is the last, last, last thing of all — on top of all the other things — that the hasty letter I should scribble in such a panic to you, while on the train away from London where we never met, should remain unposted until today: 26 days after your wedding. I have no excuses, but that I was so flurried and anxious, so tired, so miserable, that I put the train-letter into my pocket, arrived in New Quay after an 8 hour journey, imagined, in a kind of delirium, that it was posted, & then waited, perhaps without much hope of ever hearing, to hear from you that, though I was not forgiven, my explanation was understood. What can you think of me? Today I found the letter,

From *Letters to Vernon Watkins* by Dylan Thomas, edited by Vernon Watkins. Copyright © 1957 by New Directions. Reprinted by permission of New Directions, Publishers.

crumpled, unposted, in my overcoat. Please, please do try to understand. I shall let you have these two letters now, & a poem I meant also to send weeks ago, without another word of apology or abasement. All our love to you both, for your happiness forever.

Your worst man,

DYLAN

[Sent with letter dated 28 October 1944]

[Pencil] The Train to Wales, 1.30 Wed.

On Not Turning up to Be Best Man at the Wedding of One's Best Friend

Reeking & rocking back from a whirled London where nothing went right, all duties were left, and my name spun rank in the whole old smoky nose, I try, to a rhythm of Manchester pocket-handkerchers, and Conk him on the mousetrap, Conk him on the mousetrap, from the London-leaving wheels, to explain to you both, clearly & sincerely, why I never arrived, in black overcoat & shiny suit, rose-lapelled, breathing cachous & great good will, at lunch and church. But the train's stacked tight, I'm tabling a bony knee for this little pad, and am stuck, in the windy corridor, between many soldiers, all twelve foot high & commando-trained to the last lunge of the bayonet. It's not easy to think, or write, or be, and my explanations, true as air, sound, when I try to marshall them, like a chapter of accidents written in a dream by a professor of mathematics who has forgotten all formulas but the wrong one that 2 & 2 make 5. First, then, I arrived in London on Thursday & was sent straightaway, that is, on Friday morning, to Coventry: the City of Coventry, where the company who pay me occasionally are making a film called 'Building The Future', a subject on which I particularly should have no say. In Coventry I arranged to catch a train back on Sunday night, which would carry me to London in time to meet you both at the station. That train, owing to no fault of my own but to callous & diffident members of the hotel staff, who did not trouble to get the train-times straight, but only late, I missed. There was no other train until the next morning, which was Monday, & that train would reach London at an hour just convenient for me to be able to get into a cab & race for the church. I could not, at that hour of Sunday night, reach my office to leave a message for someone there to spend Monday morning ringing up you & your people & making my — by this time — frantic excuses; I could, indeed, have reached the office by telephone, but there would be no-one there to answer, except some celluloid rat

From *Letters to Vernon Watkins* by Dylan Thomas, edited by Vernon Watkins. Copyright © 1957 by New Directions. Reprinted by permission of New Directions, Publishers.

or other. So I waited until Monday morning & then, before catching the train, rang up the office & told a secretary girl to ring Charing Cross Hotel straight away, get in touch with anyone called Watkins & explain the whole position to him or her. I had not, myself, got the time to ring up Charing X Hotel, as it wd take hours, & as my call to the office could be, & was, made Priority, thereby saving those hours during which, by the nicotine-stained skin of my few teeth, I caught the wedding-going & troop-crammed horribly slow train. On arriving in London I managed, by the fervour of my heart only, I am sure, to snatch a cab. I sat back, wheezing in it. "Where to?" the driver said. And — this is the real God-help-me — I couldn't remember the name of the church. It was after half past one. I looked in all my pockets but had left your last letter, I suppose, in wood-&-asbestos Majoda, New Quay. I tried, in my head, every church name I knew. I explained to the driver: "A Church in the City. Very Old." Suddenly something came & I said, "I think it's Godolphin. Or something like that. Yes, Godolphin." We went to the City, the driver was dubious. We asked policemen: they were certain. By now, after two, & you too, I feared & hoped, married without my presence but with all my love, I went back to the office to find the secretary-girl out for lunch & the few people still there surprisingly cool and ignorant of all the infernal muddle that had been clotting up the wheels of the world for over a day. There was nothing to do. When the girl came in I asked her, though I was terrified to ask, if her little side of the whole business had gone well. She had tried the Charing X Hotel all the morning. The Watkins were out. She had left my name. The Watkins were out.

Later that evening, feeling wretcheder than ever before, alone in my beast of a studio, I remembered the church. Of course I remembered the church. Not Godolphin but St. Bartholomew the Great — too late! O what a prize of prize pickles & I'll understand always if you never want to see me again. I know this hasty jumble can't explain all the somersaulting & backspinning of circumstances against my being where I most wanted to be: at your wedding. God bless you both, & do try to forgive me.

All my love,

DYLAN

ONE OF THE WORLD's great artists writes a business letter.

Having, most illustrious lord, seen and considered the experiments of all those who pose as masters in the art of inventing instruments of war, and finding that their inventions differ in no way from those in common use, I am emboldened, without prejudice to anyone, to solicit an appointment of acquainting your Excellency with certain of my secrets.

1. I can construct bridges which are very light and strong and very portable, with which to pursue and defeat the enemy; and others more solid, which resist fire or assault, yet are easily removed and placed in position; and I can also burn and destroy those of the enemy.

2. In case of a siege I can cut off water from the trenches and make pontoons and scaling ladders and other similar contrivances.

3. If by reason of the elevation or the strength of its position a place cannot be bombarded, I can demolish every fortress if its foundations have not been set on stone.

4. I can also make a kind of cannon which is light and easy of transport, with which to hurl small stones like hail, and of which the smoke causes great terror to the enemy, so that they suffer heavy loss and confusion.

5. I can noiselessly construct to any prescribed point subterranean passages either straight or winding, passing if necessary underneath trenches or a river.

6. I can make armoured wagons carrying artillery, which shall break through the most serried ranks of the enemy, and so open a safe passage for his infantry.

7. If occasion should arise, I can construct cannon and mortars and light ordnance in shape both ornamental and useful and different from those in common use.

8. When it is impossible to use cannon I can supply in their stead catapults, mangonels, *trabocchi,* and other instruments of admirable efficiency not in general use — In short, as the occasion requires I can supply infinite means of attack and defense.

9. And if the fight should take place upon the sea I can construct many engines most suitable either for attack or defense and ships which can resist the fire of the heaviest cannon, and powders or weapons.

10. In time of peace, I believe that I can give you as complete satisfaction as anyone else in the construction of buildings both public and private, and in conducting water from one place to another.

I can further execute sculpture in marble, bronze or clay, also in painting I can do as much as anyone else, whoever he may be. Moreover, I would undertake the commission of the bronze horse, which shall endue with immortal glory and eternal honour the auspicious memory of your father and of the illustrious house of Sforza. —

And if any of the aforesaid things should seem to anyone impossible or impracticable, I offer myself as ready to make trial of them in your park or in whatever place shall please your Excellency, to whom I commend myself with all possible humility.

LEONARDO DA VINCI

BOTH FORMALITY AND warm sympathy are present in this famous novelist's letter to the widow of a beloved poet.

To Mrs. Robert Louis Stevenson

[Dec. 1894]

My dear Fanny Stevenson,

What can I say to you that will not seem cruelly irrelevant or vain? We have been sitting in darkness for nearly a fortnight,[1] but what is *our* darkness to the extinction of your magnificent light? You will probably know in some degree what has happened to us — how the hideous news first came to us via Auckland, etc., and then how, in the newspapers, a doubt was raised about its authenticity — just enough to give one a flicker of hope; until your telegram to me via San Francisco — repeated also from other sources — converted my pessimistic convictions into the wretched knowledge. All this time my thoughts have hovered round you all, around *you* in particular, with a tenderness of which I could have wished you might have, afar-off, the divination. You are such a visible picture of desolation that I need to remind myself that courage, and patience, and fortitude are also abundantly with you. The devotion that Louis inspired — and of which all the air about you must be full — must also be much to you. Yet as I write the word, indeed, I am almost ashamed of it — as if anything could be 'much' in the presence of such an abysmal void. To have lived in the light of that splendid life, that beautiful, bountiful being — only to see it, from one moment to the other, converted into a fable as strange and romantic as one of his own, a thing that *has* been and has ended, is an anguish into which no one can enter with you fully and of which no one can drain the cup for you. You are nearest to the pain, because you were nearest the joy and the pride. But if it is anything to you to know that no woman was ever more felt *with* and that your personal grief is the intensely personal grief of innumerable hearts — know it well, my dear Fanny Stevenson, for during all these days there has been friendship for you in the very air. For myself, how shall I tell you how much poorer and shabbier the whole world seems, and how one of the closest and strongest reasons for going on, for trying and doing, for planning and dreaming of the future, has dropped in an instant out of life. I was haunted indeed with a sense that I should never again see him — but it was one of the best things in life that he was *there*, or that one had him — at any rate one heard him, and felt him and awaited him and counted him into everything one most loved and lived for. He lighted up one whole side of the globe, and

[1] Robert Louis Stevenson had died suddenly in Samoa on December 3, 1894.

From *The Selected Letters of Henry James,* edited by Leon Edel. Copyright © 1955 by Leon Edel. Reprinted by permission of Paul R. Reynolds, Inc., 599 Fifth Avenue, New York 17, New York.

was in himself a whole province of one's imagination. We are smaller fry and meaner people without him. I feel as if there were a certain indelicacy in saying it to you, save that I know that there is nothing narrow or selfish in your sense of loss — for himself, however, for his happy name and his great visible good fortune, it strikes one as another matter. I mean that I feel him to have been as happy in his death (struck down that way, as by the gods, in a clear, glorious hour) as he had been in his fame. And, with all the sad allowances in his rich full life, he had the best of it — the thick of the fray, the loudest of the music, the freshest and finest of himself. It isn't as if there had been no full achievement and no supreme thing. It was all intense, all gallant, all exquisite from the first, and the experience, the fruition, had something dramatically complete in them. He has gone in time not to be old, early enough to be so generously young and late enough to have drunk deep of the cup. There have been — I think — for men of letters few deaths more romantically right. Forgive me, I beg you, what may sound cold-blooded in such words — or as if I imagined there could be anything for you 'right' in the rupture of such an affection and the loss of such a presence. I have in my mind in that view only the rounded career and the consecrated work. When I think of your own situation I fall into a mere confusion of pity and wonder, with the sole sense of your being as brave a spirit as he was (all of whose bravery you shared) to hold on by. Of what solutions or decisions you see before you we shall hear in time; meanwhile please believe that I am most affectionately with you. . . . More than I can say. I hope your first prostration and bewilderment are over, and that you are feeling your way in feeling all sorts of encompassing arms — all sorts of outstretched hands of friendship. Don't, my dear Fanny Stevenson, be unconscious of *mine*, and believe me more than ever faithfully yours,

HENRY JAMES

THE LETTERS OF St. Paul are noted for their arresting figures of speech and for their organization. Some are straightforward and businesslike; others are distinctly poetic. The following letter has a marked lyric quality, which is due in part to the choice of words and images and in part to the rhythmic sentence structure. The text is that of the King James Bible.

from *The New Testament*

FIRST CORINTHIANS, CHAPTER 13

Though I speak with the tongues of men and of angels, and have not charity, I am become as sounding brass, or a tinkling cymbal. And though I have the gift of prophecy, and understand all mysteries, and all knowledge; and though I have all faith, so that I could remove mountains, and have not charity, I am nothing. And though I bestow all my goods to feed the poor, and though I give my body to be burned, and have not charity, it profiteth me nothing. Charity suffereth long, and is kind; charity envieth not; charity vaunteth not itself, is not puffed up, Doth not behave itself unseemly, seeketh not her own, is not easily provoked, thinketh no evil; Rejoiceth not in iniquity, but rejoiceth in the truth; Beareth all things, believeth all things, hopeth all things, endureth all things. Charity never faileth: but whether there be prophecies, they shall fail; whether there be tongues, they shall cease; whether there be knowledge, it shall vanish away. For we know in part, and we prophesy in part. But when that which is perfect is come, then that which is in part shall be done away. When I was a child, I spake as a child, I understood as a child, I thought as a child: but when I became a man, I put away childish things. For now we see through a glass, darkly; but then face to face: now I know in part; but then shall I know even as also I am known. And now abideth faith, hope, charity, these three; but the greatest of these is charity.

✱ Bibliography

Cowley, Malcolm (ed.). *Writers at Work: The "Paris Review" Interviews.* New York: The Viking Press, 1961. Compass Books edition, C52.

A collection of interviews on "How Writers Write." Sixteen interviews offer a range of styles and interests from E. M. Forster to Françoise Sagan.

Fiedler, Leslie (ed.). *The Art of the Essay: Edited with Introduction, Notes and Exercise Questions.* New York: Thomas Y. Crowell Company, 1958.

An extensive collection of essays and travel accounts.

Hook, J. N., and E. G. Matthews. *Modern American Grammar and Usage.* New York: The Ronald Press, 1956.

A textbook on grammar and modern American usage with particular attention to how language is used by contemporary writers.

Ludwig, Richard M. (ed). *Essays Today, II.* New York: Harcourt, Brace and Company, 1956.

A collection of twenty-five essays from leading periodicals ranging from biographical sketches to reflective essays.

Reed, Herbert. *English Prose Style.* London: G. Bell and Son, Ltd., 1949.

Still the most complete discussion of prose style *per se.* The approach is first from the standpoint of composition and then of rhetoric.

Thomas, Wright, and Stuart Gerry Brown. *Reading Prose: An Introduction to Critical Study.* New York: Oxford University Press, 1952.

An extensive collection of essays grouped thematically, with a brief section on experimental prose. The final section is a compact directive for developing a critical approach. Helpful chronological index.

Thompson, Craig R., and John Hicks. *Thought and Experience in Prose.* New York: Oxford University Press, 1951.

A collection of essays ranging from Chesterfield's letters to his son to critical comments on selected literature.

6

Description

Though description sometimes exists for its own sake, it is most frequently found in conjunction with some other type of writing — as a means of implementing narrative, for example. Because it qualifies by expanding or limiting, a skilled writer uses description to control his readers' reactions and to focus their attention on selected facets of his subject. Description helps clarify factual prose and provides clear indications of attitude in more personal writing. It adds suggestion to both setting and character in narration. It makes an important contribution to harmony and is a chief source of variety and contrast. In short, without description a piece of literature lacks the full warmth and color of life.

Descriptive writing depicts the qualities of a person, place, or object in terms of the senses. It tells how something looks, sounds, smells, or tastes. It may describe texture or pressure, heat or cold. It may show how a person or thing moves. It can produce in the reader a feeling of tension or relaxation as an accompanying response to any one or a combination of these appeals to the senses. It is a valuable asset to the interpreter because it encourages his audience to respond physically and emotionally as well as mentally and thus share the totality of the selection. Inexperienced interpreters are often tempted to skip the descriptive sections, but the skilled interpreter takes great care to use them as the author has to insure vividness and clarity and to help control and enrich suggestion.

FACTUAL DESCRIPTION

The strength of sensory appeal in description depends partly, of course, on the author's skill in selecting references which evoke sights, sounds, smells, and tastes which are universal, rich in suggestion, and still highly individual. In some kinds of writing, however, description is not used primarily to evoke sensory or emotional response but to inform the mind. Factual writing, for example, which informs, defines, or explains, necessarily makes some use of description as a practical means of presenting information and increasing understanding. In factual prose the descriptions will be much more neutral than in imaginative prose — that is, they will have less sensory appeal and will arouse little or no emotional response. Their purpose is to help the mind explore new material by reference to that with which it is already familiar.

Even when the words taken by themselves seem to have rather strong sensory connotations, the over-all factual purpose for which they are used neutralizes the sensory appeal. For example, if one had occasion to read aloud from the *Encyclopaedia Britannica* the article on hydrogen sulphide, he would come across the following sentence: "Hydrogen sulphide, a colourless, poisonous gas having the odour of rotten eggs, is moderately soluble in water. . . ." Here, because of the context, the words "odour of rotten eggs" are not intended to arouse strong sensory response; rather, they serve the purpose of definition. The writer is concerned with telling what hydrogen sulphide is, not with conveying any feeling about it. For this reason, the person reading the passage aloud would properly present it in a straightforward fashion, and would not attempt to re-create a sensory response in his listeners. The oral interpreter is unlikely to be working with strictly factual prose. Nonetheless, he will encounter bits of factual description even in imaginative prose, and it is sometimes as important for him to know when the terms of a description do not carry strong sensory appeal as to use that appeal when it is intended.

EVOCATIVE DESCRIPTION

The interpreter's main concern will be with evocative description, by means of which the writer wants to arouse some feeling in the reader. When this is his purpose, the effectiveness of the description depends upon the writer's ability to elicit the sensory response and upon the reader's powers of perception — and further, in interpretation, upon the interpreter's ability to re-create the sensory appeal for his listeners.

Description can be extremely persuasive, for it helps to make abstract ideas concrete so that they stir the emotions and encourage the reader to link the ideas to his own specific experiences. The skillful writer of didactic prose, therefore, is careful to condense his description so that it gains power by directness and does not distract the reader from the main theme. He usually chooses a familiar object which requires very little elaboration of detail to bring it well within the realm of any reader's experience. Bacon's reference to keeping wounds green, in the essay quoted in the preceding chapter, is an excellent example of this technique.

Description plays an especially important part in narration; indeed, narration without description would be practically impossible. It usually introduces character or setting, or both, and may establish the relationship between character and setting. It may create a mood or stir the reader's sympathy for a character's situation. All these factors come into play in the opening paragraph of a short story by Mark Schorer, "What We Don't Know Hurts Us."

> The midafternoon winter sun burned through the high California haze. Charles Dudley, working with a mattock in a thicket of overgrowth, felt as steamy and as moldy as the black adobe earth in which his feet kept slipping. Rain had fallen for five days with no glimmer of sunshine, and now it seemed as if the earth, with fetid animation, like heavy breath, were giving all that moisture back to the air. The soil, or the broom which he was struggling to uproot, had a disgusting, acrid odor, as if he were tussling with some obscene animal instead of with a lot of neglected vegetation, and suddenly an overload of irritations — the smell, the stinging sweat in his eyes, his itching skin, his blistering palms, made him throw the mattock down and come diving out of the thicket into the clearing he had already achieved.

This description gives the setting, introduces the principal character, establishes the relationship between this character and the setting, and through that relationship sets a mood and creates an attitude toward the character. The reference to the "disgusting, acrid odor" is an emotion-arousing sense appeal that helps the reader share and sympathize with Charles Dudley's sense of a hostile environment; it is not a factual, definitive use like that of "rotten eggs" in the *Britannica's* description of hydrogen sulphide.

Another function of description in narrative is to advance the action or stop it momentarily, to create suspense or relax the reader's tension for the sake of greater emphasis when the action is resumed. Edgar Allan Poe is an acknowledged master of this technique.

The oral interpreter needs to understand how description is used in the selection he is to present if he is to make full and proper use of it in re-creating the material for an audience. When he feels that he understands the relation of the descriptive elements to the purpose of the whole, he must then turn to a detailed analysis of the way descriptive writing appeals to the perceiver's senses.

SENSORY APPEAL THROUGH IMAGERY

The sensory appeal of description is made through imagery. An image is inherent in any word or group of words which affects the senses and thus creates a sensory response. The amount, complexity, and vividness

From *The State of Mind* by Mark Schorer. Reprinted by permission of the author.

of imagery depend first of all on the author's purpose. In a piece of scientific writing that appeals primarily to the intellect, there will be relatively few images. On the other hand, in poetry, which of all forms of writing makes the strongest, most compressed appeal to the emotions and the senses, imagery reaches its highest development. The degree to which imagery is effectively used depends on the author's reservoir of experiences and his ability to recapture specific details of those experiences and put them into appropriate words.

Imagery has become a very popular — and occasionally confusing — word in the literary criticism of this century. In general it refers to language which describes, but within this category there are four common variations of usage. The first, and the one with which we shall be primarily concerned when we speak of imagery, is language which appeals to the senses and to motor responses. The second is language which gives concreteness to abstractions by describing them or endowing them with qualities which appeal to the senses. The third broadens the term to include a condensation of a series of the first two, so that it becomes in reality a symbol, such as Faulkner's use of heat and dryness throughout many of his writings. The fourth commonly accepted meaning of imagery makes it synonymous with idea or vision. Although all four concepts are closely related, we shall give specific attention only to the first two.

The use of language to give concreteness to an abstraction is often referred to as the use of figures of speech. The more common figures — similes, metaphors, and the like — are the very fabric of poetry and will be discussed in some detail in Chapter 10. For the understanding of descriptive prose, it is enough to consider imagery as any word or group of words which appeals to the senses.

The interpreter's skill in handling imagery depends first upon his responsiveness to the words of the author. As the writer calls upon his own memory for a concrete object which he can translate into sense-apprehended terms and thus enable the reader to create a similar image out of his own experience, so the interpreter, on encountering the word-symbol that stands for the image, reaches back to a selected experience and re-creates it in concrete terms. He then subjects that personal experience to the expansion or limitation dictated by the writer and makes a sensory response. Finally, he uses his physical and vocal techniques to convey that response to his hearers along with the image, so that they may complete the cycle by re-creating and responding in terms of *their* experiences.

This chain of perception and response is simply an extension of the process by which an actual object or sound is the stimulus for a mental and emotional response. When a person sees a tree, for example, the stimulus of light, shade, color, and form which his eye receives produces the image of a tree in his mind. This process becomes automatic as his familiarity with the object increases. He begins to make classifications of trees, as pine tree or elm tree. As his experience increases, the likelihood of his mistaking a pine for an elm becomes negligible. Perhaps the image "pine tree" or "elm tree" has special, personal associations for him; if so, these too are carried over into his response. In short, he receives the stimulus through his senses, transmits it to his brain, classifies and perhaps enlarges it, and finally makes a response.

In the case of imagery in literature, a preliminary step is necessary. The stimulus comes from a word or group of words rather than from an object. This word-stimulus strikes the eye of the reader, or the ear of the listener. The symbols of the letters, in the former case, or the sounds in the latter, must then be translated into the object or quality they represent to the perceiver. Thus the stimulus comes actually from a re-creation of the concrete object within the mind of the reader and of the listener. From this point, the process of translation, elaboration, classification, and evaluation is much as outlined above.

No two people will re-create an image in exactly the same terms. No two mental elm trees are quite the same, or are visualized against the same background. But all images of "elm tree" will have enough elements in common so that all persons to whom the words "elm tree" mean anything at all can respond in similar fashion. The author will supply whatever qualifying elements are needed to direct the universal response to his individual purpose.

VARIETIES OF SENSORY APPEAL

As we have noted, description achieves its effect through sensory images. Images that appeal predominantly to the sense of sight are called *visual;* to the sense of hearing, *auditory;* to the sense of taste, *gustatory;* to the sense of smell, *olfactory*. The sense of touch is appealed to in *tactual* (or tactile) imagery, which evokes a sensation of physical contact, pressure, or texture, and in *thermal* imagery, which refers to the feeling of heat and cold.

Imagery can also appeal to the so-called motor sense. There are two types of imagery in this category. The first is *kinetic* imagery, a large, overt action of the muscles such as "ran," "jumped," "sat down," or "walked away." The second is *kinesthetic* imagery, which refers to muscle tension and relaxation. It is closely related to empathy and is likely to be present in any particularly rich appeal, although it can also stand alone and is found in references to height and distance, for example, or in kinetic imagery, as in "sat down nervously," "walked away casually," or "ran breathlessly."

Rarely does an image appeal to one and only one sense. In much of the best literature, certainly in all literature rich in suggestion, the images carry a complex of appeals. In addition to the primary sense appeal of a word or phrase or thought unit, there will be one or more additional or secondary appeals as well. The senses of taste and smell, for example, are so closely allied that it is frequently impossible to affect one and not the other. Again, it is highly improbable that kinetic or action imagery would not be accompanied by kinesthetic or muscle-tension imagery. But complexity of appeal goes beyond these natural pairings. A skillful writer will frequently blend many secondary appeals with a primary appeal, or will allow the primary appeal to shift to secondary position within a single unit.

With this in mind, let us examine a portion of an essay by Lin Yutang. The phrases especially rich in imagery have been italicized.

> . . . To the soldier returning on leave the most common sights of city or country life — *a hot-dog stand, the neon lights at night,* even *the traffic lights* — seem good and reassuring. Even *being a lazy louse lying in bed* without the *hallucination of the reveille* seems to constitute an august virtue and a permanent achievement of human civilization.
>
> In fact, one suddenly realizes that all the good things of life — *the morning coffee, fresh air, a stroll in the afternoon,* even *dashing for the subway* or *dodging friends among commuters in the morning train* — constitute civilization because they constitute the very end of living. War makes us realize the importance of the things we ordinarily take for granted. No one values a *luxurious shave in a barber shop* more than a soldier returning from the front.

By his use of the word "sights," the author indicates that he intends the primary appeal of the opening sentence to be visual. For example, the reader forms a mental picture of a "hot-dog stand," primarily as an image to be seen. But out of his remembered experiences of hot-dog stands he summons associated imagery, though it is probably less strong than the primary visual image: olfactory, because of the smell of the hot dogs sizzling on the grill; gustatory, because of the remembered taste, perhaps enhanced by pickle relish or mustard; thermal, not only because of the suggestion of "hot," but also because the perceiver's memories may be associated with summer; auditory, because of the

From *With Love and Irony* by Lin Yutang. Reprinted by permission of the author.

voices of the customers, the rush of passing traffic and honking of horns on a state highway — or perhaps, if the remembered hot-dog stand is visualized at an amusement park, the music of a merry-go-round or the squeals of the roller-coaster riders in the background. In the same way, the primarily visual images "neon lights at night" and "traffic lights" carry associated secondary appeals to other senses. In the second sentence, the author abandons visual images and shifts his primary emphasis to motor response, the "lazy louse lying in bed," and to auditory appeal, "hallucination of the reveille," an image with strong secondary kinesthetic overtones.

The second paragraph presents a still more complex array of imagery, beginning with "morning coffee" (primary appeals, olfactory and gustatory; secondary appeals, thermal, visual, and kinesthetic, the last because of the suggestion of "well being") and continuing through a number of predominantly kinetic and kinesthetic images, to "among commuters in the morning train" (primary appeal, visual; secondary appeals, auditory and — more or less! — olfactory). The image of a "luxurious shave" is an excellent example of difference in point of view, depending, one may surmise, on whether or not one has ever had a shave. It is important to remember that Lin Yutang is a man, and the reader must attempt to make his, or more particularly her, response sympathetic with the author's. The feminine reader might derive approximately the same sensation of luxurious well-being from an oil shampoo — an interesting illustration of the fact that, though the details of the perceived images may differ, there can be enough basic similarity of sensation to arouse comparable responses.

Obviously, the interpreter cannot stop after each image and check to be sure his audience has had time to see, taste, smell, and hear all the accompanying appeals. All the images work together to produce the total effect. However, the more completely the interpreter has responded to the complexity of the appeals during preparation, and consequently during performance, the more force they will carry as he uses subtle variety of vocal technique and empathy to help the imagery fulfill its function of clarifying and making vivid.

An author's use of imagery will often affect his style and give important clues to his attitude. The writings of Thomas Wolfe contain innumerable examples of this relationship, including this fragment of remembered sense experience:

> . . . and the exciting smell of chalk and varnished desks; the smell of heavy bread-sandwiches of cold fried meat and butter . . .

and then the paragraph rushes on to other sense-vignettes not connected with the schoolroom — and we become conscious of a vigorous personality, with an almost insatiable physical appetite for life, hurrying through a catalogue of remarkably sharp sense impressions, piling image on image as though striving desperately to pin down some of the heady, crowding sense memories before they escape.

By way of contrast, compare this with George Santayana's recall of a schoolroom out of his boyhood experiences:

> No blackboard was black; all were indelibly clouded with ingrained layers of old chalk; the more you rubbed it out, the more you rubbed it in. Every desk was stained with generations of inkspots, cut deeply with initials and scratched drawings. What idle thoughts had been wandering for years through all those empty heads in all those tedious school hours!

In this description we sense the reflective mind of one who stands a little aloof from active participation in life, who uses images not as means of embracing life in all its physical manifestations but as springboards to reflection on the meaning that lies behind all that the senses apprehend.

Both Wolfe and Santayana have let their memories touch on similar aspects of experience, but each has selected the details to which he himself responds most completely, the one as a voracious liver of life, the other as an esthete and philosopher.

All the elements examined in the discussion of prose style must be considered as we analyze the handling of imagery in prose description. Word choice and length and structure of sentences are very important in setting up relationships and establishing rhythm of both content and structure. The relationship of adjacent words limits or expands the connotation. The cadences and degrees of stress growing out of the need for emphasis will enhance the empathic effect and help set the appropriate tone for the audience's response.

TONE COLOR

For the interpreter the sounds of the words which carry the sensory appeal are especially important since he will be translating the word symbols into sound symbols for his listeners. Writers who are concerned with appealing to the senses and emotions of their readers will take care that there is harmony between what they are describing and the sounds of the words they choose to describe it. Of course it is the

From *Persons and Places* by George Santayana. Reprinted by permission of Charles Scribner's Sons.

words, not the separate sounds, which carry the meaning, and it is the connotation of the words themselves that influence the interpreter's use of pace, quality, and all the rest of the elements of vocal technique. There are, for instance, more things affecting the way one would say "sleep," "slap," "slip," and "slop" than the mere changing of the vowel. Nevertheless, certain combinations of sounds produce articulation problems which slow the pace or give a sharpness to separate words, while others lend themselves to smooth linking and help produce a flowing effect. The manipulation of vowels and consonants to achieve a particular effect is called *tone color.* There is excellent use of contrasting tone color within the auditory imagery in the following excerpt from Katherine Mansfield's "At The Bay."

> Ah-Aah! sounded the sleepy sea. And from the bush there came the sound of little streams flowing, quickly, lightly, slipping between smooth stones, . . .

Tone color is part of a writer's style, since how words sound when they are put together influences his choice of words, the way he arranges them in a sentence, and, ultimately, the rhythm of the entire selection. It is the interpreter's responsibility to make full use of tone color to help support the imagery the author has provided. It is, moreover, a powerful aid to empathy since it underscores connotation and enriches suggestion.

IMAGERY AND THE INTRINSIC FACTORS

When the interpreter begins to examine a selection in detail he will be aware that imagery contributes strongly to the intrinsic factors — that it helps to produce unity and harmony, variety and contrast, balance and proportion, and rhythm. Perhaps a few examples will be useful here.

One of the most obvious methods of achieving unity through imagery is the use of visual or kinetic and kinesthetic progression from place to place. This use of imagery is very effectively illustrated in the excerpt from "St. Mark's" (see page 194). As Ruskin moves down the narrow alley, past the black eagle, etc., he stops for a detailed visual description at each focal point, creating a rhythm of tension and relaxation and of visual and motor appeal which is particularly helpful to the oral interpreter and to the listeners as well.

Sometimes the imagery displays very little unity of type but is held together by restrictions to a limited locale. This was true of the excerpt from "June Recital" (see page 192). Or similarly, the imagery may all be slanted toward one person or object, as in "Dry September" (see page 197), or to the parts of a series of details which relate to one object, place, or person. In the latter case, the effect is usually cumulative and must be handled so as to achieve the strongest ultimate impression. Charles Dickens uses this cumulative technique to describe a battle in *A Tale of Two Cities:*

> With a roar that sounded as if all the breath in France had been shaped into the detested word, the living sea rose, wave on wave, depth on depth, and overflowed the city to that point. Alarm-bells ringing, drums beating, the sea raging and thundering on its new beach, the attack begun. . . .
>
> Cannon, muskets, fire and smoke. . . . Flashing weapons, blazing torches, smoking waggon-loads of wet straw, hard work at neighboring barricades in all directions, shrieks, volleys, execrations, bravery without stint, boom, smash and rattle, and the furious sounding of the living sea. . . .

The author begins with the auditory appeal, to which he adds complexity that reaches its height in "cannon, muskets, fire and smoke"; then he shifts to the visual and kinetic imagery of "flashing weapons," returning almost at once to the auditory appeal in "shrieks, volleys," which comes to a climax in "boom, smash and rattle." Finally, he blends all this into "the furious sounding of the living sea."

Thomas Wolfe's "The Golden World" gives the interpreter a complex problem in unity through imagery. The following sentence illustrates his use of the cumulative technique.

> He knew the good male smell of his father's sitting-room; of the smooth worn leather sofa, with the gaping horse-hair rent; of the blistered varnished wood upon the hearth; of the heated calf-skin bindings; of the flat moist plug of apple tobacco, stuck with a red flag; of wood-smoke and burnt leaves in October; of the brown tired autumn earth; of honey-suckle at night; of warm nasturtiums; of a clean ruddy farmer who comes weekly with printed butter, eggs and milk; of fat limp underdone bacon and of coffee; of a bakery-oven in the wind; of large deep-hued stringbeans smoking-hot and seasoned well with salt and butter; of a room of old pine boards in which books and carpets have been stored, long closed; of Concord grapes in their long white baskets.

In this one long sentence the imagery is predominantly olfactory, but within this unity of appeal there is a variety of place. The progression from interior to exterior and back to interior may prove troublesome to the interpreter unless he is careful to group the objects which appeal to the senses. The excerpt opens in the sitting-room, where it remains

From *Look Homeward, Angel* by Thomas Wolfe. Reprinted by permission of Charles Scribner's Sons.

through mention of the visual detail of "a red flag." Without warning or apparent motivation the scene shifts to the outdoors, but the olfactory motif remains strong and there is unity of appeal in the focus of attention on the earth and its produce. The "ruddy farmer" with his "butter, eggs and milk" sets up the train of thought which centers on the smell of food and calls up the rest of the images within the sentence, including the "room of old pine boards in which books and carpets have been stored," an image which for the author belongs with these others, but to the interpreter may seem like an interpolation among the many references to food. The unifying factor here might best be classed as "stream of consciousness." The oral interpreter may experience some trouble in keeping the transitions clear and acceptable, unless he is careful to group the images by association, either by place or by sense appeal, keeping in mind the importance of the olfactory appeals and the fact that the memories cluster around a single house.

Obviously the type and vividness of the imagery must be in harmony with the total intention of the piece of literature: harmonious with the character and setting in a narrative, and with the tastes and experiences of the intended audience in didactic writing and essays. Even the adjectives used to give the objects added richness must be highly appropriate, such as "heated calf-skin bindings," "burnt leaves," and many others in the excerpt from "The Golden World." Books bound in watered silk would certainly not be harmonious with the "good male smell."

A skillful author is acutely aware, consciously or subconsciously, of the speed with which the senses tire. Everyone knows from experience that it is possible to become so accustomed to a smell, a sound, or a taste that it loses its initial impact or even passes into the realm of the subconscious and goes unnoticed. Thus, as Thomas Wolfe does here with his "red flag," an author will suddenly vary his appeal to allow the reader to shift his response to another sense. When he returns to the original appeal, the reader's response is heightened because of this momentary relief. The same relieving function can be accomplished by contrast as well. Thus imagery makes a particularly rich contribution to both variety and contrast and is itself intensified by variation and contrast. It is one of the interpreter's problems not to allow the variety to overshadow or violate the essential unity, but rather to use it to fulfill its purpose of relief.

Usually an author will provide help with this problem. On close observation, the interpreter will discover that the author has not really abandoned the primary appeal but has only allowed it to shift momentarily to a secondary position. He may also keep a fairly consistent relationship between two types of imagery. This was done most successfully in the excerpt from *With Love and Irony,* quoted earlier in this chapter (page 184), in which the visual and kinesthetic-kinetic images appear quite consistently in either the primary or secondary position, thus carrying out the author's intent of presenting familiar sights and implying their effect of muscle relaxation after the tension of a period of military service.

In the matter of balance and proportion, imagery is often used to weight a unit so that by its added vividness it is able to hold its own with a much larger unit. In this case, imagery is usually combined with other factors as well — especially to heighten a climax or sharpen a contrast.

In some selections imagery provides an interesting rhythm of logical content and emotional quality. In the excerpt quoted above, Lin Yutang neatly alternates imagistic appeals with statements directed primarily to the mind, so that the appeal to the reader is first intellectual, then sensory, then intellectual again. This rhythm is especially important in the case of kinetic and kinesthetic imagery. An excellent example of this has already been noted in the progression and cessation of movement in Ruskin's "St. Mark's."

THE INTERPRETER'S USE OF DESCRIPTION

The interpreter's first response to imagery will probably be strongly subjective. This is followed, however, by an examination which must be as objective as possible, based on what is known of the author and his individual experiences, and on the organization and style of the piece of writing under analysis. Objective analysis will help the interpreter see the author's purpose and base his primary response on the author's obvious intent, but within the limits the writer has imposed it is the interpreter's part as a re-creative artist to color the imagery with his own experiences. For although no two people respond in exactly the same way to any phrases which carry sensory appeal, the perceivers' experiences seldom differ so widely as to destroy the basic purpose of the appeal. For example, we have seen that Lin Yutang's reference to a "luxurious shave in a barber shop" is definitely a masculine image, but that it matters very little whether the reader is a man or woman, since as perceiver he or she can draw on some experience that connotes the pleasant relaxation and well-being of the "luxurious shave."

In giving detailed consideration to each image and its related tone color, it is important to keep in mind the sense of the entire thought unit. Consider, for instance, the thermal implications of the word "hot."

When used in a phrase like "hot bath after a cold walk," there is a natural tendency to let the accompanying suggestion of relaxation show in the muscles, in the slower tempo of the words, and in a more relaxed vocal tone. If on the other hand, the word is used in such a context as "Ouch! That water is hot!" the muscles will become tense, the tempo of the words will quicken, and the vocal force and tension will increase. In short, the image-bearing word or phrase must never be divorced from the whole unit of thought.

Response to imagery will have a definite effect upon the interpreter's muscle tone, and consequently on the empathic and emotional response of his audience. This is particularly true in the case of appeals to the motor responses, but the attendant emotional associations which the author has achieved through references to sights and sounds, tastes and smells will also make an empathic contribution.

After the interpreter has worked out the description through the various images, the next step is to consider what aspects of the imagery contribute most to the whole — how to express particular images in such a way that they are not a catalogue of separate items but a unifying force instead. Having exhausted the possibilities of complexity in the appeals, the interpreter must next evaluate them in terms of the author's over-all purpose. When the images are considered in relation to the whole, he will see that some contribute much more than others to the total effect and hence will need to be stressed, while those which provide variety within this unity may be played down. Against the desirability of responding completely in order to make use of the vividness which imagery adds to the writing and hence to his performance, the interpreter must balance the ever-present danger of allowing this vividness of descriptive detail to destroy the essential unity of his material.

In performance, the descriptive elements, like every other aspect of content and form, must be used subtly and unobtrusively to achieve the over-all effect, of the entire selection. They are only part of the whole, and their importance will be dictated by the author's larger purpose. The interpreter must never forget that the final step in preparation is to put the material back together so that all parts are coordinated, and that the final test of his performance is its seeming artlessness and the completeness of his communication to his audience.

SELECTIONS FOR ANALYSIS AND ORAL INTERPRETATION

In addition to the brief excerpts here, you will find some interesting descriptive passages in the selections at the ends of earlier chapters and within the narratives in Chapter 7.

Practically every kind of sensory appeal is to be found in this brief excerpt. Be careful to preserve the unity and make effective use of the style.

from *At The Bay*

Very early morning. The sun was not yet risen, and the whole of Crescent Bay was hidden under a white sea-mist. The big bush-covered hills at the back were smothered. You could not see where they ended and the paddocks and bungalows began. The sandy road was gone and the paddocks and bungalows the other side of it; there were no white dunes covered with reddish grass beyond them; there was nothing to mark which was beach and where was the sea. A heavy dew had fallen. The grass was blue. Big drops hung on the bushes and just did not fall; the silvery, fluffy toi-toi was limp on its long stalks, and all the marigolds and the pinks in the bungalow gardens were bowed to the earth with wetness. Drenched were the cold fuchsias, round pearls of dew lay on the flat nasturtium leaves. It looked as though the sea had beaten up softly in the darkness, as though one immense wave had come rippling, rippling — how far? Perhaps if you had waked up in the middle of the night you might have seen a big fish flicking in at the window and gone again. . . .

Ah-Aah! sounded the sleepy sea. And from the bush there came the sound of little streams flowing, quickly, lightly, slipping between the smooth stones, gushing into ferny basins and out again; and there was the splashing of big drops on large leaves, and something else — what was it? — a faint stirring and shaking, the snapping of a twig and then such silence that it seemed some one was listening.

Katherine Mansfield

The style here is as packed as the recital room. Pay particular attention to the shift in imagery as you reach the last paragraph.

from *June Recital*

The night of the recital was always clear and hot; everyone came. The prospective audience turned out in full oppression.

In the studio decorated like the inside of a candy box, with "material" scalloping the mantel shelf and doilies placed under every movable object, now thus made immovable, with streamers

Copyright, 1922 by Alfred A. Knopf, Inc. Renewed, 1950 by J. Middleton Murry. Reprinted from *The Short Stories of Katherine Mansfield,* by permission of Alfred A. Knopf, Inc.

Copyright, 1949, by Eudora Welty. Reprinted from her volume *The Golden Apples* by permission of Harcourt, Brace & World, Inc.

of white ribbons and nosegays of pink and white Maman Cochet roses and the last MacLain sweetpeas dividing and re-dividing the room, it was as hot as fire. No matter that this was the first night of June; no electric fans were to whir around while music played. The metronome, ceremoniously closed, stood on the piano like a vase. There was no piece of music anywhere in sight.

When the first unreasoning hush — there was the usual series — fell over the audience, the room seemed to shake with the agitation of palmetto and feather fans alone, plus the occasional involuntary tick of the metronome within its doors. There was the mixture together of agitation and decoration which could make every little forthcoming child turn pale with a kind of ultimate dizziness. Whoever might look up at the ceiling for surcease would be floundered within a paper design stemming out of the chandelier, as complicated and as unavailing as a cut-out paper snowflake.

Now Miss Eckhart came into the room all changed, with her dark hair pulled low on her brow, and gestured for silence. She was wearing her recital dress which made her look larger and closer-to than she looked at any other times. It was an old dress: Miss Eckhart disregarded her own rules. People would forget that dress between times and then she would come out in it again, the untidy folds not quite spotlessly clean, gathered about her bosom and falling heavy as a coat to the sides; it was a tawny crepe-back satin. There was a bodice of browning lace. It was as rich and hot and deep-looking as a furskin. The unexpected creamy flesh on her upper arms gave her a look of emerging from it.

Miss Eckhart, achieving silence, stood in the shadowy spot directly under the chandelier. Her feet, white-shod, shod by Mr. Sissum for good, rested in the chalk circle previously marked on the floor and now, she believed, perfectly erased. One hand, with its countable little muscles so hard and ready, its stained, blue nails, went to the other hand and they folded quite still, holding nothing, until they lost their force by lying on her breast and made a funny little house with peaks and gables. Standing near the piano but not near enough to help, she presided but not with her whole heart on guard against disaster; while disaster was what remained on the minds of the little girls. Starting with the youngest, she called them out.

So they played, and except Virgie, all played their worst. They shocked themselves. Parnell Moody burst into tears on schedule. But Miss Eckhart never seemed to notice or to care. How forgetful she seemed at exactly the moments she should have been agonized! You expected the whip, almost, for forgetting to repeat before the second ending, or for failing to count ten before you came around the curtain at all; and instead you received a strange smile. It was as though Miss Eckhart, at the last, were grateful to you for *anything.*

EUDORA WELTY

THE DESCRIPTIVE details must be carefully unified if a complete picture is to result. Pay particular attention to the organization. The long, involved sentences and numerous dependent clauses present an interesting problem to the interpreter. Tone color will help provide variety in some instances and will also help unify certain series of details.

St. Mark's

We find ourselves in a paved alley, some seven feet wide where it is widest, full of people, and resonant with cries of itinerant salesmen, — a shriek in their beginning, and dying away into a kind of brazen ringing, all the worse for its confinement between the high houses of the passage along which we have to make our way. Over-head, an inextricable confusion of rugged shutters, and iron balconies and chimney flues, pushed out on brackets to save room, and arched windows with projecting sills of Istrian stone, and gleams of green leaves here and there where a fig-tree branch escapes over a lower wall from some inner cortile, leading the eye up to the narrow stream of blue sky high over all. . . .

A yard or two farther, we pass the hostelry of the Black Eagle, and, glancing as we pass through the square door of marble, deeply moulded, in the outer wall, we see the shadows of its pergola of vines resting on an ancient well, with a pointed shield carved on its side; and so presently emerge on the bridge and Campo San Moisè, whence to the entrance into St. Mark's Place, called the Bocca di Piazza (mouth of the square) . . . We will push fast . . . into the shadow of the pillars at the end of the "Bocca di Piazza," and then we forget them all; for between those pillars there opens a great light, and, in the midst of it, as we advance slowly, the vast tower of St. Mark seems to lift itself visibly forth from the level field of chequered stones; and, on each side, the countless arches prolong themselves into ranged symmetry, as if the rugged and irregular houses that pressed together above us in the dark alley had been struck back into sudden obedience and lovely order, and all their rude casements and broken walls had been transformed into arches charged with goodly sculpture, and fluted shafts of delicate stone.

And well may they fall back, for beyond those troops of ordered arches there rises a vision out of the earth, and all the great square seems to have opened from it in a kind of awe, that we may see it far away; — a multitude of pillars and white domes, clustered into a long low pyramid of coloured light; a treasure-heap, it seems, partly of gold, and partly of opal and mother-of-pearl, hollowed beneath into five great vaulted porches, ceiled with fair mosaic, and beset with sculpture of alabaster, clear as amber and delicate as ivory, — sculpture fantastic and involved, of palm leaves and lilies, and grapes and pomegranates, and birds clinging and fluttering among

From *The Stones of Venice* by John Ruskin.

the branches, all twined together in an endless network of buds and plumes; and, in the midst of it, the solemn forms of angels, sceptred, and robed to the feet, and leaning to each other across the gates, their figures indistinct among the gleaming of the golden ground through the leaves beside them, interrupted and dim, like the morning light as it faded back among the branches of Eden, when first its gates were angel-guarded long ago. And round the walls of the porches there are set pillars of variegated stones, jasper and porphyry, and deep-green serpentine spotted with flakes of snow, and marbles, that half refuse and half yield to the sunshine, Cleopatra-like, "their bluest veins to kiss" — the shadow, as it steals back from them, revealing line after line of azure undulation, as a receding tide leaves the waved sand; their capitals rich with interwoven tracery, rooted knots of herbage, and drifting leaves of acanthus and vine, and mystical signs, all beginning and ending in the Cross; and above them, in the broad archivolts, a continuous chain of language and of life — angels, and the signs of heaven, and the labours of men, each in its appointed season upon the earth; and above these, another range of glittering pinnacles, mixed with white arches edged with scarlet flowers, — a confusion of delight, amidst which the breasts of the Greek horses are seen blazing in their breadth of golden strength, and the St. Mark's Lion, lifted on a blue field covered with stars, until at last, as if in ecstasy, the crests of the arches break into a marble foam, and toss themselves far into the blue sky in flashes and wreaths of sculptured spray, as if the breakers on the Lido shore had been frost-bound before they fell, and the sea-nymphs had inlaid them with coral and amethyst.

JOHN RUSKIN

THOMAS WOLFE PREPARES us for complexity of imagery by mentioning "mixed odors and sensations." Take your cue from him. Use care in keeping the images, and the associations which lead from one to another, clearly unified.

The Golden World

He had heard already the ringing of remote church bells over a countryside on Sunday night; had listened to the earth steeped in the brooding symphony of dark, and the million-noted little night things; and he had heard thus the far retreating wail of a whistle in a distant valley, and faint thunder on the rails; and he felt the infinite depth and width of the golden world in the brief seductions of a thousand multiplex and mixed mysterious odors and sensations, weaving, with a blinding interplay and aural explosions, one into the other.

From *Look Homeward, Angel* by Thomas Wolfe. Reprinted by permission of Charles Scribner's Sons.

He remembered yet the East India Tea House at the Fair, the sandalwood, the turbans, and the robes, the cool interior and the smell of India tea; and he had felt now the nostalgic thrill of dew-wet mornings in Spring, the cherry scent, the cool clarion earth, the wet loaminess of the garden, the pungent breakfast smells and the floating snow of blossoms. He knew the inchoate sharp excitement of hot dandelions in young Spring grass at noon; the smell of cellars, cobwebs, and built-on secret earth; in July, of watermelons bedded in sweet hay, inside a farmer's covered wagon; of cantaloupe and crated peaches; and the scent of orange rind, bitter-sweet, before a fire of coals. He knew the good male smell of his father's sitting-room; of the smooth worn leather sofa, with the gaping horse-hair rent; of the blistered varnished wood upon the hearth; of the heated calf-skin bindings; of the flat moist plug of apple tobacco, stuck with a red flag; of wood-smoke and burnt leaves in October; of the brown tired autumn earth; of honey-suckle at night; of warm nasturtiums; of a clean ruddy farmer who comes weekly with printed butter, eggs and milk; of fat limp underdone bacon and of coffee; of a bakery-oven in the wind; of large deep-hued stringbeans smoking-hot and seasoned well with salt and butter; of a room of old pine boards in which books and carpets have been stored, long closed; of Concord grapes in their long white baskets.

THOMAS WOLFE

KALYMNOS IS ONE of the numerous islands in the Aegean Sea. Notice how skillfully Durrell combines imaginative metaphor with almost factual description. Compare this description with the excerpt by the same author at the end of Chapter 5.

Kalymnos

In Kalymnos the infant's paint-box has been at work again on the milky slopes of the mountain. Carefully, laboriously it has squared in a churchyard, a monastery, and lower down repeated the motif: a church, a monastery, a town; then, simply for the sake of appropriateness, a harbour with a shelf of bright craft at anchor, and the most brilliant, the most devastatingly brilliant houses. Never has one seen anything like it — the harbour revolving slowly round one as one comes in. Plane after stiff cubistic plane of pure colour. The mind runs up and down the web of vocabulary looking for a word which will do justice to it. In vain. Under the church the half-finished caieques stand upon a slip — huge coops of raw wood looking for all the world like the skeletons of dismembered whales.

From *Reflections of a Marine Venus* by Lawrence Durrell. Reprinted by permission of E. P. Dutton & Co., Inc. and Faber and Faber, Ltd.

Three little girls in crimson dresses stand arm in arm and watch us. The harbour liquefies under the keel as we throttle down and move towards the port, our engines now puffy and subdued, yet quickened like our heartbeats as we sit and watch the island. The echo of our passage — the hard *plam-plam-plam* of the exhaust — bounces gravely off the rusted iron hull of a steamer which lies on its side in the shallows, its funnels sticking up like nostrils, but all the rest of it submerged in water as clear as the purest white gin. This is Kalymnos. High up, under the walls of the Church of the Golden Hand a woman is singing, slowly, emphatically, while from the wharves across the way a man in a blue overall is hammering at a coffin. Uncanny isolation of sound and object, each dissimilar, each entire to itself. Detached from the temporal frame. A song and a hammering which exist together but never mix or muddle the hard outlines of each other.

LAWRENCE DURRELL

THERE IS REMARKABLE unity of focus here. Notice how the descriptive details and the progress of time work together. The sentence structure is characteristic of Faulkner's style. Close attention to imagery and the relationship of descriptive words to each other will help untangle it.

from *Dry September*

II

She was thirty-eight or thirty-nine. She lived in a small frame house with her invalid mother and a thin, sallow, unflagging aunt, where each morning between ten and eleven she would appear on the porch in a lace-trimmed boudoir cap, to sit swinging in the porch swing until noon. After dinner she lay down for a while, until the afternoon began to cool. Then, in one of the three or four new voile dresses which she had each summer, she would go downtown to spend the afternoon in the stores with the other ladies, where they would handle the goods and haggle over the prices in cold, immediate voices, without any intention of buying.

She was of comfortable people — not the best in Jefferson, but good people enough — and she was still on the slender side of ordinary looking, with a bright, faintly haggard manner and dress. When she was young she had had a slender, nervous body and a sort of hard vivacity which had enabled her for a time to ride upon the crest of the town's social life as exemplified by the high school party and church social period of her contemporaries while still children enough to be unclassconscious.

She was the last to realize that she was losing ground; that those

Copyright 1930 and renewed 1958 by William Faulkner. Reprinted from *Collected Stories of William Faulkner,* by permission of Random House, Inc.

among whom she had been a little brighter and louder flame than any other were beginning to learn the pleasure of snobbery — male — and retaliation — female. That was when her face began to wear that bright, haggard look. She still carried it to parties on shadowy porticoes and summer lawns, like a mask or a flag, with that bafflement of furious repudiation of truth in her eyes. One evening at a party she heard a boy and two girls, all schoolmates, talking. She never accepted another invitation.

She watched the girls with whom she had grown up as they married and got homes and children, but no man ever called on her steadily until the children of the other girls had been calling her "aunty" for several years, the while their mothers told them in bright voices about how popular Aunt Minnie had been as a girl. Then the town began to see her driving on Sunday afternoons with the cashier in the bank. He was a widower of about forty — a high-colored man, smelling always faintly of the barber shop or of whisky. He owned the first automobile in town, a red runabout; Minnie had the first motoring bonnet and veil the town ever saw. Then the town began to say: "Poor Minnie." "But she is old enough to take care of herself," others said. That was when she began to ask her old schoolmates that their children call her "cousin" instead of "aunty."

It was twelve years now since she had been relegated into adultery by public opinion, and eight years since the cashier had gone to a Memphis bank, returning for one day each Christmas, which he spent at an annual bachelors' party at a hunting club on the river. From behind their curtains the neighbors would see the party pass, and during the over-the-way Christmas day visiting they would tell her about him, about how well he looked, and how they heard that he was prospering in the city, watching with bright, secret eyes her haggard, bright face. Usually by that hour there would be the scent of whisky on her breath. It was supplied her by a youth, a clerk at the soda fountain: "Sure; I buy it for the old gal. I reckon she's entitled to a little fun."

Her mother kept to her room altogether now; the gaunt aunt ran the house. Against that background Minnie's bright dresses, her idle and empty days, had a quality of furious unreality. She went out in the evenings only with women now, neighbors, to the moving pictures. Each afternoon she dressed in one of the new dresses and went downtown alone, where her young "cousins" were already strolling in the late afternoons with their delicate, silken heads and thin, awkward arms and conscious hips, clinging to one another or shrieking and giggling with paired boys in the soda fountain when she passed and went on along the serried store fronts, in the doors of which the sitting and lounging men did not even follow her with their eyes any more.

William Faulkner

THIS EXCERPT IS, it could be argued, basically narrative, since the author himself subtitles it "An Apologue," but the progression is carried forward by remarkably clear and detailed description. Notice how it moves from almost factual statements to the "horrible loneliness" of the closing sentence.

from *The Man of Adamant—An Apologue*

Above a century afterwards, when the trackless forest of Richard Digby's day had long been interspersed with settlements, the children of a neighboring farmer were playing at the foot of a hill. The trees, on account of the rude and broken surface of this acclivity, had never been felled, and were crowded so densely together as to hide all but a few rocky prominences, wherever their roots could grapple with the soil. A little boy and girl, to conceal themselves from their playmates, had crept into the deepest shade, where not only the darksome pines, but a thick veil of creeping plants suspended from an overhanging rock, combined to make a twilight at noonday, and almost a midnight at all other seasons. There the children hid themselves, and shouted, repeating the cry at intervals, till the whole party of pursuers were drawn thither, and pulling aside the matted foliage, let in a doubtful glimpse of daylight. But scarcely was this accomplished, when the little group uttered a simultaneous shriek, and tumbled headlong down the hill, making the best of their way homeward, without a second glance into the gloomy recess. Their father, unable to comprehend what had so startled them, took his axe, and by felling one or two trees, and tearing away the creeping plants, laid the mystery open to the day. He had discovered the entrance of a cave, closely resembling the mouth of a sepulchre, within which sat the figure of a man, whose gesture and attitude warned the father and children to stand back, while his visage wore a most forbidding frown. This repulsive personage seemed to have been carved in the same gray stone that formed the walls and portal of the cave. On minuter inspection, indeed, such blemishes were observed, as made it doubtful whether the figure were really a statue chiselled by human art, and somewhat worn and defaced by the lapse of ages, or a freak of Nature, who might have chosen to imitate, in stone, her usual handiwork of flesh. Perhaps it was the last unreasonable idea, suggested by this strange spectacle, that the moisture of the cave possessed a petrifying quality, which had thus awfully embalmed a human corpse.

There was something so frightful in the aspect of this Man of Adamant, that the farmer, the moment that he recovered from the fascination of his first gaze, began to heap stones into the mouth of the cavern. His wife, who had followed him to the hill, assisted her husband's efforts. The children, also, approached as near as they durst, with their little hands full of pebbles, and cast them on the pile. Earth was then thrown into the crevices, and the whole fabric overlaid with sods. Thus all traces of the discovery were obliterated, leaving only a marvelous legend, which grew wilder from one generation to another, as the children told it to their grandchildren, and they to their posterity, till few believed that there had ever been a cavern or a statue, where now they saw but a grassy patch on the shadowy hill-side. Yet, grown people avoid the spot, nor do children play there. Friendship, and Love, and Piety, all human and celestial sympathies, should keep aloof from that hidden cave; for there still sits, and, unless an earthquake crumble down the roof upon his head, shall sit forever, the shape of Richard Digby, in the attitude of repelling the whole race of mortals — not from heaven — but from the horrible loneliness of his dark, cold sepulchre!

NATHANIEL HAWTHORNE

✶ Bibliography

Since description is an integral part of narration, the interpreter will find his best sources for further reading on descriptive prose in the books listed at the end of Chapter 7.

7

Narration

Narration provides the interpreter with material which has a high degree of audience appeal. Myths, folk tales, and legends of every civilization testify to the fact that the enjoyment of a story is as old as human speech. The interpreter has no problem in finding narratives suitable for presentation. His only difficulty is in selecting one or two from the vast store of available material. In this he will be guided by his own interests and those of the audience he has in mind, and by his standards of literary excellence.

The primary purpose of narration, whether in prose or poetry, is to relate an incident or a series of incidents. As always, the interpreter must thoroughly acquaint himself with the logical content, emotional quality, method of organization, and various aspects of literary craftsmanship peculiar to the form in which it is written. When the narrative is in prose, he must evaluate it for style in the same manner he analyzes any other type of prose. He must consider the special problems of plot, setting, motivation, and characterization inherent in narration. The relative importance of these four factors — what happened, when and where, why and how, and to whom — will vary from selection to selection, but they are always present and require careful attention in preparation and special emphasis in presentation.

In its broadest sense, narration includes description of a single action, fables, allegories, parables, legends, fairy tales, anecdotes, diaries, history, biography and autobiography, travel and adventure, short stories, and novels. These various types of narration differ in length and complexity and in degree of concentration on one or more of the factors of plot, setting, motivation, or character. The discussion in this chapter will be confined largely to the short story, a form that embodies many of the special problems to be found in the novel and yet is brief enough to be handled conveniently. It is more complex in structure and implication than the less sophisticated forms such as the fable, the allegory, and the legend, and does not require special attention to actual personalities as do histories, biographies, and autobiographies.

Before discussing the elements peculiar to narration, it might be well to clarify four terms often found in critical discussions like those listed in the bibliography at the end of this chapter: *subject matter, theme, action,* and *plot.*

Subject matter is, in a broad sense, what the story is about. It controls the readers' and the writer's focus or center of interest. For example, "Mice and Birds and Boy" is "about" Mrs. May. On the other hand, the subject matter of "The Lottery" is the lottery itself.[1]

Theme is the underlying "why" of the story. It is a way of managing the subject matter so that it says something in particular about human relationships and human values. That "something" is not always specifically stated but is carefully suggested by selection of details, so that the reader can draw upon his own experiences to help identify with the characters and events and thus understand the universal implications.

Action is the sequence of visible or discernible physical happenings. The action in "The Lottery" is deliberately ordered and inevitable. It is more complex in "Mice and Birds and Boy" because although Mrs. May's actions contribute strongly to our response, it is William's comings and goings that provide the real core of the action.

Plot is a sequence of changes in human relations which runs parallel to the sequence of physical happenings that make up the action. Plot is occasioned by and manifested in the action. Plot, therefore, is the meshing of subject matter controlled by theme and manipulated by action.

ORGANIZATION

The ultimate achievement of a narrative lies in its plot. But in order for the plot to exist at all, there must be someone to whom the events happen and a segment of time and space in which they occur. And certain details relating to character and setting must be given the reader before the plot itself can begin to materialize. How to disclose the necessary information is one of the most difficult problems facing the writer of narration. How much does the reader need to know about character and setting for the action to be effective and logical? How and where should such information be presented? The author's answers to these two

[1] To help the student hold the separate elements in properly focused relation to the narrative as a whole, all specific illustrations throughout this chapter will be taken from the complete selections given at the end of the chapter.

questions will determine to a large degree his method of organizing his story.

Some authors prefer to make the necessary explanations at the outset, either objectively or through the speech of one of the characters. When this method is used, the interpreter will have little difficulty in deciding where the introduction ends and the main action of the plot begins. In most short stories these introductory units are brief and compact, and the interpreter must be sure that he has grasped the important elements and can present them in such a way that his listeners get an immediate, clear, and complete picture of everything they will need to know about who is involved in the action and when and where it takes place. This seems too obvious to mention, perhaps, to the interpreter who has had experience with introductory material in expository and didactic writing. In narration, however, the discovery of what the audience must know is not always so simple.

The first difficulty may arise from the fact that the selection and arrangement of details are not ordered by logic alone but are governed primarily by emotional and psychological implication, which may not be apparent until the story is completed. Sometimes we are told a great deal by what the author has deliberately left out. As we noted earlier, literature is not *exactly like* life. An author exercises the right of selectivity to underscore theme and to insure that action results in plot. Miss Jackson does an excellent job of this in "The Lottery" with the explicit details of date, time of day, specific location, and even population figures, so that we are ready for a local custom which leads inevitably to the final horror. Moreover, part of the horror comes from the skillful early description of these people and their ordinary "neighborly" actions.

Frequently, especially in modern writing, the essential background is not concentrated in a unit at the opening of the story but is inserted after the action has begun, or at various intervals throughout the narrative. The author may even use the "flash-back" technique to take the reader into the past. This gives the interpreter a problem in unity, since the present action must not be forgotten during the sections of explanation but merely suspended while still being held in clear focus. The problem is even more difficult when the technique of foreshadowing is used. Frequently an author will insert key details which seem unimportant at the time but which are vital to the totality of the plot. This is the case with the smooth, round stones which the boys collect early in "The Lottery." It is also true of the stuffed parrot in Mrs. May's house. The details of John's home life and of Thelma's in "Friends from Philadelphia" make a contrast without which the ending would be almost meaningless. The interpreter must be sure that these key units register with his audience without calling undue attention to them until such time as their significance is revealed.

There may be numerous key situations within a piece of narrative writing. They are signposts that point the direction the action and plot will take. Each key situation will probably contain a minor climax and will frequently have an introductory paragraph or two and its own conclusion. The interpreter will need to discover what motivates each minor climax, what changes in character or condition it brings about, and in what way it implements the final outcome. He will be careful to emphasize it just enough — not so much that the main climax will be overshadowed. He must not give away the plot, and yet he must be certain that the audience is properly prepared to accept it. Thus key words and phrases must always be handled in terms of the entire story development.

The conclusion is that part of the series of events which is the inevitable, or at least acceptable, aftermath of the crisis. It is the completion or resolution of the pattern of action and conflict begun in the introduction and brought to culmination at the climax. It is the tying-in of all the loose threads — "and they lived happily ever after," or the reverse. It completes the series of events, and the interpreter must use it for this purpose. Sometimes the conclusion is not explicitly stated but is left to the reader's imagination, as in the famous story of "The Lady or the Tiger"; or, especially in contemporary writing, indicated but not completely stated, as in "Mice and Birds and Boy."

CLIMAX

Some degree of conflict is essential to plot. This conflict may take place between man and an exterior force, such as another person, environment, society, nature, or even, in modern works, machinery. It may subsist between the main character and interior forces such as his will, his ideas, or his frustrations. Frequently external and internal conflict are combined, the one giving rise to the other. In any case, the writer will select and organize his materials in a way that will give his plot speed, suspense, continuity, concreteness, and credibility. We do not ask for absolute realism or for factual logic in a plot. We ask only that it be acceptable and logical as it relates to the particular characters in the particular situation. The logic of events must always be tested in terms of each character's development and of the motivations which result from the kind of person he is and the kind of person he becomes.

The major climax is the point of culmination in the complete selection, though there may be several minor climaxes preceding and following the main climax. These climaxes may be high points of action or of emotional impact. Frequently the two types come together, as they do in "The Lottery," and are so closely interrelated that there is no need to consider them separately. Sometimes they follow each other very quickly, as in "The Banal Miracle." Often the climax of action sets up and motivates the highest point of emotional impact, as in "The Foghorn." Or the arrangement may be reversed, with the highest point of emotional impact leading to the culmination of the action.

The writer may build his climax in numerous ways. In an extremely short narrative, he may open near the culmination of the action, set his background swiftly, and move immediately to the single climax. This gives the interpreter no particular problem except that of sustaining the steady build. A more common method of building climax is to use a series of incidents which lead like stair steps to the main incident. In this case, each minor incident will have its own beginning, its high point, and its conclusion. The interpreter must use these minor climaxes as focal points. They provide him with an interesting emotional rhythm and require him to give attention to the shifts in interest from one aspect of the story to another. Sometimes, for example, an author will follow one character for an entire incident, take another through the same process, and bring the two together for the final conflict and its resolution. It would be impossible to mention here every type of problem which might arise in thousands of examples of narrative writing. The interpreter must examine each selection for its individual problems and make himself aware of the minor climaxes within each of the incidents which combine to make up the plot, and of their relationship to the main climax of action and of emotional tension.

The interpreter will do well to take careful note of the kinetic and kinesthetic images which are present in the climactic moments. The former will help him in communicating the feeling of speed and activity, the latter in creating suspense and tension. Often a change in style of writing will help set off the climax. There may be a general tightening of thought units, shortening of sentences, and increase of words with high imagery content. Gertrude Atherton used this technique effectively in narrating the accident in "The Foghorn."

TRANSITIONS

Plot is largely a matter of cause and effect. Readers, and consequently an audience, want to know the *why* as well as the *what*. Whether an author chooses to give the necessary background information at the very beginning of his tale, or at intervals within the narrative, he may still be faced with the problem of transitions which establish the immediate cause of a new development in the plot. These transitions often coincide with and are inseparable from description of setting and character. On the other hand, they may differ slightly in that they are used primarily to carry the reader from the conclusion of one episode to the introduction of another. They may be unified by progression of time or place, or by the characters' physical or psychological development. The transitions may be provided by a narrator or expressed through a character. In any case, the interpreter must give them some attention so that he can lead his audience subtly and surely into the next key situation without loss of motivation.

Besides providing bridges between key situations, transitions have other important functions to perform. A transitional unit may intensify atmosphere and increase suspense. On the other hand, it may simply allow the audience to relax momentarily after an episode. Such relaxation sets up a rhythm between activity and passivity which is necessary for fullest comprehension and response. Furthermore, it permits both reader and audience to approach the next incident refreshed and to be more responsive to the climax when it comes.

The problem is quite complex in "The Foghorn" because there is no clear pattern of alternation of exterior forces and interior associations. The elements of time and place are confused, as they should be for the character involved, and the author indicates the precise stimulus for a new thought only by an occasional reference to the fog or the sound of the foghorn. This is particularly true in the early part of the story. The transitions become less complex toward the close when the character reacts to the sight of the room and of various parts of her body. This is in keeping with the woman's gradual return to mental clarity and comprehension of her situation as its actually exists. The interpreter must make the seemingly unrelated recollections plausible by supplying in his own mind the transitions which the author has purposely omitted. This requires particular attention to organization and to the selection of important words and phrases, since the association reveals everything we are to know of character and setting and plot. The mind of the woman involved jumps from a detail, seemingly unimportant in itself, directly into a key situation. She then goes back to fill in necessary background. Sometimes the key situation itself is unified by place or progression of time, or both, but the transitions from episode to episode are pure stream of consciousness. Hence the interpreter, by skillful use of pause and inflection, will need to indicate clearly to his audience that the first episode is concluded but that another is to follow. During the pause he must reconstruct in his own mind the passage of time and the new scene and situation. Obviously he does not tell his hearers that he is doing this, but he can get the idea across to them if he remembers to keep them with him by concentrating on the progression of time into the next episode as soon as the preceding one is completed. His pause will, of course, be relatively brief, but it is important. During the transition he will do well to keep his eyes on his audience and be prepared to move into the following unit without referring to the manuscript, so that he holds his listeners' attention even though he is not speaking.

POINT OF VIEW

Another element peculiar to narration is *point of view.* Point of view is the physical and psychological position and degree of involvement which the narrator takes in relation to the action and resultant plot.

There are, broadly speaking, four degrees of involvement, although there are variations of degree within each one. The first and simplest from the interpreter's standpoint is that of the "objective observer," in which the author records only what might be seen and heard by someone able to observe the characters without being observed. In this case the interpreter assumes for his audience the same "objective" point of view that the writer has assumed for his readers. He reports directly and in his own person whatever details and general outlines the author has given him. The author's control over what the narrator sees and hears must not be overlooked or underestimated, however. If the narrator were totally objective, there would be neither theme nor plot. Again, "The Lottery" gives us an excellent example of the "objective observer" narrator. The interpreter will need to work for vividness and clarity, skillful handling of the organization, and intelligent use of emphasis. He will need to establish the important points in the minds of his listeners, as well as the proper relationships between the units. He must also consider the relative importance of the details and use his voice and body to provide pointing where it is needed.

The second degree of involvement allows the author to enter into the minds and thoughts of one or all of the characters. He thus becomes omniscient and reports in his own person their thoughts and reactions. Such a point of view requires skillful handling on the part of the interpreter to keep the thread of the thoughts and speculations which the characters do not share even with each other. This is basic in "Mice and Birds and Boy."

Frequently in this direct, omniscient narration the author will reveal his own partisanship and his own set of values to so great an extent that the narrative assumes an almost didactic purpose. He may even write in the first person. More often, however, his personal comment will not be stated directly but will be reflected in the sympathy which he elicits for a certain character or in his distaste for or delight in a particular setting.

Third, the author may be involved in the plot as a minor character who observes and evaluates at the same time. Such a story usually employs a first-person narrator. This point of view requires the interpreter to establish enough characterization for the narrator to be believable in the situation, and at the same time to keep the focus of attention on the major characters.

The fourth degree of involvement is the use of a first-person narrator who is the main character in the plot. This use of "I" is an important aid to the interpreter, not only because it unifies the story but also because it allows him to establish the appropriate character for the narrator and thus insure a high degree of vividness. There are almost limitless possibilities for variety within this area. The narrator who is also the main character in the plot may be an ordinary person, and our concern may be almost entirely with the sequence of events. On the other hand, he may be a character whose very complexities give credence to the events. In any case, whenever a story is told in the first person, it will be necessary for the interpreter to make a complete analysis of the physical and psychological background of the narrator. Frequently the effect of this background cannot be completely established until all the other aspects of narrative and their relationship to that character have been evaluated. Whenever the point of view is that of a person involved in the action, certain specific qualities of characterization may need to be communicated to the audience by means of vocal and physical suggestion.

Miss Atherton's story "The Foghorn" is a particularly complex study of point of view. It is written entirely in the third person, a technique which, under ordinary circumstances, would indicate considerable objectivity on the part of the author and consequently of the interpreter. This is not, however, exactly the case. Miss Atherton not only knows what her character is feeling and thinking but follows her stream of associations and uses it as the main device for unity, entering into her thoughts and emotions so completely that the effect is almost that of a monologue. Unless the interpreter suggests the type of character clearly, as well as the emotional responses to the incidents and the exterior forces of environment, the audience will have difficulty in accepting the climax as well as the key situations which lead up to it. Moreover, there is a sharp, dramatic shift in point of view at the end of the story.

A careful consideration of point of view will help the interpreter judge accurately whether the attitude which underlies the story is that of the author, of a narrator or a character created outside the author, or a combination of both. This knowledge will be useful in helping him discover the key words and phrases as well as the key situations and the climaxes.

Thus it is extremely important to consider the point of view adopted by the author to reveal background as well as to develop the events which make up the plot. Point of view helps dictate the organization, the selection of details, the type of imagery, and the style of writing, both in the descriptive units and in the direct and indirect discourse. The resulting changes of pace help the interpreter achieve variety and sharpen contrasts; and the interesting interplay of rhythms is invaluable in holding attention and building to the climaxes. Point of view is the interpreter's clue to the relationship which he will take to his audience, varying from objective, direct reporting to the sharing of an emotional experience through a character involved in the sequence of events. It is a basic consideration in Chamber Theatre, which we shall discuss later in this chapter.

SETTING

It is difficult to establish the setting subtly and unobtrusively. This difficulty must, of course, be solved first by the writer. The interpreter in turn must be aware of its importance in the total effect of the story and must apply his knowledge of unity and harmony, variety and contrast, balance and proportion in order to achieve the author's intention.

The setting must bear a clear and acceptable relation to the action as well as to the characters who are involved. Sometimes, especially in travel and adventure stories, it is necessary to establish the geographical location and the physical aspects of the landscape and climate. In biographies and histories as well as in historical fiction, the period in which the action takes place is of vital importance. In modern stories it is usually sufficient to establish the general area, since most contemporary writers are more concerned with the psychological implications of the setting than with its physical details.

In any case, the scene must be created swiftly and concretely. Since the author does not wish to delay the all-important action for detailed description, he depends heavily upon suggestion. He concentrates on those aspects of setting which will implement his action and character development. They may be largely external, such as season, climate, urban or rural locale, or a particular type of neighborhood or building. On the other hand, they may be primarily psychological and depend upon the characters' attitudes toward social customs, conventions, or atmosphere of a locale not specifically identified. As we noted earlier, a consideration of point of view is basic in evaluating the details of setting. Almost always, however, the action is motivated to a greater or lesser degree by the reaction of the character to his environment, and the author will select those details which give the surroundings their proper associational value for the characters he has in mind.

Consequently, the interpreter is likely to encounter a degree of condensation which makes it imperative that he give careful attention to each attribute mentioned. The author of a short story must create his appeals to perception swiftly and accurately. He will most likely make liberal use of sense imagery as a means of achieving this concreteness and vividness. He may, of course, allow the setting to evolve gradually as the story unfolds. In any event, the imagery serves to advance the story and must be so used by the interpreter. The interpreter must perform the same function for his audience as the author does for the reader. He must make sure of the underlying motor responses, and hence the degree of tension or relaxation, activity or passivity produced by the more obvious sensory appeals.

The details and appeals to perception used in establishing setting may be governed by the unity of time or place, or both. A particularly interesting example of unity of place is to be found in "The Lottery," where all of the story takes place within a single specifically described area.

Progression of time is another commonly used method of unifying setting. A writer of narrative may have his clock and his calendar move at any rate he chooses, backward as well as forward. The progression may cover seconds, years, or generations. Unification by the passage of time is particularly useful because it can combine subtly with the action and help keep the plot moving steadily.

Far more difficult for the writer to achieve and for the interpreter to sustain is unity which depends upon the stream of consciousness in the mind of a character. "The Foghorn" depends entirely upon this method, even though the story is written in the third person.

> What an absurd vanity to sleep on a hard pillow and forego that luxurious burrowing into the very depths of a mass of baby pillows! . . .

From *The Foghorn* by Gertrude Atherton. Copyright 1934 by Gertrude Atherton, renewed © 1962 by Muriel Atherton Russel. Reprinted by permission of Houghton Mifflin Company.

> Fog on the Bay. Since childhood she had loved to hear that long-drawn-out, almost-human moan of the foghorn as she lay warm and sheltered in bed. It was on a night of fog they had spoken for the first time, although they had nodded at three or four formal dinners given to the newcomers who had brought letters to the elect. Bostonians were always popular in San Francisco; they had good manners and their formality was only skin-deep.

The first sentence, which opens the story, suggests the time of day, indicates the immediate surroundings, and gives strong hints as to the physical and psychological condition of the character. The second paragraph, which comes about two pages later, completes the setting and sketches in the background for an episode out of the past. It is the interpreter's problem to make these seemingly unrelated details plausible, by allowing his own recollections of lying in bed on a foggy morning to produce the empathic response, and by adapting his response to that of the character involved. Then he must jump immediately to the key situation, the memory of the first meeting, with only the fog to provide the transition.

The style of "The Foghorn" follows remarkably well the irregular, wandering rhythm of a stream of consciousness. Most of the sentences are long and tenuous with no sharp distinction between past and present, between reality and situations created by the character's imagination. The single abrupt phrase, "Fog on the Bay," breaks the previous train of thought just as a sound might do, and immediately sets up another flow of associations. This particular style is, of course, dictated by the fact that the necessary revelations of setting are being made through the character's consciousness, although the third-person narrator is used.

CHARACTER

As important as setting is, the delineation of character is even more important. Unless the interpreter and his audience know what kind of person is involved in the action of the story, setting becomes largely window dressing. The characters give the plot life and meaning.

The problem of providing information about character is much the same as that involved in creating the setting. It is, however, even more important to make the characters three-dimensional and credible because, while many stories could happen in almost any setting, very few situations would call up *exactly* the same response from different individuals. Thus it is important to establish clearly and concisely what traits of personality, habits of thought, and responses will motivate each character's reaction to the forces with which he will come in contact.

As we saw in our discussion of point of view, an author may tell us in his own person what he wants us to know about a character, describing his appearance, behavior, or speech, or recording his thoughts. Or the character may be described by another character, or even by himself. We may be given a dramatic characterization *showing* us the character in action; from that action we make our deductions as to his personality, background, and attitudes. Characters may be static as Mrs. May is, or may develop as William does, in "Mice and Birds and Boy." It is, of course, this static versus developing relationship which lies at the heart of the story, and which implements the contrasting effect of the setting at Mrs. May's house as well as in William's home where Mrs. May imagines one sort of life while William finds it considerably less attractive.

A character has two aspects: his inner responses, which are his feelings, his interests, and his thoughts; and the exterior manifestations of these responses, which are his activities. He is complete only when the interior forces and the exterior manifestations are logically related. Sometimes the physical characteristics are the more important, and sometimes the psychological characteristics are primary. Frequently they are interdependent, and the essential conflict of the plot depends upon which is the driving force and determining factor for the other.

In considering the total effect of any narrative, it is important to discover the focus of character, and to answer the question, "Whose story is it?" This is a particularly fascinating question in "Friends from Philadelphia." In a long work such as a novel the focus of character may shift from one episode to another. In most cases, however, there is a single character or a closely knit group, such as a family, on whom the center of attention is fixed throughout the progression of events. This focus of attention will help the interpreter establish the logic of events, keep the setting in its proper proportion, and show the other characters moving in and out of the spotlight as they affect the main character.

Although it is useful to examine setting and character as separate items, they cannot really be divorced. As soon as the interpreter puts the story back together, he is aware that the author, if he is skillful, has woven setting and character together in almost every instance. The interpreter's problem, then, becomes one of keeping the two in balance and putting the proper emphasis on whichever element the author has stressed. A good example of clarifying this relationship is found in the opening paragraph of "The Foghorn." Miss Atherton suggests much about the woman and her surroundings in just four sentences. In fact, each of the stories at the end of this chapter provides interesting examples of this all-important relationship between character and setting.

DIALOGUE

In our discussion of character, we gave most of our attention to the ways in which a writer might choose to reveal the physical and psychological aspects of his characters and their relationship to the setting and the plot. The interpreter needs to be aware of these techniques because he will use them in exactly the same way to make development and relationship clear to his listeners, since he assumes the same position with respect to them as the writer of narration does toward his readers. But in addition, the interpreter will encounter problems which demand special techniques of body and voice. One of the most common is the handling of dialogue.

Dialogue is almost always an integral part of a narrative. It is extremely useful in revealing what the writer wishes his readers to know. It provides variety by introducing different personalities and speech rhythms. It makes for vividness and aids in the delineation of character. Because it is fast-moving and condensed, it helps to speed the key situations along by eliminating the necessity for comment by the author. Certainly, then, dialogue is a convenient technique for the writer, but it is one that occasionally proves troublesome for the interpreter.

Dialogue may be in the form of direct or indirect discourse. Direct discourse is easily recognized because it is set off by quotation marks. The interpreter cannot depend upon this typographical device in communicating to his audience, however. Nor can he derive much help from dialogue tags, like "he said," for they do not always precede the speeches like warning bells; and even if they did, the effect would be monotonous, and the interpreter would have to consider cutting many of them. He must, then, use some other means of making it clear that a character is speaking. This he does by suggesting the personality of the character through skillful use of his body and voice and appropriate mental attitude.

In any piece of prose fiction it is necessary to give some thought to who is speaking to whom. In general, we may say that the third-person narrator speaks to the reader and hence through the interpreter directly to the audience. In first-person narration he may be speaking to the reader and also to other characters. In dialogue, on the other hand, the character is speaking to one or more other characters, frequently with an added comment by the narrator. Variations within these general categories will demand shifts in mental and physical directness as well as in projection. "Friends from Philadelphia" is largely direct discourse, and the interpreter must be very careful that its dramatic quality does not overshadow the simple, brief final sentences which are in third-person narration.

Dialogue depends to a large extent on an interchange of comments or questions and answers. Whenever one character is addressing another, the audience must be aware that the speech is being directed to someone. This requires a focus of attention on the part of the interpreter which must be both physical and mental. He may wish to re-create in his own mind the person being addressed and place that person somewhere in the audience for greater directness. This device may help the interpreter to feel and convey the illusion of direct address, but it may also embarrass the member of the audience who happens to occupy in the flesh that space in which the interpreter has placed the character. Hence it is better to establish the position of the character addressed somewhere on the back wall, between the heads of listeners and about shoulder level. This will help the interpreter to be sure that he is not appearing to single out any member of his audience, that his mental projection and his voice are strong enough to carry to the last row, and that he can differentiate between his role as narrator, when he includes the entire audience in his circle of concentration, and his role in presenting the speech of one character addressed to another. It might be helpful in this connection to review the material on projection in Chapter 4. When several characters are speaking in rapid succession, the interpreter may need to select a separate area of focus for each. This problem of focus of character will be developed in more detail in the section on drama, where it becomes a most essential technique.

Obviously, the degree of forcefulness intended will make a difference in the intensity of the physical and mental directness. If the speech is to carry great conviction or a suggestion of command, the eye contact will be sharply focused. If, however, the remark is more casual or of a general or reflective nature, it will be enough to locate the character addressed as to area, since in real-life situations one does not usually fix one's companions with a piercing and unwavering eye in ordinary conversation. It is important, however, to keep the mental focus sharp in order to give spontaneity and proper motivation for reply.

If the speech is intended to be shouted at someone, the interpreter must also take the matter of distance into consideration. It is probably neither necessary nor desirable to shout as loudly as one might in a comparable real-life situation, but some suggestion of distance must be given in the combined mental and vocal projection.

In addition to direct address, the writer of narrative commonly uses indirect discourse, either in the ordinary grammatical sense of the term, in such instances as "He said that . . ." and others like it, or in somewhat more complex instances, such as "He thought that . . . ," "She hoped that . . . ," "She remembered having heard him say that . . . ," and innumerable others.

When a character speaks directly, he is usually projecting to one or more persons who are present. His speech is prompted by an immediate situation or remark. In indirect discourse the degree of direct projection is less strong, or may be absent altogether, as in the case of thoughts, fears, and hopes which the character expresses to no one but himself. It must, however, be colored by the character's personality, his mental state, and the degree of reflection which is implied. For example, consider the incident of the stale chocolate in "Mice and Birds and Boy" when William imagines his mother saying "Curiosity killed the cat." Although this would be direct discourse in the narrowest definition, it functions as indirect discourse here, and carries William's state of mind at the moment and his memory of hearing this saying often from his mother. The abrupt change to direct discourse which ends this episode is also effective.

Frequently indirect discourse will be sharpened by an implication of activity to follow. In such a statement as "Finally he decided that he'd go and see for himself," there is a clear appeal to muscle response. This particular example also indicates a positive decision, which serves as a turning point from passivity to activity, from reflection to immediacy. The degree of suggestion will depend to some extent, of course, on whether the author has taken over as narrator or whether the revelation continues to be made through the character's consciousness.

The shift into direct discourse at the end of "The Foghorn" is most effective. Up to that point there has been only the stream-of-consciousness technique except for a single speech from the lover. Suddenly we are brought to reality by the doctor's "brisk and businesslike and deeply mature" voice answering the nurse's question. From that moment until the final sentence, the direct discourse is abrupt, factual, and swift.

Thus style is also an important consideration in getting at the interior qualities of a character. His choice of words and the way they are put together help reveal his background, attitude, and degree of mental and emotional tension under the circumstances of the moment.

Any specific directions for projecting character and dialogue to the audience can plunge both giver and receiver into extremely deep and dangerous waters. This section should not, therefore, be interpreted as a collection of mechanical rules or tricks for dividing characters into categories and then drawing upon the set of techniques which most neatly fits that category. All character suggestion must stem from the author's obvious intent. A writer of narrative will usually state his intentions more or less clearly, through what might be termed "stage directions." But to realize these intentions the interpreter will need to understand the whole story; focusing on the whole, he will see dialogue in its proper perspective as a means of advancing the movement of plot and the revelation of character, not as an excuse for a display of virtuosity on the platform.

Probably the first things to consider about a character who is speaking are his sex and maturity. The next step is to discover personal characteristics which establish him as an individual — his attitudes, his degree of emotional intensity at the moment, and any significant vocal and physical traits. Usually the writer will supply specific clues, either explicitly by describing how the speech was said or what state of mind prompted it, or implicitly through the character's mode of speech.

Often the oral presentation will profit by omission of some phrases and sentences which the author included as a guide to characterization. The interpreter may be able to suggest a state of mind by his voice and body and thus make the explanation unnecessary. Extreme care must be used, however, not to eliminate important information about background, thus obscuring the relationships among characters and the motivation of the plot.

It is usually wise to retain the dialogue tags until the character's individuality has been established. After this has been done, the interpreter may wish to eliminate most of the "he saids" and the accompanying stage directions. For instance, a trained interpreter might very well eliminate all but the direct address in " 'Push on the pedal,' Mr. Lutz sang, staring straight ahead and smiling, 'and away we go. And ah, ah, waay we go.' " The decision would rest on his ability to pick up Mr. Lutz's character and suggest his feeling of pride so that the "sang, staring straight ahead" clearly reflected his attitude at the moment.

As we have already said, these specific comments should be taken not as directives for interpreting dialogue but as guides for carrying out the author's intent in character suggestion through dialogue. If the interpreter does not understand the author's intent, or if he ignores it, he may be led into a display of his own versatility as an artist — and then, of course, he will be no artist at all. For instance, the interpreter might be tempted to exaggerate the childishness of the little boy in "Mice and Birds and Boy" or Mrs. May's advanced age to the point of caricature by too much vocal or physical technique. These excesses must be avoided for several reasons. The most important, of course, is that such exaggeration would call attention to itself and to the interpreter, and hence detract from the material. In the second place, while age is an important factor in the story, the child is not an infant, and Mrs. May is not completely senile. If she were, the story would lose most of its impact.

In the chapters on drama considerably more attention will be given to vocal and physical techniques to suggest age and sex as well as more individual aspects of character. For the moment, the interpreter should concentrate on communicating the mental attitude and degree of emotional tension which the author has indicated, rather than attempting to be specific about physical characteristics.

In general, then, the interpreter must use his body and voice skillfully and unobtrusively in handling dialogue, so that the audience will be immediately aware that a certain character is speaking instead of the author. Moreover, he must communicate the mental attitude and distinguishing traits of that character. It is impossible to attempt to set down rules for the vocal and physical projection of a character who displays any degree of complexity and individuality. The final decision rests on the requirements of the material and on the skill of the interpreter, who will be guided by the principle that it is his responsibility to *suggest* through dialogue, with sufficient clarity so that the audience can re-create both character and situation in their proper relationship.

CUTTING

Because of their brevity, most short stories need very little cutting. Mention has already been made of the possibility of eliminating some of the dialogue "tags" and "stage directions." Sometimes, of course, the interpreter may wish to use only a single key situation from a longer story. If so, he will usually need to tell his audience what takes place before the unit he is using so that they may pick up the story at the proper point of development. This is usually done most effectively by simply addressing them directly in one's own person and then taking up the thread of the story after the introductory remarks are completed.

The interpreter will not always wish to confine himself to short stories, however, for many longer narratives provide valuable and interesting material for an audience. Considerable abridgment is necessary in making a novel, a biography, or an autobiography suitable for oral presentation, since an audience will seldom be able to follow, mentally or physically, a performance which lasts longer than an hour. Thus the interpreter will need to limit his reading of a longer narrative to an abridgment of perhaps thirty or forty pages, depending upon his natural rate of reading and the requirements of the material.

If a novel is so constructed that he can choose a single climactic episode, he will analyze the excerpt as a unit just as though it were a short story. He must be sure, however, to take care of whatever background information is necessary to an understanding of the incident he has chosen. If the excerpt does not in itself have an adequate introduction, he can provide his audience with this information by summarizing in his own words what has gone before. The episode must, of course, have a point of climax.

If the interpreter wishes to use an abridgment of the entire novel, he will first of all find the focal point without which the narrative would not achieve its purpose. He will then analyze and treat the climactic episode in the same way as any other narrative. Any details not relevant to that climactic unit should be cut. The next step is to time the unit carefully, to be sure it is within the prescribed time limit. The material should always be read aloud with as much attention to proper pace and other factors of performance as possible. Returning to a consideration of the total effect desired by the author, the interpreter will then decide what scenes or background material and which key situations must precede the climactic incident. They may be condensed, if necessary, and should then be timed by reading aloud, with particular attention to balance and proportion. The same procedure holds for the preparation of the concluding units. Finally, the story must again be considered as a whole and a decision made as to which transitions must be included to keep the introduction, climax, and conclusion logically and emotionally related. These transitions may be handled entirely in the interpreter's own words, or they may be a condensation of the transitions given by the writer.

Frequently a long narrative will treat one or more sub-plots in addition to the main plot. The interpreter's decision to include or exclude these sub-plots will depend, first, upon the length of time he has for performance, and second, upon the effectiveness of the sub-plots in themselves and in their relation to the total effect. The same determinants will help him decide whether to eliminate any of the characters. It is usually wise, however, to keep the attention focused sharply on the main plot and on the principal characters involved in it.

All units to be eliminated should be clearly marked in such a way as to cause no difficulty in performance. If many pages are to be omitted, they should be clipped together. Transitions should be typed and clipped to the page preceding the next unit to be read. The interpreter need only remember that all marking should help him move smoothly through the printed material. As he gains experience, he will inevitably work out his own system of marking.

CHAMBER THEATRE

Although our concern in this chapter is primarily with the individual interpreter, some mention should be made of the relatively new method of handling narrative fiction called Chamber Theatre. It will be impossible to do more than touch on a few of the basic principles of this mode of performance here, but interpreters will find Chamber Theatre a useful, exciting area of group performance well worth investigating more fully.[1]

Earlier in this chapter, we noted that point of view is a basic consideration in Chamber Theatre. Indeed, since point of view controls and dictates the entire concept of a performance in this medium, Chamber Theatre has been defined as "a technique for dramatizing the point of view of narrative fiction."

In Dr. Breen's words, "The techniques of the Chamber Theatre were devised to present the novel, or narrative fiction, on the stage so that the dramatic action would unfold with full and vivid immediacy, as it does in a play, but at the same time allowing the sensibility of the narrator, or the central intelligence in the form of a character, to so condition our view of that action that we who listen and watch would receive a highly organized and unified impression of it."

The "dramatic action" of a piece of narration is, of course, made up of the dialogue and the discernible physical actions. These units are presented in dramatic form as if they were part of a play, with a separate "actor" for each character and appropriate but minimal properties, settings, and costumes. The characters move freely about the acting area. Their circle of concentration shifts from the scene created around them in direct discourse, during which they speak directly to each other and "play" together, to the audience area for much of the indirect discourse. Thus the dramatic devices of plot, character, action, dialogue, and climax "unfold with full and vivid immediacy."

The heart of Chamber Theatre, however, is the careful, intelligent use of the narrator through whom the author controls point of view. Not only does point of view govern the author's selectivity; it also conditions the listeners' responses to the characters and the action. When the narration is closely integrated with the action, there is an effect of simultaneity and a sharpening of motivation.

Care must be taken to use the narrator — whether he be an objective

[1] For an authoritative discussion of the intricacies and possibilities of Chamber Theatre, see *Chamber Theatre* by Robert S. Breen, scheduled for publication in 1966. I am indebted to Dr. Breen for many of the ideas presented here. The quotations are from his unpublished manuscript and are used with his permission.

observer speaking in the third person or a character involved in the action speaking in the first person — exactly as the author has used him, or in the case of some long novels, them. If the narrator is involved in the action, he takes his assigned role in the "dramatized" scene and moves in and out of it as the script indicates. If he is not so involved, he may move into the scene for some of his comments and then move out again, both physically and mentally, to address the audience directly. He must, of course, be careful to retain the person and tense used in the text as well as the proper attitude for the action which the audience observes as he speaks, or for which he is preparing them.

Chamber Theatre is *not* making a novel into a play. It is the presentation of a piece of fiction on stage *as it was written*, with the narrator fulfilling his proper function so that point of view is made to operate vividly as it controls action and response. "Chamber Theatre is dedicated to the proposition that the ideal literary experience is one in which the simultaneity of the drama, representing the illusion of actuality . . . be combined with the novel's privilege of examining human motivation at the moment of action."

SELECTIONS FOR ANALYSIS AND ORAL INTERPRETATION

ALL OF THE FOLLOWING stories require careful attention to the matters we have been discussing within the chapter. Each contains units which are brief enough to use for class work, but the interpreter should remember that any key situation must be considered in its relationship to the entire story.

THE POINT OF VIEW and style of this story were both touched on within the chapter. Give special attention to the varying degrees of indirect discourse. Be careful not to give away the ending, which requires careful control of balance.

The Foghorn

What an absurd vanity to sleep on a hard pillow and forego that last luxurious burrowing into the very depths of a mass of baby pillows! . . . her back was already as straight as — a chimney? . . . who was the Frenchman that said one must reject the worn counters? . . . but this morning she would have liked that sensuous burrowing, and the pillow had never seemed so hard, so flat . . . yet

From *The Foghorn* by Gertrude Atherton. Copyright 1934 by Gertrude Atherton, renewed © 1962 by Muriel Atherton Russel. Reprinted by permission of Houghton Mifflin Company.

how difficult it was to wake up! She had had the same experience once before when the doctor had given her veronal for insomnia . . . could Ellen, good creature, have put a tablet in the cup of broth she took last thing at night: "as a wise precaution," the doctor had said genially. What a curse insomnia was! But she had a congenital fear of drugs and had told no one of this renewal of sleeplessness, knowing it would pass.

And, after all, she didn't mind lying awake in the dark; she could think, oh, pleasant lovely thoughts, despite this inner perturbation — so cleverly concealed. How thankful she was to be tall enough to carry off the new fashion in sleeves! If trains would only come in again, she would dress her hair high some night (just for fun) and look — not like her beloved Mary Stuart, for Mary was almost ugly if one analyzed her too critically. Charm? How much more charm counted than mere beauty, and she herself had it "full measure and running over," as that rather fresh admirer had announced when drinking her health at her coming-out party . . . what was his name? . . . six years ago. He was only a college boy . . . how could one remember? There had been so many since.

Ninon de l'Enclos? She was passable in her portraits, but famous mainly for keeping young . . . Diane de Poictiers? She must have needed charm double-distilled if she looked anything like an original portrait of her hung at a loan exhibition in Paris: flaxen hair, thin and straight, drawn severely from a bulging brow above insufferably sensual eyes — far too obvious and "easy" for the fastidious male of today — a flaxen complexion, no high lights; not very intelligent. Interesting contrast in taste centuries apart — perhaps.

Madame Récamier? Better-looking than most of the historic beauties: hair piled high — but then she wore a slip of an Empire gown . . . well, never mind . . .

She ranked as a beauty herself, although perhaps charm had something to do with it. Her mouth was rather wide, but her teeth were exquisite. Something rather obscure was the matter in that region of brilliant enamel this morning. A toothache? She had never had a toothache. Well, there was no pain . . . what matter? . . . something wrong, though; she'd go to the dentist during the day. Her nose was a trifle tip-tilted, but very thin and straight, and anyhow the tilt suited the way she carried her head, "flung in the air." Her complexion and hair and eyes were beyond all cavil . . . she was nothing so commonplace as a downright blonde or brunette . . . how she should hate being catalogued! The warm, bright waving masses of her hair had never been cut since her second birthday. They, too, were made for burrowing.

Her mother's wedding dress had a long train. But the delicate ivory of the satin had waxed with time to a sickly yellow. Her mother hadn't pressed the matter when she was engaged to John St. Rogers, but she had always expressed a wish that each of her daughters should wear the dress to the altar. Well, she had refused outright, but had consented to have her own gown trimmed with the lace: yards and yards of *point d'Alençon* — and a veil that reached halfway down the train. What a way to spend money! Who cared for lace now? Not the young, anyhow. But Mother was rather a dear, and she could afford to be quite unselfish for once, as it certainly would be becoming. When the engagement was broken, they told the poor old darling that she cried because she would have another long wait before watching all that lace move up the aisle on a long slender figure that made her think pridefully of the graceful skeleton hidden within one hundred and seventy resented pounds.

Well, she would never wear that lace — nor any wedding gown. If she were lucky enough to marry at all, the less publicity the better . . . a mere announcement (San Francisco papers please copy) . . . a quiet return from Europe . . . a year or two in one of those impersonal New York apartment-houses where no one knew the name of his nextdoor neighbor . . . no effacement in a smaller city for her!

How strange that she of all girls should have fallen in love with a married man — or, at all events, accepted the dire consequences. With a father that had taken to drugs and then run off with another woman — luckily before Mother had come in for Granddad's fortune — and . . . what was it Uncle Ben had once said, queer twists in this family since "way back." It had made her more conventional than her natural instincts would have prompted; but, no, let her do herself justice: she had cultivated a high standard of character and planted her mind with flowers both sturdy and fair — that must have been the reason she had fallen in love at last, after so many futile attempts. No need for her to conceal from him the awful truth that she read the Greek and Latin classics in the original text, attended morning classes over at the University . . . odd, how men didn't mind if you "adored" music and pictures, but if they suspected you of being intellectual, they either despised or feared you, and faded away . . .

Fog on the Bay. Since childhood she had loved to hear that long-drawn-out, almost-human moan of the foghorn as she lay warm and sheltered in bed. It was on a night of fog they had spoken for the first time, although they had nodded at three or four formal dinners given to the newcomers who had brought letters to the elect. Bostonians were always popular in San Francisco; they had good manners and their formality was only skin-deep. The men were very smart; some of the women, too; but as a rule they lacked the meticulous grooming and well-set-up appearance of their men. She had been impressed the first time she had met him: six feet (she herself was five feet six), somewhere in the thirties, very spare, said to be a first-rate tennis player, and had ranked as an all-round athlete at Harvard; had inherited a piece of property in San Francisco which was involving him in litigation, but he was in no haste to leave, even before they met.

That had been at the Jeppers', and as the house commanded a fine view of the Bay, and she was tired of being torn from some man every time they circled the ballroom, she had managed to slip away and had hidden behind the curtains of the deep bow window at the end of the hall. In a moment she was aware that someone had followed her, and oddly enough she knew who it was, although she didn't turn her head; and they stood in silence and gazed together at the sharp dark outlines of the mountains on the far side of the Bay; the glittering spheroids of golden light that were ferryboats, the islands with their firm, bold outlines, now almost visibly drooping in slumber . . . although there always seemed to her to be an atmosphere of unrest about Alcatraz, psychic emanation of imprisoned men under rigid military rule, and officials no doubt as resentful in that dull monotonous existence on a barren rock . . . A light flickered along a line of barred upper windows; doubtless a guard on his round . . .

The band of pulsing light on the eastern side of the Bay: music made visible . . . stars as yellow and bright above, defying the thin silver of the hebetic moon . . . lights twinkling on Sausalito opposite, standing out boldly from the black mass of Tamalpais high-flung above. Her roving eyes moved to the Golden Gate, narrow entrance between two crouching forts, separating that harbor of arrogant beauty from the gray waste of the Pacific — ponderous, rather stupid old ocean . . .

For the first time he spoke: "The fog! Chief of San Francisco's many beauties."

She had nodded, making no other reply, watching that dense yet imponderable white mass push its way through the Golden Gate like a laboring ship . . . then riding the waters more lightly, rolling a little, writhing, whiffs breaking from the bulk of that ghostly ship to explore the hollows of the hills, resting there like puffs of white smoke. Then, over the cliffs and heights on the northern side of the Bay, a swifter, more formless, but still lovely white visitant that swirled down and over the inland waters, enshrouding the islands, Sausalito, where so many Englishmen lived, the fulgent zone in the east; but a low fog — the moon and stars still visible . . . the foghorns, one after another, sending forth their long-drawn-out moans of utter desolation . . .

With nothing more to look at, they had seated themselves on a small sofa, placed there for reticent couples, and talked for an hour — a desultory exploring conversation. She recalled none of it. A few mornings later they had met on the Berkeley ferryboat, accidentally no doubt, and he had gone on with her in the train and as far as the campus . . . Once again. . . . After that, when the lecture was over, in the Greek Theatre . . . wonderful hours . . . how easy to imagine themselves in Greece of the fifth century B.C., alone in that vast gray amphitheatre, the slim, straight tenebrous trees above quivering with the melody of birds!

Never a word of love — not for months. This novel and exciting companionship was enough . . . depths of personality to explore — in glimpses! Sometimes they roamed over the hills, gay and care-free. They never met anyone they knew.

Winter. Weeks of pouring rain. They met in picture galleries, remote corners of the Public Library, obscure restaurants of Little Italy under the shadow of Telegraph Hill. Again they were unseen, undiscovered.

He never came to the house. Since her mother's death and the early marriages of the girls, Uncle Ben had come to live with her in the old house on Russian Hill; the boys were East at school; she was free of all family restrictions, but her old servants were intimate with all the other servants on the Hill. She barely knew his wife. He never spoke of her.

Spring. A house-party in the country, warm and dry after the last of the rains. After dinner they had sat about on the terraces, smoking, drinking, listening to a group singing within, admiring the "ruins" of a Roman temple at the foot of the lawn lit by a blazing moon.

He and she had wandered off the terrace, and up an almost perpendicular flight of steps on the side of the mountain that rose behind the house . . . dim aisles of redwoods, born when the earth was young, whose long trunks never swayed, whose high branches rarely sang in the wind — unfriendly trees, but protective, sentinel-like, shutting out the modern world; reminiscent were those closely planted aisles of ancient races . . . forgotten races . . . god-like races, perhaps.

Well, they had felt like gods that night. How senseless to try to stave off a declaration of love . . . to fear . . . to wonder . . . to worry . . . How inevitable . . . natural . . . when it came! Hour of hours . . .

They had met the next day in a corner of their favorite little restaurant, over a dish of spaghetti, which she refused to eat as it had liver in it, and talked the matter out. No, she would not enter upon a secret intrigue; meeting him in some shady quarter of the town, where no questions were asked, in some horrible room which had sheltered thousands of furtive "lovers" before them . . . she would far rather never see him again . . . He had smiled at the flight taken by an untrained imagination, but nodded. . . . No, but she knew the alternative. He had no intention of giving her up. No hope of a divorce. He had sounded his wife; tentatively at first, then told her outright he loved another woman. She had replied that he could expect no legal release from her. It was her chance for revenge and she would take it. . . . A week or two and his business in San Francisco would be settled . . . he had an independent fortune . . . would she run away with him? Elope in good old style? Could she stand the gaff? All Europe for a perpetual honeymoon

— unless his wife were persuaded by her family later on to divorce him. Then he would return and work at something. He was not a born idler.

She had consented, of course, having made up her mind before they met. She had had six years of "the world." She knew what she wanted. One might "love" many times, but not more than once find completion, that solidarity which makes two as one against the malignant forces of life. She had no one to consider but herself. Her mother was dead. Her sisters, protected by husbands, wealth, position, would merely be "thrilled." The boys and Uncle Ben, of course, would be furious. Men were so hopelessly conservative.

For the rest of the world she cared exactly nothing.

That foghorn. What was it trying to tell her? A boat . . . fog . . . why was it so hard to remember? So hard to awaken? Ellen must have given her an overdose. Fragmentary pictures . . . slipping down the dark hill to the wharf . . . her low delighted laugh echoed back to her as he helped her into the boat . . . one more secret lark before they flung down the gage. . . . How magnificently he rowed . . . long, sweeping, easy strokes as he smiled possessively into her eyes and talked of the future. . . . No moon, but millions of stars that shed a misty golden light . . . rows of light on the steep hillsides of the city. The houses dark and silent . . . a burst of music from Fort Mason . . .

Out through the Golden Gate, still daring . . . riding that oily swell . . . his chuckle as she dared him to row straight across to China . . . Her sharp anxious cry as she half-rose from her seat and pointed to a racing mountain of snow-white mist.

He had swept about at once and made for the beach below Sutro Heights. Too late. Almost as he turned, they were engulfed. Even an old fisherman would have lost his sense of direction.

And then the foghorns began their warnings. The low, menacing roar from Point Bonito. The wailing siren on Alcatraz. Sausalito's throaty bass. The deep-toned bell on Angel Island. She knew them all, but they seemed to come from new directions.

A second . . . a moment . . . an hour . . . later . . . a foreign but unmistakable note. Ships — two of them. . . . Blast and counterblast. . . . She could barely see his white rigid face through the mist as he thrust his head this way and that trying to locate those sounds. . . . Another abrupt swerve . . . crash . . . shouts . . . her own voice shrieking as she saw his head almost severed — the very fog turned red . . .

She could hear herself screaming yet. It seemed to her that she had been screaming since the beginning of time.

She sat up in bed, clasping her head between her hands, and rocked to and fro. This bare small room, just visible in the gray dawn. . . . She was in a hospital, of course. Was it last night or the night before they had brought her here? She wondered vaguely that she felt no inclination to scream any more, now that she had struggled to full consciousness. . . . Too tired, perhaps . . . the indifference of exhaustion. . . . Even her eyes felt singularly dry, as if they had been baked in a hot oven. She recalled a line, the only memorable line, in Edwin Arnold's "Light of Asia," "Eyepits red with rust of ancient tears." . . . Did her eyes look like that? But she did not remember crying . . . only screaming . . .

Odd that she should be left alone like this. Uncle Ben and the girls must have been summoned. If they had gone home, tired out, they should have left a nurse in constant attendance . . . and surely they might have found her a better room. . . . Or had she been carried into some emergency hospital? . . . Well, she could go home today.

Her hands were still clasping her head when another leaf of awareness turned over, rattling like parchment. Hair. Her lovely abundant hair. . . . She held her breath as her hands moved exploringly over her head. Harsh short bristles almost scratched them.

She had had brain fever, then. Ill a long time . . . weeks . . . months, perhaps. . . . No wonder she felt weak and spent and indifferent! But she must be out of danger, or they would not leave her like this. . . . Would she suffer later, with renewed mocking strength? Or could love be burnt out, devoured by fever germs? A short time before, while not yet fully conscious, she had relived all the old hopes, fears, dreams, ecstasies; reached out triumphantly to a wondrous future, arrogantly sure of herself and the man, contemptuous of the world and its makeshift conventions. . . . And now she felt nothing . . .

But when she was well again? Twenty-four! Forty, fifty, years more; they were a long-lived family. Her mother had been killed at a railroad crossing. . . . Well, she had always prided herself on her strength. She would worry through the years somehow.

Had the town rung with the scandal when the newspapers flared forth next morning? No girl goes rowing at night with a married man unless there is something between them. Had his wife babbled? Were the self-righteous getting off the orthodoxies of their kind? Punished for their sin. Retributive justice meted out to a girl who would break up a home and take a married man for her lover.

Retributive justice! As if there were any such thing in life as justice. All helpless victims of the law of cause and effect. Futile, aspiring, stupidly confident links in the inexorable chain of Circumstance. . . . Commonplace minds croaking, "Like father like daughter." . . .

How she hated, hated, *hated*, self-righteousness, smug hypocrisy . . . illogical minds — one sheep bleating like another sheep — not one of them with the imagination to guess that she never would have stooped to a low secret intrigue . . .

She had been pounding her knee with her fist in a sudden access of energy. As it sputtered out and she felt on the verge of collapse, her hand unfolded and lay palm down on the quilt. . . . She felt her eyes bulging. . . . She uttered her first sound: a low almost inarticulate cry.

Her hand? That large-veined, skinny thing? She had beautiful long white hands, with skin as smooth as the breast of a dove. Of no one of her beauty's many parts had she been prouder, not even when she stood now and then before the cheval glass and looked critically, and admiringly, at the smooth, white, rounded perfection of her body. She had given them a golden manicure set on one of their birthdays, a just tribute; and they were exquisitely kept, although she hated conspicuous nails. . . .

A delusion? A nightmare? She spread the other hand beside it . . . side by side the two on the dingy counterpane . . . old hands . . . Shorn hair will grow again . . . but hands . . .

Mumbling. Why mumbling? She raised one of those withered yellow hands to her mouth. It was empty. Her shaking fingers unbuttoned the high nightgown, and she glanced within. Pendant dugs, brown and shriveled.

Brain fever! The sun had risen. She looked up at the high barred window. She understood.

Voices at the door. She dropped back on the pillow and closed her eyes and lay still. The door was unlocked, and a man and woman entered: doctor and nurse, as was immediately evident. The doctor's voice was brisk and business-like and deeply mature; the woman's, young and deferential.

"Do you think she'll wake again, doctor?"

"Probably not. I thought she would be gone by now, but she is still breathing." He clasped the emaciated wrist with his strong fingers. "Very feeble. It won't be long now."

"Is it true, doctor, that sometimes, just before death, reason is restored and they remember and talk quite rationally?"

"Sometimes. But not for this case. Too many years. Look in every hour, and when it is over, ring me up. There are relatives to be notified. Quite important people, I believe."

"What are they like?"

"Never seen them. The law firm in charge of her estate pays the bills. Why should they come here? Couldn't do her any good, and nothing is so depressing as these melancholia cases. It's a long time now since she was stark raving. That was before my time. Come along. Six wards after this one . . . Don't forget to look in. Good little girl. I know you never forget."

They went out and locked the door.

GERTRUDE ATHERTON

OPENING AS IT DOES on a speech from William, this story demands a careful analysis of the young boy's attitude toward the old lady. Remember that he is a character in his own right and must not become a stereotype.

His individuality is very important to the relationship upon which the story turns.

Mice and Birds and Boy

"Was this when you were pretty?" William asked, holding the photograph in both hands and raising his eyes to the old lady's with a look of near certainty.

"I was thought to be beautiful," she said; and she wondered, How long ago was that? Who had been the last person to comment upon her beauty, and how many years ago? She thought that it might have been her late husband, from loyalty or from still seeing what was no longer there. He had been dead for over twenty years and her beauty had not, by any means, been the burden of his dying words.

The photograph had faded to a pale coffee color, but William could distinguish a cloud of fair hair, a rounded face with lace at the chin, and the drooping, sad mouth so many beautiful women have. Poor Mrs. May, he thought.

The photographs were all jumbled up in a carved sandalwood box lined with dusty felt. There was a large one, mounted on stiff cardboard, of the big house where Mrs. May had lived as a child. It had been pulled down between the wars, and on its grounds was built a housing estate, a row of small shops by the bus stop, and a children's playground, with swings and slides. William could look out of the narrow window of the old gardener's lodge where Mrs. May lived now and watch the shrieking toddlers climbing the frames, swinging on the swings. He never went to the playground himself now that he was six.

"It was all fields," Mrs. May would often say, following his glance. "All fields and parkland. I used to ride my pony over it. It was a different world. We had two grooms and seven indoor servants and four gardeners. Yet we were just ordinary people. Everybody had such things in those days."

"Did every child have a pony?" William asked.

"All *country* children had one," she said firmly.

His curiosity endeared him to her. It was so long since anyone had asked her a question and been interested in the answer. His curiosity had been the beginning of their friendship. Going out into her overgrown little garden one afternoon, she had found him leaning against the rickety fence, staring at her house, which was round in shape and had attracted his attention. It was made of dark flint and had narrow, arched windows and an arched door studded with big square-headed nails. A high twisted chimney stack rose from the center of the roof. Surrounded by the looped and tangled growth of the garden — rusty, black-leaved briars and crooked

Mice and Birds and Boy by Elizabeth Taylor. Copyright © 1963 by The New Yorker Magazine, Inc. Reprinted by permission of Brandt & Brandt.

apple trees — the place looked as menacing as an Arthur Rackham drawing, he thought. Then the door had opened and the witch herself had come out, leaning on a stick. She had untidy white hair and a face crosshatched with wrinkles; but her eyes weren't witch-like, not black and beady and evil but large and milky blue and kind, though crows had trodden about them.

"How can your house be round inside?" William asked, in his high, clear voice. She looked about her and then saw his red jersey through the fence and, above it, his bright face with its straight fringe of hair. "How can rooms be round?" he asked. He came up to the broken gate and stood there.

Beyond a row of old elm trees which hid the lodge from the main road, a double-decker bus went by, taking the women from the estate to Market Swanford for their afternoon's shopping. When it had gone, William turned back to the old lady and said, "Or are they like this shape?" He made a wedge with his hands.

"You had better come and see," she said.

He opened the gate at once and went in. She might pop me into the oven, he thought.

One room was half a circle, the other two were quarters. All three were dark and crammed with furniture. A mouse streaked across the kitchen floor. The sink was stacked with dirty china, the table littered with odds and ends of food in torn paper wrappings.

"Do you live here alone?" he asked.

"Except for the mice; but I should prefer to be alone."

"You are more like a hermit than a witch."

"And should prefer to be," she said.

He examined a dish of stewed fruit which had a greenish-gray mantling of mold.

"Pooh! It smells like beer," he said.

"I meant to throw it away, but it seemed such a criminal waste when the natives are starving everywhere."

In the sitting room, with frail and shaking hands, she offered to him a chocolate box; there was one chocolate left. It was stale and had a bloom on it, and might be poisoned, he thought, but he took it politely and turned it about in his mouth. It was very hard and tasted musty. "Curiosity killed the cat," his mother would say when his body was discovered.

Mrs. May began then to tell him about the fields and park and her pony. He felt drowsy and wondered if the poison was taking effect. She had such a beautiful voice — wavering, floating — that he could not believe in his heart that she would do him any harm. The room was airless and he sat in a little spoon-shaped velvet chair and stared up at her, listening to a little of her story, here and there. Living alone, except for the mice, she had no one to blame her when she spilled egg and tea down her front, he supposed; and she had taken full advantage of her freedom. She was really very dirty, he decided dispassionately. But smelled nice. She had the cozy smell that he liked so much about his guinea pigs — a warm, stuffy, old smell.

"I'd better go," he said suddenly. "I might come back again tomorrow."

She seemed to understand at once, but like all grown-up people was compelled to prolong the leave-taking a little. He answered her questions briefly, anxious to be off once he had made up his mind to go.

"There," he said, pointing up the hill. "My house is there." The gilt weather vane, veering round, glittered in the sun above the slate roofs.

"Our old stables," Mrs. May said quite excitedly. "Oh, the memories."

He shut the gate and sauntered off, between piles of bricks and tiles on the site where more houses were being built. Some trees had been left standing, looking strange upon the scarred, untidy landscape. William walked around the foundations of a little house, stood in the middle of a rectangle, and tried to imagine a family sitting at a table in the middle of it, but it seemed far too small. The walls were only three bricks high. He walked round them, on the top of the bricks, one foot before the other, his arms lifted to keep his balance. Some workmen shouted at him. They were tiling the roof of a nearby house. He took no notice, made a completed round of the walls, and then walked off across the rough grass, where Mrs. May had ridden her pony when she was a little girl.

"Do you *hear* me?" his mother said again, her voice shrill with anxiety and vexation. She even took William's shoulder and shook him. "You are *not* to talk to strangers."

His sister, Jennifer, who was ballet-mad, practiced an arabesque and watched the scene without interest, her mind on her own schemes.

William looked gravely at his mother, rubbing his shoulder.

"Do you understand?"

He nodded.

"That's right, remember what your mother told you," his father said, for the sake of peace.

The next morning, William took a piece of cheese from the larder and a penknife and went to the building site. His mother was having an Italian lesson. Some of the workmen were sitting against a wall in the sun, drinking tea and eating bread and cheese, and William sat down amongst them, settling himself comfortably with his back against the wall. He cut pieces of cheese against his thumb as the others did and popped them neatly into his mouth. They drew him into solemn conversation, winking at one another above his head. He answered them politely, but knew that they were making fun of him. One wag, going too far, grimacing too obviously, asked, "And what is your considered opinion of the present emergency?"

"I don't know," William replied, and he got up and walked away — more in sorrow than in anger, he tried to convey.

He lingered for a while, watching a bulldozer going over the uneven ground, opening wounds in the fields where Mrs. May had ridden her pony; then he wandered on toward the main road. Mrs. May came out to her front doorstep and dropped an apronful of crumbs onto the path. Thrushes and starlings descended about her.

"So you're back again," she called. "I am shortly off to the shops. It will be nice to have a boy go with me." She went inside, untying her apron.

He tried to swing on the gate, but it was lopsided. When she came out after a long time, she was wearing a torn raincoat, although it was quite hot already. It had no buttons and hung open. Her dirty jersey was held to her flat chest with rows of jet beads.

William noted that they were much stared at as they passed the bus queue and, in the butcher's shop, Mrs. May was the subject of the same knowing looks and gravely kept straight faces that he himself had suffered from the builders. He felt, uncomfortably, that this behavior was something that children came to expect but that an older person should neither expect nor tolerate. He could not find words to explain his keen uneasiness on Mrs. May's account.

He watched the butcher unhook a drab piece of liver, slap it on the counter, and cut off a slice.

"When I think of the saddles of mutton, the suckling pigs . . ." said Mrs. May vaguely, counting out coppers.

"Yes, I expect so," said the butcher's wife, with a straight face turned toward her husband.

Outside the shop, Mrs. May continued the list. "And ribs of beef, green goose at Michaelmas," she chattered on to herself, going past the dairy, the grocer's, the draper's with quick herringbone steps. William caught glimpses of themselves reflected in the shopwindows, against a pyramid of syrup tins, then a bolt of sprigged cotton.

"And what are *you* going to tell *me*?" Mrs. May suddenly asked. "I can't do all the entertaining, you know. Are you quite warm up there in the stables? Have you beds and chairs and all you need?"

"We have even more beds than we need."

"Well, don't ask me to imagine it, because I can't. Shall we turn back? I'll buy an egg at the dairy, and I might get some stale bread for the birds. 'My only friends,' I say to them, as they come to greet me."

"You have the mice as well."

"I can't make friends with mice. The mice get on my nerves, as a matter of fact."

"You could get a cat," he suggested.

"And seem more like a witch than ever?"

There appeared to be no stale bread at the baker's. At sight of Mrs. May, the woman behind the counter seemed to shutter her face, stood waiting with lowered eyes for them to go.

When they reached Mrs. May's broken gate — with only the slice of meat and the egg — William would not go in. He ran home as fast as he could over the uneven ground, his heart banging, his throat aching.

When he reached it, the house was quiet and a strange, spicy smell he could not identify came from the kitchen. His mother, in addition to her Italian lessons, had taken up Japanese cooking. His sister, returning from ballet class, with her shoes hanging from her neck by their ribbons, found him lying on the floor pushing a toy car back and forth. Her suspicions were roused, for he was pretending to be playing, she was convinced, with an almost cross-eyed effort at concentration. He began to hum unconcernedly. Jennifer's nose wrinkled. "It smells as if we're going to have that horrid soup with stalks in it."

"I like it," he murmured.

"You would. What have you been doing, anyway?"

Still wearing her coat, she practiced a few *pliés*.

Never waste a moment, he thought. "Nothing."

But she was not interested in him; had been once — long ago, it seemed to her, when his birth, she had hoped, would brighten up the house. The novelty of him had soon worn off.

"The death duties," Mrs. May explained. Because of them, she could not light a fire until the really chilly days and sometimes had only an egg to eat all day. These death duties William thought of as moral obligations which both her father and husband had insisted on discharging while dying — some charitable undertakings, plainly not approved of by Mrs. May. He was only puzzled by the varying effect of this upon her day-to-day life; sometimes she was miserably conscious of her poverty, but at other times she bought peppermint creams for herself and William and digestive biscuits for the birds.

Every time she opened or shut the garden gate she explained how she would have had it mended if it were not for the death duties. *The* death duties made them sound a normal sort of procedure, a fairly usual change of heart brought about perhaps by the approach of death and clearly happening not only in Mrs. May's family.

The days were beginning to grow chilly, too chilly to be without a fire. The leaves on the great chestnut trees about the building site turned yellow and fell. William went back to school and called on Mrs. May on Saturday mornings. He did not miss her. His life was suddenly very full, and some weeks he did not go at all and she fretted for him, watching from a window like a lovesick girl, postponing her visit to the shops. She missed not only him but her glimpses — from his conversation — of the strange life going on up in the old stables. His descriptions — in answer to her questions — and what she read into them formed a bewildering picture. She imagined the family sitting round the bench in the old harness room, drinking a thin soup with blades of grass in it — the brisk mother, the gentle, dreamy father, and an objectionable little girl who kept getting down from the frugal meal to practice *pas de chats* across the old, broken brick floor. She had built the scene from his phrases — "My mother will be cross if I'm late" (more polite, he thought, than "My mother will be cross if she knows I came to see you") and "My father wouldn't mind." His sister, it seemed, complained about the soup; apart from this, she only talked of Margot Fonteyn. But confusions came into it — in William's helping to clean silver for a dinner party and having been sent to bed early for spilling ink on a carpet. Silver and carpets were hard to imagine as part of the old stables.

She had forgotten what a family was like, and had never had much chance of learning — only child and childless wife. William was too young to be a satisfactory informant. He was haphazardly selective, interested too much in his own separate affairs, unobservant and forgetful of the adult world; yet she managed to piece something together and it had slowly grown — a continuous story, without direction or catharsis — but could no longer grow if he were not to visit her.

Holding the curtains, her frail hands shook. When he did come, he was enticed to return. On those mornings now, there were always sweets. But her questions tired him, as they tire and antagonize all children, who begin to feel uneasily in the wrong role. He had by now satisfied his curiosity about her and was content to let what he did not understand — the death duties, for instance — lie at peace.

"You shall have this when I'm gone," she began to say, closing the lid of the sandalwood box in which she kept the old photographs. Also promised was her father's sword and scabbard, in which William was more interested, and a stuffed parrot called Bertha — once a childhood pet and still talked to as if no change had taken place.

One morning, she saw him playing on the building site and went out to the gate and called to him, lured him into the garden and then the house with witchlike tactics, sat him down on the spoon-shaped chair, and gave him a bag of sweets.

"And how is your mother?" she inquired. She had a feeling that she detested the woman. William nodded absent-mindedly, poking about in the sweets bag. His hair was like gold silk, she thought.

"People have always lost patience with me," she said, feeling his attention wandering from her. "I only had my beauty."

She was going on to describe how her husband's attention had also wandered, then thought it perhaps an unsuitable subject to discuss with a child. She had never discussed it with anyone else. Such a vague marriage, and her memories of it were vague, too — seemed farther away than her childhood.

A mouse gnawed with a delicate sound in the wainscot and William turned his gaze toward it, waiting for the minutes to pass until the time when he could rise politely from the dusty chair and say goodbye.

If only he would tell me, Mrs. May thought in despair. Tell me what there was for breakfast, for instance, and who said what and who went where, so that I could have something to think about in the evening.

"Oh, well, the winter will come if it means to," she said aloud. Rain had swept in a gust upon the window, as if cast upon the little panes in spite. "Nothing we can do can stop it. Only dig in and make ourselves comfortable — roast chestnuts on my little coal shovel." William glanced from the wainscot to the empty grate, but Mrs. May seemed not to see its emptiness. "Once, when I had a *nice* governess, we roasted some over the schoolroom fire. But the next governess would never let me do anything that pleased me. 'Want must be your master,' she said. She had many low phrases of that kind. Yes, want must be your master," she said again, and sighed.

The visit was running down and her visitor simply sitting there until he could go. Courageously, when he had refused another peppermint cream and showed that he did not want to see again the photograph of her home, she released him; she even urged him to go, speeding him on his way, and watched him from the open door, her hands clasped close to her flat chest. He was like a most beloved caged bird that she had set at liberty. She felt regret and yet a sense of triumph, seeing him go.

She returned to the room and looked dully at the stuffed parrot, feeling a little like crying, but she had been brought up not to do so. "Yes, want must be your master, Bertha," she said, in a soft but serene voice.

"I can't see harm in it," William's father told his wife. Jennifer had seen William leaving Mrs. May's and hurried to tell her mother, who began complaining the moment her husband returned for lunch.

"She's stark, staring mad and the place is filthy; everybody says so."

"Children sometimes see what we can't."

"I don't know what you mean by that. I forbade him to go there and he repeatedly disobeyed me. You should speak to him."

So his father spoke to William — rather offhandedly, over his shoulder, while hanging his coat up in the hall, as William passed through.

To be reprimanded for what he had not wanted to do, for what he looked on as a duty, did not vex William. It was the kind of thing that happened to him a great deal, and he let it go, rather than tie himself up in explanations.

"You did hear what I said?" his father asked.

"Yes, I heard."

"Your mother has her reasons. You can leave it at that."

It happened that he obeyed his parents. His father, one day, passing Mrs. May's garden, came on her feeding her birds there. He raised his hat and saw, as she glanced up, her ruined face, bewildered eyes, and was stirred by pity as he walked on.

As the nights grew colder, Mrs. May was forced to light a fire, and she wandered about the building site collecting sawed-off pieces of batten and wood shavings. She met William there once, playing with another boy. He returned her greeting, answered her questions unwillingly, knowing that his companion had ducked his head, trying to hide a smile. When she had wandered on at last, there were more questions from his friend. "Oh, she's only an old witch I know," he replied.

The truth was that he could hardly remember how once he had liked to go to see her. Then he tired of her stories about her childhood, grew bored with her photographs, became embarrassed by her, and realized, in an adult way, that the little house was filthy. One afternoon, on his way home from school, he had seen her coming out of the butcher's shop ahead of him and had slackened his pace, almost walked backward not to overtake her.

She was alone again, except for the birds in the daytime, the mice at night. The deep winter came and the birds grew fewer and the mice increased. The cold-weather birds, double their summer size, hopped dottily about the crisp, rimed grass, jabbing their beaks into frozen puddles, bewildered as refugees. Out she hurried, first thing in the mornings, to break the ice and scatter crumbs. She found a dead thrush and grieved over it. "Oh, Bertha, one of ours," she mourned.

Deep snow came and she was quite cut off — the garden was full of strange shapes, as if heaped with pillows and bolsters, and the birds made their dagger tracks across the drifts. She could not open her door.

Seeing the untrodden path, William's father, passing by, went to borrow a shovel from the nearest house and cleared the snow from the gateway to the door. He saw her watching from a window, and when at last she could, she opened the door to thank him.

"I'm afraid I don't know who you are," she began.

"I live in the old stables up on the hill."

"Then I know your little boy. He used to visit me. It was very kind of you to come to my rescue."

William's father returned the shovel and then walked home, feeling sad and ashamed. "Oh dear, that house," he said to his wife. "It is quite filthy — what I glimpsed of it. You were perfectly right. Someone ought to do something to help her."

"She should help herself. She must have plenty of money. All this building land."

"I think she misses William."

"It was just a passing thing," said his wife, who was a great one herself for passing things. "He simply lost interest."

"Lost innocence, perhaps. The truth is, I suppose, that children grow up and begin to lose their simple vision."

"The truth is," she said tartly, "that if people don't wash themselves they go unloved." Her voice was cold and disdainful. She had summed up many other lives than Mrs. May's and knew the tone to use.

The thaw began, then froze in buds upon the red twigs of the dogwood in Mrs. May's untidy hedge. The hardening snow was pitted with drips from the branches.

Mrs. May was afraid to venture on her frozen path beyond her doorway, and threw her remaining bits of bread from there. There was no one to run an errand for her. The cold drove her inside, but she kept going to the window to see if the ice was melting. Instead, the sky darkened. Both sky and earth were iron.

"It's my old bones," she said to Bertha. "I'm afraid for my old bones."

Then she saw William running and sliding on the ice, his red scarf, his cheeks bright. He fell, and scrambled up, laughing.

"It's falling I'm afraid of," Mrs. May whispered to the windowpane. "My old bones are too brittle."

She went to the front door and opened it. Standing shivering on the step, she called to William. He seemed not to hear and she tried to raise her voice. He took a run and, with his arms flung up above his head, slithered across a patch of ice. He shouted to someone out of sight and dashed forward.

Mrs. May shut the door again. "Someone will come," she told Bertha briskly. She straightened her father's sword, suspended above the fireplace, and bustled about, trying to make the room ready for an unknown visitor. "There's no knowing what might happen. Anyone might call," she murmured.

ELIZABETH TAYLOR

MAKE A CAREFUL STUDY of point of view here as well as motivation for the telling of the parable. The ending will require careful balance. The text is from the King James Bible.

from *The New Testament*

St. Luke 10: 25–38

And, behold, a certain lawyer stood up, and tempted him, saying, Master, what shall I do to inherit eternal life? He said unto him, What is written in the law? how readest thou? And he answering said, Thou shalt love the Lord thy God with all thy heart, and with all thy soul, and with all thy strength, and with all thy mind; and thy neighbor as thyself. And he said unto him, Thou hast answered right: this do, and thou shalt live. But he, willing to justify himself, said unto Jesus, And who is my neighbor?

And Jesus answering said, A certain man went down from Jerusalem to Jericho, and fell among thieves, which stripped him of his raiment, and wounded him, and departed, leaving him half dead. And by chance there came down a certain priest that way; and when he saw him, he passed by on the other side. And likewise a Levite, when he was at the place, came and looked on him, and passed by on the other side.

But a certain Samaritan, as he journeyed, came where he was; and when he saw him, he had compassion on him, And went to him, and bound up his wounds, pouring in oil and wine, and set him on his own beast, and brought him to an inn, and took care of him. And on the morrow when he departed, he took out two pence, and gave them to the host, and said unto him, Take care of him: and whatsoever thou spendest more, when I come again, I will repay thee. Which now of these three, thinkest thou, was neighbor unto him that fell among the thieves? And he said, He that showed mercy on him. Then said Jesus unto him, Go, and do thou likewise.

Be sure you understand the reason for including the name and vintage year of the wine. The climax will take careful handling to maintain balance and proportion.

Friends from Philadelphia

In the moment before the door was opened to him, he glimpsed her thigh below the half-drawn shade. Thelma was home, then. She was wearing the Camp Winniwoho T shirt and her quite short shorts.

"Why, my goodness: Janny!" she cried. She always pronounced his name, John, to rhyme with Ann. Earlier that vacation, she had visited in New York City, and tried to talk the way she thought they talked there. "What on earth ever brings you to me at this odd hour?"

"Hello, Thel," he said. "I hope — I guess this is a pretty bad time." She had been plucking her eyebrows again. He wished she wouldn't do that.

Thelma extended her arm and touched her fingers to the base of John's neck. It wasn't a fond gesture, just a hostesslike one. "Now, Janny. You know that I — my mother and I — are always happy to be seeing you. Mother, who do you ever guess is here at this odd hour?"

"Don't keep John Nordholm standing there," Mrs. Lutz said. Thelma's mother was settled in the deep red settee watching tele-

Copyright, 1954 by John Updike, "Friends from Philadelphia" first appeared in The New Yorker. Reprinted from *The Same Door* by John Updike, by permission of Alfred A. Knopf, Inc.

vision and smoking. A coffee cup being used as an ashtray lay in her lap, and her dress was hiked up so that her knees showed.

"Hello, Mrs. Lutz," John said, trying not to look at her broad, pale knees. "I really hate to bother you at this odd hour."

"I don't see anything odd about it." She took a deep-throated drag on her cigarette and exhaled through her nostrils, the way men do. "Some of the other kids were here earlier this afternoon."

"I would have come in if anybody had told me."

Thelma said, "Oh, Janny! Stop trying to make a martyr of yourself. Keep in touch, they say, if you want to keep up."

He felt his face grow hot and knew he was blushing, which made him blush all the more. Mrs. Lutz shook a wrinkled pack of Herbert Tareytons at him. "Smoke?" she said.

"I guess not, thanks a lot."

"You've stopped? It's a bad habit. I wish I had stopped at your age. I'm not sure I even *begun* at your age."

"No, it's just that I have to go home soon, and my mother would smell the smoke on my breath. She can smell it even through chewing gum."

"Why must you go home soon?" Thelma asked.

Mrs. Lutz sniffled. "I have sinus. I can't even smell the flowers in the garden or the food on the table any more. Let the kids smoke if they want, if it makes them feel better. I don't care. My Thelma, she can smoke right in her own home, her own living room, if she wants to. But she doesn't seem to have the taste for it. I'm just as glad, to tell the truth."

John hated interrupting, but it was close to five-thirty. "I have a problem," he said.

"A problem — how gruesome," Thelma said. "And here I thought, Mother, I was being favored with a social call."

"Don't talk like that," Mrs. Lutz said.

"It's sort of complex," John began.

"Talk like what, Mother? Talk like what?"

"Then let me turn this off," Mrs. Lutz said, snapping the right knob on the television set.

"Oh, Mother, and I was listening to it!" Thelma toppled into a chair, her legs flashing. John thought when she pouted, she was delicious.

Mrs. Lutz had set herself to give sympathy. Her lap was broadened and her hands were laid palms upward in it.

"It's not much of a problem," John assured her. "But we're having some people up from Philadelphia." He turned to Thelma and added, "If anything is going on tonight, I can't get out."

"Life is just too, too full of disappointments," Thelma said.

"Look, is there?"

"Too, too full," Thelma said.

Mrs. Lutz made fluttery motions out of her lap. "These Philadelphia people."

John said, "Maybe I shouldn't bother you about this." He waited, but she just looked more and more patient, so he went on. "My mother wants to give them wine, and my father isn't home from teaching school yet. He might not get home before the liquor store closes. It's at six, isn't it? My mother's busy cleaning, so I walked in."

"She made you walk the whole mile? Poor thing, can't you drive?" Mrs. Lutz asked.

"*Sure* I can drive. But I'm not sixteen yet."

"You look a lot taller than sixteen."

John looked at Thelma to see how she took that one, but Thelma was pretending to read a rented novel wrapped in cellophane.

"I walked all the way in to the liquor store," John told Mrs. Lutz, "but they wouldn't give me anything without written permission. It was a new man."

"Your sorrow has rent me in twain," Thelma said, as if she was reading it from the book.

"Pay no attention, Johnny," Mrs. Lutz said. "Now Frank will be home any time. Why not wait until he comes and let him run down with you for a bottle?"

"That sounds wonderful. Thanks an awful lot, really."

Mrs. Lutz's hand descended upon the television knob. Some smiling man was playing the piano. John didn't know who he was; there wasn't any television at his house. They watched in silence until Mr. Lutz thumped on the porch outside. The empty milk bottles tinkled, as if they had been nudged. "Now don't be surprised if he has a bit of a load on," Mrs. Lutz said.

Actually, he didn't act at all drunk. He was like a happy husband in the movies. He called Thelma his little pookie-pie and kissed her on the forehead; then he called his wife his big pookie-pie and kissed her on the mouth. Then he solemnly shook John's hand and told him how very, very happy he was to see him here and asked after his parents. "Is that goon still on television?" he said finally.

"Daddy, please pay attention to somebody else," Thelma said, turning off the television set. "Janny wants to talk to you."

"And *I* want to talk to *Johnny*," Thelma's father said. He spread his arms suddenly, clenching and unclenching his fists. He was a big man, with shaved gray hair above his tiny ears. John couldn't think of the word to begin.

Mrs. Lutz explained the errand. When she was through, Mr. Lutz said, "People from Philadelphia. I bet their name isn't William L. Trexler, is it?"

"No. I forget their name, but it's not that. The man is an engineer. The woman went to college with my mother."

"Oh. College people. Then we must get them something very, very nice, I should say."

"Daddy," Thelma said. "*Please*. The store will close."

"Tessie, you hear John. People from college. People with diplomas. And it is very nearly closing time, and who isn't on their way?" He took John's shoulder in one hand and Thelma's arm in the other and hustled them through the door. "We'll be back in one minute, Mamma," he said.

"Drive carefully," Mrs. Lutz said from the shadowed porch, where her cigarette showed as an orange star.

Mr. Lutz drove a huge blue Buick. "I never went to college," he said, "yet I buy a new car whenever I want." His tone wasn't nasty, but soft and full of wonder.

"Oh, Daddy, not *this* again," Thelma said, shaking her head at John, so he could understand what all she had to go through. When she looks like that, John thought, I could bite her lip until it bleeds.

"Ever driven this kind of car, John?" Mr. Lutz asked.

"No. The only thing I can drive is my parents' Plymouth, and that not very well."

"What year car is it?"

"I don't know exactly." John knew perfectly well it was a 1940 model. "We got it after the war. It has a gear shift. This is automatic, isn't it?"

"Automatic shift, fluid transmission, directional lights, the works," Mr. Lutz said. "Now, isn't it funny, John? Here is your father, an educated man, with an old Plymouth, yet at the same time I, who never read more than twenty, thirty books in my life . . . it doesn't seem as if there's justice." He slapped the fender, bent over to get into the car, straightened up abruptly, and said, "Do you want to drive it?"

Thelma said, "Daddy's asking you something."

"I don't know how," John said.

"It's very easy to learn, very easy. You just slide in there — come on, it's getting late." John got in on the driver's side. He peered out of the windshield. It was a wider car than the Plymouth; the hood looked wide as a boat.

Mr. Lutz asked him to grip the little lever behind the steering wheel. "You pull it toward you like *that,* that's it, and fit it into one of these notches. 'P' stands for 'parking' — I hardly ever use that one. 'N,' that's 'neutral,' like on the car you have, 'D' means 'drive' — just put it in there and the car does all the work for you. You are using that one ninety-nine per cent of the time. 'L' is 'low,' for very steep hills, going up or down. And 'R' stands for — what?"

"Reverse," John said.

"Very, very good. Tessie, he's a smart boy. He'll never own a new car. And when you put them all together, you can remember their order by the sentence, Paint No Dimes Light Red. I thought that up when I was teaching my oldest girl how to drive."

"Paint No Dimes Light Red," John said.

"Excellent. Now, let's go."

A bubble was developing in John's stomach. "What gear do you want it in to start?" he asked Mr. Lutz.

Mr. Lutz must not have heard him, because all he said was "Let's go" again, and he drummed on the dashboard with his fingertips. They were thick, square fingers, with fur between the knuckles.

Thelma leaned up from the back seat. Her cheek almost touched John's ear. She whispered, "Put it at 'D.' "

He did, then he looked for the starter. "How does he start it?" he asked Thelma.

"I never watch him," she said. "There was a button in the last car, but I don't see it in this one."

"Push on the pedal," Mr. Lutz sang, staring straight ahead and smiling, "and away we go. And ah, ah, waay we go."

"Just step on the gas," Thelma suggested. John pushed down firmly, to keep his leg from trembling. The motor roared and the car bounded away from the curb. Within a block, though, he could manage the car pretty well.

"It rides like a boat on smooth water," he told his two passengers. The metaphor pleased him.

Mr. Lutz squinted ahead. "Like a what?"

"Like a boat."

"Don't go so fast," Thelma said.

"The motor's so quiet," John explained. "Like a sleeping cat."

Without warning, a truck pulled out of Pearl Street. Mr. Lutz, trying to brake, stamped his foot on the empty floor in front of him. John could hardly keep from laughing. "I see him," he said, easing his speed so that the truck had just enough room to make its turn. "Those trucks think they own the road," he said. He let one hand slide away from the steering wheel. One-handed, he whipped around a bus. "What'll she do on the open road?"

"That's a good question, John," Mr. Lutz said. "And I don't know the answer. Eighty, maybe."

"The speedometer goes up to a hundred and ten." Another pause — nobody seemed to be talking. John said, "Hell. A baby could drive one of these."

"For instance, you," Thelma said.

There were a lot of cars at the liquor store, so John had to double-park the big Buick. "That's close enough, close enough," Mr. Lutz said. "Don't get any closer, whoa!" He was out of the car before John could bring it to a complete stop. "You and Tessie wait here," he said. "I'll go in for the liquor."

"Mr. Lutz. Say, Mr. Lutz," John called.

"Daddy!" Thelma shouted.

Mr. Lutz returned. "What is it, boys and girls?" His tone, John noticed, was becoming reedy. He was probably getting hungry.

"Here's the money they gave me." John pulled two wadded dollars from the change pocket of his dungarees. "My mother said to get something inexpensive but nice."

"Inexpensive but nice?" Mr. Lutz repeated.

"She said something about California sherry."

"What did she say about it? To get it? Or not to?"

"I guess to get it."

"You guess." Mr. Lutz shoved himself away from the car and walked backward toward the store as he talked. "You and Tessie wait in the car. Don't go off somewhere. It's getting late. I'll be only one minute."

John leaned back in his seat and gracefully rested one hand at the top of the steering wheel. "I like your father."

"You don't know how he acts to Mother," Thelma said.

John studied the clean line under his wrist and thumb. He flexed his wrist and watched the neat little muscles move in his forearm. "You know what I need?" he said. "A wrist-watch."

"Oh, Jan," Thelma said. "Stop admiring your own hand. It's really disgusting."

A ghost of a smile flickered over his lips, but he let his strong nervous fingers remain as they were. "I'd sell my soul for a drag right now."

"Daddy keeps a pack in the glove compartment," Thelma said. "I'd get them if my fingernails weren't so long."

"*I'll* get it open," John said, and did. They fished one cigarette out of the old pack of Luckies they found and took alternate puffs. "Ah," John said, "that first drag of the day, clawing and scraping its way down your throat."

"Be on the lookout for Daddy. They hate my smoking."

"Thelma."

"Yes?" She stared deep into his eyes, her face half masked by blue shadow.

"Don't pluck your eyebrows."

"I think it looks nice."

"It's like calling me 'Jan.'" There was a silence, not awkward, between them.

"Get rid of the 'rette, Jan. Daddy just passed the window."

Being in the liquor store had put Mr. Lutz in a soberer mood. "Here you be, John," he said, in a businesslike way. He handed John a tall, velvet-red bottle. "Better let me drive. You drive like a veteran, but I know the roads."

"I can walk from your house, Mr. Lutz," John said, knowing Mr. Lutz wouldn't make him walk. "Thanks an awful lot for all you've done."

"I'll drive you up. Philadelphians can't be kept waiting. We can't make this young man walk a mile, now can we, Tessie?" In the sweeping way the man asked the question there was an energy and a hint of danger that kept the young people quiet all the way out of town, although several things were bothering John.

When the car stopped in front of his house, he forced himself to ask, "Say, Mr. Lutz. I wonder if there was any change?"

"What? Oh. I nearly forgot. You'll have your daddy thinking I'm a crook." He reached into his pocket and without looking handed John a dollar, a quarter and a penny.

"This seems like a lot," John said. The wine must be cheap. His stomach squirmed; maybe he had made a mistake. Maybe he should have let his mother phone his father, like she had wanted to, instead of begging her to let him walk in.

"It's your change," Mr. Lutz said.

"Well, thanks an awful lot."

"Goodbye now," Mr. Lutz said.

"So long." John slammed the door. "Goodbye, Thelma. Don't forget what I told you." He winked.

The car pulled out, and John walked up the path. "Don't forget what I told you," he repeated to himself, winking. In his hands the bottle was cool and heavy. He glanced at the label; it read *Château Mouton-Rothschild 1937.*

JOHN UPDIKE

THERE IS AN INTERESTING challenge here in point of view and character suggestion. The dialogue will take careful handling to keep it within the framework established by the point of view.

A Banal Miracle

Linda Vanelli died suddenly and unobtrusively. She was seated at the foot of the kitchen table — she would never have assumed Angelo's chair, even when he was out on the boat — and the children were squabbling, yelling, whining, pecking at and mishmashing spaghetti, squirming in their chairs, spilling milk down their already messy shirts, blouses and chests, when she made unexpectedly a curiously awkward movement, a wide stiff sweep of the right arm as though reaching clumsily for something she wanted, and knocked Jason's plate to the floor. For a moment the attention was all on the broken plate, and by the time the children looked up again their mother was dead.

There was no good reason for Mrs. Vanelli to die, that anyone could see; on the other hand, there was no particularly good reason for her not to. She had left no loose ends to speak of. Most of the housework in the past two years had been taken care of by Ginny and Vicky, since arthritis and two operations had left Mrs. Vanelli's right hand almost entirely useless and pretty well crippled the other too. She had brought up eleven out of fourteen born, kept clothes on their backs and food in their bellies most of the time, saw that each boy went to school as long as he wanted to, until he quit to get a job (hoping maybe that one of her children would go somewhere; but none ever did), protected them as well as she was able from her husband Angelo's infrequent but maniacally violent explosions; and had protected Angelo himself in his turn the time, three years before, when in such a rage he had beaten a child too hard and

"A Banal Miracle" by Tim Reynolds originally appeared in *New World Writing 20.* It is reprinted by permission of the author and J. B. Lippincott Company.

too long. She had been a good wife, then, and a good mother, and a good Catholic, and had spent most of her life unhappy, worried and in pain; so, although she was not yet fifty, people said or might have said, It was a blessing, as one says of old people or the incurably ill.

People felt that Angelo should have left it at that. He was out on the boat, which was a little seiner without a radio, so didn't know anything until he got home, the day after Linda Vanelli's sudden death. The neighbors had taken care of things; the house was pretty much in order, Ginny and Vicky were taking care of the little ones, and Mrs. Vanelli's body had been moved to the Boronis' where there was a bigger living room and fewer children.

Angelo walked in around ten in the morning. Right away the children felt not only frightened but guilty, as though they were responsible, as if they had broken something belonging to him while he was gone and were afraid to tell him but couldn't lie to him, could never conceive of defying Angelo.

Stinking of sardine, with four days' worth of beard on his face and two hours' worth of red wine in his belly, he looked ominously around the living room at the too-silent children. He felt threatened; they were always subdued when he came home, but he had never seen them so thoroughly chastened.

— Where's your ma, he asked them.

The little ones looked at the middle ones, the middle ones at the bigger ones, and finally everyone was looking at Ginny, who was oldest. Ginny took a deep breath.

— Ma's dead, she told her father.

— Hell you say, said Angelo.

— She's dead, Ginny said. They took her over to the Boronis'.

Angelo thought about it a while. Hell's bells, he said, and thought some more, and then said, She'll keep, and went on into the cluttered bedroom to lie down, as he always did when he came home. Mrs. Vanelli wasn't there to keep the children quiet while he slept, but it wasn't necessary. He slept until nine o'clock that evening.

When Angelo woke up he went over to the Boronis', three doors away, without even bothering to shave. The women, chatting over coffee, subsided when he came in. He paid no attention to them. Mrs. Vanelli was lying in a black coffin with silver handles lying across two chairs, and Angelo walked over and stood looking down at her.

Mrs. Boroni, later, maintained he had said it quietly, almost gently and lovingly; her daughter Frances claimed it was masterfully; Mrs. Corona thought it was desperate, as though he were pleading; of the other two ladies, one heard nothing and the other said Angelo had just said it, the way Angelo said anything, when he did, which was rarely: Get up and come home with me.

Then he turned and walked out the door. By the time Mrs. Vanelli had managed to scramble out of the coffin without overturning everything and hurriedly thank Mrs. Boroni and the other ladies for taking care of her, Angelo was almost halfway home. She had to run to catch up with him.

There was a good deal of talk at first; in a neighborhood where weddings were actively planned by everyone two months in advance and dissected for two weeks afterwards, it would have been odd if there hadn't been. But after a few days it was pretty well accepted; nothing had changed: Mrs. Vanelli's complexion, some said, was a little worse, but otherwise she was the same, and Angelo was as surly as ever and as little liked, so there was really nothing to talk *about.*

The general consensus initially inclined toward a "rare disease," but Doctor Karpov, who had examined Mrs. Vanelli and made out the certificates and such, denied it vehemently.

— There's no such disease, he said. I've made misdiagnoses, but I've never yet diagnosed a living woman as dead. It was heart failure pure and simple, not a rare disease or any disease. That woman was dead when I examined her, and if she was dead then she's dead now. But he refused to go see her, and after a time refused to talk about it any more.

That made it, evidently, a miracle. People looked oddly at Angelo Vanelli in the streets: they recalled mutterings of "Mafista" when he had first come to Monterey — he was a Siciliano, while most of the others were second- and third-generation — and later mutterings concerning some unpleasantness with a child's death a few years back; they didn't think they'd ever seen him in church; there was nothing specific to say against him, at least out loud, but no one had anything to say in his favor either; it all seemed very odd. The two boys on the seiner started to call him Mr. Vanelli Sir instead of plain Mr. Vanelli when they spoke to him; and that was, and always had been, as little as they could help.

If it *was* a miracle, however, it was in Father Martin's department. He put it off as long as he could, but with a nagging certainty that it would eventually have to be tended to. As far as anyone seemed to know, this Angelo Vanelli had raised his wife from the dead. The worst of it was that there was apparently no question at all that it had taken place. Father Martin was certain there was a perfectly rational explanation, such as mass hypnosis or hysteria, but in the meantime he had what amounted to a miracle on his hands.

He went to speak with Linda Vanelli when most of the children were in school and Angelo out on the seiner, on a Tuesday. One of the little ones let him in, yelled over his shoulder *Maaaa!,* and returned immediately to the center of the floor, dropping cross-legged between two other children, one scantily diapered, and returned his attention to the massive television set in the corner by the kitchen door.

The room seemed perfectly familiar to the priest; although he had never been in this particular home, he had been in a hundred like it: a constellation of tinted photographs, children and weddings mostly, among whom Christ demonstrated his bleeding heart and Mary her sorrows as though members of the family, a blanket-swathed sofa, an armchair, an ungainly collection of rachitic chairs and stools, all aimed at the television set, a glimpse through the kitchen door of a cramped sink and a woodstove; and, he knew as well as if he had been conducted on a guided tour, beyond the closed door to his right a double bed, a crib and a cot to hold at night, with the sofa, an entire family of perhaps a dozen, tumbled like puppies in a cardboard carton. He noted, however, with approval, that although the furnishings were scuffed and worn everything was clean and moderately well ordered.

Mrs. Vanelli was a stout dull-eyed woman, like her house considerably frayed, considerably used, but well tended; although Father Martin had never had personal dealings with her save in the confessional, he knew her face well; she was a conscientious churchgoer.

— Coffee, Father? she asked hovering over the sofa, waiting his answer to either drop into it or retire to the kitchen for refreshments.

— No, thank you, Mrs. Vanelli. Mrs. Vanelli dropped. Father Martin leaned forward from the armchair, fingers interlaced. Mrs. Vanelli, I've come to speak to you in reference to an incident that occurred, I'm told, some two weeks ago. It appears that . . . He didn't quite know how to phrase it, and stopped, raising his eyebrows and leaning back to indicate that he was awaiting an answer more complete than the question.

— Oh, it's got nothing to do with you, Father. She seemed actually surprised. He waited. Mrs. Vanelli, eyes on the floor, or on her knees, searching ineptly for words. That's just between me and Mr. Vanelli, kind of, Father. You could talk to him, she added hopefully.

— I may have to, he answered. But right now I'd like to hear your view of the matter.

Mrs. Vanelli's brow creased thoughtfully. — It's just how Angelo *is,* she said at last. When he first came to town he was like that. He'd been here maybe a month, two months, and he came to my father's house and I was just sitting there, I was fifteen years old, almost sixteen, and he just looked at me and said, Get up and come home with me, and Pa was scared to say nothing on account of all the talk about Angelo, *you* know, so I went home with him.

— You mean, Father Martin interrupted, you mean . . . Just went home?

— Umhuh, she said. And maybe five years later I found out he was with another woman in Salinas and I was sick a lot and he'd get drunk and come home and be mean to me and the kids, *you* know, so I took the kids and went back home back to my pa. And a week, two weeks later, Angelo walks in and says, You get up and come home with me, so I did.

And that's how it is, Father, I mean how Angelo is. I just couldn't say no to him, ever. Did I do wrong, Father?

Father Martin considered. — I suppose not, he said.

— You see how it's got nothing to do with you, she pressed.

— I suppose not, he said again. Perhaps, as they say, love is stronger than death.

Mrs. Vanelli shrugged wearily. Her crushed and broken hands lay like gnarled cypress roots on her broad lap.

— Well, she said dubiously, anyway habits.

There was a long pause. There seemed nothing more to say. Father Martin rose from the armchair and Mrs. Vanelli walked three steps with him to the door. — Watch the step, she said, it's broken. But the priest stopped in the doorway and turned to her.

— What was it like? he asked cautiously.

— Being dead? I don't know, she said, holding the bellied-out rusty screen door open with one warped hand. It was like nothing; it wasn't so bad; it was like nothing at all. *You* know.

He stepped out and down, watching out for the broken step, and turned again. — Well, good-by, Mrs. Vanelli, he said; and thank you for talking with me.

— That's all right, she said. Her wide face looked dim and far away through the sagging mesh of the screen. Good-by. I'll tell Angelo you was here.

TIM REYNOLDS

THIS FAMOUS STORY moves slowly but inexorably to its climax. Make full use of the key phrases and minor climaxes along the way. Let style and kinetic and kinesthetic imagery help with the final unit.

The Lottery

The morning of June 27th was clear and sunny, with the fresh warmth of a full-summer day; the flowers were blossoming profusely and the grass was richly green. The people of the village began to gather in the square, between the post office and the bank, around ten o'clock; in some towns there were so many people that the lottery took two days and had to be started on June 26th, but in this village, where there were only about three hundred people, the whole lottery took only about two hours, so it could begin at ten o'clock in the morning and still be through in time to allow the villagers to get home for noon dinner.

The children assembled first, of course. School was recently over

Reprinted from *The Lottery* by Shirley Jackson, by permission of Farrar, Straus & Company, Inc. Copyright 1948 by The New Yorker Magazine, 1949 by Shirley Jackson.

for the summer, and the feeling of liberty sat uneasily on most of them; they tended to gather together quietly for a while before they broke into boisterous play, and their talk was still of the classroom and the teacher, of books and reprimands. Bobby Martin had already stuffed his pockets full of stones, and the other boys soon followed his example, selecting the smoothest and roundest stones; Bobby and Harry Jones and Dickie Delacroix — the villagers pronounced this name "Dellacroy" — eventually made a great pile of stones in one corner of the square and guarded it against the raids of the other boys. The girls stood aside, talking among themselves, looking over their shoulders at the boys, and the very small children rolled in the dust or clung to the hands of their older brothers or sisters.

Soon the men began to gather, surveying their own children, speaking of planting and rain, tractors and taxes. They stood together, away from the pile of stones in the corner, and their jokes were quiet and they smiled rather than laughed. The women, wearing faded house dresses and sweaters, came shortly after their menfolk. They greeted one another and exchanged bits of gossip as they went to join their husbands. Soon the women, standing by their husbands, began to call to their children, and the children came reluctantly, having to be called four or five times. Bobby Martin ducked under his mother's grasping hand and ran, laughing, back to the pile of stones. His father spoke up sharply, and Bobby came quickly and took his place between his father and his oldest brother.

The lottery was conducted — as were the square dances, the teenage club, the Halloween program — by Mr. Summers, who had time and energy to devote to civic activities. He was a round-faced, jovial man and he ran the coal business, and people were sorry for him, because he had no children and his wife was a scold. When he arrived in the square, carrying the black wooden box, there was a murmur of conversation among the villagers, and he waved and called, "Little late today, folks." The postmaster, Mr. Graves, followed him, carrying a three-legged stool, and the stool was put in the center of the square and Mr. Summers set the black box down on it. The villagers kept their distance, leaving a space between themselves and the stool, and when Mr. Summers said, "Some of you fellows want to give me a hand?," there was a hesitation before two men, Mr. Martin and his oldest son, Baxter, came forward to hold the box steady on the stool while Mr. Summers stirred up the papers inside it.

The original paraphernalia for the lottery had been lost long ago, and the black box now resting on the stool had been put into use even before Old Man Warner, the oldest man in town, was born. Mr. Summers spoke frequently to the villagers about making a new box, but no one liked to upset even as much tradition as was represented by the black box. There was a story that the present box had been made with some pieces of the box that had preceded it, the one that had been constructed when the first people settled down to make a village here. Every year, after the lottery, Mr. Summers began talking again about a new box, but every year the subject was allowed to fade off without anything's being done. The black box grew shabbier each year; by now it was no longer completely black but splintered badly along one side to show the original wood color, and in some places faded or stained.

Mr. Martin and his oldest son, Baxter, held the black box securely on the stool until Mr. Summers had stirred the papers thoroughly with his hand. Because so much of the ritual had been forgotten or discarded, Mr. Summers had been successful in having slips of paper substituted for the chips of wood that had been used for generations. Chips of wood, Mr. Summers had argued, had been all very well when the village was tiny, but now that the population was more than three hundred and likely to keep on growing, it was necessary to use something that would fit more easily into the black box. The night before the lottery, Mr. Summers and Mr. Graves made up the slips of paper and put them into the box, and it was then taken to the safe of Mr. Summers' coal company and locked up until Mr. Summers was ready to take it to the square next morning. The rest of the year, the box was put away, sometimes one place, sometimes another; it had spent one year in Mr. Graves' barn and another year underfoot in the post office, and sometimes it was set on a shelf in the Martin grocery and left there.

There was a great deal of fussing to be done before Mr. Summers declared the lottery open. There were the lists to make up — of heads of families, heads of households in each family, members of each household in each family. There was the proper swearing-in of Mr. Summers by the postmaster, as the official of the lottery; at one time, some people remembered, there had been a recital of some sort, performed by the official of the lottery, a perfunctory, tuneless chant that had been rattled off duly each year; some people believed that the official of the lottery used to stand just so when he said or sang it, others believed that he was supposed to walk among the people, but years and years ago this part of the ritual had been allowed to lapse. There had been, also, a ritual salute, which the official of the lottery had had to use in addressing each person who came up to draw from the box, but this also had changed with time, until now it was felt necessary only for the official to speak to each person approaching. Mr. Summers was very good at all this; in his clean white shirt and blue jeans, with one hand resting carelessly on the black box, he seemed very proper and important as he talked interminably to Mr. Graves and the Martins.

Just as Mr. Summers finally left off talking and turned to the assembled villagers, Mrs. Hutchinson came hurriedly along the path to the square, her sweater thrown over her shoulders, and slid into place in the back of the crowd. "Clean forgot what day it was," she said to Mrs. Delacroix, who stood next to her, and they both laughed softly. "Thought my old man was out back stacking wood," Mrs. Hutchinson went on, "and then I looked out the window and the kids was gone, and then I remembered it was the twenty-seventh and came a-running." She dried her hands on her apron, and Mrs. Delacroix said, "You're in time, though. They're still talking away up there."

Mrs. Hutchinson craned her neck to see through the crowd and found her husband and children standing near the front. She tapped Mrs. Delacroix on the arm as a farewell and began to make her way through the crowd. The people separated good-humoredly to let her through; two or three people said, in voices just loud enough to be heard across the crowd, "Here comes your Mrs. Hutchinson," and "Bill, she made it after all." Mrs. Hutchinson reached her husband, and Mr. Summers, who had been waiting, said cheerfully, "Thought we were going to have to get on without you, Tessie." Mrs. Hutchinson said, grinning, "Wouldn't have me leave m'dishes in the sink, now, would you, Joe?," and soft laughter ran through the crowd as the people stirred back into position after Mrs. Hutchinson's arrival.

"Well, now," Mr. Summers said soberly, "guess we better get started, get this over with, so's we can go back to work. Anybody ain't here?"

"Dunbar," several people said. "Dunbar, Dunbar."

Mr. Summers consulted his list. "Clyde Dunbar," he said. "That's right. He's broke his leg, hasn't he? Who's drawing for him?"

"Me, I guess," a woman said, and Mr. Summers said, "Don't you have a grown boy to do it for you, Janey?" Although Mr. Summers and everyone else in the village knew the answer perfectly well, it was the business of the official of the lottery to ask such questions formally. Mr. Summers waited with an expression of polite interest while Mrs. Dunbar answered.

"Horace's not but sixteen yet," Mrs. Dunbar said regretfully. "Guess I gotta fill in for the old man this year."

"Right," Mr. Summers said. He made a note on the list he was holding. Then he asked, "Watson boy drawing this year?"

A tall boy in the crowd raised his hand. "Here," he said. "I'm drawing for m'mother and me." He blinked his eyes nervously and ducked his head as several voices in the crowd said things like "Good fellow, Jack," and "Glad to see your mother's got a man to do it."

"Well," Mr. Summers said, "guess that's everyone. Old Man Warner make it?"

"Here," a voice said, and Mr. Summers nodded.

A sudden hush fell on the crowd as Mr. Summers cleared his throat and looked at the list. "All ready?" he called. "Now, I'll read the names — heads of families first — and the men come up and take a paper out of the box. Keep the paper folded in your hand without looking at it until everyone has had a turn. Everything clear?"

The people had done it so many times that they only half listened to the directions; most of them were quiet, wetting their lips, not looking around. Then Mr. Summers raised one hand high and said, "Adams." A man disengaged himself from the crowd and came forward. "Hi, Steve," Mr. Summers said, and Mr. Adams said, "Hi, Joe." They grinned at one another humorlessly and nervously. Then Mr. Adams reached into the black box and took out a folded paper. He held it firmly by one corner as he turned and went hastily back to his place in the crowd, where he stood a little apart from his family, not looking down at his hand.

"Allen," Mr. Summers said. "Anderson. . . . Bentham."

"Seems like there's no time at all between lotteries any more," Mrs. Delacroix said to Mrs. Graves in the back row. "Seems like we got through with the last one only last week."

"Time sure goes fast," Mrs. Graves said.

"Clark. . . . Delacroix."

"There goes my old man," Mrs. Delacroix said. She held her breath while her husband went forward.

"Dunbar," Mr. Summers said, and Mrs. Dunbar went steadily to the box while one of the women said, "Go on, Janey," and another said, "There she goes."

"We're next," Mrs. Graves said. She watched while Mr. Graves came around from the side of the box, greeted Mr. Summers gravely, and selected a slip of paper from the box. By now, all through the crowd there were men holding the small folded papers in their large hands, turning them over and over nervously. Mrs. Dunbar and her two sons stood together, Mrs. Dunbar holding the slip of paper.

"Harburt. . . . Hutchinson."

"Get up there, Bill," Mrs. Hutchinson said, and the people near her laughed.

"Jones."

"They do say," Mr. Adams said to Old Man Warner, who stood next to him, "that over in the north village they're talking of giving up the lottery."

Old Man Warner snorted. "Pack of crazy fools," he said. "Listening to the young folks, nothing's good enough for *them.* Next thing you know, they'll be wanting to go back to living in caves, nobody work any more, live *that* way for a while. Used to be a saying about 'Lottery in June, corn be heavy soon.' First thing you know, we'd all be eating stewed chickweed and acorns. There's *always* been a lottery," he added petulantly. "Bad enough to see young Joe Summers up there joking with everybody."

"Some places have already quit lotteries," Mrs. Adams said.

"Nothing but trouble in *that,*" Old Man Warner said stoutly. "Pack of young fools."

"Martin." And Bobby Martin watched his father go forward. "Overdyke. . . . Percy."

"I wish they'd hurry," Mrs. Dunbar said to her older son. "I wish they'd hurry."

"They're almost through," her son said.

"You get ready to run tell Dad," Mrs. Dunbar said.

Mr. Summers called his own name and then stepped forward precisely and selected a slip from the box. Then he called, "Warner."

"Seventy-seventh year I been in the lottery," Old Man Warner said as he went through the crowd. "Seventy-seventh time."

"Watson." The tall boy came awkwardly through the crowd. Someone said, "Don't be nervous, Jack," and Mr. Summers said, "Take your time, son."

"Zanini."

After that, there was a long pause, a breathless pause, until Mr. Summers, holding his slip of paper in the air, said, "All right, fellows." For a minute, no one moved, and then all the slips of paper were opened. Suddenly, all the women began to speak at once, saying, "Who is it?," "Who's got it?," "Is it the Dunbars?," "Is it the Watsons?" Then the voices began to say, "It's Hutchinson. It's Bill," "Bill Hutchinson's got it."

"Go tell your father," Mrs. Dunbar said to her older son.

People began to look around to see the Hutchinsons. Bill Hutchinson was standing quiet, staring down at the paper in his hand. Suddenly, Tessie Hutchinson shouted to Mr. Summers, "You didn't give him time enough to take any paper he wanted. I saw you. It wasn't fair!"

"Be a good sport, Tessie," Mrs. Delacroix called, and Mrs. Graves said, "All of us took the same chance."

"Shut up, Tessie," Bill Hutchinson said.

"Well, everyone," Mr. Summers said, "that was done pretty fast, and now we've got to be hurrying a little more to get done in time." He consulted his next list. "Bill," he said, "you draw for the Hutchinson family. You got any other households in the Hutchinsons?"

"There's Don and Eva," Mrs. Hutchinson yelled. "Make *them* take their chance!"

"Daughters draw with their husbands' families, Tessie," Mr. Summers said gently. "You know that as well as anyone else."

"It wasn't *fair,*" Tessie said.

"I guess not, Joe," Bill Hutchinson said regretfully. "My daughter draws with her husband's family, that's only fair. And I've got no other family except the kids."

"Then, as far as drawing for families is concerned, it's you," Mr. Summers said in explanation, "and as far as drawing for households is concerned, that's you, too. Right?"

"Right," Bill Hutchinson said.

"How many kids, Bill?" Mr. Summers asked formally.

"Three," Bill Hutchinson said. "There's Bill, Jr., and Nancy, and little Dave. And Tessie and me."

"All right, then," Mr. Summers said. "Harry, you got their tickets back?"

Mr. Graves nodded and held up the slips of paper. "Put them in the box, then," Mr. Summers directed. "Take Bill's and put it in."

"I think we ought to start over," Mrs. Hutchinson said, as quietly as she could. "I tell you it wasn't *fair*. You didn't give him time enough to choose. *Every*body saw that."

Mr. Graves had selected the five slips and put them in the box, and he dropped all the papers but those onto the ground, where the breeze caught them and lifted them off.

"Listen, everybody," Mrs. Hutchinson was saying to the people around her.

"Ready, Bill?" Mr. Summers asked, and Bill Hutchinson, with one quick glance around at his wife and children, nodded.

"Remember," Mr. Summers said, "take the slips and keep them folded until each person has taken one. Harry, you help little Dave." Mr. Graves took the hand of the little boy, who came willingly with him up to the box. "Take a paper out of the box, Davy," Mr. Summers said. Davy put his hand into the box and laughed. "Take just *one* paper," Mr. Summers said. "Harry, you hold it for him." Mr. Graves took the child's hand and removed the folded paper from the tight fist and held it while little Dave stood next to him and looked up at him wonderingly.

"Nancy next," Mr. Summers said. Nancy was twelve, and her school friends breathed heavily as she went forward, switching her skirt, and took a slip daintily from the box. "Bill, Jr.," Mr. Summers said, and Billy, his face red and his feet overlarge, nearly knocked the box over as he got a paper out. "Tessie," Mr. Summers said. She hesitated for a minute, looking around defiantly, and then set her lips and went up to the box. She snatched a paper out and held it behind her.

"Bill," Mr. Summers said, and Bill Hutchinson reached into the box and felt around, bringing his hand out at last with the slip of paper in it.

The crowd was quiet. A girl whispered, "I hope it's not Nancy," and the sound of the whisper reached the edges of the crowd.

"It's not the way it used to be," Old Man Warner said clearly. "People ain't the way they used to be."

"All right," Mr. Summers said. "Open the papers. Harry, you open little Dave's."

Mr. Graves opened the slip of paper and there was a general sigh through the crowd as he held it up and everyone could see that it was blank. Nancy and Bill, Jr., opened theirs at the same time, and both beamed and laughed, turning around to the crowd and holding their slips of paper above their heads.

"Tessie," Mr. Summers said. There was a pause, and then Mr.

Summers looked at Bill Hutchinson, and Bill unfolded his paper and showed it. It was blank.

"It's Tessie," Mr. Summers said, and his voice was hushed. "Show us her paper, Bill."

Bill Hutchinson went over to his wife and forced the slip of paper out of her hand. It had a black spot on it, the black spot Mr. Summers had made the night before with the heavy pencil in the coal-company office. Bill Hutchinson held it up, and there was a stir in the crowd.

"All right, folks," Mr. Summers said. "Let's finish quickly."

Although the villagers had forgotten the ritual and lost the original black box, they still remembered to use stones. The pile of stones the boys had made earlier was ready; there were stones on the ground with the blowing scraps of paper that had come out of the box. Mrs. Delacroix selected a stone so large she had to pick it up with both hands and turned to Mrs. Dunbar. "Come on," she said. "Hurry up."

Mrs. Dunbar had small stones in both hands, and she said, gasping for breath, "I can't run at all. You'll have to go ahead and I'll catch up with you."

The children had stones already, and someone gave little Davy Hutchinson a few pebbles.

Tessie Hutchinson was in the center of a cleared space by now, and she held her hands out desperately as the villagers moved in on her. "It isn't fair," she said. A stone hit her on the side of the head.

Old Man Warner was saying, "Come on, come on, everyone." Steve Adams was in the front of the crowd of villagers, with Mrs. Graves beside him.

"It isn't fair, it isn't right," Mrs. Hutchinson screamed, and then they were upon her.

SHIRLEY JACKSON

✶ Bibliography

Brooks, Cleanth, and Robert Penn Warren. *Understanding Fiction.* New York: F. S. Crofts and Company, 1943.

Clear and usable approach to the analysis of fiction with an anthology of relevant stories.

Brown, E. K. *Rhythm in the Novel.* Toronto: University of Toronto Press, 1963.

A modern expansion of E. M. Forster's method of analysis.

Edel, Leon. *The Psychological Novel, 1900–1950.* Philadelphia: J. B. Lippincott Company, 1955.

Discussion of the psychological theories as they relate to the writer and the reader of modern fiction.

Isaacs, Neil D., and Louis Leiter (eds.). *Approaches to the Short Story.* San Francisco: Chandler Publishing Company, 1963.

A varied collection of short stories with critical comments on the thesis that the short story is a work of literary art.

James, Henry. *The Art of Fiction.* New York: Oxford University Press, 1948.

James, Henry. *The Art of the Novel: Critical Prefaces.* New York: Charles Scribner's Sons, 1934, 1950.

The two classic works by an author who was himself a master in the field of fiction.

Mizener, Arthur. *The Sense of Life in the Modern Novel.* Boston: Houghton Mifflin Company, 1964.

An important study whose purpose is "to examine one aspect of the novel . . . the relation of the represented life to 'nature,' and the effects this relation has on the novel's expression of values." Novels by Trollope, Hardy, Cozzens, Faulkner, Fitzgerald, Hemingway, Salinger, Updike, and Tate are discussed.

Scholes, Robert. *Approaches to the Novel.* San Francisco: Chandler Publishing Company, 1961.

A collection of essays on the novel grouped under appropriate headings such as "Mimesis," "Plot," "Narrative Structure," etc.

Thompson, David W., and Virginia Fredricks. *Oral Interpretation of Fiction: A Dramatistic Approach.* Minneapolis: Burgess Publishing Company, 1964.

A brief text stressing a "dramatistic" approach to oral interpretation, based on the theory that "the total symbolic action in literature and in the reader's oral interpretation of it can be discovered only from exploring all the interacting relationships of Scene-Role-Gesture."

In addition to the writers suggested at the end of this chapter, you would also enjoy the works of the following novelists and short story writers:

Conrad Aiken
Sherwood Anderson
James Joyce
Stephen Vincent Benét
Kay Boyle
Anton Chekhov
Stephen Crane
Elizabeth Bowen
Fyodor Dostoevsky
Thomas Hardy
Ernest Hemingway
Graham Greene
Henry James
Franz Kafka
D. H. Lawrence
Nancy Hale
Frank O'Connor
F. Scott Fitzgerald
Rebecca West
Irwin Shaw
J. D. Salinger
Virginia Woolf

PART 3

The Interpretation of Drama

8

The Interpreter's Approach to Drama

Many of the characteristics of narration are also common to drama. As a matter of fact, the elements of plot, character, and setting are as basic to one as to the other. Consequently, much of the discussion of narration in the previous chapter is equally applicable here. The chief difference for the interpreter lies in the form in which these three elements are presented. There are numerous highly literary definitions of "drama," but for the purposes of this chapter, attention will be focused on that type of writing which takes the form of a play.

Much stress has been laid, in previous chapters, on fidelity to the author's purpose. How, then, can one justify the use of drama for interpretation, since the material was obviously written to be presented on a stage, with scenery, costumes, make-up, lights, and a number of actors? The justification rests upon the interpreter's ability to suggest the visual aspects of a play so completely that the listeners will re-create the necessary details in their minds as he reads. A trained interpreter can accomplish this difficult feat so perfectly that the audience has the sense of knowing how the characters look, and of mentally seeing them move about in a clearly imagined setting.

The interpretation of drama requires a particularly strong emphasis on technique, which, as always, must serve the literature and be so carefully and skillfully developed that it is completely unobtrusive in performance. Because of the form of the material, depending as it does on what the characters say and do, with no comment from the author to explain motivations and emotional responses, the interpreter must give particular attention to clear, unmistakable characterization. The audience must know immediately who is speaking, what prompted the speech, and to whom it is addressed. The interpreter cannot rely on a narrative device such as ". . . she said gently," or ". . . she said impatiently." He is on his own, with only the stage directions, his complete understanding of the material, and his body and voice to help him re-create *in the minds of his listeners* what actors, technicians, and director achieve in a dramatic performance.

ACTING AND INTERPRETATION

The actor and the interpreter have many things in common. There are, however, some basic differences in the art of acting and the art of interpreting drama. They are differences not of degree but of kind.

The printed page, as a medium for conveying the author's thought, is the point at which both interpreter and actor begin the process of re-creation. It is true that the actor memorizes his material, whereas the interpreter frequently does not; but this is not a fundamental difference, for the actor, like the interpreter, remains faithful to the author's words. Both the actor and the oral interpreter of drama must study the characters and come to understand what kind of person each one is, how he thinks and feels, what motivations drive him. Both must be aware of a character's language, of his speech rhythms, and of his choice of words, as all these things reflect personality and emotional state. Both must analyze the entire play carefully so that they will use their vocal and physical techniques to project the appropriate characterization to the audience. Thus the actor and the interpreter of drama have many responsibilities in common.

The actor completely memorizes his material and asks his audience to believe that he is actually the person to whom the events are happening. He normally portrays only one character and is aided in his portrayal by other members of the cast, as well as by scenery, costumes, make-up, and properties. His scene is *on stage* and exists around him. He moves about the stage; he sits down; he enters and exits through doors that open and close; and in general, he strives for physically complete and explicit characterization. Theoretically, he has no direct contact with the audience, for his circle of concentration is limited to the acting area. He is, of course, conscious of his audience to the degree that he senses their response, waits for laughs, and takes care to project so that his voice can be heard in the last row of the balcony. The audience, however, must not be aware that he is conscious of their presence; they should feel that a fourth wall has been removed from an actual location and that they are observing the events on that location without being observed.

The interpreter, on the other hand, places his scene *out front.* His area of concentration goes out from himself to include the entire audience. He focuses his speeches out front and receives his motivations, in terms of others' speeches and actions, from out front. He creates a scene in the minds of his audience, and through suggestion creates characters which move about that scene. He asks his audience to accept him as an instrument through which all the characters, their actions, their physical, mental, and vocal characteristics, and their relationships are *suggested*, not represented. Through his skill in suggestion, the audience re-creates mentally the visual aspects which in a staged performance are concretely given through action, scenery, costumes, make-up, and properties. The interpreter, like the actor, is responsible for complete mental and emotional characterization. His presentation, however, must of necessity be less physically explicit. In the first place, he is not limiting himself to a single character. He may suggest a dozen or more during the course of a play. And he cannot change costumes and make-up for each line of dialogue. Moreover, he does not have doors to open and close; and if he did, he could not very convincingly take himself offstage as one character and then come bounding back, in the person of another character, to talk about himself after he had gone. After one or two such exhibitions, any audience would be reduced to a state of total confusion or uncontrollable laughter.

One of the most important problems for the interpreter of drama is the matter of audience contact. His circle of concentration is not limited to the reading stand, but must be wide enough to include all his listeners, although his direct eye contact is with the visualized character he is addressing. Some ways of communicating to the audience without losing the immediacy required in dialogue were mentioned briefly in direct discourse (Chapter 7) and will be given more attention in the next chapter. The important point here is that the interpreter's contact with his audience is conscious and constant, whereas the actor's is theoretically non-existent.

It must now be apparent that the question which students often ask, "How far can you go in interpretation of drama before it becomes acting?" is in reality putting the cart before the horse. Interpretation does not "come before" acting. Acting does not "go farther" than interpretation of drama. Both arts follow the same path in preparation. The actor and the interpreter of drama follow the same procedure of analysis and rehearsal, except that the interpreter must analyze all the characters and rehearse each one in turn until he has complete control of all of them, whereas an actor need concentrate on only one. The actor then puts himself, physically and visibly, into the scenery, costumes, and make-up, and begins to blend his performance with that of the other actors and with the concept of the entire production. His scene is around him. The interpreter, on the other hand, goes on to those details which will enable him to present a three-dimensional character, and incorporates into his muscle responses and vocal qualities whatever is important for *suggesting* character and action. His scene and characters are in the minds of his audience.

Thus the actor and the interpreter of drama differ primarily in degree of emphasis on certain techniques. In performance, the actor strives for the utmost physical explicitness, while the interpreter relies upon suggestion.

Somewhere between acting and the oral interpretation of drama falls the art of impersonation, or monodrama. In this form of presentation, one person focuses attention on a single character in a single situation. He will probably use a minimum of properties, such as a chair or a table. He may suggest costume by a hat or a pair of gloves or some such article which will facilitate his business. This business will be limited, but he will be almost as explicit as the actor in handling properties and establishing entrances and exits. His circle of concentration, like the actor's, is limited to the area established by the set he has created, and his contact with the audience is secondary. The audience is allowed to overhear the scene. This differs from a soliloquy, in which a single actor in a play delivers a speech alone on the stage, for in a soliloquy a character thinks aloud, talks to himself, whereas a monologue or monodrama assumes the presence of other characters, who move in and out of the scene and motivate changes in the speaker's thoughts and actions. The minor characters are not, of course, seen by the audience, but the mono-actor must be aware of their presence and react to them.

In summary, then, an actor usually portrays only one character and is vocally and physically explicit in that portrayal, aided by make-up, costumes, scenery, and the presence of other actors. The mono-actor also concentrates on only one character; selects and uses appropriate properties, costumes, make-up, and scenery; and creates the other actors in imagination, while keeping the focus of attention constantly on the single character that is visible to the audience. The interpreter, on the other hand, presents many characters by suggesting them, basing his suggestion on complete understanding of the material and on an intelligent selection of physical and vocal characteristics. He is the instrument through which the printed page comes alive and the means of re-creating in the mind of his audience the details which are physically present in a dramatic production.

It might be well to point out that although these three areas — acting, mono-acting, and interpretation of drama — are mutually related, each is a distinct art in itself. No one is "higher" than the others. The versatile artist will be able to handle all three. His decision as to which he wishes to use in approaching drama will be governed by practical considerations (such as the availability of other actors, and the availability and physical equipment of a theater) and by his own interests and inclinations. But having decided which of these three dramatic arts he wishes to practice, he must be true to the principles of that art.

Our concern here, obviously, is with interpretation. The basic principles of the interpretation of drama are the same as those applied to the interpretation of any other type of literature. The variations come in the degree and the mechanics of technique, always judged in terms of the vital word *suggestion*. The first step is to decide what elements are to be suggested; the second, to determine how these elements may best be handled by a voice and body governed by an alert, informed, and disciplined mind.

STRUCTURAL CONSIDERATIONS

The interpreter who wishes to present a play will of course be guided by his standards of literary worth, and by the interests of his audience, in choosing one of the countless dramas available to him. After making his final choice, he must then undertake careful, objective analysis to discover all the aspects of content and form which make up the whole. His procedure in studying the content and organization of a play parallels, to some extent, the one he used with narrative prose. He follows the thread of the action and accepts the unifying principles of time, place, and character as the writer has established them.

Plays are organized on the principles of unity and probability, and their basic ingredient is conflict. The ways in which conflict is presented, developed, and resolved vary widely. In general, however, the opening scenes are devoted to exposition through action and dialogue. Following the clarification of the preliminary situation, there is the challenge which introduces the inciting or exciting force. There may be several such units as the play develops. The primary challenge may already have been touched on in the exposition and be re-introduced and intensified by developing action or relationship so that it becomes more acute. This will usually be followed by moves and counter-moves between the two characters most involved, thus producing a tightening of conflict and what is often termed the rising action. The rising action comes to a point of decision in the crisis. The *crisis* is the moment of recognition and limitation which directs the action to its final outcome. The crisis brings about the *climax*, which is the point of highest culmination of all the elements of conflict. This is followed by the dénouement or resolution, or, in tragedy, the inevitable catastrophe. Thus a play has an over-all pattern of rhythm of content growing out of emotional builds, pace of action, and intensity of conflict.

The rhythm of a play is extremely interesting and somewhat complex. In the first place, at the stylistic level there is the individual speech rhythm of each character. Second, in terms of both content and form, there are the important fluctuations in emotional tension. Third, there is the inevitable alternation of "action" scenes and "static" scenes. This alternation is comparable to the rhythm of activity and passivity in other forms of writing, though of course no part of a good play is ever really passive inasmuch as a play depends upon action for its development. Some scenes, or portions of scenes, may consist primarily of exposition and fulfill much the same function as transitional units in narrative writing. They may clarify cause and effect or present necessary relationships, allow the playwright to plead his case through one of his characters, or provide needed relaxation or suspense in preparation for a climax. This alternation between the active and the passive elements will affect the tempo at which the various scenes and speeches move, and the speed with which they build toward minor climaxes and finally toward the main climax, whether in terms of action, character development, or both. In a well-written modern play, these transitional "static" scenes are used sparingly and present nothing which does not bear upon the ultimate outcome of the action. The playwright's arrangement of these scenes will probably be governed by the same principles which influence the writer of narrative prose; that is, he has to consider how much the audience must know about background and where that background material can be most effectively inserted.

The preceding discussion and much that follows is in terms of the presentation of a cutting of an entire play. Clearly, the average classroom situation will not permit a performance of this length, but the popularity of play cuttings for club audiences makes such a discussion valid. If the interpreter chooses only a single scene or a portion of a scene from a full-length play for his performance, he will be governed by principles of cutting and condensation similar to those suggested for the novel in Chapter 7. Although the time spent in preparation will be in proportion to the length of the selection, the general plan of working for complete understanding is basic, since it is impossible to do justice to a scene without knowing where it fits into the play.

PLOT

In using drama, the interpreter's most important task, though not his most difficult one, is to keep the events which make up the plot in clear focus and in consecutive order, following whatever progression of time and place the author has adopted. In narrative, it will be remembered, the action and the author's comments on background material are often woven together. In a play, the plot never begins until the curtain has gone up, because it depends upon the speeches of the characters and their actions. Whereas the writer of narrative may devote several paragraphs to the introductory units of the story in careful preparation for his plot, a playwright cannot truly take up his job until the action begins. Consequently, the introductory units in a play or in a single scene, as they are presented by an interpreter to his audience, must be swifter and more sharply focused than is necessary in a narrative. They must be checked carefully for key speeches. The same is true of the conclusion. A writer of narrative may step in and explain how it all came out — that "they lived happily ever after." A playwright cannot take this direct approach, unless he is willing to have one of his characters speak an epilogue, as Tom does in *The Glass Menagerie.*

Again, the main climax will be preceded by minor climaxes, just as in narrative. Early in his preparation the interpreter will become conscious of the focal points of meaning and emotion, and of the units which form the lead-in and conclusion to each. In drama, these focal points may consist of only a single speech or perhaps a seemingly unimportant action which nevertheless becomes a steppingstone to the next unit of development or a means of resolving a much later episode. In narrative, the writer can, and often does, prepare the reader for the climaxes by his own comments or by detailed description. In drama, the writer must depend upon his characters — their dialogue, which reflects their mental comment, and their actions, which are motivated by their complex responses. Consequently, the interpreter must keep in mind every signpost along the way and judge its importance in the light of the final outcome. Hedda's action in placing the manuscript in the bookcase, after persuading Tesman to delay returning it to Lövborg, is an excellent example of a focal point which must be sharpened by the interpreter so that his audience can follow the plot development of Ibsen's *Hedda Gabler.* If the single scene of the burning of the manuscript is selected for interpretation, it will be necessary to sketch in relevant background and to summarize the events which led to Hedda's possession of the papers in order that the audience may understand the motivation for the action and Hedda's emotional response to it.

In analyzing a play for interpretation, it is necessary to be aware of two kinds of action. The first, which may be termed practical business, is intended primarily as guidance for a director when the play is presented on the stage. It is the action which moves a character from one area to another in order to free the first area for an entrance or to make a pictorially effective grouping for a climactic moment. The interpreter is not usually concerned with this sort of action, since he does not have to worry about getting the characters together or out of one another's way. Sometimes, however, such a piece of business will give him valuable clues to the degree of tension or focus of attention which he can and should incorporate into his empathic responses.

The second type of action is used primarily to reveal mental attitude or emotional response. For instance, a playwright may indicate that a character is to pace nervously about the stage throughout the greater part of a scene. In preparation the interpreter will probably work on this action in detail. Obviously, in performance he will not pace about as one character, then stop in his tracks to reply to himself, then start pacing again. This explicit action would be both distracting and ridiculous; it would shatter the play which his listeners are re-creating in their own minds. Moreover, it is completely unnecessary in performance, since by his vocal quality, tempo, muscle tone, and mental comment as he reads the speeches of that character, he can suggest the same nervous tension that is visually conveyed by the physical act of pacing. Usually he will not even need to tell his audience specifically that the character is pacing about, but will let his voice and body alone suggest the mental tension. In the case of an important bit of action, however — something that motivates a climactic scene, such as the placing of the manuscript in the bookcase in *Hedda Gabler* — it is usually safer and simpler to tell the audience directly, and as briefly as possible, that the business is taking place. Frequently a direct quotation from the printed stage directions will be sufficient.

Transitional scenes, or "static" scenes, must be kept in their proper relation to the whole so that they serve the intended purpose and no more. When the interpreter is cutting a long play, he might do well to include at least a few of them, since they are an important attribute of rhythm and allow the audience to relax before and after the more active scenes. Again, he may often summarize them in his own words and give them directly to the audience in his capacity as narrator. When he chooses the latter course, he should be careful to preserve the mood of the scene by keeping the style and choice of words close to the spirit of the original.

The summary must be truly transitional, both logically and emotionally, in order to prepare the listeners for whatever changes of place, time, train of thought, and emotional tone they will encounter in the scene to follow.

CHARACTER

After thorough examination of the play as a whole and of the scenes which make up the whole, it is time to consider character specifically. There are numerous ways of arriving at complete understanding of character, and each interpreter must find the one which best suits him. No matter what method is used, however, there are certain important factors which must be investigated, incorporated into the presentation, and suggested by body and voice, by mental comment, and by attitude. The following method has proved useful and is offered as a suggestion until the interpreter feels able to establish his own.

The first steps in the analysis of character must always be taken in terms of the entire play. This, of course, goes back directly to understanding of logical content and of the principles of organization. In short, what does each character say, in what circumstances does he say it, and how does what he says further the development of the plot?

After the relationship of the characters to the plot progression has been clearly established, it will be helpful to consider the relationship of characters to setting. Here again, one starts with the play as a whole. The playwright had a definite purpose in placing his action in the particular setting he used. How does this locale affect the characters who are portrayed against it? Different people respond in different ways to the same environment, and a character's acceptance or rejection of the social standards and conventions of his milieu may be the motivating factor in the action and in the ultimate outcome of the plot. A knowledge of period and custom is often necessary to the understanding and appreciation of a character — the old nurse in *Romeo and Juliet,* for example, and indeed Juliet herself. Clothes affect manner and movement; hence some knowledge and awareness of period costume will help the interpreter in his physical suggestion of character and in the pace with which he handles some of the scenes.

Next comes the problem of the relationships among the characters. We will delay for a moment the all-important psychological relationships and consider first simply how the characters compare, contrast, and balance in point of sex, maturity, and cultural background. These three elements contribute to the variety and contrast of the play as a whole and also help to establish the prevailing emotional tone.

After the characters have been carefully considered in terms of the entire play and of their relationships to each other, the interpreter begins his more detailed analysis. From his study of the play he should already have determined which are the important characters, and which is the key character around whom the incidents revolve. He next evaluates the others by classifying them as those who are directly concerned in the plot, those who implement it, and those who can be eliminated in his cutting without interruption of the series of events. This last consideration is important, since it is not often practicable for the interpreter to do an unabridged performance of a full-length play. Before any characters are eliminated by cutting, however, an objective analysis should be made of the purpose of each in terms of the whole. This holds equally true for a single scene which is to be presented as a unit in itself. Frequently, of course, a character who might be important in the outcome of the plot can be eliminated from an isolated scene.

The next step is to focus attention on one character at a time in much the same way that a cameraman brings his lens from a group picture to a close-up. Starting with the person around whom the plot — or the chosen scene — revolves, the interpreter applies to the speeches of that character the now-familiar process of understanding logical content, giving careful attention to the climaxes and focal points, to style and rhythm, and to the denotations and connotations of all the words. When he has the content of the speeches clear in his mind, he will be ready to study the exterior and interior traits which the character exhibits.

Exterior or outward traits are the physical aspects which are immediately apparent to an observer: as "young man, about twenty-three, blond, tall, rather frail physique, holds one shoulder higher than the other, moves with nervous, jerky motions." These traits include the character's sex, age, and any outstanding physical characteristics or mannerisms. In a play they are revealed by whatever stage directions the playwright has inserted, by what the character does, and by what others say about him. Obviously these physical characteristics provide only a skeleton of the character, but they must be examined to discover what they reflect of his inner qualities and how they affect his responses to his environment and to other characters. Moreover, they will help the interpreter suggest the character in performance, just as they guide the actor and director in representation when the play is staged.

Interior, psychological aspects of character are much more complex. They are sometimes touched on in the stage directions, especially of the more elaborate, analytical type, but they are more completely revealed by what the character does and says, how he says it, and by what other characters say about him. They include his point of view; his attitude toward himself, toward others, and toward his surroundings; his emotional stability; his habitual degree of tension; his responses, both mental and emotional; and any variation from a "normal" set of values.

The writer of narrative can insert several paragraphs to tell about previous events and persons which have helped make his characters what they are. A playwright cannot allow himself this luxury unless he wishes to use a flash-back technique. More frequently he must be content with drawing his characters so completely in dialogue and action that there can be no doubt about their earlier environment. The interpreter, in order to achieve this same completeness of characterization, must often go back and reconstruct much of the action which precedes the play proper. Of Hedda Gabler, for example, we are told through dialogue in the opening scene that she is the daughter of General Gabler, that she has been accustomed to a life that in Miss Tesman's eyes is exciting and glamorous, and that she was sought after by many suitors before she married George Tesman. These details of her earlier life are important in making credible her utter selfishness and her impatience with the simple things that delight George and his aunt. Her age — nearly thirty — and her father's death obviously influenced her decision to marry Tesman, despite the fact that she can barely tolerate him. Period and locale, too, probably contributed to this decision, since a satisfactory career outside of marriage would have been difficult for her to achieve.

The interpreter of drama must follow much the same method which a conscientious actor adopts. He will need to know how his character looked, lived, thought, and behaved long before the play or scene itself takes place. The playwright does not always give this complete information, and the interpreter may need to depend upon his knowledge of human nature to supply him with the omitted details. He must develop an ability to observe life about him, and then to go behind the exterior manifestations in people in an attempt to discover motivations. He is dealing with human actions and reactions, and the more he knows of his fellow creatures the more easily he can understand and communicate the complexities of drama to his audience. Only after he has thoroughly understood the characters as people can he hope to apply his techniques for the purpose of full communication.

Having filled in the physical, mental, and emotional background, the interpreter is ready to begin his study of each character as he is involved in the incident of the play. What stage of development has the character reached by the time he makes his first entrance? What has he been doing immediately before his entrance? Has he been dozing in the garden, or attending a football game? Is he happy or depressed as the result of this activity? Does he expect to find the situation as it exists on stage, and is he thus prepared to become a part of it immediately, or is he unprepared for the events which have taken place during his absence?

When Hedda Gabler (or rather, Hedda Tesman) makes her first appearance, she has just gotten up on her first morning in her new home. She has taken time, however, to dress carefully, has apparently breakfasted, and is somewhat in control of herself and ready to begin her day. She is, of course, fundamentally discontented and impatient with the life that lies ahead, and to be confronted immediately with her husband and his aunt underlines her discontent and impatience. In the excerpt from *King Oedipus* at the end of this chapter (page 289) it is important to remember that Oedipus has sent for Teiresias, the blind prophet, and has been waiting for him with the citizens of Thebes, including a company of elders. It is a public, official occasion. Prior relationship is particularly vital to the scene from *Mary Stuart* as well (page 284). Although the two queens have not met previously, they are well aware of each other as royal, political enemies. The estate is Elizabeth's. It is Mary's place of detention, and she has not been warned of Elizabeth's being in the vicinity.

Because interrelationships play a vital part in character development, it is impractical to take a single character through an entire play while disregarding the others involved in the various scenes. Therefore, it might be well to follow the above procedure only to the end of the first key scene, and then go back to repeat it with the next most important character in that scene, evaluating his relation to the leading character and trying to discern what forces have shaped him over the years before the play begins, especially what attitude toward the main character he has already developed. The interpreter should note carefully how this attitude is revealed and whether or not it changes during the scene. He should continue this process with each character, studying each as an individual and evaluating his relationship to every other individual, so that in performance each segment will fit into the over-all pattern, and both plot and character development will reach their intended destinations.

In the opening scenes of *Hedda Gabler,* for example, there are three attitudes to consider besides Hedda's. The maid, Berta, is the least important character in these scenes, since she is primarily a tool used by Ibsen to give certain information and act as a foil for Miss Tesman. She does, however, provide some significant clues to Hedda's personality. She comments on how much the young mistress had to unpack before she could go to bed and confesses that she is "mortally afraid" she cannot please Hedda. She also points out that even though the couple arrived very late the night before, Hedda has already told her to change her manner of addressing Tesman and has also given some directions for rearranging the furniture.

Miss Tesman is an interesting person, both in her own pathetic right and in her influence upon George. She and George ally themselves very quickly, but quite unintentionally, as a single force for conflict with Hedda. George is the more dominant character, both because of his position as Hedda's husband and because of his prominence in the entire fabric of the play. His years with his two aunts have had a lasting effect upon his emotional stability and his attitude toward himself and others. In these respects, he shares some characteristics of Miss Tesman's. He has, however, made considerable progress on his own, not only in his marriage to Hedda but in his professional life. This gives him an added dimension which must be understood. He is an interesting mixture of pride and humility, authority and impotence, achievement and frustration. The more positive of these elements come into focus in his relationship with his aunt, while his tentativeness and frustration are most in evidence when Hedda is present.

The opening dialogue between Miss Tesman and Berta tells us a good deal about Hedda, and after George enters he fills in more details; thus we are well prepared for Hedda when she finally appears. But we learn much more about her from her own speeches and actions in the seemingly unimportant scene which follows. We are told by Ibsen that she is twenty-nine, that her face and figure show refinement and distinction, and that her steel-gray eyes express a cold, unruffled repose. Her rudeness and complete self-concentration, her irritation at the little things which mean much to George, and her unconcealed impatience with her surroundings and associates are revealed by her manner of speaking and of moving about the room.

After the interpreter has the first key scene firmly established in his mind, with all the aspects of content and form which must be considered, he returns again to his main character and goes to the next key scene, repeating the process he used in analyzing the first one. This time he watches for any changes in the playwright's focus of attention, in the development of the separate characters, and in their relation to each other and to the setting; and in so doing he becomes aware, also, of the increase or decrease in emotional tension and in activity. As new characters are introduced, he catches them up, too, in his process of analysis and evaluation. Finally, after going through the entire play in this manner, focusing attention on the key scenes — those which are necessary to the development of the plot — first in terms of the most important character and then of the lesser characters, the interpreter will turn his attention to the transitional scenes and analyze them in the same way for character relationship and development.

The style in which dialogue is written often provides some assistance in character analysis. The language which a character uses should indicate a great deal about his background and his attitude, just as it does in narrative prose. The arrangement of ideas gives a clue to the clarity of his thinking and is likely to be affected by intensity of emotion. The length of the thought units may also reveal much about his personality, his forcefulness, and his authority, as well as his degree of tension. Through awareness of the harmony between content and style, the interpreter can establish an appropriate tempo and over-all rhythm which will enable him to communicate a character's traits through his speeches. The language must always be considered in terms of the period in which the play was written, yet the well-written play of any time will convey strong indications of character through the length of the thought groups and through the rhythms and stresses within the units. Style is a most interesting consideration in an "anti-drama" like *Rhinoceros,* where the language is deliberately bare and reduced to its lowest level of suggestion to help achieve the dehumanization of the characters.

As a matter of fact, many of the plays of the sixties present interesting problems for the interpreter. Most of the so-called "absurd" plays have as their basic concept man's inability to communicate with his fellow man and even to put into words the frustrations and fears in his own mind. Thus, motivation and character interaction must be examined in quite a different fashion than in the traditional play. The motivation for both speech and action is most often confined within the character's own mind and is formed by his sense of isolation from the world or the resultant acceptance of the belief that man, the world, life, love, and death are equally "absurd." The dialogue often takes the form of extremely long near-monologues or soliloquies. These are difficult to sustain, partly because they are subjectively motivated but also because they are highly repetitious, which is one of the devices for anti-climax in the structure of these plays. Likewise, the action is often either violent and almost stylized or statically impotent, and the shifts of muscle tone are swift and sharp.

SETTING AND PROPERTIES

The matter of setting is much simpler for the dramatist than for the writer of narrative prose, for the dramatist can put the necessary information into the stage directions which precede each scene. These notations of time and place are included on the printed program when the play is given on stage and are emphasized through the skill of the scene designer, costumer, and lighting expert. Playwrights vary in the number of details which they give about period and locale. Shakespeare's plays, for example, frequently give no more indication of setting than "A public place" or "A room in ———'s house." Many contemporary playwrights, however, are more explicit in their directions and may include as many as a thousand words on setting and atmosphere. George Bernard Shaw was one of the most voluble, but even he was limited by the form in which he had chosen to work.

The author of a narrative has time and opportunity to dwell on the associational values he wishes to emphasize, and he gives the interpreter numerous clues to his intention by using various types of imagery. A playwright, on the other hand, relies heavily upon visual appeal in his stage directions. He is primarily concerned with the scene as the audience is to see it, and he allows the characters to reveal their more complex reactions to it as the dialogue progresses. This formula is necessary for the practical reason that the audience does not see the complete set of stage directions. They are intended for the actors and technicians involved in staging the play.

How, then, does the interpreter of drama handle this background material and make it clear to his listeners? Obviously, since he does not have the help of technicians who design scenery and control lighting effects, and of actors who use stage properties and react to the setting, he must be, in a sense, actor, technician, and director, as well as narrator.

In the role of narrator, he can easily and legitimately give most of the necessary stage directions directly to his audience before the curtain goes up on the action, as it were. The condensation and careful selection of detail that characterize most stage directions require him to make the most of his brief opportunity to create the scene. He therefore must emphasize important aspects of the time and place so that they etch themselves in the minds of the listeners, and he must give his listeners time to set up their own associational values. These values will result in part from the relationship of the setting to the social position, taste, and financial situation of the characters who are placed in it. Whenever a playwright has included abundant notes on production in his preliminary directions, the interpreter must decide which elements need to be presented directly to the audience and which ones can be handled by skillful suggestion of character as the play progresses.

In George Bernard Shaw's *Candida,* for example, nearly a thousand words of introductory material, in the form of stage directions, precede the rise of the curtain on Act I. Some of this information is of immediate interest to the audience, but a great deal of it is aimed primarily at establishing the background out of which the characters have come and against which they developed, and can be revealed through the interpreter's mental comment as he handles the dialogue. Consequently, in giving the stage directions, the interpreter would do well to omit much of the detailed information, and use it instead for his own guidance in showing plot motivation and character development. Since the scene cannot be presented visually to the listening audience, the interpreter, by selecting only the important details, can enable his listeners to focus on essential background information. On the other hand, the audience will need the description of the lion in the prologue from Shaw's *Androcles and the Lion* (page 342), although the specific description of Androcles might well be omitted except for the last sentence.

The time or period in which a play is laid is of extreme importance when social customs and economic conditions play a vital part in making the plot credible. This is true of *Romeo and Juliet,* for instance. The love story is universal to all times and places; but the family enmity is emphasized by the period, and the duels, the famous potion scene, and the entombment of Juliet could hardly happen in modern times.

Occasionally, a playwright will allow much of the information about the setting to come from someone who speaks directly to the audience as a narrator. In Thornton Wilder's *Our Town,* for example, there is a "Stage Manager" who explains the general location and atmosphere, sets each new scene, introduces the characters, establishes the time progression, and finally brings the play to its conclusion with:

> . . . Mm . . . Eleven o'clock in Grover's Corners. — You get a good rest, too. Good night.

Such devices as these simplify the interpreter's job because neither the "Stage Manager" nor the "Chorus" becomes a part of the play as a character caught up in the action, but is used only as a link between audience and actors. Hence the interpreter can assume the same relation to the audience and deliver the speeches directly to his listeners as narrator, giving only enough suggestion of character to make the narrator fit into the spirit of the play while conveying the desired philosophical quality.

A more complicated example of the narrator technique is found in Tennessee Williams' memory play, *The Glass Menagerie.* Here the author himself gives some suggestion of setting, but much of it is left to Tom, Amanda Wingfield's son. Combining the detached narrator and the participating character into one person lays greater demands on the interpreter than does the simple narrator device. Tom develops as the play proceeds, and the closing narration must take this development into account.

This narrator technique, which in fact dates back to the chorus of the Greek theater, is not, however, the general practice among modern playwrights. Usually the stage directions are quite brief and objective, and the interpreter handles them simply by speaking to the audience directly and in his own person.

Another aspect of setting in drama which the interpreter must not overlook, either in preparation or performance, is the effect of the setting on the characters. The writer of narrative can and often does remind his readers, and consequently the interpreter and his audience, of the physical aspects and psychological impact of the surroundings. The playwright, on the other hand, does not ordinarily intrude after his play has begun but, rather, counts on the physical setting to keep itself and its effect upon the characters in the consciousness of the audience. The interpreter, then, must see to it that he is as constantly aware of the surroundings he is attempting to suggest as the actor is of the set against which he plays. Suppose, for example, the character or characters are portrayed against an overcrowded room, elaborate with knickknacks, heavy draperies, and much furniture. It might well be that this atmosphere would produce a feeling of psychic suffocation in one character and a feeling of security in others. This will affect the mental attitude of each of them as well as their kinetic and kinesthetic responses. In *Romeo and Juliet,* for example, the lovers are affected by the gaiety and size of the ballroom; by the night, the distance between them, and the attendant details of setting in the balcony scene; by the intimacy and privacy of the bedchamber; and finally by the suffocating enclosure of the tomb.

Not only must the interpreter be aware of the area and specific location in which the various scenes take place, he must also exercise some care in using the setting for whatever purpose it was intended — whether for realism, establishing a mood, motivating significant action, or all three. The more skillful the playwright, the more important this consideration is likely to be. *The Cherry Orchard* by Chekhov (page 346) is an excellent example of a play in which setting contributes to all three of these factors. The house and its furnishings are important for realism because they establish the historical period and the financial and social background of the characters. But the setting performs an even more important function in strengthening mood and in motivating action. The house itself, interestingly enough, is less significant than the view of the orchard from the windows, for the orchard has become a symbol to most of the characters involved, and it provides a vital force in plot motivation. Thus care must be taken to establish the existence of the orchard along with the opening description of the interior in which the action takes place. The interpreter must remember that a play does not happen in a vacuum; although he does not have the actual scenery around him, he must nevertheless be constantly aware of its effect upon the characters he is portraying. To be successful in creating the setting in the minds of others, he must first create it for himself. The playwright intended it to be a part of the whole, and the degree of emphasis placed upon it is dictated by that intention.

Properties and various details of stage dressing may also play an important part in the action. In Ibsen's *Hedda Gabler*, the stove, which is included as a seemingly decorative detail in the description of Tesman's drawing room, assumes considerable importance when Hedda uses it to dispose of Lövborg's manuscript. If the interpreter has not mentioned the stove to his audience and thus enabled them to accept and visualize it as a part of the setting, it will be thrust too suddenly and confusingly into their consciousness in the manuscript-burning scene. The manuscript itself, first introduced when Lövborg takes it from his pocket and shows it to Hedda, is sufficiently pointed by the dialogue and will require no added emphasis. The next time the packet of papers is introduced as a property, the dialogue makes it very clear that Tesman has brought it in, having found it and deliberately kept it from its owner. Hedda places it, quite logically, in the bookcase. This last action, which is given as a stage direction, must be pointed slightly because it explains how she can fail to produce the manuscript when Lövborg returns and yet have it at hand to destroy immediately after his exit. Another property which is most important to the plot, though not emphasized when first introduced, is the pistol case, because the pistols it holds become increasingly significant as the play progresses. Hedda gives one of them to Lövborg for his suicide in the fourth act; and, partly because it has been recognized by Judge Brack, she uses the other for her own self-destruction in the last act. In the theatre of the absurd, the properties and settings are primarily to underscore the mood of starkness and distortion. Therefore, the interpreter will want to describe them for his audience, though he will rarely be called upon to "use" them in any practical sense.

The interpreter, then, must evaluate the details of setting and properties for their importance to plot and character motivation, as well as for their contribution to the visual aspects of time and place. Since he takes his cue from the playwright's objectivity, he will probably exhibit little or no muscular tension when he is giving stage directions, but will depend upon tempo, pause, force, stress, and inflection to give the appropriate degree of pointing to the significant details. When, however, he is suggesting background — or its effect on the characters — through dialogue, he will make empathic response through muscle tone as well as through voice.

CHARACTER SUGGESTION AND MUSCLE MEMORY

The interpreter's primary concern is with what goes on *inside* the characters as they operate in relation to each other and to the events which take place. Nevertheless, as we have already seen, interior characteristics and responses are reflected in certain discernible exterior traits.

It is sometimes helpful to go through the entire cutting to be used and develop technique for one character at a time, concentrating wholly on his speeches and actions just as if one were going to act that part — and only that part — on the stage. In making this type of study, the interpreter uses the other characters merely as linefeeders until such time as he feels that the main character is clearly and lastingly instilled in his mind, muscles, and voice. Then one by one the other characters are allowed to emerge with their individualities, progressions, and interrelationships. The interpreter will probably find it helpful to "walk" the main character, and the others in their turn — to rehearse relevant business exactly as if he were going to do it with properties and scenery. All this is an invaluable aid to timing, pace, and muscle tension, as well as to the motivation of changes in thought; and these are means by which he can suggest the character to his audience. Since this suggested procedure is time-consuming, the student should select for his classroom assignment a brief scene which contains relatively few characters, so that he may prepare thoroughly and work toward a stimulating performance. After these habits of preparation are set up, the process becomes less demanding because the interpreter knows what he is looking for and where to find it. Drama is built upon complexity, and the interpreter who wishes to handle this type of material must be willing to discover the intricate shadings of the characters and their relationships to every other aspect of the play, and to use his technique to make those shadings clear to his audience.

After the character is "set," the next step is vocal and physical selectivity. It is here that the paths of actor and interpreter of drama separate. The interpreter, like the actor, has created an explicit character with individual mental, emotional, physical, and vocal traits. He now decides which vocal elements — such as tempo, rhythm, inflection, range, and quality of voice

— will most accurately and swiftly suggest the character to the audience for whom he is preparing his performance. Abandoning the overt actions he has been using, he depends primarily upon posture, muscle tone, and kinesthetic response to suggest physical characteristics, although he may of course use gestures appropriate to the characters whenever they aid communication.

The time spent in rehearsing the actual business is by no means lost, however, because his *memory* of it will add to the vitality of his performance, to the pace and general effectiveness. This principle of muscle memory is sometimes referred to as the theory of remembered action. Muscle memory affects the reader's empathy and allows him to suggest hurry or leisure, activity or passivity, tension or relaxation as the scenes progress, thus enabling him to build his climaxes more effectively.

To test the effectiveness of this theory of muscle memory, read the following scene aloud, ignoring the stage directions for the moment. Of course, it is necessary to consider this scene in the context of the entire play before complete character development will emerge. Nevertheless this excerpt as it stands will serve our purpose as an illustration.

BRACK: No. But you will have to answer the question: Why did you give Eilert Lövborg the pistol? And what conclusions will people draw from the fact that you did give it to him?

HEDDA: (*Lets her head sink*) That is true. I did not think of that.

BRACK: Well, fortunately, there is no danger, so long as I say nothing.

HEDDA: (*Looks up at him*) So I am in your power, Judge Brack. You have me at your beck and call, from this time forward.

BRACK: (*Whispers softly*) Dearest Hedda — believe me — I shall not abuse my advantage.

HEDDA: I am in your power none the less. Subject to your will and your demands. A slave, a slave then! (*Rises impetuously*) No, I cannot endure the thought of that! Never!

BRACK: (*Looks half-mockingly at her*) People generally get used to the inevitable.

HEDDA: (*Returns his look*) Yes, perhaps. (*She crosses to the writing table.*)

After having analyzed the elements of content and style and the relationship of the characters so that you are certain of their interplay, go through the excerpt again and follow fully the directions for action which Ibsen has given. Start perhaps with Brack since he does not change his position. Assume that he is standing, leaning against a chair. Get the feeling in your muscles of one who leans on a chair, perfectly in control of the situation. Let Brack look down at Hedda, who is seated. He will probably straighten slightly and shift his focus with her movement when she rises. Act out the business exactly as you would if you were rehearsing his lines for the stage. Next, take Hedda from a sitting position, through the drooping of her head and the upward look that follows, her sudden rising and her cross to the table. Repeat as often as necessary to perfect the timing. You will note that it is easier to vary pace and inflection, as well as muscle tone and emotional tension, when the action accompanies the words. Now, applying the theory of muscle memory, re-read the scene without making the overt physical movements for either character. You will be able to retain the vocal variety as well as the physical variety for a strong degree of suggested activity.

Perhaps the most difficult thing about the interpretation of drama, aside from the purely mechanical or technical problems of suggesting character and action, is keeping the numerous threads of character development and reaction separated and yet related. This demands careful preparation and a high degree of concentration during performance. The interpreter must keep careful check, especially during his preparation, to make sure that he is not doing merely a series of character sketches, each complete in itself but almost totally unrelated to the others. For besides a thorough knowledge of each character, a constant awareness of relationships and of progressions in these relationships is required.

Thus the interpreter will need to select for each character enough significant physical and vocal details so that his hearers can themselves fill in the outline to make a three-dimensional, believable person. These details must, of course, be inherent in the character as the author has created him. The interpreter will need to use subtle variations in inflection and vocal quality, in the tempo and rhythm of his speech, to indicate changes in emotional response. He will find it necessary to vary his muscle tone and sometimes even his posture as the tension mounts or decreases.

It is impractical and even dangerous to offer specific directions for achieving this final communication of character, because each personality in each play presents its own slightly different problems. Some suggestions for handling mechanical details — and they are suggestions only — will be given in the next chapter. For the moment, however, it is enough for the interpreter to be aware that he will need to spend considerable time and effort in preparation to perfect his control of voice and body, and that he will have to exert extreme care in performance to keep these techniques from calling attention to themselves.

SELECTIONS FOR ANALYSIS AND ORAL INTERPRETATION

THE PLAY *Hedda Gabler*, from which the following excerpt is taken, was mentioned from time to time within the chapter.

Lövborg is — or rather was — a writer whom Hedda knew before her marriage to George Tesman. During the first act of the play it is revealed that Mrs. Elvsted has left her husband to be near Lövborg, and through her love has exerted considerable influence upon him. He has given up his drinking and has just completed a book of which they are both very proud. She confesses to Hedda, however, that there is always the shadow of a woman whom Lövborg cannot forget — a woman Hedda recognizes as herself.

Driven by a consuming ambition and selfishness heightened by her boredom and discontent with Tesman, Hedda will not endure Mrs. Elvsted's hold over Lövborg. When he calls late one afternoon, she plays upon his emotions until he breaks his promise not to drink and leaves in anger to join Tesman and others at a supper party. During an evening of drinking and merrymaking, he loses the manuscript of his book. Tesman finds it and brings it home.

When Lövborg returns much later in the evening, he is very drunk. He cannot recall what he did with his manuscript and confesses that he has disgraced himself and Mrs. Elvsted by an evening of debauchery. In desperation he talks of suicide, and Hedda, realizing his weaknesses, gives him one of the pistols with which she had threatened him in the past, saying, " . . . use it now . . . and beautifully, Eilert Lövborg. Promise me that!" As soon as Lövborg leaves, Hedda begins to burn his manuscript, thus giving vent to her jealousy and destroying the tangible evidence of Mrs. Elvsted's influence.

The scene below is from the fourth act. It is evening of the next day. Judge Brack, friend of George Tesman, and one of Hedda's admirers who understands her better than most of the others, brings some details of the death of Lövborg. Mrs. Elvsted and Tesman are arranging some notes in an attempt to reconstruct the manuscript which they believe Lövborg himself destroyed.

As the scene progresses, watch carefully for indications of Hedda's recognition of the fact that instead of being in control herself (her own feeling of power is expressed in her opening speech) it is Brack who really has the upper hand. Be sure to keep the tension building in Hedda in her offstage speeches. Remember that neither Mrs. Elvsted nor Tesman suspects the truth. Be careful not to underestimate Tesman's reaction because of his "Fancy that!" It is a characteristic expression of his.

from *Hedda Gabler*

ACT IV

(. . . HEDDA *crosses to the stove and sits in the arm-chair. Presently* BRACK *goes up to her.*)

HEDDA: (*In a low voice*) Oh, what a sense of freedom it gives one, this act of Eilert Lövborg's.

"Hedda Gabler" by Henrik Ibsen, translated by William Archer (1904), is reprinted with the permission of Charles Scribner's Sons from *The Collected Works of Henrik Ibsen,* Volume X.

BRACK: Freedom, Hedda? Well, of course, it is a release for him —

HEDDA: I mean for me. It gives me a sense of freedom to know that a deed of deliberate courage is still possible in this world, — a deed of spontaneous beauty.

BRACK: (*Smiling*) H'm — my dear Hedda —

HEDDA: Oh, I know what you are going to say. For you are a kind of specialist, too, like — you know!

BRACK: (*Looking hard at her*) Eilert Lövborg was more to you than perhaps you are willing to admit to yourself. Am I wrong?

HEDDA: I don't answer such questions. I only know that Eilert Lövborg has had the courage to live his life after his own fashion. And then — the last great act, with its beauty! Ah! that he should have the will and the strength to turn away from the banquet of life — so early.

BRACK: I am sorry, Hedda, — but I fear I must dispel an amiable illusion.

HEDDA: Illusion?

BRACK: Which could not have lasted long in any case.

HEDDA: What do you mean?

BRACK: Eilert Lövborg did not shoot himself — voluntarily.

HEDDA: Not voluntarily?

BRACK: No. The thing did not happen exactly as I told it.

HEDDA: (*In suspense*) Have you concealed something? What is it?

BRACK: For poor Mrs. Elvsted's sake I idealized the facts a little.

HEDDA: What are the facts?

BRACK: First, that he is already dead.

HEDDA: At the hospital?

BRACK: Yes — without regaining consciousness.

HEDDA: What more have you concealed?

BRACK: This — the event did not happen at his lodgings.

HEDDA: Oh, that can make no difference.

BRACK: Perhaps it may. For I must tell you — Eilert Lövborg was found — in Mademoiselle Diana's boudoir.

HEDDA: (*Makes a motion as if to rise, but sinks back again*) That is impossible, Judge Brack! He cannot have been there again to-day.

BRACK: He was there this afternoon. He went there, he said, to demand the return of something which they had taken from him. Talked wildly about a lost child —

HEDDA: Ah — so that was why —

BRACK: I thought probably he meant his manuscript; but now I hear he destroyed that himself. So I suppose it must have been his pocket-book.

HEDDA: Yes, no doubt. So he was found — there?

BRACK: Yes, there. With a pistol in his breast-pocket, discharged. The ball had lodged in a vital part.

HEDDA: In the breast — yes.

BRACK: No — in the bowels.

HEDDA: (*Looks up at him with an expression of loathing*) That, too! Oh, what curse is it that makes everything I touch turn ludicrous and mean?

BRACK: There is one point more — another disagreeable feature in the affair.

HEDDA: And what is that?

BRACK: The pistol he carried —

HEDDA: (*Breathless*) Well? What of it?

BRACK: He must have stolen it.

HEDDA: (*Leaps up*) Stolen it! That is not true! He did not steal it!

BRACK: No other explanation is possible. He must have stolen it —

HEDDA: Why stolen it?

BRACK: Because every other explanation ought to be impossible, Hedda.

HEDDA: Indeed?

BRACK: (*Glances at her*) Of course, Eilert Lövborg was here this morning. Was he not?

HEDDA: Yes.

BRACK: Were you alone with him?

HEDDA: Part of the time.

BRACK: Did you not leave the room whilst he was here?

HEDDA: No.

BRACK: Try to recollect. Were you not out of the room a moment?

HEDDA: Yes, perhaps just a moment — out in the hall.

BRACK: And where was your pistol-case during that time?

HEDDA: I had it locked up in —

BRACK: Well, Hedda?

HEDDA: The case stood there on the writing-table.

BRACK: Have you looked since, to see whether both the pistols are there?

HEDDA: No.

BRACK: Well, you need not. I saw the pistol found in Lövborg's pocket, and I knew it at once as the one I had seen yesterday — and before, too.

HEDDA: Have you it with you?

BRACK: No; the police have it.

HEDDA: What will the police do with it?

BRACK: Search till they find the owner.

HEDDA: Do you think they will succeed?

BRACK: (*Bends over her and whispers*) No, Hedda Gabler — not so long as I say nothing.

HEDDA: (*Looks frightened at him*) And if you do not say nothing, — what then?

BRACK: (*Shrugs his shoulders*) There is always the possibility that the pistol was stolen.

HEDDA: (*Firmly*) Death would be better than that.

BRACK: (*Smiling*) People say such things — but they don't do them.

HEDDA: (*Without replying*) And supposing the pistol was not stolen, and the owner is discovered? What then?

BRACK: Well, Hedda — then comes the scandal.

HEDDA: The scandal!

BRACK: Yes, the scandal — of which you are so mortally afraid. You will, of course, be brought before the court — both you and Mademoiselle Diana. She will have to explain how the thing happened — whether it was an accidental shot or murder. Did the pistol go off as he was trying to take it out of his pocket, to threaten her with? Or did she tear the pistol out of his hand, shoot him, and push it back into his pocket? That would be quite like her; for she is an able-bodied young person, this same Mademoiselle Diana.

HEDDA: But I have nothing to do with all this repulsive business.

BRACK: No. But you will have to answer the question: Why did you give Eilert Lövborg the pistol? And what conclusions will people draw from the fact that you did give it to him?

HEDDA: (*Lets her head sink*) That is true. I did not think of that.

BRACK: Well, fortunately, there is no danger, so long as I say nothing.

HEDDA: (*Looks up at him*) So I am in your power, Judge Brack. You have me at your beck and call, from this time forward.

BRACK: (*Whispers softly*) Dearest Hedda — believe me — I shall not abuse my advantage.

HEDDA: I am in your power none the less. Subject to your will and your demands. A slave, a slave then! (*Rises impetuously*) No, I cannot endure the thought of that! Never!

BRACK: (*Looks half-mockingly at her*) People generally get used to the inevitable.

HEDDA: (*Returns his look*) Yes, perhaps. (*She crosses to the writing-table where* TESMAN *and* MRS. ELVSTED *are arranging papers. Suppressing an involuntary smile, she imitates* TESMAN'S *intonations.*) Well? Are you getting on, George? Eh?

TESMAN: Heaven knows, dear. In any case it will be the work of months.

HEDDA: (*As before*) Fancy that! (*Passes her hands softly through* MRS. ELVSTED'S *hair*) Doesn't it seem strange to you, Thea? Here are you sitting with Tesman — just as you used to sit with Eilert Lövborg?

MRS. ELVSTED: Ah, if I could only inspire your husband in the same way!

HEDDA: Oh, that will come, too — in time.

TESMAN: Yes, do you know, Hedda — I really think I begin to feel something of the sort. But won't you go and sit with Brack again?

HEDDA: Is there nothing I can do to help you two?

TESMAN: No, nothing in the world. (*Turning his head*) I trust to you to keep Hedda company, my dear Brack.

BRACK: (*With a glance at* HEDDA) With the very greatest of pleasure.

HEDDA: Thanks. But I am tired this evening. I will go in and lie down a little on the sofa.

TESMAN: Yes, do dear — eh?

(HEDDA *goes into the back room and draws the curtains. A short pause. Suddenly she is heard playing a wild dance on the piano.*)

MRS. ELVSTED: (*Starts from her chair*) Oh — what is that?

TESMAN: (*Runs to the doorway*) Why, my dearest Hedda — don't play dance-music to-night! Just think of Aunt Rina! And of Eilert, too!

HEDDA: (*Puts her head out between the curtains*) And of Aunt Julia. And of all the rest of them. — From now on I will be quiet. (*Closes the curtains again.*)

TESMAN: (*At the writing-table*) It's not good for her to see us at this distressing work. I'll tell you what, Mrs. Elvsted, — you shall take the empty room at Aunt Julia's, and then I will come over in the evenings, and we can sit and work there — eh?

HEDDA: (*In the inner room*) I hear what you are saying, Tesman. But how am *I* to get through the evenings out here?

TESMAN: (*Turning over the papers*) Oh, I daresay Judge Brack will be so kind as to look in now and then, even though I am out.

BRACK: (*In the arm-chair, calls out gaily*) Every blessed evening, with all the pleasure in life, Mrs. Tesman! We shall get on capitally together, we two!

HEDDA: (*Speaking loud and clear*) Yes, don't you flatter yourself we will, Judge Brack? Now that you are the one cock in the basket — (*A shot is heard within.* TESMAN, MRS. ELVSTED, *and* BRACK *leap to their feet*)

TESMAN: Oh, now she is playing with those pistols again.

(*He throws back the curtains and runs in, followed by* MRS. ELVSTED. HEDDA *lies stretched on the sofa, dead. Confusion and cries.*)

TESMAN: (*Shrieks to* BRACK) Shot herself! Shot herself in the temple! Fancy that!

BRACK: (*Dropping into the arm-chair*) Good God! — people don't do such things.

HENRIK IBSEN

THESE SCENES FROM the third act of *Mary Stuart* are laid in the garden outside the castle at Fotheringay where Mary has been held prisoner for a long time by Elizabeth's order. The charges are political, but despite innumerable requests Mary has been unable to gain an audience with Elizabeth. Lord Leicester and Lord Shrewsbury, along with numerous other members of Elizabeth's court, have conspired to bring the queens together as Elizabeth rides home from a hunting expedition. Shrewsbury has just told Mary that her long-sought audience is about to take place. Mary, who has planned for years what she wishes to say to Elizabeth, is caught unawares and has almost no time to compose herself before Elizabeth enters with Leicester. The relationship between Mary and Leicester is a political one but highly charged with personal involvement as well. Hannah Kennedy (Scene 5) is Mary Stuart's nurse.

In the excerpt which follows, some stage directions have been deleted, and some of the language has been modernized. Ellipses show where non-essential lines of dialogue have been omitted.

from *Mary Stuart*

Act III, Scene 4

ELIZ: What place is this, my lord?
LEIC: 'Tis Fotheringay.
ELIZ: My lord, send back our retinue to London;
The people crowd too eager in the roads,
We'll seek a refuge in this quiet park.
My honest people love me overmuch.
These signs of joy are quite idolatrous.
Thus should a god be honoured, not a mortal.
MARY: O God! from out these features speaks no heart.
ELIZ: What lady's that? —
LEIC: You are at Fotheringay,
My liege.
ELIZ: Who has done this, my Lord of Leicester?
LEIC: 'Tis done my queen; — and now that Heaven has led
Your footsteps hither, be magnanimous;
And let sweet pity be triumphant now.
SHREW: O royal mistress! yield to our entreaties;
And look with mercy on this anguished one, . . .
ELIZ: How, my lords!
Which of you then announced to me a prisoner
Bowed down by woe? I see a haughty one,
By no means humbled by calamity.
MARY: Well, be it so: — to this I will submit.
Reject high thought, and pride of noble mind!
I will forget my dignity, and all
My sufferings; I will fall before *her* feet
Who has reduced me to this wretchedness.
The voice of Heaven decides for you, my sister.
Your happy brow is now with triumph crowned,
I bless the Power Divine, which thus has raised you.
But in your turn be merciful, my sister.
Let me not lie before you thus disgraced;
Stretch forth your hand, your royal hand, to raise
Your sister from the depths of her distress.

ELIZ: You are where it becomes you, Lady Stuart;
And thankfully I prize my God's protection,
Who has not suffered *me* to kneel a suppliant
Thus at *your* feet, as you now kneel at mine.

MARY: Oh! There are gods who punish haughty pride;

. . .

Before these strangers' eyes, dishonour not
Yourself in me: profane not, nor disgrace
The royal blood of Tudor. In my veins
It flows as pure a stream as in your own.
O! for God's pity, stand not so estranged
And inaccessible, like some tall cliff,
Which the poor shipwrecked mariner in vain
Struggles to seize, and labours to embrace.
My all, my life, my fortune now depends
Upon the influence of my words and tears,
That I may touch your heart, O! set mine free.
If you regard me with those icy looks, . . .
My tears do freeze, and frigid horror chains
The words of supplication in my bosom!

ELIZ: What would you say to me, my Lady Stuart?
You wished to speak with me; and I, forgetting
The queen, and all the wrongs I have sustained,
Fulfil the pious duty of the sister,
And grant the boon you wished for of my presence.
Yet I . . . expose myself
To rightful censure, that I stoop so low.
For well you know, you would have had me murdered.

MARY: O! how shall I begin? O, how shall I
So artfully arrange my cautious words,
That they may touch, yet not offend your heart? —
. . . Alas! I cannot speak
In my own cause, without impeaching you; . . .
You have not, as you ought, behaved to me;
I am a queen, like you, yet you have held me
Confined in prison. As a suppliant
I came to you, yet *you* in me insulted
The pious use of hospitality,
Slighting in me the holy law of nations,
Immured me in a dungeon — tore from me
My friends and servants. I was exposed
To most unseemly want, and hurried to the court
Of a disgraceful, insolent tribunal.
No more of this; — in everlasting silence
Let us bury all the wrongs I suffered!
See — I will throw the blame of all on fate,
'Twas not your fault, no more than it was mine. . . .
This is the curse

Of kings, that they, divided, tear the world
In pieces with their hatred, and let loose
The raging furies of all hellish strife!
No foreign tongue is now between us, sister,
Now we stand face to face; now, sister, speak;
Name but my crime, I'll fully satisfy you, —
Alas! had you vouchsafed to hear me then, . . .
It never would have come to this, nor would,
Here in this mournful place, have happened now
This so distressful, this so mournful meeting.

ELIZ: My better stars preserved me. I was warned. . . .
The blow was aimed full at my head,
But yours it is which falls!

MARY: . . . You never will
Exert so cruelly the power heaven gives you.

ELIZ: Who shall prevent me? Say, did not your uncle
Set all the kings of Europe the example
How to conclude a peace with those they hate. . . .
Say then, what surety can be offered me,
Should I magnanimously loose your bond?
Say, with what lock can I secure your faith,
Which by St. Peter's keys cannot be opened?
Force is my only surety. No alliance
Can be concluded with a race of vipers.

MARY: O! this is but your wretched, dark suspicion!
For you have constantly regarded me
But as a stranger, and an enemy.
Had you declared me heir to your dominions,
As is my right, then gratitude and love
In me had fixed, for you, a faithful friend
And kinswoman.

ELIZ: Your friendship is abroad,
Your house is papacy, the monk your brother.
Name *you* my successor! . . .

MARY: O sister, rule your realm in peace!
I give you every claim to these domains — . . .
Greatness entices me no more: your point
Is gained; I am but Mary's shadow now —
My noble spirit is at last broke down
By long captivity: — you've done your worst! . . .
Now, end your work, my sister; — speak at length
The word, which to pronounce has brought you hither;
For I will not believe, that you have come,
To mock unfeelingly your hapless victim.
Pronounce this word; — say, "Mary, you are free;
You have already felt my power, — learn now
To honour too my generosity."

Say this, and I will take my life, will take
My freedom, as a present from your hands.
One word makes all undone; — I wait for it; —
O let it not be needlessly delayed. . . .

ELIZ: And you confess at last, that you are conquered;
Are all your schemes run out? No more assassins
Now on the road? Will no adventurer
Attempt again, for you, the sad achievement?
Yes, madam, it is over: — You will seduce
No mortal more. The world has other cares;
None is ambitious of the dangerous honour
Of being your fourth husband: — You destroy
Your wooers like your husbands.

MARY: Sister, sister! —
Grant me forbearance, all ye powers of heaven!

ELIZ: These then, my Lord of Leicester, are the charms
Which no man with impunity can view,
Near which no woman dare attempt to stand?
In sooth, this honour has been cheaply gained;
She who to all is common, may with ease
Become the common object of applause.

MARY: This is too much!

ELIZ: You show us now indeed,
Your real face; till now 'twas but the mask.

MARY: My sins were human, and the faults of youth: . . .
I have never denied or sought to hide it. . . .
The worst of me is known, and I can say,
That I am better than the fame I bear.
Woe to you! when, in time to come, the world
Shall draw the robe of honour from your deeds,
With which your arch-hypocrisy has veiled
The raging flames of lawless secret lust.
Virtue was not your portion from your mother;
We well know what it was which brought the head
Of Anne Boleyn to the fatal block.

SHREW: . . . Alas, and must it come to this!
Is this the moderation, the submission,
My lady? —

MARY: Moderation! I've supported
What human nature can support! . . . A bastard soils,
Profanes the English throne! The generous Britons
Are cheated by a juggler, whose whole figure
Is false and painted, heart as well as face!
If right prevailed, you now would in the dust
Before me lie, for I'm your rightful monarch!

(*Exit Elizabeth and Leicester*)

SCENE 5

HANNAH: What have you done? She has gone hence in wrath,
All hope is over now!
MARY: Gone hence in wrath!
She carries death within her heart! I know it.
But after years of sorrow and abasement,
One moment of victorious revenge!
A weight falls off my heart, a weight of mountains. . . .
HANNAH: . . . 'Tis she who wields the light'ning! She is queen. . . .
MARY: I have abased her before Leicester's eyes;
He saw it. He was witness of my triumph.
How I did hurl her from her haughty height.
He saw it, and his presence strengthened me.

FRIEDRICH VON SCHILLER

OEDIPUS, KING OF THEBES, who once answered the riddle of the Sphinx and thus destroyed her power, has been visited by the elders and townsmen begging him to deliver them once again from famine and pestilence. He tells them that he has sent his brother-in-law, Creon, to the oracle to find out what he might do to save the state. When Creon returns, he reveals that the oracle has said the curse will not be lifted until the murderer of King Laius, who held the throne before Oedipus, is found and driven from Thebes. Oedipus has issued a proclamation to carry out this task. Moreover, he has sent for the blind prophet Teiresias in the hope that he can help identify the murderer through his powers of divination. Oedipus stands on the steps of his palace surrounded by his citizens, waiting for the arrival of the revered man.

from *King Oedipus*

Enter TEIRESIAS, *blind, led by an attendant.*

OEDIPUS: Teiresias, we know there is nothing beyond your ken;
Lore sacred and profane, all heavenly and earthly knowledge
Are in your grasp. In your heart, if not with the eye,
You see our city's condition: we look to you
As our only help and protector. We have sent —
They may have told you — to Phoebus, and he has answered.
The only way of deliverance from our plague
Is for us to find out the killers of Laius
And kill or banish them.
Now, sir, spare not your skill
In bird-lore or whatever other arts
Of prophecy you profess. It is for yourself,
It is for Thebes, it is for me. Come, save us all,

From *King Oedipus* by Sophocles, translated by E. F. Watling. Reprinted by permission of Penguin Books, Ltd.

Save all that is polluted by this death.
We look to you. To help his fellow-men
With all his power is man's most noble work.
TEIRESIAS: Wise words, but O, when wisdom brings no profit,
To be wise is to suffer. And why did I forget this,
Who knew it well? I never should have come.
OEDIPUS: It seems you bring us little encouragement.
TEIRESIAS: Let me go home. It will be easier thus
For you to bear your burden, and me mine.
OEDIPUS: Take care, sir. You show yourself no friend to Thebes,
Whose son you are, if you refuse to answer.
TEIRESIAS: It is because I see your words, sir, tending
To no good end; therefore I guard my own.
OEDIPUS: By the gods! If you know, do not refuse to speak!
We all beseech you; we are all your suppliants.
TEIRESIAS: You are all deluded. I refuse to utter
The heavy secrets of my soul — and yours.
OEDIPUS: What? Something you know, and will not tell? You mean
To fail us and to see your city perish?
TEIRESIAS: I mean to spare you, and myself. Ask me
No more. It is useless. I will tell you nothing.
OEDIPUS: Nothing? Insolent scoundrel, you would rouse
A stone to fury! Will you never speak?
You are determined to be obstinate to the end?
TEIRESIAS: Do not blame me; put your own house in order.
OEDIPUS: Hear him! Such words — such insults to the State
Would move a saint to anger.
TEIRESIAS: What will be
Will be, though I should never speak again.
OEDIPUS: What is to be, it is your trade to tell.
TEIRESIAS: I tell no more. Rage with what wrath you will.
OEDIPUS: I shall; and speak my mind unflinchingly.
I tell you I do believe *you* had a hand
In plotting, and all but doing, this very act.
If you had eyes to see with, I would have said
Your hand, and yours alone, had done it all.
TEIRESIAS: You would so? Then hear this: upon your head
Is the ban your lips have uttered — from this day forth
Never to speak to me or any here.
You are the cursed polluter of this land.
OEDIPUS: You dare to say it! Have you no shame at all?
And do you expect to escape the consequence?
TEIRESIAS: I have escaped. The truth is my defence.
OEDIPUS: Whose work is this? This is no soothsaying.
TEIRESIAS: You taught me. You made me say it against my will.
OEDIPUS: Say it again. Let there be no mistake.
TEIRESIAS: Was it not plain? Or will you tempt me further?
OEDIPUS: I would have it beyond all doubt. Say it again.

TEIRESIAS: I say that the killer you are seeking is yourself.
OEDIPUS: The second time. You shall be sorry for this.
TEIRESIAS: Will you have more, to feed your anger?
OEDIPUS: Yes!
More, and more madness. Tell us all you know.
TEIRESIAS: I know, as you do not, that you are living
In sinful union with the one you love,
Living in ignorance of your own undoing.
OEDIPUS: Do you think you can say such things with impunity?
TEIRESIAS: I do — if truth has any power to save.
OEDIPUS: It has — but not for you; no, not for you,
Shameless and brainless, sightless, senseless sot!
TEIRESIAS: You are to be pitied, uttering such taunts
As all men's mouths must some day cast at you.
OEDIPUS: Living in perpetual night, you cannot harm
Me, nor any man else that sees the light.
TEIRESIAS: No; it is not for me to bring you down.
That is in Apollo's hands, and he will do it.
OEDIPUS: (*scenting a possible connection with Creon's embassy*)
Creon! Was this trick his, then, if not yours?
TEIRESIAS: Not Creon either. Your enemy is yourself.
OEDIPUS: What was your vaunted seercraft ever worth?
And where were you, when the Dog-faced Witch was here?
Had you any word of deliverance then for our people?
There was a riddle too deep for common wits;
A seer should have answered it; but answer came there none
From you; bird-lore and god-craft all were silent.
Until *I* came — I, ignorant Oedipus, came —
And stopped the riddler's mouth, guessing the truth
By mother-wit, not bird-lore. This is the man
Whom you would dispossess, hoping to stand
Nearest to Creon's throne. You shall repent,
You and your fellow-plotter, of your zeal
For scapegoat-hunting. Were you not as old
As you appear to be, sharp punishment
Would soon convince you of your wickedness.
CHORUS: Sir, to our thinking, both of you have spoken
In the heat of anger. Surely this is not well,
When all our thought should be, how to discharge
The god's command.
TEIRESIAS: King though you are, one right —
To answer — makes us equal; and I claim it.
It is not you, but Loxias, whom I serve;
Nor am I bound to Creon's patronage.
You are pleased to mock my blindness. Have you eye
And do not see your own damnation? Eyes,
And cannot see what company you keep?
Whose son are you? I tell you, you have sinned —

And do not know it — against your own on earth
And in the grave. A swift and two-edged sword,
Your mother's and your father's curse, shall sweep you
Out of this land. Those now clear-seeing eyes
Shall then be darkened, then no place be deaf,
No corner of Cithaeron echoless,
To your loud crying, when you learn the truth
Of that sweet marriage-song that hailed you home
To the fair-seeming haven of your hopes —
With more, more misery than you can guess,
To show you what you are, and who they are
That call you father. Rail as you will at Creon,
And at my speaking — you shall be trodden down
With fouler scorn than ever fell on man.

OEDIPUS: Shall I bear more of this? Out of my sight!
Go! Quickly, go! Back where you came from! Go!

TEIRESIAS: I will. It was your wish brought me here, not mine.

OEDIPUS: Had I known what madness I was to listen to,
I would have spared myself the trouble.

TEIRESIAS: Mad I may seem
To you. Your parents would not think me so.

OEDIPUS: What's that? My parents? Who then . . . gave me birth?

TEIRESIAS: This day brings you your birth; and brings you death.

OEDIPUS: Man, must you still wrap up your words in riddles?

TEIRESIAS: Were you not famed for skill at solving riddles?

OEDIPUS: You taunt me with the gift that is my greatness?

TEIRESIAS: Your great misfortune, and your ruin.

OEDIPUS: No matter!
I have saved this land from ruin. I am content.

TEIRESIAS: Well, I will go. Your hand, boy. Take me home.

OEDIPUS: We well can spare you. Let him take you home.

TEIRESIAS: When I have said my all. Thus, to your face,
Fearful of nothing you can do to me:
The man for whom you have ordered hue and cry,
The killer of Laius — that man is here;
Passing for an alien, a sojourner here among us;
But, as presently shall appear, a Theban born,
To his cost. He that came seeing, blind shall he go;
Rich now, then a beggar; stick-in-hand, groping his way
To a land of exile; brother, as it shall be shown,
And father at once, to the children he cherishes; son,
And husband, to the woman who bore him; father-killer,
and father-supplanter.
Go in, and think on this.
When you can prove me wrong, then call me blind.

Exeunt

SOPHOCLES

These scenes do not run consecutively in Archibald MacLeish's play about a modern Job. They do, however, all deal with his relationship with his wife and her involvement in his sufferings and struggle to accept God's will. With a careful transition they can work very well as a unit, or each can stand alone.

J.B. and Sarah have suffered a succession of tragedies. They have gone from wealth, prosperity, and a happy family life to degradation, poverty, illness, and the loss by horrible accident and murder of their five children. As a final catastrophe their whole world now lies in rubble around them, peopled only by a few survivors huddled on trash heaps.

Nickles, who has worn the Satan mask in the dramatic commentary on the story, operates almost as a Greek chorus, commenting to the audience, indeed to the world in general, rather than entering into the scene itself.

from *J.B.*

Scene 8

There is no light but the glow on the canvas sky, which holds the looming, leaning shadows. They fade as a match is struck. It flares in Sarah's hand, showing her face, and glimmers out against the wick of a dirty lantern. As the light of the lantern rises, J.B. is seen lying on the broken propped-up table, naked but for a few rags of clothing. Sarah looks at him in the new light, shudders, lets her head drop into her hands. There is a long silence and then a movement in the darkness of the open door where four women and a young girl stand, their arms filled with blankets and newspapers. They come forward slowly into the light.

. . . . .

The women settle themselves on their newspapers off at the edge of the circle of light. Nickles has perched himself on a chair at the side.

. . . . .

Silence. Out of the silence, felt rather than heard at first, a sound of sobbing, a muffled, monotonous sound like the heavy beat of a heart.

J.B.: If you could only sleep a little
Now they're quiet, now they're still.

SARAH: *her voice broken*
I try. But oh I close my eyes and . . .
Eyes are open there to meet me!

Silence. Then Sarah's voice in an agony of bitterness.

My poor babies! Oh, my poor babies!

J.B. pulls himself painfully up, sits huddled on his table in the feeble light of the lamp, his rags about him.

From *J.B.* by Archibald MacLeish. Copyright © 1956, 1957, 1958 by Archibald MacLeish. Reprinted by permission of Houghton Mifflin Company.

J.B.: *gently* Go to sleep.

SARAH: *Go!* Go where?
If there were darkness I'd go there.
If there were night I'd lay me down in it.
God has shut the night against me.
God has set the dark alight
With horror blazing blind as day
When I go toward it . . .
close my eyes.

J.B.: I know. I know those waking eyes.
His will is everywhere against us —
Even in our sleep, our dreams . . .

NICKLES: *a snort of laughter up toward the dark of the platform*

Your will, *his* peace!
Doesn't seem to grasp that, does he?
Give him another needling twinge
Between the withers and the works —
He'll understand you better.

J.B.: If I
Knew . . . If I knew why!

NICKLES: If he knew
Why he wouldn't be there. He'd be
Strangling, drowning, suffocating,
Diving for a sidewalk somewhere . . .

J.B.: What I *can't* bear is the blindness —
Meaninglessness — the numb blow
Fallen in the stumbling night.

SARAH: *starting violently to her feet*

Has death no meaning? Pain no meaning?

She points at his body.

Even these suppurating sores —
Have they no meaning for you?

NICKLES: Ah!

J.B.: *from his heart's pain*

God will not punish without cause.

Nickles doubles up in a spasm of soundless laughter.

J.B.: God is just.

SARAH: *hysterically* God is just!
If God is just our slaughtered children
Stank with sin, were rotten with it!

She controls herself with difficulty, turns toward him, reaches her arms out, lets them fall.

Oh, my dear! my dear! my dear!
Does God demand deception of us? —
Purchase His innocence by ours?
Must we be guilty for Him? — bear
The burden of the world's malevolence
For Him who made the world?

J.B.: *He*
Knows the guilt is mine. He must know:
Has He not punished it? He knows its
Name, its time, its face, its circumstance,
The figure of its day, the door,
The opening of the door, the room, the moment . . .

SARAH: *fiercely*
And you? Do you? You do not know it.
Your punishment is all you know.

She moves toward the door, stops, turns.

I will not stay here if you lie —
Connive in your destruction, cringe to it:
Not if you betray my children . . .
I will not stay to listen . . .
They are
Dead and they were innocent: I will not
Let you sacrifice their deaths
To make injustice justice and God good!

J.B.: *covering his face with his hands*
My heart beats. I cannot answer it.

SARAH: If you buy quiet with their innocence —
Theirs or yours . . .
softly I will not love you.

J.B.: I have no choice but to be guilty.

SARAH: *her voice rising*
We have the choice to live or die,
All of us . . .
curse God and die . . .

Silence.

J.B.: God is God or we are nothing —
Mayflies that leave their husks behind —
Our tiny lives ridiculous — a suffering
Not even sad that Someone Somewhere
Laughs at as we laugh at apes.
We have no choice but to be guilty.
God is unthinkable if we are innocent.

Sarah turns, runs soundlessly out of the circle of light, out of the door. The women stir.

. . . . . .

Gradually the women gather up their few belongings and leave the stage. J.B. is left alone lying on a pile of rubble. Nickles crosses and stands looking down at him.

from SCENE 10

. . . . . .

NICKLES: Oh come off it.
You don't have to act with me.

J.B. is silent.

O.K. Carry on.
All I wanted was to help.
Professional counsel you might call it . . .

J.B. is silent.

Of course you know how all this ends? . . .

J.B. is silent.

I wondered how you'd play the end.

J.B.: Who knows what the end is, ever?

NICKLES: I do. You do.

J.B.: Then don't tell me.

NICKLES: What's the worst thing you can think of?

J.B.: I have asked for death. Begged for it. Prayed for it.

NICKLES: Then the worst thing can't be death.

J.B.: Ah!

NICKLES: You know now.

J.B.: No. You tell me.

NICKLES: Why should I tell you when you know?

J.B.: Then don't. I'm sick of mysteries. Sick of them.

NICKLES: He gives it back to you.

J.B.: What back?

NICKLES: All of it.
Everything He ever took:
Wife, health, children, everything.

J.B.: I have no wife.

NICKLES: She comes back to you.

J.B.: I have no children.

NICKLES: *a nasty laugh* You'll have better ones.

J.B.: My skin is . . .

He breaks off, staring at the skin of his naked arms.

NICKLES: Oh come on! I know the
Look of grease paint!

J.B.: . . . whole! It's healed!

NICKLES: *heavily ironic*

You see? You see what I mean? What He plans for you?

J.B., staring at his arms, is silent.

NICKLES: *leaning forward, urgently*

Tell me how you play the end.
Any man was screwed as Job was! . . .

J.B. does not answer.

I'll tell you how you play it. Listen!
Think of all the mucked-up millions
Since this buggered world began
Said, No!, said, Thank you!, took a rope's end,
Took a window for a door,
Swallowed something, gagged on something . . .

J.B. lifts his head: he is listening but not to Nickles.

None of them knew the truth as Job does.
None of them had his cause to know.

J.B.: Listen! Do you hear? There's someone . . .

NICKLES: *violently*

Job won't take it! Job won't touch it!
Job will fling it in God's face
With half his guts to make it spatter!
He'd rather suffocate in dung —
Choke in ordure —

J.B.: *rising* There is someone —
Someone waiting at the door.

NICKLES: *pulling his cap down, rising slowly*

I know.

The dangling lights dim out.

SCENE 11

A light comes from the canvas door. It increases as though day were beginning somewhere. Nickles has gone.

J.B.: Who is it?

He crosses toward the door walking with his old ease. Stops.

Is there someone there?

There is no answer. He goes on. Reaches the door.

Sarah!

The light increases. She is sitting on the sill, a broken twig in her hand.

SARAH: Look, Job: the forsythia,
The first few leaves . . .
not leaves though . . .
petals . . .
J.B.: *roughly* Get up!
SARAH: Where shall I go?
J.B.: Where you went!
Wherever!
She does not answer.
More gently. Where?
SARAH: Among the ashes.
All there is now of the town is ashes.
Mountains of ashes. Shattered glass.
Glittering cliffs of glass all shattered
Steeper than a cat could climb
If there were cats still . . .
And the pigeons —
They wheel and settle and whirl off
Wheeling and almost settling . . .
And the silence —
There is no sound there now — no wind sound —
Nothing that could sound the wind —
Could make it sing — no door — no doorway . . .
Only this.
She looks at the twig in her hands.
Among the ashes!
I found it growing in the ashes,
Gold as though it did not know . . .
Her voice rises hysterically.
I broke the branch to strip the leaves off —
Petals again! . . .
She cradles it in her arms.
But they so clung to it!
J.B.: Curse God and die, you said to me.
SARAH: Yes.
She looks up at him for the first time, then down again.
You wanted justice, didn't you?
There isn't any. There's the world . . .
She begins to rock on the doorsill, the little branch in her arms.
Cry for justice and the stars
Will stare until your eyes sting. Weep,
Enormous winds will thrash the water.
Cry in sleep for your lost children,
Snow will fall . . .
snow will fall . . .

J.B.: Why did you leave me alone?

SARAH: I loved you.
I couldn't help you any more.
You wanted justice and there was none —
Only love.

J.B.: He does not love. He
Is.

SARAH: But we do. That's the wonder.

J.B.: Yet you left me.

SARAH: Yes, I left you.
I thought there was a way away . . .
Water under bridges opens
Closing and the companion stars
Still float there afterwards. I thought the door
Opened into closing water.

J.B.: Sarah!

He drops on his knees beside her in the doorway, his arms around her.

SARAH: Oh, I never could!
I never could! Even the forsythia . . .

She is half laughing, half crying.

Even the forsythia beside the
Stair could stop me.

They cling to each other. Then she rises, drawing him up, peering at the darkness inside the door.

J.B.: It's too dark to see.

She turns, pulls his head down between her hands and kisses him.

SARAH: Then blow on the coal of the heart, my darling.

J.B.: The coal of the heart . . .

SARAH: It's all the light now.

Sarah comes forward into the dim room, J.B. behind her. She lifts a fallen chair, sets it straight.

Blow on the coal of the heart.
The candles in churches are out.
The lights have gone out in the sky.
Blow on the coal of the heart
And we'll see by and by . . .

J.B. has joined her, lifting and straightening the chairs.

We'll see where we are
The wit won't burn and the wet soul smoulders
Blow on the coal of the heart and we'll know . . .
We'll know . . .

The light increases, plain white daylight from the door, as they work.

CURTAIN

ARCHIBALD MACLEISH

VOLPONE IS ONE of the most famous of the seventeenth century plays of deception and counter-deception used to satirize an excess of a common human trait — in this instance, greed. Volpone is a rich and powerful man. Mosca, a parasite, is determined to inherit all the old man's wealth and prestige. Voltore is a lawyer who himself has designs on Volpone's estate. Volpone lies in bed feigning a fatal illness, overhearing all the conversations between Mosca and the various visitors who come to call their devotion to the attention of the dying man and his "devoted" attendant. Mosca and Volpone have set up the scenes with care and enjoy them fully. Remember that Volpone is actually "in scene" even after he pretends to lose consciousness and that Mosca knows of his trick.

from *Volpone*

ACT I, SCENE 3

MOSCA, VOLTORE, VOLPONE

MOS. You still are what you were, sir. Only you,
Of all the rest, are he commands his love:
And you do wisely to preserve it, thus,
With early visitation and kind notes
Of your good meaning to him, which, I know,
Cannot but come most grateful. Patron, sir,
Here's Signior Voltore is come —
VOLP. [*faintly*] What say you?
MOS. Sir, Signior Voltore is come this morning
To visit you.
VOLP. I thank him.
MOS. And hath brought
A piece of antique plate, bought of St. Mark,
With which he here presents you.
VOLP. He is welcome.
Pray him to come more often.
MOS. Yes.
VOLT. What says he?
MOS. He thanks you, and desires you see him often.
VOLP. Mosca.
MOS. My patron?
VOLP. Bring him near, where is he?
I long to feel his hand.

From *Volpone* by Ben Jonson, edited by J. M. Morrell. Reprinted by permission of Penguin Books, Ltd.

MOS. The plate is here, sir.
VOLT. How fare you, sir?
VOLP. I thank you, Signior Voltore.
  Where is the plate? Mine eyes are bad.
VOLT. [*putting it into his hands*] I'm sorry
  To see you still thus weak.
MOS. That he is not weaker. [*Aside*
VOLP. You are too munificent.
VOLT. No, sir, would to heaven,
  I could as well give health to you, as that plate.
VOLP. You give, sir, what you can. I thank you. Your love
  Hath taste in this, and shall not be unanswered:
  I pray you see me often.
VOLT. Yes, I shall, sir.
VOLP. Be not far from me.
MOS. Do you observe that, sir?
VOLP. Hearken unto me still; it will concern you.
MOS. You are a happy man, sir; you know your good.
VOLP. I cannot now last long —
MOS. You are his heir, sir.
VOLT. Am I?
VOLP. I feel me going; uh! uh! uh! uh!
  I am sailing to my port. Uh! uh! uh! uh!
  And I am glad I am so near my haven.
MOS. Alas, kind gentleman. Well, we must all go —
VOLT. But, Mosca —
MOS. Age will conquer.
VOLT. Pray thee, hear me.
  Am I inscribed his heir for certain?
MOS. Are you?
  I do beseech you, sir, you will vouchsafe
  To write me i' your family. All my hopes
  Depend upon your worship. I am lost,
  Except the rising sun do shine on me.
VOLT. It shall both shine, and warm thee, Mosca.
MOS. Sir,
  I am a man that hath not done your love
  All the worst offices: here I wear your keys,
  See all your coffers and your caskets locked,
  Keep the poor inventory of your jewels,
  Your plate and monies, am your steward, sir,
  Husband your goods here.
VOLT. But am I sole heir?
MOS. Without a partner, sir, confirmed this morning;
  The wax is warm yet, and the ink scarce dry
  Upon the parchment.
VOLT. Happy, happy, me!
  By what good chance, sweet Mosca?

MOS. Your desert, sir;
I know no second cause.
VOLT. Thy modesty
Is not to know it: well, we shall requite it.
MOS. He ever liked your course, sir, that first took him.
I oft have heard him say how he admired
Men of your large profession, that could speak
To every cause, and things mere contraries,
Till they were hoarse again, yet all be law;
That, with most quick agility, could turn,
And re-turn; make knots, and undo them;
Give forked counsel; take provoking gold
On either hand, and put it up; these men,
He knew, would thrive with their humility.
And for his part he thought he should be blest
To have his heir of such a suffering spirit,
So wise, so grave, of so perplex'd a tongue,
And loud withal, that would not wag, nor scarce
Lie still, without a fee; when every word
Your worship but lets fall, is a *cecchine!*[1] —
[*Another knocks.*
Who's that? One knocks, I would not have you seen, sir.
And yet — pretend you came, and went in haste:
I'll fashion an excuse. And, gentle sir,
When you do come to swim in golden lard,
Up to the arms in honey, that your chin
Is borne up stiff with fatness of the flood,
Think on your vassal; but remember me;
I have not been your worst of clients.
VOLT. Mosca —
MOS. When will you have your inventory brought, sir?
Or see a copy of the will? — Anon —
I'll bring them to you, sir. Away, be gone,
Put business i' your face. [*Exit Voltore.*
VOLP. [*springing up*] Excellent, Mosca!
Come hither, let me kiss thee.
MOS. Keep you still, sir.
Here is Corbaccio.
VOLP. Set the plate away:
The vulture's gone, and the old raven's come!

BEN JONSON

THE SETTING OF *A Raisin in the Sun* is the crowded apartment of the Younger family on Chicago's South Side. Ruth and Walter Younger, about

[1] *Cecchine* — a Venetian gold coin of the 13th century, i.e., *golden.*

From *A Raisin in the Sun*, by Lorraine Hansberry. © Copyright, as an unpublished work, 1958 by Lorraine Hansberry. © Copyright 1959 by Lorraine Hansberry. Reprinted by permission of Random House, Inc.

thirty, are husband and wife. Travis, their son, is a sturdy, handsome little boy of ten or eleven. Mama, to whom the apartment originally belonged, is his paternal grandmother. She is in her early sixties.

During the first act we have learned that Mama has received a check for ten thousand dollars from a life insurance policy which her late husband somehow managed to keep up. There has been considerable quarrelling about the use of the money. Walter wants to invest it in a liquor store with his friend Willy Harris. Ruth insists the money is Mama's. Mama cannot bring herself to become involved in what seems to her a very questionable business. At the beginning of this scene Mama has gone out. Walter has obviously been drinking and is in a quarrelsome mood.

There are sharp builds of emotion within this excerpt. Make careful use of the rhythm of content.

from *A Raisin in the Sun*

Act II, Scene 1

RUTH Walter—
(She stops what she is doing and looks at him)

WALTER (*Yelling*) Don't start!

RUTH Start what?

WALTER Your nagging! Where was I? Who was I with? How much money did I spend?

RUTH (*Plaintively*) Walter Lee—why don't we just try to talk about it . . .

WALTER (*Not listening*) I been out talking with people who understand me. People who care about the things I got on my mind.

RUTH (*Wearily*) I guess that means people like Willy Harris.

WALTER Yes, people like Willy Harris.

RUTH (*With a sudden flash of impatience*) Why don't you all just hurry up and go into the banking business and stop talking about it!

WALTER Why? You want to know why? 'Cause we all tied up in a race of people that don't know how to do nothing but moan, pray and have babies!
(The line is too bitter even for him and he looks at her and sits down)

RUTH Oh, Walter . . . (*Softly*) Honey, why can't you stop fighting me?

WALTER (*Without thinking*) Who's fighting you? Who even cares about you?
(This line begins the retardation of his mood)

RUTH Well—(*She waits a long time, and then with resignation starts to put away her things*) I guess I might as well go on to bed . . . (*More or less to herself*) I don't know where we lost it . . . but we have . . . (*Then, to him*) I—I'm sorry about this new baby, Walter. I guess maybe I better go on and do what I started . . . I guess I just didn't realize how bad things was with us . . . I guess I just didn't really realize — (*She starts out to the bedroom and stops*) You want some hot milk?

WALTER Hot milk?

RUTH Yes — hot milk.

WALTER Why hot milk?

RUTH 'Cause after all that liquor you come home with you ought to have something hot in your stomach.

WALTER I don't want no milk.

RUTH You want some coffee then?

WALTER No, I don't want no coffee. I don't want nothing hot to drink. (*Almost plaintively*) Why you always trying to give me something to eat?

RUTH (*Standing and looking at him helplessly*) What else can I give you, Walter Lee Younger?

(*She stands and looks at him and presently turns to go out again. He lifts his head and watches her going away from him in a new mood which began to emerge when he asked her "Who cares about you?"*)

WALTER It's been rough, ain't it, baby? (*She hears and stops but does not turn around and he continues to her back*) I guess between two people there ain't never as much understood as folks generally thinks there is. I mean like between me and you — (*She turns to face him*) How we gets to the place where we scared to talk softness to each other. (*He waits, thinking hard himself*) Why you think it got to be like that? (*He is thoughtful, almost as a child would be*) Ruth, what is it gets into two people ought to be close?

RUTH I don't know, honey. I think about it a lot.

WALTER On account of you and me, you mean? The way things are with us. The way something done come down between us.

RUTH There ain't so much between us, Walter . . . Not when you come to me and try to talk to me. Try to be with me . . . a little even.

WALTER (*Total honesty*) Sometimes . . . sometimes . . . I don't even know how to try.

RUTH Walter —

WALTER Yes?

RUTH (*Coming to him, gently and with misgiving, but coming to him*) Honey . . . life don't have to be like this. I mean sometimes people can do things so that things are better . . . You remember how we used to talk when Travis was born . . . about the way we were going to live . . . the kind of house . . . (*She is stroking his head*) Well, it's all starting to slip away from us . . .

(MAMA *enters, and* WALTER *jumps up and shouts at her*)

WALTER Mama, where have you been?

MAMA My — them steps is longer than they used to be. Whew!

(*She sits down and ignores him*) How you feeling this evening, Ruth?

(RUTH *shrugs, disturbed some at having been prematurely interrupted and watching her husband knowingly*)

WALTER Mama, where have you been all day?

MAMA (*Still ignoring him and leaning on the table and changing to more comfortable shoes*) Where's Travis?

RUTH I let him go out earlier and he ain't come back yet. Boy, is he going to get it!

WALTER Mama!

MAMA (*As if she has heard him for the first time*) Yes, son?

WALTER Where did you go this afternoon?

MAMA I went downtown to tend to some business that I had to tend to.

WALTER What kind of business?

MAMA You know better than to question me like a child, Brother.

WALTER (*Rising and bending over the table*) Where were you, Mama? (*Bringing his fists down and shouting*) Mama, you didn't go do something with that insurance money, something crazy?

(*The front door opens slowly, interrupting him, and* TRAVIS *peeks his head in, less than hopefully*)

TRAVIS (*To his mother*) Mama, I —

RUTH "Mama I" nothing! You're going to get it, boy! Get on in that bedroom and get yourself ready!

TRAVIS But I —

MAMA Why don't you all never let the child explain hisself.

RUTH Keep out of it now, Lena.

(MAMA *clamps her lips together, and* RUTH *advances toward her son menacingly*)

RUTH A thousand times I have told you not to go off like that —

MAMA (*Holding out her arms to her grandson*) Well — at least let me tell him something. I want him to be the first one to hear . . . Come here, Travis. (*The boy obeys, gladly*) Travis — (*She takes him by the shoulder and looks into his face*) — you know that money we got in the mail this morning?

TRAVIS Yes'm —

MAMA Well — what you think your grandmama gone and done with that money?

TRAVIS I don't know, Grandmama.

MAMA (*Putting her finger on his nose for emphasis*) She went out and she bought you a house! (*The explosion comes from* WALTER *at the end of the revelation and he jumps up and turns away from all of them in a fury.* MAMA *continues, to* TRAVIS) You glad about the house? It's going to be yours when you get to be a man.

TRAVIS Yeah — I always wanted to live in a house.

MAMA All right, gimme some sugar then — (TRAVIS *puts his arms around her neck as she watches her son over the boy's shoulder. Then, to* TRAVIS, *after the embrace*) Now when you say your prayers tonight, you thank God and your grandfather — 'cause it was him who give you the house — in his way.

RUTH (*Taking the boy from* MAMA *and pushing him toward the bedroom*) Now you get out of here and get ready for your beating.

TRAVIS Aw, Mama —

RUTH Get on in there — (*Closing the door behind him and turning radiantly to her mother-in-law*) So you went and did it!

MAMA (*Quietly, looking at her son with pain*) Yes, I did.

RUTH (*Raising both arms classically*) *Praise God!* (*Looks at* WALTER *a moment who says nothing. She crosses rapidly to her husband*) Please, honey — let me be glad . . . you be glad too. (*She has laid her hands on his shoulders, but he shakes himself free of her roughly, without turning to face her*) Oh, Walter . . . a home . . . *a home.* (*She comes back to* MAMA) Well — where is it? How big is it? How much it going to cost?

MAMA Well —

RUTH When we moving?

MAMA (*Smiling at her*) First of the month.

RUTH (*Throwing back her head with jubilance*) *Praise God!*

MAMA (*Tentatively, still looking at her son's back turned against her and* RUTH) It's — it's a nice house too . . . (*She cannot help speaking directly to him. An imploring quality in her voice, her manner, makes her almost like a girl now*) Three bedrooms — nice big one for you and Ruth. . . . Me and Beneatha still have to share our room, but Travis have one of his own — and (*With difficulty*) I figure if the — new baby — is a boy, we could get one of them double-decker outfits . . . And there's a yard with a little patch of dirt where I could maybe get to grow me a few flowers . . . And a nice big basement . . .

RUTH Walter honey, be glad —

MAMA (*Still to his back, fingering things on the table*) 'Course I don't want to make it sound fancier than it is . . . It's just a plain little old house — but it's made good and solid — and it will be *ours.* Walter Lee — it makes a difference in a man when he can walk on floors that belong to *him* . . .

RUTH Where is it?

MAMA (*Frightened at this telling*) Well — well — it's out there in Clybourne Park —

(RUTH'S *radiance fades abruptly, and* WALTER *finally turns slowly to face his mother with incredulity and hostility*)

RUTH Where?

MAMA (*Matter-of-factly*) Four o six Clybourne Street, Clybourne Park.

RUTH Clybourne Park? Mama, there ain't no colored people living in Clybourne Park.

MAMA (*Almost idiotically*) Well, I guess there's going to be some now.

WALTER (*Bitterly*) So that's the peace and comfort you went out and bought for us today!

MAMA (*Raising her eyes to meet his finally*) Son — I just tried to find the nicest place for the least amount of money for my family.

RUTH (*Trying to recover from the shock*) Well — well — 'course I ain't one never been 'fraid of no crackers, mind you — but — well, wasn't there no other houses nowhere?

MAMA Them houses they put up for colored in them areas way out all seem to cost twice as much as other houses. I did the best I could.

RUTH (*Struck senseless with the news, in its various degrees of goodness and trouble, she sits a moment, her fists propping her chin in thought, and then she starts to rise, bringing her fists down with vigor, the radiance spreading from cheek to cheek again*) Well — well! — All I can say is — if this is my time in life — *my time* — to say good-bye — (*And she builds with momentum as she starts to circle the room with an exuberant, almost tearfully happy release*) — to these Goddamned cracking walls! — (*She pounds the walls*) — and these marching roaches! — (*She wipes at an imaginary army of marching roaches*) — and this cramped little closet which ain't now or never was no kitchen! . . . then I say it loud and good, *Hallelujah! and good-bye misery . . . I don't never want to see your ugly face again!* (*She laughs joyously, having practically destroyed the apartment, and flings her arms up and lets them come down happily, slowly, reflectively, over her abdomen, aware for the first time perhaps that the life therein pulses with happiness and not despair*) Lena?

MAMA (*Moved, watching her happiness*) Yes, honey?

RUTH (*Looking off*) Is there — is there a whole lot of sunlight?

MAMA (*Understanding*) Yes, child, there's a whole lot of sunlight.
(*Long pause*)

RUTH (*Collecting herself and going to the door of the room* TRAVIS *is in*) Well — I guess I better see 'bout Travis. (*To* MAMA) Lord, I sure don't feel like whipping nobody today!
(*She exits*)

MAMA (*The mother and son are left alone now and the mother waits a long time, considering deeply, before she speaks*) Son — you — you understand what I done, don't you? (WALTER *is silent and sullen*) I — I just seen my family falling apart today . . . just falling to pieces in front of my eyes . . . We couldn't of gone on like we was today. We was going backwards 'stead of forwards — talking 'bout killing babies and wishing each other was dead . . . When it gets like that in life — you just got to do something different, push on out and do something bigger . . . . . . (*She waits*) I wish you say something, son . . . I wish you'd say how deep inside you you think I done the right thing —

WALTER (*Crossing slowly to his bedroom door and finally turning there and speaking measuredly*) What you need me to say you done right for? *You* the head of this family. You run our lives like you want to. It was your money and you did what you wanted with it. So what you need for me to say it was all right for? (*Bitterly, to hurt her as deeply as he knows is possible*) So you butchered up a dream of mine — you — who always talking 'bout your children's dreams . . .

MAMA Walter Lee —

(*He just closes the door behind him.* MAMA *sits alone, thinking heavily*)

CURTAIN

LORRAINE HANSBERRY

✱ Bibliography

Since this chapter and the one which follows are so closely related in cause and effect, it seems wise to include here books which are applicable to both discussions.

Altenbernd, Lynn, and Leslie L. Lewis. *Introduction to Literature: Plays.* New York: The Macmillan Company, 1963.

One of a series of three books dealing with poetry, prose, and drama. An anthology of plays from Sophocles to Ionesco with an introduction covering the elements of drama, hints on the silent reading of plays, and a brief discussion of traditional and modern modes of dramatic writing.

Boleslavsky, Richard. *Acting: The First Six Lessons.* New York: Theatre Arts Books, 1949.

A delightful, sound book on the basic principles of observation and character analysis.

Brooks, Cleanth, and Robert B. Heilman (eds.). *Understanding Drama.* New York: Holt, Rinehart and Winston, Inc., 1945.

A companion to *Understanding Fiction.* Elementary but sound.

Corrigan, Robert W., and James L. Rosenberg. *The Art of the Theatre: A Critical Anthology of Drama.* San Francisco: Chandler Publishing Company, 1964.

Plays from Sophocles to Ionesco with selected critical essays preceding each play.

Corrigan, Robert W. *The Context and Craft of Drama: An Anthology of Critical Essays on the Nature of Drama and Theatre.* San Francisco: Chandler Publishing Company, 1964.

A collection of contemporary dramatic criticism presented in two divisions. *Context* includes discussions of the nature, language, structure, and criticism of drama; *craft* discusses the role of the playwright, actors, director, designer, and critic.

Gassner, John. *Form and Idea in Modern Theatre.* New York: Holt, Rinehart and Winston, Inc., 1956.

Considerations of dramatic structure and style within a historical development.

Kerr, Walter. *How Not to Write a Play.* New York: Simon and Schuster, 1955.

Witty, practical discussion of dramatic structure by a successful professional critic.

Magarshack, David. *Stanislavsky on the Art of the Stage.* New York: Hill and Wang, 1961.

A translation of this famous classic with an introductory essay on the Stanislavsky system.

McGaw, Charles. *Acting Is Believing: A Basic Method for Beginners.* New York: Holt, Rinehart and Winston, Inc., 1953.

Clear, practical statement on basic theories and techniques of acting. Exercises from well-known plays and two complete plays for analysis and practice.

Seyler, Athene, and Stephen Haggard. *The Craft of Comedy.* Second Edition. New York: Theatre Arts Books, 1957.

One of the standard books on structure and devices in comedy.

Wellwarth, George E. *The Theatre of Protest and Paradox: Developments in the Avant-Garde Drama.* New York: New York University Press, 1964.

Discussion of contemporary playwrights' use of the themes of protest developed through the technique of paradox. Analyses of selected plays.

9

Some Suggestions on Technique

In the preceding chapter we noted that during the early phases of preparation the interpreter of drama and the actor follow the same general procedure. Both first seek to understand and respond mentally, emotionally, and physically to all the aspects of the play. After this is achieved, the actor goes forward into explicit physical and vocal representation; the interpreter, into selectivity and suggestion. The question, then, for the interpreter of drama, is not so much how far to go as where to go. The accuracy of his selectivity will depend upon the completeness of his understanding. The effectiveness of his suggestion will depend, in large measure, on the perfection of certain techniques. This chapter will be concerned with some specific technical problems inherent in the interpretation of drama. The brief suggestions for solving these problems are not, however, to be taken as rules. They are intended simply as practical suggestions which have been found effective. The only unbreakable rule is that there must be communication of the total achievement of the playwright, whether the entire play is being used or a single scene as an entity in itself.

THE ROLE OF TECHNIQUE IN THE INTERPRETATION OF DRAMA

The interpretation of drama demands the utmost in alertness and in mental, emotional, vocal, and physical flexibility. Although a play usually revolves around one or two characters, the others are vitally important in their relationship to the main characters and must emerge as individuals without any objective reminder from the author as to the elements which make up that individuality. The threads of each character's development must remain unmistakable and unbroken and must be woven together to produce the whole fabric of the play. The interpreter must therefore be able to respond to every shade of mental and emotional activity for each character. Moreover, he must be able to pick up each character exactly as he has already suggested him in the previous scene or speech.

This extreme flexibility can be achieved only through careful, conscientious preparation. The process of analysis must be thorough and detailed. The interpreter will need to spend much time and effort in disciplining his voice and body to respond without visible coaching and with split-second timing to the dictates of the material. He may often have to go over and over a difficult speech or scene, working it out as a musician practices a complex passage or as a dancer perfects a complicated step. Only by such exercises can he bring his technique to the point where it becomes a tool to help him communicate rather than an embellishment to be exhibited. He must have his technique so completely under control that he can forget about it in performance, secure in the knowledge that his muscles will respond. As experience increases, the degree of carry-over from preparation to performance will also increase. He will have reached his goal only when the audience is completely unaware of any effort on his part and is held by the material he is communicating to them. In performance, he must concentrate steadily on communication and on progressions and relationships.

Everything the interpreter chooses to do by way of technique must spring from an alert and disciplined mind. Mental discipline is perhaps more important in handling drama than in handling any other form of writing, both because of the special demands of drama, already noted, and because of the ever-present temptation toward display.

Techniques are not tricks. A trick deceives in order to puzzle or amuse. Technique, on the other hand, is skill in execution. The interpreter, who is an artist in his own right, is necessarily concerned with technique. It is wise to test one's artistic integrity from time to time in preparation to be sure one makes and observes the distinction. There is always a strong temptation to adopt certain physical and vocal mannerisms for their own sake, rather than allowing them to grow out of the needs of the material. A character is what he is because of numerous underlying mental and emotional qualities. He speaks and moves as he does because of those qualities. Only when the bases of characterization are clearly understood can the interpreter begin to work on the techniques which will honestly communicate the desired effects. Every interpreter who has a sense of performance and enjoys his position before his audience must occasionally ask himself, "Why am I doing this character in this particular way? Is it because of the demands of the material, or because I am being tempted to charm or impress my audience?" The need to ask the question is no reflection on the interpreter's integrity. But strict honesty in answering it is absolutely imperative. Self-discipline and a firm set of artistic values will keep the interpreter from exhibitionism.

In no other area of interpretation is it more important to recall that "great art conceals art." The moment the audience becomes conscious of the way an interpreter is achieving an effect, the effect itself is weakened. It detracts from the total achievement by calling attention to the interpreter instead of to the play he is attempting to communicate. The effectiveness of performance will depend directly upon the interpreter's ease and unobtrusiveness. Ease will result from painstaking preparation and from discipline of vocal and physical technique. Unobtrusiveness, too, depends upon thorough preparation and disciplined technique, and also upon concentration and honesty of purpose in performance.

Intensity and Control of Emotion

These remarks on discipline and control should not be read as an indication that the interpreter of drama does not respond emotionally to his material. On the contrary, the intensity of his response is as great as the actor's. There is a difference between suppressing an emotion and controlling its outward manifestations. The intensity is present according to the demands of the material, but the control of that intensity is an important artistic discipline. An actor who became so caught up with his emotional responses to a scene that he neglected to give the proper cues to the other characters, or sank into a chair and wept when he was supposed to go offstage, would certainly be in for an after-performance lecture from the director, for he would have violated the principles of his art. In the same way, an interpreter who allows himself to be so completely caught up in one character that he neglects to give the others the proper degree of importance and clarity is not interpreting. He is not being true to the principles of any art. If he becomes so emotionally involved that his eyes fill with tears and his voice cannot be heard, he will embarrass the people close enough to see the tears and irritate those who cannot hear what he is saying. He will be calling attention to himself and concentrating on his own response instead of on the material and the audience's response to that material. As soon as he embarks on an emotional orgy, the audience becomes uneasy and embarrassed, for the emotion no longer belongs to the character but to the interpreter. A public display of personal emotion is in bad taste on any occasion, but in this case the interpreter is committing the further sin of inviting the audience to divide its attention between the character and the interpreter as a person.

The principle of controlled intensity is sometimes referred to as "aesthetic distance." It means, in the words of an old theater axiom, keeping a cool head over a warm heart. It is a matter of increased control, not of lessened intensity. Emotional intensity must be strong when the material demands it, if the interpreter is to draw a suitable response from his audience. Yet this intensity must be kept under firm control, so that the audience will respond to the emotional impact of the material, not to the performer's extreme sensibility.

The interpreter's circle of emotional response, like his mental circle of concentration, is not limited to the reading stand but includes the entire audience in its sweep. The principle of emotional rapport with an audience is an extremely difficult one to define in words, but once the interpreter has experienced it he will never doubt its value and effectiveness in oral interpretation. We are all familiar with the process of projecting an emotion to a single person so that response is engendered in him and returns to us. The same process applies to a group of people. It is the interpreter's business to make his audience *feel* as well as *think* with the characters in a drama, and in this connection the already familiar principle of empathy is, of course, basic.

Memorizing

Closely allied with the interrelations among the interpreter, the dramatic materials he is presenting, and the audience is the question of memorizing. With drama, the interpreter needs to come closer to a complete memorization of his material than with any other type of writing, because of the speed with which he must handle the interplay of characters. He is without the prop of the explanatory dialogue tag, ". . . said Mr. So-and-So . . . ," such as he finds in narrative. He is given only the character's name at the beginning of each speech, which, of course, he does not repeat to the audience. Though the audience must always know who is speaking, identifying the character by name at the beginning of each speech would soon become tiresome. Moreover, it would constantly break the train of thought and emotion, and destroy the total effect. The interpreter, then, must be able to establish the character's identity immediately by a skillful use of technique. He must not only have the speeches and their progression clearly in mind, but who speaks them, what prompts them, and to whom they are addressed. He cannot afford to look down after each speech for his next cue. This would slow the performance — and worse still, it would break his own concentration on the continuity of the scene and destroy most of the necessary interplay between the characters. For these reasons, he would do best to have his material fairly well memorized, using the printed page to refresh his memory from time to time.

PRESENTING THE CAST

Each person who attends a theater performance is provided with a printed program which lists the members of the cast. When an interpreter is doing a play, he must assume the responsibility of introducing the cast to his listeners. This he does directly as narrator.

If the cast is small, he may include all of them in his first remarks, indicating perhaps which ones appear somewhat later than the others. On the other hand, when a play has a large number of characters, it is neither practical nor necessary for the interpreter to attempt to introduce all of them. He will be guided by the cuts he has made in the material, and he will mention only those characters he will be using in his cutting. He may lump several together as "guests at the tea." When the cast is a large one, it is usually wise to introduce the minor characters when they appear, rather than to burden the audience with too many names at the outset. As a start, it will be enough to give only the names of and a word or two of identification for the characters needed for the first key scene or two. The others may be introduced as they enter.

Many plays published in book form give on the cast page a notation of the date and place of first performance and the names of the complete original cast. This information will hardly be needed for the interpreter's purposes. Indeed, it is usually unwise to remind an audience that certain roles have been created or made famous by certain actors. After all, the interpreter is not attempting to suggest a famous portrayal of the main role, but rather the characters around whom the play revolves.

STAGE DIRECTIONS

The problem of handling preliminary stage directions was touched on in the preceding chapter in relation to the establishment of background and setting. We have seen that the interpreter can give the essential information directly to the audience before the action of the play begins, and can incorporate other elements from the stage directions into his analysis of character and eventually into his handling of the dialogue.

When a play is divided into scenes and acts, it will usually be simplest to make a similar break in the handling of the material for interpretation. The interpreter does not normally leave the platform, but indicates the division by general relaxation, effective use of pause, and a return to conversational directness with his audience. Thus he makes the best possible use of the playwright's principles of organization by concluding large units of action and clearly establishing their conclusion for the audience. This technique, moreover, enables the interpreter and the listeners to relax momentarily and go smoothly into the next large unit.

Each scene and act will have its own indication of time and place. When the location remains the same throughout the play, the interpreter may establish that fact in his first narration to the audience, and thereafter cope merely with time changes. When there are changes in location as well as time, it is most helpful to call them to the attention of the audience immediately before the units to which they apply.

It is smoother, more direct, and more conversational to use complete sentences for stage directions instead of the literal wording of the script, "Act One. Living room in the Martin home, Washington, D.C." Sometimes, of course, the stage directions may be used almost exactly as they are printed. If there are two or more scenes within a single act, these can be taken care of neatly and simply by a brief statement before each: "The first scene of Act Two takes place in John Martin's study"; "The second scene of Act Two is again in the living room."

The matter of time is handled in equally simple fashion. The cast page often gives the progression in terms of months, noting, for example, that the first act takes place in December, the second in January and February, and the last act in March. This information can most conveniently be given to the audience at the beginning of each scene and act. One may use the months as mentioned, or such phrases as "a few weeks later," "a month later," or any other wording which will make clear that sufficient time has elapsed to make the action and the development of character credible.

The same principles apply to stage directions at the end of an act. Just as a director times his curtain to harmonize with the mood of the scene, so an interpreter gives some attention to his choice of words in closing a scene. In *Androcles and the Lion* (page 342), for example, the prologue ends with a suggestion of continuing activity on the part of Androcles and his lion as well as a change of locale. Androcles' wife, however, has just revived from her faint and has a speech after their exit. The skilled interpreter who has already carefully established Megaera's character could probably suggest her revival without the stage direction, and indicate by vocal projection that she is shouting after her husband and his waltzing partner. The closing stage direction, "She rushes off after them into the jungle," however, makes an excellent curtain line. In *Rhinoceros* (page 348), on the other hand, most of the scenes end on a piece of stage direction which must be included for both mood and clarity of action. Sometimes the playwright's words can be used almost verbatim, but the interpreter will need to smooth the transition to "Curtain" in such a close as this:

> [*He goes once more to the various exits, but the spectacle of the rhinoceros halts him. When he gets back to the bathroom door it seems about to give way.* BERENGER *throws himself against the back wall, which yields; the street is visible in the background; he flees, shouting:*]
>
> Rhinoceros! Rhinoceros!
>
> [*Noises. The bathroom door is on the point of yielding.*]
>
> CURTAIN

Entrances and exits during the course of a scene may occasionally cause some difficulty. If a character's exit occurs at the close of his speech and indicates the completion of a key scene, the interpreter may easily assume the role of narrator and tell his audience directly, "And he goes out." Sometimes it may be advisable to add some explanatory remark to maintain a mood or to complete an action, as "He hesitated for a moment, looking back at her, then went out closing the door behind him." If the attention is to remain with the character or characters on stage, the wording can be changed slightly to accomplish this shift of focus: "He hesitated for a moment, looking back at her; then went out, closing the door behind him. As soon as she was left alone, Mary opened her eyes."

A character who enters will usually have to be identified — or re-identified. On a first entrance, the playwright will probably give a description of the character. The interpreter may use whatever he needs of that description to help in identifying the character for his audience. On later entrances, the character's name will probably be sufficient, with a brief reference to any relevant changes of costume or mood. Usually there is no need to specify the direction from which an entrance is made unless some definite plot motivation is involved. One might wish to say, "He enters from the porch," but it would not be necessary to say, "He enters from up center," because the interpreter's scene is not on stage and he is not concerned with physical layout beyond indicating an entrance into the scene.

Sometimes the interpreter will need to insert the name of an entering character when a speech is addressed to him. This might be a helpful device in the opening speeches of *Hedda Gabler*. Although it is very clear that only Miss Tesman and Berta are on stage, the audience has not yet identified either one. The speeches read:

> MISS TESMAN: (*Stops close to the door, listens, and says softly*) Upon my word, I don't believe they are stirring yet!
>
> BERTA: (*Also softly*) I told you so, Miss. Remember how late the steamboat got in last night . . .

The stage directions can be eliminated, and suggested instead by the manner of speaking, and the characters can be made to identify each other. Thus the speeches might well be changed to read:

> MISS TESMAN: Upon my word, Berta, I don't believe they are stirring yet!
>
> BERTA: I told you so, Miss Tesman. Remember how late the steamboat got in last night . . .

This identification through dialogue need not be continued once the identities have been established, but it is a device that may prove useful whenever a character re-enters the scene, if he is not sufficiently identified by stage directions, as might be the case when several characters enter at once. The interpreter's own judgment will dictate whether this device is necessary for clarity or would seriously alter the style of the speech, as it certainly would in poetic drama.

PHYSICAL ACTION

In the case of a specific physical action, it is important to remember that suggestion rather than explicitness is the goal. It is never wise to underestimate the audience's ability and willingness to accept suggestion if it is clear and shows the proper motivation and empathic response. Listeners tend to accept a presentation on its own terms, so long as it is consistent and not obtrusive.

If an action is necessary to plot motivation, it is usually better to make use of the narrative technique.[1] If the action is primarily important for its revelation of attitude or of emotional state, then the audience should be made aware of the cause rather than the action itself. The action is the outward manifestation of an interior response, and this gives the interpreter an important clue to the way it should be handled. It is not so much *what* the character does as *how* he does it that will reveal what he is thinking and feeling. If, for example, a character sinks dejectedly into a chair, it is not the mere process of sitting down that is important, but rather the dejection pointed up by the action. This dejection will show

[1] As suggested for the placing of the manuscript in the bookcase, in *Hedda Gabler;* see page 266.

itself in the muscle tone of the entire body, in the pace of speech, in the vocal quality, and in numerous other ways. In preparation, the business should certainly be rehearsed in detail, and the act of sitting synchronized with the speech so that voice and body are saying the same thing. In performance, however, the explicit act of sinking into a chair would pull the scene up on stage instead of keeping it out front. Moreover, it would be impractical and would cause needless complications. In the first place, the interpreter would need a chair to sink into. If he uses a chair, he may logically need a table, a mantel to lean against, a window to open, and a door to slam. To use one and not the others would be to meander back and forth between acting and interpretation, and the result would be an interruption of the audience's attention and an illogical if not ludicrous situation. Moreover, once the character was seated, there would always be the problem of getting him up again. This action, too, would need to be properly motivated by something the character said or thought, and the motivation might not occur for some time. Meanwhile, there is the question of what to do about the characters who speak from another position. The safest plan is to continue standing throughout and to suggest repose not by an overt bodily act but by empathy, muscle tone, and whatever aspects of vocal technique are appropriate.

When, occasionally, an interpreter is confronted with a scene in which the character loses consciousness, effective presentation and good taste alike require of him a particular control and a nice discrimination. The end of the scene from *Romeo and Juliet* presents this problem. Obviously, any explicit action such as dropping the head onto the lectern or relaxing in an exaggerated slump would be difficult to achieve subtly and would call attention to the interpreter. During the pause that follows Juliet's closing words, the physical tension can be held for a moment and then visibly relaxed. The pause should be sufficiently long to enable the audience to complete the piece of action *in their own minds* before the interpreter closes his manuscript or speaks directly as a narrator to tell them "the curtain falls," or some such appropriate phrase to end the scene.

Properties

Certain properties which must be suggested can also cause difficulty. In fact, the whole matter of properties requires of the interpreter a very sure sense of degree of suggestion.

Many modern plays, for example, make use of a telephone. The excerpt from *Rhinoceros* depends in part on effective handling of this property. Placing one clenched hand to the ear and the other below the chin, which for some reason seems to be a popular way to suggest a telephone conversation, can be ludicrous and create unnecessary complications — especially if one hand is occupied with a book or script. If the interpreter wishes to suggest so explicitly that he is holding a telephone, then he must also pick it up from somewhere and put it back on the hook when he has finished the conversation. Instead of going through these motions in mid-air, it is far better to insert the word "Operator" or "Hello" before giving the number. The audience will immediately know that a telephone is being used. When the use of a dial telephone is indicated, it is simpler to translate the action into words as if the connection were being made through an operator. The type of telephone being used is, after all, a matter of very little consequence. There is also a distinct difference in degree of directness between a telephone conversation and a conversation with someone who is present. Thus, the quality of attention and the manner of speaking will help set the telephone speeches off from the others, as will the handling of the pauses to indicate the other half of the dialogue which the audience does not hear.

But the problem of properties is by no means confined to modern plays. In one of the most familiar scenes from *Romeo and Juliet* — Scene Three of Act Four, in which Juliet drinks the potion Friar Laurence has given her — the interpreter must cope with both a vial and a dagger. The first part of Juliet's speech presents some difficulties in focus as well. It opens with "Farewell!" as Lady Capulet and the Nurse leave Juliet's room. Of course, the interpreter may assume that they have already gone and that the "Farewell!" is primarily reflective. The audience can be helped to visualize the scene more clearly, however, and the stage directions can be simplified as well, if Juliet calls this parting after them as they leave the room and then waits a moment, as she watches the door close behind them, before continuing with, "God knows when we shall meet again." Four lines later Juliet calls to the Nurse, and then immediately decides against having her return, something which can be suggested by attention to projection. The interpreter can suggest the decisions by the principle of muscle memory, which will motivate a change in muscle tone, and by appropriate timing and use of pauses.

But what about the passage beginning "Come, vial," in which Juliet voices her doubts as she looks at the mixture? Clearly, she picks up the vial with the intention of drinking it. It is traditional and practical for an actress on the stage to hold the vial high enough to be seen by the audience. But the interpreter does not have a vial. For this reason, it is sufficient — and considerably more effective — to keep the hand low, on the reading stand or level with the book, and visualize a small vial lying in the palm of the hand, or even lying on the stand itself. The interpreter is not trying to make the audience believe he actually is holding a vial; he is merely establishing the idea of the vial in the minds of the audience since it is essential to the plot. The barely sketched gesture of holding it in his palm will help him visualize it and project the muscle response which will enable the audience to accept the idea that Juliet has a potion in her hand and is about to drink it. Muscle tone and emotional tensions are the important considerations, not an overt manipulation of an imaginary object.

A few lines later attention turns to the dagger, which Juliet does not mention specifically though it is logically implied by the words "This shall forbid it. Lie thou there." When the play is staged, the weapon is held so that the audience can see it. But again, the interpreter does not have a dagger. A slight gesture comparable to the one used to indicate the vial will satisfy a desire for action on the line, and will establish the presence of the dagger in the minds of the listeners. If it is assumed that Juliet picks up the dagger, looks at it a moment, and then lays it down, the interpreter will need to draw on his muscle memory for his timing. His hand, kept low on the reading stand or level with the book, may merely turn from palm up while holding the dagger to palm down on "Lie thou there." The focus of attention is held for a moment on the dagger and then returns to the vial.

If the interpreter has fallen into the trap of the too-explicit gesture, he will find himself in trouble as he shuttles his imaginary properties from hand to hand, or plucks them from mid-air and lays them down on nothingness — especially if he has no reading stand and has one hand occupied with an all too solid book! Since there is much activity and a high degree of tension in this scene which must be allowed to come through, the interpreter is very likely to feel the need for some bodily expression that goes beyond muscle tension. Even so, he should guard against overt representation. He wants to catch the audience up with him, enable them to see the scene in their minds and feel it in their muscles. But he does not want to step across the boundary from suggestion to explicitness, presenting not Juliet in her agonized moment of decision but the spectacle of himself plucking at the air. *Suggestion* and *controlled intensity* are the keynotes.

The last words of the speech, and of the scene, "This do I drink to thee," make it very clear that the vial has been lifted to Juliet's lips and that she swallows the potion. This is a dramatic moment for the actress. But the interpreter is not *being* Juliet; he is helping the audience to *see* Juliet. Because it is the close of a scene and a high point, and because

Juliet is the only character to be considered, the interpreter may be unendurably tempted to raise the vial to his mouth in a grand final gesture. If he chooses to do so, he must pause while the potion takes effect, because an important key action, once begun, must be completed. But he must remember that no curtain will fall to rescue him! He must consider also whether he will not miss his effect by the shock his listeners will feel at this sudden total identification of interpreter with character, for he has previously been suggesting a Juliet to their mind's eye, not acting the role himself. The scene may be brought to a most effective close without the use of the lifted hand. This method requires swift changes in mental comment and a build to the emotional peak, followed by a suggestion, at least, of faltering consciousness — probably by slackening the muscle tone and dropping the head. As we noted earlier, this can be accomplished during the pause which must follow the speech and can be perfectly timed for climactic effect. It requires maximum concentration and control. The interpreter will need to rehearse the full action in his early preparation, to get the feel and timing of coordinated bodily action and speech, but he will be wise to experiment until he can do the scene in performance without the overt action of drinking the poison. There is, of course, no reason why he cannot use appropriate gestures during a performance, but raising an imaginary vial in *his* hand to *his* lips would pull the scene up on stage and distract the audience from the one they have in their minds. As he grows in skill, the interpreter will become increasingly able to distinguish between valid bodily movement and tension which suggest, and the explicit, physical representation of an action.

Physical Contact

Action which requires physical contact with another character should probably be translated into narration. A handshake, for example, is most difficult to make convincing when only one hand is involved. To reach out into space as one character, grasp a hand that is not there and give it a firm clasp, then jump into the other character and complete the greeting is both awkward and unnecessary. A straightforward manner of speaking, an increased directness, and a sharpening of focus are enough to suggest the greeting.

A kiss, which is more difficult to suggest, cannot always be cut, since it is often a key action; when retained, however, it can usually be translated into narration. In no case should a kiss be an explicit action, for an interpreter who purses his lips and closes his eyes for a fond caress with empty air can most charitably be described as an amusing spectacle.

Usually the playwright provides stage directions to indicate the physical contact and to serve as a guide to actors and director. When these can be appropriately used, the interpreter may give them directly to the audience as narration. In Tennessee Williams' *The Glass Menagerie,* for example, the Gentleman Caller has been telling Laura what she should do about her inferiority complex, and he comes to the conclusion that

> Somebody — ought to —
> Ought to — *kiss* you, Laura!
> (*His hand slips slowly up her arm to her shoulder.*)
> (*He suddenly turns her about and kisses her on the lips.*)
> (*When he releases her, Laura sinks on the sofa with a bright, dazed look.*)
> (*Jim backs away and fishes in his pocket for a cigarette.*)

The playwright has successfully maintained the proper mood through these brief directions. He reaches the climax swiftly in the second parenthetical sentence. The interpreter would probably hold this climax for a moment to allow the audience to complete the picture and the emotional implications. The playwright provides for a gradual release of tension in the next sentence, keeping the attention focused on Laura. The last sentence comes back to reality, as attention turns to the Gentleman Caller. When the playwright's stage directions do not coincide so happily with the interpreter's needs as Williams' do in this case, the interpreter had best re-write the directions so that they preserve the mood established and prepare the audience for whatever change is to follow.

Physical contact growing out of anger usually comes at a climactic moment. Thus, to interrupt a speech with the parenthetical information that "He slapped her" or "He hit him" would often break the build-up. This type of action, of course, carries with it a high degree of muscle tension and a sharp kinetic imagery. The interpreter's mental comment, emotional intensity, facial expression, and entire posture will help considerably in suggesting not only the anger which motivates the action but even the thrust of the blow. The character receiving the blow will react with a sudden muscle reflex, and with either increased muscle tension or total relaxation depending upon the force and effect of the blow. Because they depend on the visual spectacle for their effectiveness and are longer in duration, duels and wrestling are best covered by narration. The narration can help create suspense and eliminate the problem of simultaneous activity by two characters.

It is impossible and impractical to formulate general rules to be applied to every example of physical contact. Each instance presents its own problem, depending upon its importance in the over-all effect and upon the interpreter's skill in suggestion and his taste and discrimination. The only rule that can guide him may be summed up in two questions which he must ask himself. The first is: "How explicit *must* (not *may*) I be so that the audience will understand what I am doing and accept the action as an integral part of the total effect?" In answering this question, the interpreter must take care not to underestimate his audience. That is, he should think in terms not of how much action he can get away with, but of how little he needs to use. The second question is: "Will this technique of suggested action call attention to itself and to me, and thus detract from the material?"

The interpreter is by no means to infer that he should stand like a totem pole, not daring to move his hands. Any action which he feels is *necessary* for communication is to be used without apology or self-consciousness. He will find it useful to go to both extremes in preparation. On the one hand, specific action will insure muscle memory and thus help him to establish his timing and to motivate empathy. On the other, it is only through trying the scene without any specific action at all that he can put his artistic standards to the test. Somewhere between these extremes he will hit upon the mean which seems right to him. His decision will rest upon his ultimate purpose, which is communication.

PORTRAYAL OF CHARACTER

Drama, by its very nature and form, does not tell explicitly *about* the characters, except in brief stage directions; hence it imposes on the interpreter a greater responsibility for suggestion than do other literary forms. All outward manifestations which suggest character must spring directly from understanding of the mental and emotional characteristics of the person being suggested. A character moves and speaks as he does largely because of what he thinks and feels. Certain physical aspects, however, are important in establishing a three-dimensional character, and sex, age, and infirmity can play a strong part in forming the inner response. The following suggestions are offered to help the interpreter in handling these and other physical aspects of character. Obviously, the complexity of the characters and the importance of their physical attributes will vary from play to play. The interpreter of drama must be guided by the playwright's intention and by his own knowledge of the relationship between the interior and exterior aspects of each character. Always, however, he must remember that his aim is to *suggest* and not to *assume* character.

Sex

One of the most troublesome problems in handling drama arises out of the interpreter's need to suggest characters of both sexes. The excerpt from *Mary Stuart* at the end of the previous chapter points up this problem, for Mary and Elizabeth are of comparable importance historically and dramatically. Leicester and Shrewsbury have only a few lines to speak and are clearly observers rather than active participants in the scene. Nevertheless its effect upon them is important, and they must not become so nondescript that they fade away in contrast to the strength and vividness of the two queens. Even a woman interpreter might have some difficulty in distinguishing Mary from Elizabeth unless she remembers the importance of setting and relationship of characters in a dramatic situation. She would need to give special attention to the attitudes of Leicester and Shrewsbury and be constantly aware of their relationship to both queens. A male interpreter, on the other hand, would need to pay close attention to the relative positions of authority of the two queens and be sure they have strength rather than masculinity.

On the surface there is little to distinguish Mary from Elizabeth, and both male and female interpreters must be guided by subtle differences within the essentially feminine framework of their minds and actions. Both women are of royal blood, accustomed to the privileges and responsibilities which go with it. Mary's greater beauty, her passionate nature, and the desperateness of her situation give her daring. Elizabeth is not beautiful and knows it. She is jealous of Mary on many counts. She has the upper hand and takes full advantage of it both as a ruler and as a woman.

As to techniques of voice, the male interpreter will do well to underplay rather than overplay his suggestion of feminine character. He need not raise his voice above its natural pitch for the women's speeches. He can put across the idea of feminine speech more effectively by merely lightening the quality of his voice and allowing most of the sound to come from the top of his throat, and by establishing individual rhythms of speech for the feminine as well as for the masculine characters.

To suggest a feminine character physically, a man may allow his weight to shift very slightly forward on one foot, as women tend to stand with the weight centered on the balls of the feet rather than back on the heels. He should be very careful, however, not to go beyond the point of merely helping the audience to identify the character speaking. He is not attempting to assume the role of a woman, and he certainly does not want to set up a rhythmic rocking motion — swaying forward for a woman, back again for a man. Awareness of the part played by the smaller muscles of the neck, the waist, and the ankles and wrists may also help achieve a feeling of delicacy.

A woman interpreter will have comparable difficulties with male characters. She must also remember that she is *suggesting* and that her audience will accept even slight distinctions between masculine and feminine characters if she is consistent and sufficiently clear in establishing that difference in their minds. She, too, should underplay rather than overplay the physical and vocal attributes of a male character. An exaggerated bass voice convinces no one of masculinity; indeed, it is ridiculous to assume that a violent change in pitch or volume indicates anything to the listeners except the reader's vocal range, which is of interest only as it promotes understanding and enjoyment of the material at hand. But quality of voice, as a means of suggesting a male character, is a different matter. A fuller sound can be achieved by allowing the throat to relax so that the undertones of the voice are put to use, and by breathing fully and deeply so that a steady stream of air sustains the richer quality. Physically, the woman interpreter can suggest a male character by reversing the procedure a man uses to suggest a woman. That is, she may let the large muscles of the shoulders, legs, and upper arms give her a feeling of solidness, and allow her weight to shift backward a little more onto her heels. Few men stand with their feet extremely far apart, but they do tend to keep their weight evenly balanced, a fact which gives them a firmer stance than women usually have. This simple change in balance, combined with an almost imperceptible squaring of the shoulders, is ordinarily all that is needed by way of physical suggestion.

Age and Infirmity

The outward manifestations of age and vitality or infirmity are important if the hearers are to re-create a three-dimensional character as they listen to and watch the interpreter of drama. A subtle suggestion of age, however, is most difficult to achieve. It is neither necessary nor desirable to hump the shoulders, curl the hands helplessly across the breast, and speak in an exaggerated tremolo and falsetto. Indeed, few old people speak and hold themselves that way unless they are extremely feeble and emaciated. A person beyond middle age is not necessarily in the last stages of debility. Further, when a pattern so devoid of vitality is set up, it is almost impossible to achieve any strength or climactic builds within the development of the character. Age, like so many other things, is a relative matter. Some people are mentally and emotionally antiquated at fifty; others retain their vitality through a long and vigorous old age.

The degree of vitality should be dictated by the individual character involved, and should be related less to his chronological age as indicated in the stage directions than to his responsiveness and individuality.

Age can be suggested sufficiently by muscle memory and by certain aspects of vocal technique. An old person will move more deliberately, more cautiously than one who is in his prime. Consequently, his scenes are likely to be paced more slowly and evenly than those of a younger character. By responding empathically to the idea of stiffened joints, insecure footing, and generally decreased vigor, the interpreter can convey an impression of age to the audience; and he may also sketch a suggestion, through his body, of the physical pattern of age — the shoulders slightly drooped, the head thrust almost imperceptibly forward. In preparation, when the specific actions are rehearsed, the hands rather than full arm movements should be used wherever possible, since the big muscles of the arms and shoulders no longer have the strength of youth. The interpreter should watch old people carefully to note how they handle things without putting their arm and shoulder muscles into play, and how they minimize the use of muscles in the back and thighs. In performance, this impression of diminished muscular activity can be put across by means of muscle tone and a shift in the balance of the whole frame. The interpreter must always remember that the audience is not interested in seeing how quickly he can snap from an aged stoop to the erect posture of youth. Under-emphasis on physical details is the safer part, for any abrupt change in stance calls attention to itself and destroys the overall effect of the material. In like manner, individual characteristics of age — indecisiveness, pomposity, or any other quality which would show itself physically — must be treated with the same restraint as diminished vitality.

Vocally, old people tend to use a narrow range of inflection, partly because their responses are slower, and partly because the mental attitude of age reflects less enthusiasm than does that of youth. The rate of speech may also be slower, and the rhythm less staccato than that of a younger person.

INTERPLAY OF CHARACTERS

The interpreter who wants to work out the full values in drama will find it helpful, at least until he becomes experienced, to take one character at a time and perfect the technique to be used in suggesting him, as outlined in the previous chapter. Then comes the problem of getting all the characters together so that they are contributing parts of the whole and react to each other as the play progresses. The actor must learn not only how to speak and move in his part, but also how to listen. The interpreter of drama obviously cannot listen as one character while he is speaking as another. Perhaps, however, we may say that the interpreter must learn to "have heard." He must develop the ability to pick up the thread of thought in the person of the character who has heard the speech or seen the action. This requires a split-second response which is possible only when he has all the characters so completely under control that they seem ready and waiting to step immediately into the center of attention. In short, the interpreter is not to develop a split personality but to build a compound one. He cannot let half his mind, voice, and body lie dormant while one character speaks, thinks, and acts. He must use all his faculties for each character. He must have a clear focus of attention when he is speaking, and a sharp and immediate response in the person of the character who replies. When he has developed the art of interpreting drama to its highest point, his reaction will be as complete mentally and emotionally as the actor's, and his empathic response as genuine.

There is no quick way to accomplish this difficult feat. The only sure method is careful, painstaking preparation and complete concentration during performance. No character should be allowed to drop out of the scene or out of the fabric of the whole. Furthermore, his outlines must not become blurred; he must emerge complete and individual the moment he picks up his cue. Developing this technique takes time, effort, and experience, and the beginner can only work toward it as a goal, but it lies at the heart of a well-paced, successful performance of drama.

Picking Up Cues

The interpreter should recall that a cue can be picked up mentally and physically as well as vocally. The character need not begin to speak the second his cue is given. Pauses are often effective and necessary. Moreover, they give the audience time to assimilate the previous speech if it has been an important or complex one. Care should be taken, however, not to let the pace become labored. It is important to keep a careful check on the rhythm of the entire scene. A cue can be picked up by a glance or a facial expression or a change of muscle tone.

The interpreter's control and precision must be highly developed to avoid two common pitfalls in the shift from one character to another. One of these is the danger of allowing a sag in characterization between speeches. Inexperienced readers are sometimes guilty of completing one character and then reverting to their own personalities in the fraction of a second before they pick up another character. This slows the scene and makes the total effect labored and heavy-handed. The student should practice picking up each of the characters cleanly and sharply, as they are rehearsed individually, until his mind and muscles react without conscious prompting.

The other pitfall is the danger of a too-hurried transition, the result of imperfect timing and coordination between mind and muscles. When the interpreter leaves one character and picks up another a fraction of a second before a speech has been completed, his listeners may lose the final words of the speech. What is even more serious, they may become aware that the interpreter is anticipating the other character, and this awareness will split their attention. Thorough preparation, time and effort spent on technique, and a sure sense of timing will help the interpreter avoid either of these extremes in the transition from one character to another.

The vocal technique must become so much a part of the characterization that it is almost automatic as the mind and muscles pick up the character. This cannot be achieved in a few minutes of preparation. It is far better to begin preparation well in advance of performance, and keep working at it so that there is time to evolve the habit of each character, than to attempt the work in one long, sustained session just before a presentation. The interpreter must live with his characters; they must become part of him, and he of them.

PHYSICAL FOCUS

The degree and direction of physical focus on the characters should spring out of the interpreter's concept of his material as a whole and not be imposed on the material by external rules. There are, however, a few general techniques that may prove helpful.

It is usually safest, for example, to assume that a character being addressed is approximately one's own height, with an eye level about even with one's own. Even when a discrepancy in height may be assumed, any exaggerated angle of focus should be avoided. When a short person and a tall one converse, unless they are standing very close together the angle at which their eyes meet is not a marked one. Thus, in suggesting a tall character addressing a short one, an adult speaking to a child, or a standing character addressing a seated character, the interpreter must take care not to reduce the shorter person to a spot on the floor. For best results, he should rehearse each character specifically, and then let muscle memory dictate the angle of eye focus.

Sometimes it is necessary to indicate that the character being addressed is approaching or going away from the speaker. This situation was mentioned in connection with the "Farewell" in Juliet's speech. Since the interpreter's scene is out front, the characters approach and depart out front — *not* behind or beside him as they would on stage. The person to whom a speech is directed may be entering or leaving the room, descending or ascending stairs, or moving about in other ways which would change the distance between him and the speaker. In this case, it is well to visualize the action of the other person as he moves in the area of the back wall, allowing the eyes to follow the direction and rate of his movement. The increase or decrease of vocal and mental projection thus required will help to indicate the logical eye movements also.

Angle of Placement

It must be borne in mind that, like the other technical suggestions in this chapter, the following suggestions on angle of placement are not rules but devices that have been found useful. If the suggestions do not fit the demands of the material and the needs of the interpreter, they need not be followed.

On stage, people move about from one area to another; consequently, speeches addressed to a character must be directed to the place where he is stationed at the moment. Many interpretative artists follow this same principle and allow the direction of address to change as the character being addressed moves about. This is a logical procedure and is often handled most skillfully. It does, however, impose an added burden on the interpreter, who must remember not only which character is speaking, what prompted the speech, and to whom it is addressed, but also where the character being addressed has moved to since his earlier scenes.

It is less complicated and more effective to follow the principle that the angle of address should be dictated by the character speaking, not by the hypothetical position of the character being addressed. In the first place, an audience quickly becomes accustomed to having a certain character speak at a certain angle. It helps identify him. This is especially important when there are several characters who are hard to distinguish in terms of vocal and physical characteristics. Further, the interpreter can more easily accustom himself to the nearly automatic pick-up of focus and muscle set for each character when he retains the same relative position for all the speeches of each one.

In other words, a specific character always speaks in the same direction no matter whom he is addressing. This does not mean that he keeps his eyes glued on a single spot on the back wall. If he is addressing several people simultaneously or in succession, he will let his eye focus shift slightly to indicate that he is doing so. In actual conversation, one does not stare steadily into the eyes of another unless the degree of emotional intensity demands such concentration. Locating the character as to area of address is sufficient unless there is an unusually large cast of characters.

Since the angle widens as it extends to the rear of the audience, the interpreter should keep his areas of address sufficiently close together so that he can shift from one to the other easily. An almost imperceptible change of angle, combined with the other changes in posture, muscle tone, facial expression, and vocal characteristics, will make it clear that another character is speaking. When the characters are placed too far apart, the interpreter must turn his whole head, and the result, in fast dialogue, is much the same as the head movement of a spectator at a tennis match. Moreover, the danger of a sag between speeches is increased because the interpreter has so far to go physically before he can pick up the next speech. Any movement of this kind may become unpleasantly noticeable and detract from the effectiveness of the performance.

In deciding upon the angle of address or the area toward which each character will direct his speeches, it is usually more practical to retain exact center position for narration which will be given to the audience in the interpreter's own person. The characters may then be placed on either side of that center line, as close together as possible without confusing the audience. The principal characters, who carry much of the dialogue and have the most important speeches, may be placed on either side of the center line to facilitate their interplay. It is sometimes practical to separate similar characters so that they will not overlap as they might if placed side by side. Minor characters who play a scene together should all be placed in the same general direction to prevent any wide gap between them.

It is recommended that the interpreter adopt this method of character placement until his experience is such that he can discover his own method without the danger of confusing his audience and adding needless complications to the already complex process of interpreting drama. The most important consideration is that the audience know immediately who is speaking.

Audience Contact

How to establish and maintain contact with the audience is one of the troublesome problems in the handling of drama. Clearly, the interpreter's greatest chance for immediate contact lies in his direct narrative and explanatory material. In dialogue the problem is not so simple. Some authorities suggest selecting a member of the audience and addressing the speeches to him. Though this helps to achieve directness, we assume here that the interpreter who is ready to handle drama has already passed the stage in his development at which he would have needed such a device. As we have remarked, it often embarrasses a listener to have highly emotional speeches directed at him, and he will tend to pull away. Moreover, a direct meeting of eyes can sometimes throw the interpreter off stride for a moment and break his concentration. It is simpler and safer to visualize the characters addressed as somewhere toward the back of the room, only a few inches above the heads of the audience. In this way the interpreter can achieve direct focus on character without seeming to single out any member of the audience. During a long or particularly reflective speech, the interpreter may include an entire section of his audience in his eye contact. When one carries on a conversation in real life, the eyes occasionally move about during the speech, and the same can be true in interpretation. Care should be taken, however, to start and end the speech with the angle of address already established for the character in question, so that his identity will never merge with that of another character. The interpreter's sense of communication must remain as direct for this as for any other type of material.

THE READING STAND

An interpreter who wishes to use dramatic material outside the classroom must be adaptable. He may have a large auditorium complete with stage and reading stand. Or he may find himself in a small living room or behind a banquet table. He should practice working with and without the reading stand so that he can adapt himself to any set of circumstances without detriment to his performance. He will find, too, that reading stands vary in height, width, and lighting facilities.

An interpreter is free to use a reading stand or not, as he prefers. The only difficulty arises if he has become dependent upon one and is then placed in a situation where none is provided. If he uses a reading stand, he must guard against the temptation to remain too long behind it. He should use it as the center for whatever changes of position he may find helpful. Most of these changes can usually be made during the direct, informal, less demanding narrative sections. When the interpreter uses no reading stand, he may move as he pleases for variety and relief, being careful only to avoid any movement that might become distracting to the audience. Any repeated pattern of movement will soon become obtrusive.

The marks used in cutting a play must be particularly clear because of the speed with which the performance moves. Frequently portions of speeches will be cut, or several speeches run together. Many experienced interpreters draw a line through the cut material, connecting the end of one portion to the beginning of the next by an arrow. If for some reason the book cannot be marked, pieces of blank paper may be clipped over the speeches to be omitted. When whole speeches are cut, the character names which precede them should be crossed out so that they will not cause confusion on a quick glance. In any case, the interpreter should mark his book or typescript so that it is clear and unmistakable. He should not depend on chance; the mind does strange things under the stress of performance. Once the interpreter has established his own method of marking, he should use it consistently.

Cuttings of scenes or speeches must always be timed carefully. When a speaker is asked to give a program of specific length, it is part of his responsibility to fill the time allotted him. It is poor showmanship and bad manners to continue the program long past the time set aside for it. A selection should always be timed as it is read aloud because of the tendency to skim and omit pauses in silent reading.

READERS THEATRE

In recent years there has been an increased interest in group interpretation of drama, sometimes referred to as Readers Theatre. Readers Theatre uses all the techniques we have been discussing for the individual interpreter. The difference lies in the fact that there is usually a separate interpreter for each role just as in a fully staged production. Though each interpreter is responsible for only one character, he must, of course, make a thorough study of the entire play so that he is aware of relationships and of the contribution of each scene to the total effect. In rehearsal and performance he is bound by the same principles as the individual interpreter of drama, and he depends on suggestion rather than explicitness in bodily action and the handling of properties. However, since he is interpreting only one character, he will probably use the entire area at the back of the house for his focus in dialogue, allowing the angle to shift according to whom he is addressing. Thus the angles of focus of two characters addressing each other will cross about two-thirds of the way back in the audience area.

Despite the use of separate readers for various parts, the scene in Readers Theatre is out front. Keeping this in mind is very difficult. It is a tremendous temptation for the interpreter to turn and look at the person whose speech he is answering, but to do so brings the scene up on stage. It is often helpful during the rehearsal period to divide the cast so that half of them are working at the back of the auditorium and the members on stage can address them directly. After a few rehearsals the positions can be reversed. This encourages good visualization and directness. When all members of the cast are again on stage, they simply remember how they handled the scene when the other characters were at the back of the auditorium and continue to visualize them there.

Drama in which the literary style is especially strong adapts itself well to Readers Theatre and can often be used exactly as written. Greek dramas are especially effective. Plays which depend on stage business are more difficult to handle. When explanations must be made, many directors use a narrator at one side and in front of the proscenium who speaks directly to the audience in his own person. Such a device is very effective, but it must be carefully timed and coordinated in mood so that the narration does not break the dramatic progression.

Though a pleasing stage picture is valuable in Readers Theatre, scenery, costumes, and make-up should be kept at a minimum. It would be impossible to cover all the examples which might be considered because each play and each cast will have its own individual requirements and limitations. On the whole, it is safest to remember that in Readers Theatre, as in individual interpretation of drama, the speakers are not attempting to look like the characters but, rather, to project the mental and emotional complexities of the characters so that the audience will create the scene and action in their minds.

There is no "one way" to do Readers Theatre. The cast and the director must always be guided by the demands of the selection they are using. Many directors place the readers on stage in groups which suggest the psychological relationship of the characters. They may be either standing or sitting, in chairs or on stools. Some use reading stands; others do not. If reading stands are used, they must not be so high that they obscure the view for the people in the front row. Manuscripts may be placed on the stands or held in the hands just as in individual interpretation.

Effective entrances and exits may be handled in many ways as well. Usually the reader does not leave the stage when the character for whom he is responsible exits. Nevertheless, the audience must know who is present during the various scenes. Entrances can be suggested by having the reader rise or simply lift his head. If the stools revolve, a reader may turn slightly away from the audience until the entrance of his character, at which time he faces front and either remains seated or rises. Exits, of course, can be handled in the reverse of any of these ways. With a large cast it is often more practical to have most or all of the readers seated well upstage and bring them downstage to handle their scenes. Readers may also enter from and exit to the offstage area. Practical considerations such as the size of the cast, the area available for staging, and the number and length of scenes will influence the decisions on all these matters.

However the entrances and exits are handled, timing is extremely important, as are muscle tone, the "sense of performance," and empathy. If the entrance is a sudden one, the reader will rise quickly and "take scene" in the mood of the lines he is about to speak. For such an exit he would sit or turn quickly and then "drop scene." When the character for whom he is responsible is offstage, the reader remains absolutely quiet with his head slightly down so as to resist the temptation to look at the audience and draw attention to himself. He narrows his circle of concentration so that he is, as it were, isolated mentally in his own little area. Of course, he must be careful not to become so comfortable in his isolation that he is not ready for his cue. When he "takes stage," he widens his circle of concentration to include the entire audience and directs his thoughts and voice to the back of the auditorium. His exits reverse the procedure. This change in mental directness, and consequently in physical and vocal projection, is an extremely important part of Readers Theatre technique. When it is neglected, the audience is distracted from the scene in progress.

The interpreter should not make the mistake of thinking that Readers Theatre takes less time and effort on the part of the participants than a fully staged production. The interpreter must be as fully prepared as the actor. Since he will have his manuscript before him, whether he memorizes his lines or not is unimportant. Nevertheless, he must be completely in control of all the elements of the entire play and alert to the contribution his scenes make to the total performance. Though difficult and challenging, Readers Theatre is an effective and satisfying technique.

SELECTIONS FOR ANALYSIS AND ORAL INTERPRETATION

THE BEGINNING OF this famous scene, with its entrances and exits, will require some care to keep the abrupt stage directions from interrupting the dialogue. Juliet's speech, with its problem of properties and her loss of consciousness at the end, has been mentioned within this chapter. Watch the build of hysteria toward the end of the speech, and the resultant problem of balancing the climactic "This do I drink to thee."

from *Romeo and Juliet*

ACT IV, SCENE 3

Enter JULIET *and* NURSE

JUL. Ay, those attires are best; — but, gentle nurse,
I pray thee, leave me to myself to-night;
For I have need of many orisons
To move the heavens to smile upon my state,
Which, well thou know'st, is cross and full of sin.

Enter LADY CAPULET

LA. CAP. What, are you busy, ho? Need you my help?
JUL. No, Madam; we have cull'd such necessaries
As are behoveful for our state to-morrow.
So please you, let me now be left alone,
And let the nurse this night sit up with you;
For, I am sure, you have your hands full all,
In this so sudden business.
LA. CAP. Good-night.
Get thee to bed, and rest; for thou hast need.

(*Exeunt* LADY CAPULET *and* NURSE)

JUL. Farewell! God knows when we shall meet again.
I have a faint cold fear thrills through my veins,
That almost freezes up the heat of life.
I'll call them back again to comfort me.
Nurse! — What should she do here?
My dismal scene I needs must act alone.
Come, vial.
What if this mixture do not work at all?
Shall I be married then to-morrow morning?
No, no; this shall forbid it. Lie thou there.

(*Laying down her dagger.*)

What if it be a poison, which the friar
Subtly hath minist'red to have me dead,
Lest in this marriage he should be dishonour'd

Because he married me before to Romeo?
I fear it is; and yet, methinks, it should not,
For he hath still been tried a holy man.
How if, when I am laid into the tomb,
I wake before the time that Romeo
Come to redeem me? There's a fearful point!
Shall I not then be stifled in the vault,
To whose foul mouth no healthsome air breathes in,
And there die strangled ere my Romeo comes?
Or, if I live, is it not very like
The horrible conceit of death and night,
Together with the terror of the place, —
As in a vault, an ancient receptacle,
Where, for this many hundred years, the bones
Of all my buried ancestors are pack'd;
Where bloody Tybalt, yet but green in earth,
Lies fest'ring in his shroud; where, as they say,
At some hours in the night spirits resort; —
Alack, alack, is it not like that I,
So early waking, — what with loathsome smells,
And shrieks like mandrakes' torn out of the earth,
That living mortals, hearing them, run mad; —
O, if I wake, shall I not be distraught,
Environed with all these hideous fears,
And madly play with my forefathers' joints,
And pluck the mangled Tybalt from his shroud,
And, in this rage, with some great kinsman's bone
As with a club, dash out my desperate brains?
O, look! methinks I see my cousin's ghost
Seeking out Romeo, that did spit his body
Upon a rapier's point. Stay, Tybalt, stay!
Romeo, I come! This do I drink to thee.

(*She falls upon her bed, within the curtains.*)

William Shakespeare

In this opening scene from *Hedda Gabler,* Ibsen was interested in giving certain important background information about the characters and their relations to one another, as well as a suggestion of Hedda's incompatibility with everything George Tesman, her husband, holds dear. The numerous detailed stage directions will provide some of that background and suggestion, but many of them are intended to vitalize the stage picture when the play is presented. Be discriminating in your selection of those which must be given to the audience through narration and those which can be eliminated or suggested through dialogue and muscle memory. There is a problem of physical contact when Miss Tesman kisses Hedda. How will you handle it?

from *Hedda Gabler*

Act I

A spacious, handsome, and tastefully furnished drawing-room decorated in dark colors. . . . In front, by the wall on the right, a wide stove of dark porcelain, a high-backed arm-chair, a cushioned foot-rest, and two footstools. A settee, with a small round table in front of it, fills the upper right-hand corner. In front, on the left, a little way from the wall, a sofa. Further back than the glass door, a piano. . . . Morning light. The sun shines in through the glass door.

MISS JULIANA TESMAN, *with her bonnet on and carrying a parasol, comes in from the hall, followed by* BERTA, *who carries a bouquet wrapped in paper.* MISS TESMAN *is a comely and pleasant-looking lady of about sixty-five. She is nicely but simply dressed in a gray walking-costume.* BERTA *is a middle-aged woman of plain and rather countrified appearance.*

MISS TESMAN: (*Stops close to the door, listens, and says softly*) Upon my word, I don't believe they are stirring yet!

BERTA: (*Also softly*) I told you so, Miss. Remember how late the steamboat got in last night. And then, when they got home! — good Lord, what a lot the young mistress had to unpack before she could get to bed.

MISS TESMAN: Well, well — let them have their sleep out. . . . So you've got a new mistress now, my dear Berta. Heaven knows it was a wrench to me to part with you.

BERTA: (*On the point of weeping*) And do you think it wasn't hard for me, too, Miss? After all the blessed years I've been with you and Miss Rina.

MISS TESMAN: We must make the best of it, Berta. There was nothing else to be done. George can't do without you, you see — he absolutely can't. He has had you to look after him ever since he was a little boy.

BERTA: Ah, but, Miss Julia, I can't help thinking of Miss Rina lying helpless at home there, poor thing. And with only that new girl, too! She'll never learn to take proper care of an invalid.

MISS TESMAN: Oh, I shall manage to train her. And, of course, you know I shall take most of it upon myself. You needn't be uneasy about my poor sister, my dear Berta.

BERTA: Well, but there's another thing, Miss. I'm so mortally afraid I shan't be able to suit the young mistress.

MISS TESMAN: Oh, well — just at first there may be one or two things —

BERTA: Most like she'll be terrible grand in her ways.

MISS TESMAN: Well, you can't wonder at that — General Gabler's

"Hedda Gabler" by Henrik Ibsen, translated by William Archer (1904), is reprinted with the permission of Charles Scribner's Sons from *The Collected Works of Henrik Ibsen,* Volume X.

daughter! Think of the sort of life she was accustomed to in her father's time. Don't you remember how we used to see her riding down the road along with the General? In that long black habit—and with feathers in her hat?

BERTA: Yes, indeed—I remember well enough!—But, good Lord, I should never have dreamt in those days that she and Master George would make a match of it.

MISS TESMAN: Nor I.—But by-the-bye, Berta—while I think of it; in future you mustn't say Master George. You must say Dr. Tesman.

BERTA: Yes, the young mistress spoke of that, too—last night—the moment they set foot in the house. . . .

MISS TESMAN: . . . (*Looks around*) . . . Bless me, Berta—why have you done this? Taken the chintz covers off all the furniture?

BERTA: The mistress told me to. She can't abide covers on the chairs, she says.

MISS TESMAN: Are they going to make this their everyday sitting-room then?

BERTA: Yes, that's what I understood—from the mistress. Master George—the doctor—he said nothing.

(GEORGE TESMAN *comes from the right into the inner room, humming to himself, and carrying an unstrapped empty portmanteau. He is a middle-sized, young-looking man of thirty-three, rather stout, with a round, open, cheerful face, fair hair and beard. He wears spectacles, and is somewhat carelessly dressed in comfortable indoor clothes.*)

MISS TESMAN: Good morning, good morning, George.

TESMAN: (*In the doorway between the rooms*) Aunt Julia! Dear Aunt Julia! (*Goes up to her and shakes hands warmly*) Come all this way—so early! Eh?

MISS TESMAN: Why, of course I had to come and see how you were getting on.

TESMAN: In spite of your having had no proper night's rest?

MISS TESMAN: Oh, that makes no difference to me.

TESMAN: Well, I suppose you got home all right from the pier? Eh?

MISS TESMAN: Yes, quite safely, thank goodness. Judge Brack was good enough to see me right to my door.

TESMAN: We were so sorry we couldn't give you a seat in the carriage. But you saw what a pile of boxes Hedda had to bring with her.

MISS TESMAN: Yes, she had certainly plenty of boxes.

BERTA: (*To* TESMAN) Shall I go in and see if there's anything I can do for the mistress?

TESMAN: No thank you, Berta—you needn't. She said she would ring if she wanted anything.

BERTA: (*Going towards the right*) Very well.

TESMAN: But look here—take this portmanteau with you.

BERTA: (*Taking it*) I'll put it in the attic. (*She goes out by the hall door*)

TESMAN: . . . And now, look here —suppose we sit comfortably on the sofa and have a little chat, till Hedda comes.

(*They seat themselves. She places her parasol in the corner of the sofa.*)

MISS TESMAN: . . . To think that here are you a married man, George! — And that you should be the one to carry off Hedda Gabler — the beautiful Hedda Gabler! Only think of it — she, that was so beset with admirers!

TESMAN: (*Hums a little and smiles complacently*) Yes, I fancy I have several good friends about town who would like to stand in my shoes — eh?

MISS TESMAN: And then this fine long wedding-tour you have had! More than five — nearly six months —

TESMAN: Well, for me it has been a sort of tour of research as well. I have had to do so much grubbing among old records — and to read no end of books too, Auntie.

MISS TESMAN: Oh yes, I suppose so. . . . It must have cost a great deal of money, George?

TESMAN: Well, you see — my handsome traveling-scholarship went a good way.

MISS TESMAN: But I can't understand how you can have made it go far enough for two.

TESMAN: No, that's not so easy to understand — eh?

MISS TESMAN: And especially traveling with a lady — they tell me that makes it ever so much more expensive.

TESMAN: Yes, of course — it makes it a little more expensive. But Hedda had to have this trip, Auntie! She really had to. Nothing else would have done.

MISS TESMAN: No, no, I suppose not. . . .

TESMAN: . . . I believe I hear her coming — eh?

(HEDDA *enters from the left through the inner room. She is a woman of nine-and-twenty. Her face and figure show refinement and distinction. Her complexion is pale and opaque. Her steel-gray eyes express a cold, unruffled repose. Her hair is of an agreeable medium brown, but not particularly abundant. She is dressed in a tasteful, somewhat loose-fitting morning gown.*)

MISS TESMAN: (*Going to meet Hedda*) Good morning, my dear Hedda! Good morning, and a hearty welcome!

HEDDA: (*Holds out her hand*) Good morning, dear Miss Tesman! So early a call! That is kind of you.

MISS TESMAN: (*With some embarrassment*) Well — has the bride slept well in her new home?

HEDDA: Oh yes, thanks. Passably.

TESMAN: (*Laughing*) Passably! Come, that's good, Hedda! You were sleeping like a stone when I got up.

HEDDA: Fortunately. Of course one has always to accustom one's self to new surroundings, Miss Tesman — little by little. . . . But — won't you sit down, Miss Tesman?

MISS TESMAN: No, thank you. Now that I have seen that everything is all right here — thank heaven! — I must be getting home again. My sister is lying longing for me, poor thing.

TESMAN: Give her my very best love, Auntie; and say I shall look in and see her later in the day.

MISS TESMAN: Yes, yes, I'll be sure to tell her. But by-the-bye, George — (*Feeling in her dress pocket*) — I had almost forgotten — I have something for you here.

TESMAN: What is it, Auntie? Eh?

MISS TESMAN: (*Produces a flat parcel wrapped in newspaper and hands it to him*) Look here, my dear boy.

TESMAN: (*Opening the parcel*) Well, I declare! — Have you really saved them for me, Aunt Julia! Hedda! Isn't this touching — eh?

HEDDA: (*Beside the whatnot on the right*) Well, what is it?

TESMAN: My old morning-shoes! My slippers.

HEDDA: Indeed. I remember you often spoke of them while we were abroad.

TESMAN: Yes, I missed them terribly. (*Goes up to her*) Now you shall see them, Hedda!

HEDDA: (*Going towards the stove*) Thanks, I really don't care about it.

TESMAN: (*Following her*) Only think — ill as she was, Aunt Rina embroidered these for me. Oh, you can't think how many associations cling to them.

HEDDA: (*At the table*) Scarcely for me.

MISS TESMAN: Of course not for Hedda, George.

TESMAN: Well, but now that she belongs to the family, I thought — . . . Eh? But Auntie, take a good look at Hedda before you go! See how handsome she is!

MISS TESMAN: Oh, my dear boy, there's nothing new in that. Hedda was always lovely. (*She nods and goes towards the right*)

TESMAN: (*Following*) Yes, but have you noticed what splendid condition she is in? How she has filled out on the journey?

HEDDA: (*Crossing the room*) Oh, do be quiet — !

MISS TESMAN: (*Who has stopped and turned*) Filled out?

TESMAN: Of course you don't notice it so much now that she has that dress on. But I, who can see —

HEDDA: (*At the glass door, impatiently*) Oh, you can't see anything.

TESMAN: It must be the mountain air in the Tyrol —

HEDDA: (*Curtly, interrupting*) I am exactly as I was when I started.

TESMAN: So you insist; but I'm quite certain you are not. Don't you agree with me, Auntie?

MISS TESMAN: (*Who has been gazing at her with folded hands*)

Hedda is lovely — lovely — lovely. (*Goes up to her, takes her head between both hands, draws it downwards, and kisses her hair*) God bless and preserve Hedda Tesman — for George's sake.

HEDDA: (*Gently freeing herself*) Oh — ! Let me go.

MISS TESMAN: (*In quiet emotion*) I shall not let a day pass without coming to see you.

TESMAN: No you won't, will you, Auntie? Eh?

MISS TESMAN: Good-bye — good-bye! (*She goes out by the hall door.* TESMAN *accompanies her. The door remains half open.* TESMAN *can be heard repeating his message to Aunt Rina and his thanks for the slippers*) . . .

HENRIK IBSEN

THE INTERPRETER WILL need to decide which of the stage directions he wishes to use as narration and which he can incorporate into character suggestion. There are also some interesting problems of physical action and proximity. Style and rhythm in the dialogue add to the humor.

from *Androcles and the Lion*

Prologue

Overture: forest sounds, roaring of lions, Christian hymn faintly.

A jungle path. A lion's roar, a melancholy suffering roar, comes from the jungle. It is repeated nearer. The lion limps from the jungle on three legs, holding up his right forepaw, in which a huge thorn sticks. He sits down and contemplates it. He licks it. He shakes it. He tries to extract it by scraping it along the ground, and hurts himself worse. He roars piteously. He licks it again. Tears drop from his eyes. He limps painfully off the path and lies down under the trees, exhausted with pain. Heaving a long sigh, like wind in a trombone, he goes to sleep.

Androcles and his wife Megaera come along the path. He is a small, thin, ridiculous little man who might be any age from thirty to fifty-five. He has sandy hair, watery compassionate blue eyes, sensitive nostrils, and a very presentable forehead; but his good points go no further: his arms and legs and back, though wiry of their kind, look shrivelled and starved. He carries a big bundle, is very poorly clad, and seems tired and hungry.

His wife is a rather handsome pampered slattern, well fed and in the prime of life. She has nothing to carry, and has a stout stick to help her along.

MEGAERA [*suddenly throwing down her stick*] I won't go another step.

ANDROCLES [*pleading wearily*] Oh, not again, dear. What's the

From *Androcles and the Lion* by George Bernard Shaw. Reprinted by permission of the Society of Authors and The Public Trustee.

good of stopping every two miles and saying you won't go another step? We must get on to the next village before night. There are wild beasts in this wood: lions, they say.

MEGAERA. I don't believe a word of it. You are always threatening me with wild beasts to make me walk the very soul out of my body when I can hardly drag one foot before another. We havn't seen a single lion yet.

ANDROCLES. Well, dear, do you want to see one?

MEGAERA [*tearing the bundle from his back*] You cruel brute, you don't care how tired I am, or what becomes of me [*she throws the bundle on the ground*]: always thinking of yourself. Self! self! self! always yourself! [*She sits down on the bundle.*]

ANDROCLES [*sitting down sadly on the ground with his elbows on his knees and his head in his hands*] We all have to think of ourselves occasionally, dear.

MEGAERA. A man ought to think of his wife sometimes.

ANDROCLES. He can't always help it, dear. You make me think of you a good deal. Not that I blame you.

MEGAERA. Blame me! I should think not indeed. Is it my fault that I'm married to you?

ANDROCLES. No, dear: that is my fault.

MEGAERA. That's a nice thing to say to me. Aren't you happy with me?

ANDROCLES. I don't complain, my love.

MEGAERA. You ought to be ashamed of yourself.

ANDROCLES. I am, my dear.

MEGAERA. You're not: you glory in it.

ANDROCLES. In what, darling?

MEGAERA. In everything. In making me a slave, and making yourself a laughing-stock. It's not fair. You get me the name of being a shrew with your meek ways, always talking as if butter wouldn't melt in your mouth. And just because I look a big strong woman, and because I'm goodhearted and a bit hasty, and because you're always driving me to do things I'm sorry for afterwards, people say 'Poor man: what a life his wife leads him!' Oh, if they only knew! And you think I don't know. But I do, I do, [*screaming*] I do.

ANDROCLES. Yes, my dear: I know you do.

MEGAERA. Then why don't you treat me properly and be a good husband to me?

ANDROCLES. What can I do, my dear?

MEGAERA. What can you do! You can return to your duty, and come back to your home and your friends, and sacrifice to the gods as all respectable people do, instead of having us hunted out of house and home for being dirty disreputable blaspheming atheists.

ANDROCLES. I'm not an atheist, dear: I am a Christian.

MEGAERA. Well, isn't that the same thing, only ten times worse? Everybody knows that the Christians are the very lowest of the low.

ANDROCLES. Just like us, dear.

MEGAERA. Speak for yourself. Don't you dare to compare me to common people. My father owned his own public-house; and sorrowful was the day for me when you first came drinking in our bar.

ANDROCLES. I confess I was addicted to it, dear. But I gave it up when I became a Christian.

MEGAERA. You'd much better have remained a drunkard. I can forgive a man being addicted to drink: it's only natural; and I don't deny I like a drop myself sometimes. What I can't stand is your being addicted to Christianity. And what's worse again, your being addicted to animals. How is any woman to keep her house clean when you bring in every stray cat and lost cur and lame duck in the whole countryside? You took the bread out of my mouth to feed them: you know you did: don't attempt to deny it.

ANDROCLES. Only when they were hungry and you were getting too stout, dearie.

MEGAERA. Yes: insult me, do. [*Rising*] Oh! I won't bear it another moment. You used to sit and talk to those dumb brute beasts for hours, when you hadn't a word for me.

ANDROCLES. They never answered back, darling. [*He rises and again shoulders the bundle.*]

MEGAERA. Well, if you're fonder of animals than of your own wife, you can live with them here in the jungle. I've had enough of them and enough of you. I'm going back. I'm going home.

ANDROCLES [*barring the way back*] No, dearie: don't take on like that. We can't go back. We've sold everything: we should starve; and I should be sent to Rome and thrown to the lions —

MEGAERA. Serve you right! I wish the lions joy of you. [*Screaming*] Are you going to get out of my way and let me go home?

ANDROCLES. No, dear —

MEGAERA. Then I'll make my way through the forest; and when I'm eaten by the wild beasts you'll know what a wife you've lost. [*She dashes into the jungle and nearly falls over the sleeping lion.*] Oh! Oh! Andy! Andy! [*She totters back and collapses into the arms of Androcles, who, crushed by her weight, falls on his bundle.*]

ANDROCLES [*extracting himself from beneath her and slapping her hands in great anxiety*] What is it, my precious, my pet? What's the matter? [*He raises her head. Speechless with terror, she points in the direction of the sleeping lion. He steals cautiously towards the spot indicated by Megaera. She rises with an effort and totters after him.*]

MEGAERA. No, Andy: you'll be killed. Come back.

The lion utters a long snoring sigh. Androcles sees the lion, and recoils fainting into the arms of Megaera, who falls back on the bundle. They roll apart and lie staring in terror at one another. The lion is heard groaning heavily in the jungle.

ANDROCLES [*whispering*] Did you see? A lion.

MEGAERA [*despairing*] The gods have sent him to punish us because you're a Christian. Take me away, Andy. Save me.

ANDROCLES [*rising*] Meggy: there's one chance for you. It'll take him pretty nigh twenty minutes to eat me (I'm rather stringy and tough) and you can escape in less time than that.

MEGAERA. Oh, don't talk about eating. [*The lion rises with a great groan and limps toward them.*] Oh! [*She faints.*]

ANDROCLES [*quaking, but keeping between the lion and Megaera*] Don't you come near my wife, do you hear? [*The lion groans. Androcles can hardly stand for trembling.*] Meggy: run. Run for your life. If I take my eye off him, it's all up. [*The lion holds up his wounded paw and flaps it piteously before Androcles.*] Oh, he's lame, poor old chap! He's got a thorn in his paw. A frightfully big thorn. [*Full of sympathy*] Oh, poor old man! Did um get an awful thorn into um's tootsums wootsums? Has it made um too sick to eat a nice little Christian man for um's breakfast? Oh, a nice little Christian man will get um's thorn out for um; and then um shall eat the nice Christian man and the nice Christian man's nice big tender wifey pifey. [*The lion responds by moans of self-pity.*] Yes, yes, yes, yes, yes. Now, now [*taking the paw in his hand*], um is not to bite and not to scratch, not even if it hurts a very very little. Now make velvet paws. That's right. [*He pulls gingerly at the thorn. The lion, with an angry yell of pain, jerks back his paw so abruptly that Androcles is thrown on his back.*] Steadee! Oh, did the nasty cruel little Christian man hurt the sore paw? [*The lion moans assentingly but apologetically.*] Well, one more little pull and it will be all over. Just one little, little, leetle pull; and then um will live happily ever after. [*He gives the thorn another pull. The lion roars and snaps his jaws with a terrifying clash.*] Oh, mustn't frighten um's good kind doctor, um's affectionate nursey. That didn't hurt at all: not a bit. Just one more. Just to show how the brave big lion can bear pain, not like the little crybaby Christian man. Oopsh! [*The thorn comes out. The lion yells with pain, and shakes his paw wildly.*] That's it! [*Holding up the thorn.*] Now it's out. Now lick um's paw to take away the nasty inflammation. See? [*He licks his own hand. The lion nods intelligently and licks his paw industriously.*] Clever little liony-piony! Understands um's dear old friend Andy Wandy. [*The lion licks his face.*] Yes, kissums Andy Wandy. [*The lion, wagging his tail violently, rises on his hind legs, and embraces Androcles, who makes a wry face and cries*] Velvet paws! Velvet paws! [*The lion draws in his claws.*] That's right. [*He embraces the lion, who finally takes the end of his tail in one paw, places that tight round Androcles' waist, resting it on his hip. Androcles takes the other paw in his hand, stretches out his arm, and the two waltz rapturously round and round and finally away through the jungle.*]

MEGAERA [*who has revived during the waltz*] Oh, you coward, you haven't danced with me for years; and now you go off dancing with a great brute beast that you haven't known for ten minutes and that wants to eat your own wife. Coward. Coward! Coward! [*She rushes off after them into the jungle.*]

GEORGE BERNARD SHAW

LIKE SO MANY of Chekhov's dramas, *The Cherry Orchard* deals with the decay of a class and a social order. There is a wistful, static quality about it. The sale of the cherry orchard is a symbol of the changing times; and Lyubov, lovely, confused, almost childish (but not child-like) in her sense of values, is herself a symbol of the idle, landed class which is disappearing.

In this scene from Act III, notice particularly the swift changes of emotion, which are credible only when the play is put into its proper period (late nineteenth century) and setting. Be sure to use Petya's appearance and actions as the motivations for these swift changes in Lyubov's speeches. Anya is Lyubov's seventeen-year-old daughter, and Petya is a young student who takes himself and the world very seriously.

from *The Cherry Orchard*

ACT III

A drawing-room divided by an arch from a larger drawing-room. The orchestra is heard playing in the ante-room. It is evening. In the larger drawing-room they are dancing the grand chain. MADAME RANEVSKY (LYUBOV), *the owner of the Cherry Orchard, and* TROFIMOV (PETYA), *a student, are in the smaller drawing-room.* VARYA, *Lyubov's adopted daughter, has just left.*

. . . . . .

LYUBOV: Don't tease her, Petya. You see she has grief enough without that.

TROFIMOV: She is so very officious, meddling in what's not her business. All the summer she's given Anya and me no peace. She's afraid of a love affair between us. What's it to do with her? Besides, I have given no grounds for it. Such triviality is not in my line. We are above love!

LYUBOV: And I suppose I am beneath love. (*Very uneasily*) Why is it Leonid's not here? If only I could know whether the estate is sold or not! It seems such an incredible calamity that I really don't know what to think. I am distracted. . . . I shall scream in a minute. . . . I shall do something stupid. Save me, Petya, tell me something, talk to me!

TROFIMOV: What does it matter whether the estate is sold to-day or not? That's all done with long ago. There's no turning back, the path is overgrown. . . . You mustn't deceive yourself; for once in your life you must face the truth!

LYUBOV: What truth? You see where the truth lies, but I seem to have lost my sight, I see nothing. You settle every great problem so boldly, but tell me, my dear boy, isn't it because you're young—because you haven't yet understood one of your problems through suffering? You look forward boldly, and isn't it that you don't see and don't expect anything dreadful because life is still hidden from

Translated by Constance Garnett. Reprinted by permission of Chatto & Windus, Ltd. Also reprinted by permission of Mr. David Garnett and A. P. Watt & Son.

your young eyes? You're bolder, more honest, deeper than we are, but think, be just a little magnanimous, have pity on me. I was born here, you know, my father and mother lived here, my grandfather lived here, I love this house. I can't conceive of life without the cherry orchard, and if it really must be sold, then sell me with the orchard. My boy was drowned here. (*Weeps*) Pity me, my dear kind fellow.

TROFIMOV: You know I feel for you with all my heart.

LYUBOV: But that should have been said differently, so differently. (*Takes out her handkerchief, telegram falls on the floor*) My heart is so heavy to-day. It's so noisy here, my soul is quivering at every sound, I'm shuddering all over, but I can't go away; I'm afraid to be quiet and alone. Don't be hard on me, Petya . . . I love you as though you were one of ourselves, I would gladly let you marry Anya — I swear I would — only, my dear boy, you must take your degree, you do nothing — you're simply tossed by fate from place to place. That's so strange. It is, isn't it? And you must do something with your beard to make it grow somehow. (*Laughs*) You look so funny!

TROFIMOV: (*Picks up the telegram*) I've no wish to be a beauty.

LYUBOV: That's a telegram from Paris. I get one every day. One yesterday and one to-day. That savage creature is ill again, he's in trouble again. He begs forgiveness, beseeches me to go, and really I ought to go to Paris to see him. You look shocked, Petya. What am I to do, my dear boy, what am I to do? He is ill, he is alone and unhappy, and who'll look after him, who'll keep him from doing the wrong thing, who'll give him his medicine at the right time? And why hide it or be silent? I love him, that's clear. I love him! I love him! He's a millstone about my neck, I'm going to the bottom with him, but I love that stone and can't live without it. (*Presses Trofimov's hand*) Don't think ill of me, Petya, don't tell me anything, don't tell me. . . .

TROFIMOV: For God's sake forgive my frankness: why, he robbed you!

LYUBOV: No! No! No! You musn't speak like that. (*Covers her ears*)

TROFIMOV: He is a wretch! You're the only person that doesn't know it! He's a worthless creature! A despicable wretch!

LYUBOV: (*Getting angry, but speaking with restraint*) You're twenty-six or twenty-seven years old, but you're still a school-boy.

TROFIMOV: Possibly.

LYUBOV: You should be a man at your age! You should understand what love means! And you ought to be in love yourself. You ought to fall in love! (*Angrily*) Yes, yes, and it's not purity in you, you're simply a prude, a comic fool, a freak.

TROFIMOV: (*In horror*) The things she's saying!

LYUBOV: I am above love! You're not above love, but simply as our Firs here says, "You are a good-for-nothing." At your age not to have a mistress!

TROFIMOV: (*In horror*) This is awful! The things she is saying! (*Goes rapidly into the larger drawing-room clutching his head*) This is awful! I can't stand it! I'm going. (*Goes off, but at once returns*) All is over between us! (*Goes off into the ante-room*)

LYUBOV: (*Shouts after him*) Petya! Wait a minute! You funny creature! I was joking! Petya!

ANTON CHEKHOV

AS THIS PLAY has progressed, there has been a continuing process of dehumanization of all the characters except the two we meet here. The other members of the community have become rhinoceroses, some of them before our very eyes. The metamorphosis is painful and horrible, terminating in animal noises and violence. Daisy and Berenger are alone now. The animals have taken charge of the world.

This excerpt will divide into separate scenes for class exercises, but the steady build of disintegration must be constantly realized. The deliberate starkness of the style was mentioned in our earlier discussion. Notice how it increases as Daisy's human fear turns to spiritual and mental lethargy. The telephone and the abundance of stage directions offer a nice challenge to the interpreter.

from *Rhinoceros*

ACT III

(*The telephone rings.*)

BERENGER: Who could that be?

DAISY: (*fearful*) Don't answer.

BERENGER: Why not?

DAISY: I don't know. I just feel it's better not to.

BERENGER: It might be Mr. Papillon, or Botard, or Jean or Dudard ringing to say they've had second thoughts. You did say it was probably only a passing phase.

DAISY: I don't think so. They wouldn't have changed their minds so quickly. They've not had time to think it over. They're bound to give it a fair trial.

BERENGER: Perhaps the authorities have decided to take action at last; maybe they're ringing to ask our help in whatever measures they've decided to adopt.

DAISY: I'd be surprised if it was them.

(*The telephone rings again.*)

BERENGER: It is the authorities, I tell you, I recognize the ring—a long drawn-out ring, I can't ignore an appeal from them. It can't

Rhinoceros and Other Plays by Eugène Ionesco, translated by Derek Prouse. Copyright © 1960 by John Calder (Publishers) Ltd. Published by Grove Press, Inc. Reprinted by permission of Grove Press, Inc.

be anyone else. (*He picks up the receiver.*) Hallo? (*Trumpetings are heard coming from the receiver.*) You hear that? Trumpeting! Listen!

(DAISY *puts the telephone to her ear, is shocked by the sound, quickly replaces the receiver.*)

DAISY: (*frightened*) What's going on?

BERENGER: They're playing jokes now.

DAISY: Jokes in bad taste!

BERENGER: You see! What did I tell you?

DAISY: You didn't tell me anything.

BERENGER: I was expecting that; it was just what I'd predicted.

DAISY: You didn't predict anything. You never do. You can only predict things after they've happened.

BERENGER: Oh yes, I can; I can predict things all right.

DAISY: That's not nice of them — in fact it's very nasty. I don't like being made fun of.

BERENGER: They wouldn't dare make fun of you. It's me they're making fun of.

DAISY: And naturally I come in for it as well because I'm with you. They're taking their revenge. But what have we done to them?

(*The telephone rings again.*)

Pull the plug out.

BERENGER: The telephone authorities say you mustn't.

DAISY: Oh you never dare to do anything — and you say you could defend me!

BERENGER: (*darting to the radio*) Let's turn on the radio for the news!

DAISY: Yes, we must find out how things stand!

(*The sound of trumpeting comes from the radio.* BERENGER *peremptorily switches it off. But in the distance other trumpetings, like echoes, can be heard.*)

Things are getting really serious! I tell you frankly, I don't like it! (*She is trembling.*)

BERENGER: (*very agitated*) Keep calm! Keep calm!

DAISY: They've taken over the radio stations!

BERENGER: (*agitated and trembling*) Keep calm, keep calm!

(DAISY *runs to the up-stage window, then to the down-stage window and looks out;* BERENGER *does the same in the opposite order, then the two come and face each other centre-stage.*)

DAISY: It's no joke any longer. They mean business!

BERENGER: There's only them left now; nobody but them. Even the authorities have joined them.

(*They cross to the windows as before, and meet again centre-stage.*)

DAISY: Not a soul left anywhere.

BERENGER: We're all alone, we're left all alone.

DAISY: That's what you wanted.

BERENGER: You mean that's what you wanted!

DAISY: It was you!

BERENGER: You!

(*Noises come from everywhere at once. Rhinoceros heads fill the up-stage wall. From left and right in the house, the noise of rushing feet and the panting breath of the animals. But all these disquieting sounds are nevertheless somehow rhythmical, making a kind of music. The loudest noises of all come from above; a noise of stamping. Plaster falls from the ceiling. The house shakes violently.*)

DAISY: The earth's trembling! (*She doesn't know where to run.*)

BERENGER: No, that's our neighbours, the Perissodactyles! (*He shakes his fist to left and right and above.*) Stop it! You're preventing us from working! Noise is forbidden in these flats! Noise is forbidden!

DAISY: They'll never listen to you!

(*However the noise does diminish, merely forming a sort of musical background.*)

BERENGER: (*he, too, is afraid*) Don't be frightened, my dear. We're together — you're happy with me, aren't you? It's enough that I'm with you, isn't it? I'll chase all your fears away.

DAISY: Perhaps it's all our own fault.

BERENGER: Don't think about it any longer. We mustn't start feeling remorse. It's dangerous to start feeling guilty. We must just live our lives, and be happy. We have the right to be happy. They're not spiteful, and we're not doing them any harm. They'll leave us in peace. You just keep calm and rest. Sit in the armchair. (*He leads her to the armchair.*) Just keep calm! (DAISY *sits in the armchair.*) Would you like a drop of brandy to pull you together?

DAISY: I've got a headache.

BERENGER: (*taking up his bandage and binding* DAISY'S *head*) I love you, my darling. Don't you worry, they'll get over it. It's just a passing phase.

DAISY: They won't get over it. It's for good.

BERENGER: I love you. I love you madly.

DAISY: (*taking off the bandage*) Let things just take their course. What can we do about it?

BERENGER: They've all gone mad. The world is sick. They're all sick.

DAISY: We shan't be the ones to cure them.

BERENGER: How can we live in the same house with them?

DAISY: (*calming down*) We must be sensible. We must adapt ourselves and try and get on with them.

BERENGER: They can't understand us.

DAISY: They must. There's no other way.

BERENGER: Do you understand them?

DAISY: Not yet. But we must try to understand the way their minds work, and learn their language.

BERENGER: They haven't got a language! Listen . . . do you call that a language?

DAISY: How do you know? You're no polyglot!

BERENGER: We'll talk about it later. We must have lunch first.

DAISY: I'm not hungry any more. It's all too much. I can't take any more.

BERENGER: But you're the strong one. You're not going to let it get you down. It's precisely for your courage that I admire you so.

DAISY: You said that before.

BERENGER: Do you feel sure of my love?

DAISY: Yes, of course.

BERENGER: I love you so.

DAISY: You keep saying the same thing, my dear.

BERENGER: Listen, Daisy, there *is* something we can do. We'll have children, and our children will have children — it'll take time, but together we can regenerate the human race.

DAISY: Regenerate the human race?

BERENGER: It happened once before.

DAISY: Ages ago. Adam and Eve . . . They had a lot of courage.

BERENGER: And we, too, can have courage. We don't need all that much. It happens automatically with time and patience.

DAISY: What's the use?

BERENGER: Of course we can — with a little bit of courage.

DAISY: I don't want to have children — it's a bore.

BERENGER: How can we save the world, if you don't?

DAISY: Why bother to save it?

BERENGER: What a thing to say! Do it for me, Daisy. Let's save the world.

DAISY: After all, perhaps it's we who need saving. Perhaps we're the abnormal ones.

BERENGER: You're not yourself, Daisy, you've got a touch of fever.

DAISY: There's aren't any more of our kind about anywhere, are there?

BERENGER: Daisy, you're not to talk like that!

(DAISY *looks all around at the rhinoceros heads on the walls, on the landing door, and now starting to appear along the footlights.*)

DAISY: Those are the real people. They look happy. They're content to be what they are. They don't look insane. They look very natural. They were right to do what they did.

BERENGER: (*clasping his hands and looking despairingly at* DAISY) We're the ones who are doing right, Daisy, I assure you.

DAISY: That's very presumptuous of you!

BERENGER: You know perfectly well I'm right.

DAISY: There's no such thing as absolute right. It's the world that's right — not you and me.

BERENGER: I *am* right, Daisy. And the proof is that you understand me when I speak to you.

DAISY: What does that prove?

BERENGER: The proof is that I love you as much as it's possible for a man to love a woman.

DAISY: Funny sort of argument!

BERENGER: I don't understand you any longer, Daisy. You don't know what you're saying, darling. Think of our love! Our love . . .

DAISY: I feel a bit ashamed of what you call love — this morbid feeling, this male weakness. And female, too. It just doesn't compare with the ardour and the tremendous energy emanating from all these creatures around us.

BERENGER: Energy! You want some energy, do you? I can let you have some energy! (*He slaps her face.*)

DAISY: Oh! I never would have believed it possible . . . (*She sinks into the armchair.*)

BERENGER: Oh forgive me, my darling, please forgive me! (*He tries to embrace her, she evades him.*) Forgive me, my darling. I didn't mean it. I don't know what came over me, losing control like that!

DAISY: It's because you've run out of arguments, that's why.

BERENGER: Oh dear! In the space of a few minutes we've gone through twenty-five years of married life.

DAISY: I pity you. I understand you all too well . . .

BERENGER: (*as* DAISY *weeps*) You're probably right that I've run out of arguments. You think they're stronger than me, stronger than us. Maybe they are.

DAISY: Indeed they are.

BERENGER: Well, in spite of everything, I swear to you I'll never give in, never!

DAISY: (*she rises, goes to* BERENGER, *puts her arm round his neck*) My poor darling, I'll help you to resist — to the very end.

BERENGER: Will you be capable of it?

DAISY: I give you my word. You can trust me.

(*The rhinoceros noises have become melodious.*)

Listen, they're singing!

BERENGER: They're not singing, they're roaring.

DAISY: They're singing.

BERENGER: They're roaring, I tell you.

DAISY: You're mad, they're singing.

BERENGER: You can't have a very musical ear, then.

DAISY: You don't know the first thing about music, poor dear — and look, they're playing as well, and dancing.

BERENGER: You call that dancing?

DAISY: It's their way of dancing. They're beautiful.

BERENGER: They're disgusting!

DAISY: You're not to say unpleasant things about them. It upsets me.

BERENGER: I'm sorry. We're not going to quarrel on their account.

DAISY: They're like gods.

BERENGER: You go too far, Daisy; take a good look at them.

DAISY: You mustn't be jealous, my dear.

(*She goes to* BERENGER *again and tries to embrace him. This time it is* BERENGER *who frees himself.*)

BERENGER: I can see our opinions are directly opposed. It's better not to discuss the matter.

DAISY: Now you mustn't be nasty.

BERENGER: Then don't you be stupid!

DAISY: (*to* BERENGER, *who turns his back on her. He looks at himself closely in the mirror*) It's no longer possible for us to live together.

(*As* BERENGER *continues to examine himself in the mirror she goes quietly to the door, saying:*)

He isn't very nice, really, he isn't very nice. (*She goes out, and is seen slowly descending the stairs.*)

BERENGER: (*still looking at himself in the mirror*) Men aren't so bad-looking, you know. And I'm not a particularly handsome specimen! Believe me, Daisy! (*He turns round.*) Daisy! Daisy! Where are you, Daisy? You can't do that to me! (*He darts to the door.*) Daisy! (*He gets to the landing and leans over the banister.*) Daisy! Come back! Come back, my dear! You haven't even had your lunch. Daisy, don't leave me alone! Remember your promise! Daisy! Daisy! (*He stops calling, makes a despairing gesture, and comes back into the room.*) Well, it was obvious we weren't getting along together. The home was broken up. It just wasn't working out. But she shouldn't have left like that with no explanation. (*He looks all around.*) She didn't even leave a message. That's no way to behave. Now I'm all on my own. (*He locks the door carefully, but angrily.*) But they won't get me. (*He carefully closes the windows.*) You won't get me! (*He addresses all the rhinoceros heads.*) I'm not joining you; I don't understand you! I'm staying as I am. I'm a human being. A human being. (*He sits in the armchair.*) It's an impossible situation. It's my fault she's gone. I meant everything to her. What'll become of her? That's one more person on my conscience. I can easily picture the worst, because the worst can easily happen. Poor little thing left all alone in this world of monsters! Nobody can help me find her, nobody, because there's nobody left.

(*Fresh trumpetings, hectic racings, clouds of dust.*)

I can't bear the sound of them any longer, I'm going to put cotton wool in my ears. (*He does so, and talks to himself in the mirror.*) The only solution is to convince them—but convince them of what? Are the changes reversible, that's the point? Are they reversible? It would be a labour of Hercules, far beyond me. In any case, to convince them you'd have to talk to them. And to talk to them I'd have to learn their language. Or they'd have to learn mine. But what language do I speak? What is my language? Am I talking French? Yes, it must be French. But what is French? I can call it French if I want, and nobody can say it isn't—I'm the only one who speaks it. What am I saying? Do I understand what I'm saying? Do I? (*He crosses to the middle of the room.*) And what if it's true what Daisy said, and they're the ones in the right? (*He turns back to the mirror.*) A man's not ugly to look at, not ugly at all! (*He examines himself, passing his hand over his face.*) What a funny-looking thing! What do I look like? What? (*He darts to a cupboard, takes out some photographs which he examines.*) Photographs? Who are all these people? Is it Mr. Papillon — or is it Daisy? And is that Botard or Dudard or Jean? Or is it me? (*He rushes to the cupboard again and takes out two or three pictures.*) Now I recognize me: that's me, that's me! (*He hangs the pictures on the back wall, beside the rhinoceros heads.*) That's me, that's me!

(*When he hangs the pictures one sees that they are of an old man, a huge woman, and another man. The ugliness of these pictures is in contrast to the rhinoceros heads which have become very beautiful.* BERENGER *steps back to contemplate the pictures.*)

I'm not good-looking, I'm not good-looking. (*He takes down the pictures, throws them furiously to the ground, and goes over to the mirror.*) They're the good-looking ones. I was wrong! Oh, how I wish I was like them! I haven't got any horns, more's the pity! A smooth brow looks so ugly. I need one or two horns to give my sagging face a lift. Perhaps one will grow and I needn't be ashamed any more — then I could go and join them. But it will never grow! (*He looks at the palms of his hands.*) My hands are so limp — oh, why won't they get rough! (*He takes his coat off, undoes his shirt to look at his chest in the mirror.*) My skin is so slack. I can't stand this white, hairy body. Oh I'd love to have a hard skin in that wonderful dull green colour — a skin that looks decent naked without any hair on it, like theirs! (*He listens to the trumpetings.*) Their song is charming — a bit racuous perhaps, but it does have charm! I wish I could do it! (*He tries to imitate them.*) Ahh, Ahh, Brr! No, that's not it! Try again, louder! Ahh, Ahh, Brr! No, that's not it, it's too feeble, it's got no drive behind it. I'm not trumpeting at all; I'm just howling. Ahh, Ahh, Brr. There's a big difference between howling and trumpeting. I've only myself to blame; I should have gone with them while there was still time. Now it's too late! Now I'm a monster, just a monster. Now I'll never become a rhinoceros, never, never! I've gone past changing. I want to, I really do, but I can't, I just can't. I can't stand the sight of me. I'm too ashamed! (*He turns his back on the mirror.*) I'm so ugly! People who try to hang on to their individuality always come to a bad end! (*He suddenly snaps out of it.*) Oh well, too bad! I'll take on the whole of them! I'll put up a fight against the lot of them, the whole lot of them! I'm the last man left, and I'm staying that way until the end. I'm not capitulating!

CURTAIN

EUGÈNE IONESCO

PART 4

The Interpretation of Poetry

10

The Language of Poetry

Broadly speaking, poetry differs from prose in the emotional weight of its content and in the importance of its sound pattern. In poetry, perhaps more than in any other kind of literature, the content and the form are inseparable in achieving the total effect. The one intensifies the other. A poet's ear is attuned to the sounds of words as a composer's is to tone and the effect of tone sequences, and the poet tests his words for sound as well as for denotation and connotation. Consequently, poetry may be said to be the particular province of the oral interpreter because it reaches its ultimate objective only when it is read aloud.

The high degree of emotion in poetry requires that the interpreter make full use of all the imagery, which is usually more abundant than in other types of writing. Complete response to this imagery will affect his posture and muscle tone and help him draw an appropriate empathic response from his listeners. The principle of empathy lies at the very heart of poetry, since emotion produces, and in turn is intensified by, physical response. Because poetry is so condensed, an audience profits considerably from the trained interpreter's knowledge and control of vocal quality, inflection, force, and factors of timing that help to clarify the meaning and add richness to the associational values of the words.

The structure of poetry, which we shall examine in detail in the next chapter, has its traditional requisites of rhythm, based on an effective combination of sounds and silences and of light and heavier stresses. This pattern of flow of sound and degree of stress can of course be fully realized and appreciated only when it strikes the ear. If the poet had not been concerned with the heightened contribution of patterned sound, he might well have put his idea into prose. The interpreter will discover that poetry demands the utmost vocal flexibility and control, for it is his responsibility to communicate the content in harmony with the sound pattern in such a way that perfect balance is maintained and neither is allowed to obscure the other. The reader's response to a poem is influenced by this harmony, and the total effect of the poem is achieved only when content and structure are perfectly coordinated. Nevertheless, each presents some specific problems which may be considered separately during the process of objective analysis.

POETIC CONTENT

In previous chapters, logical content (what a piece of writing "says") and emotive content (what causes the reader's pleasure or pain, relaxation or tension) have sometimes been considered separately, although they can never be completely divorced in either prose or poetry. As we have noted, emotive content is found even in predominantly factual prose, where, however, it is not an end in itself but a means of reinforcing or making more vivid the idea being developed. In descriptive prose, there is an accompanying emotive response which intensifies and adds effectiveness to the description itself. In drama, a high degree of emotive response may grow out of the conflict and character participation. However, the development of the characters and the situation are things which hold the attention of the writer, and consequently of the interpreter, with emotion used to implement and motivate the plot.

In poetry, the logical content and the emotive content are blended so completely that it is nearly impossible to tell where the one ends and the other begins. Poetry is characterized by the greatest possible condensation. It leaves much unsaid. Nevertheless, the poet must give his readers enough clues to guide their responses; consequently, he selects every word with the utmost care. Moreover, the syntactical relationship of the words is vitally important. This principle of selectivity operates, of course, in other forms of writing, but in poetry each word must carry specific denotative meaning, rich connotative meaning, and make a harmonious contribution to the sound pattern as well. It is partly by this careful selectivity that condensation is achieved. The condensation, in turn, sharpens the emotional impact and allows the poem to move on several levels simultaneously, providing the reader with strong suggestion so that he may personally identify with the experience of the poem.

Since the poet is intent on emotive response, he uses his organization and whatever aspects of progression, character suggestion, and description he finds effective to implement and establish that emotion. The experience he wishes to share may call up a response as pleasant and delicate as Cummings' "Spring is like a perhaps hand" (page 435), or as disturbing as Emily Dickinson's poem which we looked at in Chapters 1 and 2, or Eliot's "The Love Song of J. Alfred Prufrock" (page 395).

It may be necessary, therefore, to reconsider the established concept of content, or what the author has said. Obviously, a poet must have something to say, and must say it so that his audience will understand. This does not mean, however, that a poem must be as immediately clear and factual as an essay or a newspaper article. If the poet had wished simply to inform, he would have put his idea into a prose essay or article — that is, into a form which lends itself much more easily to the development of a purely logical idea. But the poet intends to communicate something beyond fact or opinion. Indeed, much poetry does not require an opinion at all. It asks of the reader merely the acceptance of an attitude. It is not necessary that he accept this attitude as a philosophy of life. It is only necessary that he grant the poet the right to hold it, and begin his evaluation from there. The enjoyment of poetry is comparable to the enjoyment of music or of any other art. It requires a degree of cooperation from the perceiver.

Some people distrust poetry because they feel that it does not say anything. Their distrust, of course, is based on their own personal opinion of what is worth saying. There is a tendency among the pseudo-realists of this century to insist that all literature must present information, an answer to some problem of living, or a logical explanation of some contemporary phenomenon. They are so accustomed to reading for information that they fall into the trap of "message hunting."

Poetry is a record of experience to be shared. This does not mean experience to be explained, nor does it always mean totality of experience. A poet may give us only a segment of his experience which is translatable into terms of the reader's own experiences. He may certainly write of facts, but he writes of them in terms of an interpretation of those facts in the wider areas of human life. He may have been motivated to write by an "idea"; but if the "idea" had been his whole concern, he would not have needed the additional suggestion and richness of sound which are characteristic of poetry. He is usually concerned rather with an emotional or aesthetic response which grows out of that idea. Even in didactic poetry, where the idea is probably of first importance, the emotive response is the driving force by which the poet attempts to persuade the reader to action. Sometimes the poet's intention is primarily to express and give aesthetic pleasure, or he may wish merely to create a mood of excitement or repose, or to recapture the effects of a specific emotion, such as love, hate, joy, or fear. In any case, he will go beyond the confines of strictly logical content. A poet's achievement must be judged in terms of what he has chosen to do, not of what the reader thinks he should have done.

Archibald MacLeish says in his "Ars Poetica" that

> A poem should not mean
> But be.

This statement implies not that a poem needs only to exist, without meaning anything, but rather that a poem must be a complete and harmonious entity — that it does not *only* "mean" something, but has a purpose beyond meaning. It goes beyond definition into the complexity of connotation. As soon as the reader has accepted the fact that poetry is not only what it means but what it does with meaning, he will be ready to let the poet and his poem begin their communication to him.

The first step in understanding and evaluating any piece of literature is, of course, to read it over in its entirety to get a general idea of what it says. And this is the first thing to be done with a poem. This first step may be less objective, less purely "mental," with poetry, however, than with prose or even with drama. The initial response to a poem may not be in terms of idea or logical content at all, but rather in terms of pleasure or pain, activity or repose — in short, of emotive content. The interpreter should read the poem aloud — several times over — and permit himself the luxury of a completely subjective response before beginning the objective analysis. He should give full play to the sound and to the harmony between content and form. Instead of beginning at once to work on the poem, he should let the poem work on him. Enjoyment is a good starting point for appreciation, even if the reason for liking the poem cannot be put into words immediately.

The student interpreter should not be discouraged if he finds only a very simple, obvious meaning in a poem and someone else finds a quantity of implication which he has missed. As his experience with life and with poetry increases, he will be better able to enrich the core of meaning with appropriate marginal and associational meanings. Above all, he should be careful not to get so preoccupied with reading between the lines that he loses sight of the lines themselves.

Poetry has been classified by types according to innumerable systems — some based on content, some on structure, and some on combinations of both. Many of the classifications overlap, and the student will find differences of opinion as to the precise category in which certain poems should be placed. The interpreter is not concerned with technical names and categories, except as they may provide him with handles to get a firmer grasp on his material. From this standpoint, however, he will find it helpful to consider briefly some of the more common classifications in order to discover the advantages and special problems of each. He will, of course, always go beyond these generalizations to the special qualities of the individual selection.

For our purposes, poetry may be classified under three major headings: narrative, lyric, and dramatic. These distinctions are based largely on a consideration of the *persona* — the speaker in the poem. This consideration is, of course, important to the interpreter as a guide to his relation to his audience. He must know who is speaking in the poem, to whom he is speaking, and whether the experience is being revealed directly (as in a narrative poem), is overheard (as in a dramatic poem), or is the highly personal utterance of a single speaker to anyone who can share his response (as in a lyric poem).

NARRATIVE POETRY

Narrative poetry tells a story or relates a series of events leading up to a climax. In this respect it resembles narrative prose, and many of the steps suggested for complete understanding of narrative prose (Chapter 7) are equally applicable here. It will be necessary to discover the key situations, their focal points, and their relationship to the main climax. Attention must be given to the progression of time and place, to the development of character, and to the relationships between characters whenever these elements are important in furthering the plot. Setting, situation, and physical and psychological traits of character — and the interdependence of these factors — must also be considered, if the poet has made use of them. The *persona* is the narrator, and the interpreter will be very much concerned with his point of view. When dialogue occurs in narrative poetry, as it often does, the interpreter must solve the problem of handling it, just as he did in narrative prose. And as in narrative prose, there may or may not be descriptive passages where imagery is used to reinforce setting or to effect a transition from one key situation to the next.

When the interpreter elects to present a narrative poem, he must accept the twofold responsibility which this classification implies. He must be, first of all, a story-teller — that is, the progression of events leading to the climax must be his primary concern. He must analyze the content carefully to become thoroughly aware of all the aspects of organization. He must remember that he is telling *a story in poetry,* and that it is his obligation to use the poetic aspects to implement the story and enhance its movement and emotional impact.

Communicating a story in condensed poetic form, with all its suspense and activity, demands a high degree of directness. The interpreter must keep his attention on the unity of the incident or incidents which make up the plot, and allow the descriptions and transitions to provide the needed variety and emotional rhythm. He must use his knowledge of balance and proportion so that the climax will achieve its purpose. The incidents must retain their proper proportion, hold suspense, and move with speed. These two attributes, suspense and speed, can be enhanced by the condensation and high degree of suggestivity of which poetry is capable.

If it is necessary to cut a long narrative poem, the interpreter follows much the same procedure as in cutting narrative prose, except that he has to be very careful not to violate the structural pattern on which the narrative poem depends. That is, he may, if absolutely necessary, cut complete sections but not lines or parts of lines within stanzas. For example, the tag "he said" might easily be eliminated from a sentence of prose without any loss, but to cut it out of a line of poetry would be to destroy the pulse of the line and break the pattern of sound.

Of the three commonly accepted types of narrative poetry, possibly the oldest in English is the *popular ballad,* which is a folk product and always anonymous. Simple in plot and metrical structure, it is a short, swift, stark narrative told in unadorned language. There is a complete objectivity in point of view with no comment or personal attitude on the part of the narrator. The themes are elemental — love, hate, battles, revenge, and magic — and the climaxes are abrupt and powerful. The modern interpreter will need a strong sense of performance to give these stark and often bloody stories the gusto to make them convincing and interesting.

The speed with which the ballad moves is due in part to the omission of transitions of time, place, and character development. Consequently, the interpreter will need to establish these transitions for himself in order to retain the unity of progression. Dialogue is usually a prominent characteristic of ballads and must be handled with precision and clarity. The question-and-answer technique is quite common and requires a sure sense of "interplay" to keep the progression alive. This dependence on dialogue, of course, takes the interpreter into certain aspects of technique which belong primarily to drama but which are also important in handling direct discourse in any type of narrative writing.

Ballads usually have a refrain which may help to implement the plot, although often its contribution is primarily rhythmic. These refrains present the interpreter with a challenging problem in unity; they must not be allowed to break the progress of the story, yet they must be made to serve their purpose of repetition.

Even the modernized versions of the old ballads retain traces of dialect, or of archaic words and spellings. The extent to which the modern interpreter uses dialect depends partly on his own ability to make it convincing, but even more on his hearers' background, and on their willingness and ability to follow it without finding it an annoying barrier to understanding. The safest path is probably to give just a *suggestion* of dialect, pronouncing the words as they are written in order to preserve the rhythm and rhyme, but concentrating on over-all flavor and lilt rather than on individual sounds. The ballad must have an easy flow of sound, but it must also tell a fast-moving and exciting story.

The second important type of narrative poetry is the *metrical tale,* a full-length novel or short story in verse. It may be a medieval tale such as those in *The Canterbury Tales,* or a modern product like Keats' "The Eve of St. Agnes," John Masefield's "Dauber," or Robert Frost's "The Death of the Hired Man." In any case, the process of analyzing content and organization will be comparable to that used for the short story. The characters may be romanticized types, as in "The Eve of St. Agnes," and thus exhibit little more complexity than those in some of the ballads, or they may be completely realized individuals, like Mary, Warren, and Silas in "The Death of the Hired Man." Descriptions of the setting are likely to be fairly explicit, and the relationship between the characters and the setting takes on a good deal of importance. Moreover, the poet does not hesitate to express his own attitude and sympathies from time to time while still retaining his position as observer.

The third type of narrative poetry is the *epic,* which differs from an ordinary narrative in its extreme length and elevated tone, and more particularly in the type of events it relates. An epic centers on a hero of superhuman proportions, both morally and physically, and the events in which he takes part are of great significance to a tribe, race, or nation. Art-epics like the *Aeneid* and folk-epics like *Beowulf* are examples of this type of poetry. There is also the epic in which the events concern mankind's battle with the forces of evil and his struggle for a divine victory; of this, *Paradise Lost* is the prime example. Finally, the mock-epic, like Pope's "The Rape of the Lock," applies the grand epic scope and manner to trivial circumstances with amusing satirical effect.

The style of an epic is lofty, the language highly poetic and exalted, and the sentences usually complex and elaborate, with numerous clauses and inversions. The interpreter must use these aspects of style to help him suggest the scope of the episodes and the heroic proportions of the participants. Epics are not written about common men in everyday situations. They involve whole nations and heroes who are larger than life, and they must be given their proper dimension in performance.

LYRIC POETRY

The *lyric* is most typically a short poem, though it may be a long, sustained emotional utterance. It is strongly unified poetry, for all aspects of content are shaped toward the emotional focal point. The persona in a lyric poem is usually a single speaker whose primary purpose is to share an emotional experience. Whether or not the speaker is the poet himself is a matter of debate among contemporary critics. The differences of opinion grow in part out of a semantic problem. For our purposes we shall assume that the poet is speaking in a lyric poem, remembering that poets, like the rest of us, have varying moods and attitudes and complex and many-sided personalities. We shall handle the problem of someone who thinks and feels like the poet but who is a clearly distinguishable character in his own right when we come to the dramatic lyric (page 368). It might be well to point out, however, that we are not concerned in a lyric with the poet as a man with brown hair and blue eyes wearing a sport shirt, but rather with his emotional and psychological personality as it is revealed in the particular poem under consideration.

A lyric poem has been compared to a flash of lightning which illuminates some object with a moment of vividness, in this case emotional vividness. The lyric poet usually gives little or no account of what leads up to the emotional experience or what follows it, since his concern is with *sharing* the experience, not *explaining* it. The interpreter, however, will find that sketching in some appropriate background, in his own mind, enhances his appreciation and helps him set the appropriate mood, since these poems, especially the shorter ones, provide him with practically no introductory material. The high degree of association and the intensity of emotion make it imperative for him to be in complete control of his techniques before he even begins reading the poem to an audience, since the extreme condensation will allow him no time to "warm up" or to find his equilibrium. Thus his introduction becomes unusually important.

If a lyric is to achieve its purpose, the interpreter must allow himself to respond to it completely. Only through his complete response will his audience be moved. This does not mean, of course, that he becomes so carried away by his own emotions that he neglects his responsibility to his listeners. In his earliest phases of preparation, he may indulge in complete subjectivity, but in performance he must remember that his purpose is to share an experience, not to display his own sensitivity. He will attempt to call forth from his audience the emotional response which the poet obviously intended, and to this end he will keep intelligent control of his techniques. The more the listeners are moved by the material, and the less they are aware of the interpreter's presence, the greater is his success.

The reader may not have had the exact experience which the poet is sharing, but he can apply the principle of remembered or transferred emotion, calling on his own experience to guide him into the area of the poet's intention. The intensity of response desired by the poet may vary all the way from gentle relaxation to passionate mystical experience. Full appreciation of the kinesthetic imagery will help produce the proper empathy by which the audience's response will be intensified. In the lyric, the poet usually speaks his own thoughts, aspirations, and fears; hence it is useful to know as much as possible about the man who felt the impact of the lyrical emotion.

Most lyric poetry needs to be read more slowly than narrative poetry, partly because imagery is less easy to assimilate than story, and partly because a swiftly paced reading does not permit the structure to make its full contribution to both music and emotion. The audience must have time to hear the words, re-create the images, and set up the response. Lyric poetry requires less directness in presentation than does narrative writing, but the interpreter must be careful not to withdraw completely from his audience and read as though he were lost in the clouds. On the other hand, direct eye contact with the members of the audience may inhibit their response and make them self-conscious. The happy mean is to adopt an attitude of sharing the experience. The interpreter can help intensify the audience's response by skillful technique and by control. He is aware of his power to stimulate his listeners' emotions, but he knows that he cannot compel them.

The emotion that characterizes a lyric poem is often expressed in terms of reflection or description. Thus, the *reflective lyric,* as its name suggests, is the poet's emotional response through recall and reflection or contemplation. This element of an emotional experience remembered in tranquillity is important to the interpreter because it gives him a clue to the degree of activity — or, more precisely, absence of immediate physical activity — in the poem. Wordsworth's famous poem, popularly called "Daffodils," is an outstanding example of the reflective lyric.

The *elegy* is a lyric that expresses grief at death, usually the death of an individual. In Greek verse, the elegy had a definite structural form, but it was brought over into English poetry not as a form but as a quality of emotional expression. Thus an elegy may assume any conventional metrical pattern, or may even be written in free verse. Usually, however, there is a formality of language and structure which lends dignity to the expression of grief and harmonizes with the solemn mystery of death and the sense of personal loss. Auden's "In Memory of W. B. Yeats" (page 440) is an elegy which uses a combination of structural patterns that change with the tone of the separate sections.

Like the elegy, the *ode* was a recognized lyrical form in Greek verse. Designed to be accompanied by music and by a highly stylized dance, it consisted of three movements, two of which had identical music and dance patterns. But although these Greek structures have been imitated in English verse, the term "ode" has come to be applied to any sustained lyric utterance of exalted theme, often in commemoration of some important event or experience. An ode, then, is a dignified, relatively long lyric poem, formal in language, and formal though not necessarily regular in structure.

In harmony with the dignity of its inspiration, the ode moves steadily to a single philosophic-emotional focal point. The progress is often achieved by elaborating various details or attributes of the person, object, or circumstance that serves as the motivation, and the climax occurs when these are given a universal and philosophical implication. This is the method used by Keats in his famous "Ode on a Grecian Urn" (page 389). The interpreter must make full use of the imagery and keep a careful check on unity so that all details may lead to the final culmination. In general tone, the ode is more contemplative than active and suggests a restraint of movement similar to a reflective lyric—though by no means a complete passivity, for there is a sense of movement in the particularly strong kinesthetic imagery which accompanies response to an exalted theme.

Perhaps the most familiar type of lyric is the *sonnet*. This poetic form is interesting to the interpreter for several reasons. In the first place, it is widely used, with varying degrees of success, of course, but in sufficient quantity even among contemporary writers so that there is a wealth of material from which to choose. The sonnet by tradition deals with subject matter that is dignified—although not necessarily so exalted as that treated in the ode—and its greatest challenge to both poet and interpreter lies in its fixed form.

A sonnet is a fourteen-line poem, written in predominantly iambic meter, with five feet to the line. It has, moreover, a prescribed rhyme scheme. The two most common types of sonnet are the Petrarchan and the Shakespearean, which differ primarily in the arrangement of their rhyme sounds. The distinction between them is important, but it need not concern the interpreter unduly, except as it gives him certain guides to the organization of content and to the intricacy of the sound pattern. Both in content and structure, the Petrarchan sonnet is very strictly organized. The first four lines introduces the subject, and the next four develop it. In a true Petrarchan sonnet each of these quatrains completes a unit of thought, and the sentences are allowed to "run on." The next three lines introduce a new but related theme, and the last three lines bring the observation to its conclusion. The rhyme scheme, which is *abba, abba, cdc, cdc,* or *cdcdcd,* reinforces the division of content. A true Petrarchan sonnet is somewhat rare in English, however, as most poets have chosen to vary the strict form. The Shakespearean sonnet follows the same principle of organization through the first eight lines, but departs from it in devoting the last six lines to the conclusion, with the focal point occurring in the two final lines. There is also greater flexibility in the rhyme scheme of the Shakespearean sonnet — *abab, cdcd, efef, gg.* This variation in rhyme pattern concerns the interpreter because it corresponds to the divisions of the content and helps bring the poem to a firm close by introducing a rhyming couplet for the last two lines.

When a poet has accepted such traditional restrictions of organization and structure, the interpreter must also give particular attention to the way the sonnet form augments the emotion being expressed, and to the determination of his own responsibilities in retaining the sound pattern established by the rhyme scheme and the five-foot iambic lines. He will be greatly aided in his analysis by the sonnet's prescribed principles of organization of content, and he must use some care in preserving the balance and proportion.

DRAMATIC POETRY

Many contemporary critics take the position that all poetry is dramatic in that it is an action in itself which concerns a person or persons and that there is a distinct development or revelation within it. This is, of course, true and this approach to poetry can prove very helpful. Nevertheless, in line with our early classifications of literature we shall limit our discussion of dramatic poetry to those works which center on a character in conflict with a force within or outside himself, one whose development is revealed without a third-person narrator.

Dramatic poetry includes the *dramatic narrative, dramatic lyric, dramatic monologue,* and *soliloquy.* Although these terms are often used interchangeably, the four types vary slightly in emphasis on character and situation, and some attempt to differentiate them will help the interpreter in making his analysis and in deciding on the degree of characterization which will be necessary in his performance. In each case, the *persona* is an identifiable character speaking directly to an audience, to himself as he thinks aloud, or to other characters involved in a dramatic situation.

A *dramatic narrative* is a poem in which the incidents or series of incidents are related by a participant affected by the events which he relates. Byron's "The Prisoner of Chillon" is such a poem. It opens with Bonivard's brief description of his present physical state, and the purpose of this unit is obviously, first, to establish the flash-back technique by which the plot is to be revealed, and second, to indicate the point of view which will give the incidents greater vividness. After the introductory statement, Bonivard begins to draw the story out of the past. His attention is on the story, and his own reactions to events are used primarily as transitions from one key situation to the next. Thus the interpreter may assume that the personality of Bonivard is in reality a device for revealing the plot and not a motivating force for its progression, and he will suggest only enough of the prisoner's broken health and spirit to make the plot credible and prepare for the closing phrase

— even I
Regain'd my freedom with a sigh.

The *dramatic lyric,* like any other lyric poetry, is a reflection of the poet's subjective responses, thoughts, and aspirations. It is dramatic because the poet has put his thoughts and emotions into the mouth of an appropriate character who speaks for him, so that there is added force and vividness to the expression. Tennyson's "Ulysses" (page 67) and Eliot's "The Love Song of J. Alfred Prufrock" (page 395) fall into this general classification, although they also share some of the characteristics of dramatic monologues or soliloquies. The interpreter will emphasize in his suggestion of character those qualities which make the speaker an appropriate exponent of the philosophy being expressed. The essential qualities in Ulysses, for instance, are his mental vigor, his maturity and wisdom, and his authority and leadership. It is unwise to take too literally his phrase, "you and I are old," because he turns immediately to the belief that

Old age hath yet his honor and his toil,

which he reinforces with

> . . . but something ere the end,
> Some work of noble note, may yet be done,
> Not unbecoming men that strove with Gods.

The poem closes on the positive note that Ulysses is still

> . . . strong in will
> To strive, to seek, to find, and not to yield.

Prufrock's ironic awareness of his own inability to "disturb the universe" is carefully concealed by his meticulous grooming and "a face [prepared] to meet the faces that you meet."

The *dramatic monologue* is spoken by a single character created outside the poet's own personality. The speaker directly addresses other characters, who are also affected by the incident taking place and who help to motivate the speaker's reactions and train of thought. The other characters do not speak, but they are nevertheless rather fully developed as personalities, or at least as forces in relation to the speaker. Browning's "My Last Duchess" is an excellent example of this type of dramatic poetry. Anyone who knows the love story of Elizabeth and Robert Browning will be aware that Browning is not expressing his own ideas of marriage in this famous poem. The ideas are the Duke's and reflect his time and his attitude toward himself and others. He is not acting as an appropriate mouthpiece for the poet's subjective response, but is created outside the poet and speaks for himself. Therefore, the interpreter must give the audience a clear, three-dimensional picture of him in order that they will understand his thoughts and feelings.

The *soliloquy* is also spoken by a single character created outside the poet's own personality. The principal difference is that no other characters are being addressed. Since the speaker in a soliloquy is alone, his degree of directness is likely to be less pronounced. However, as in "Soliloquy of the Spanish Cloister" (page 405), he may receive direct and immediate motivations from some exterior source. Though the monk is speaking only to himself, Brother Lawrence's actions direct his thoughts.

THE POET'S ATTITUDE

Methods of discovering the author's attitude have been touched on in previous chapters. All the things we have already said are equally useful when applied to poetry. However, because of its extreme condensation as well as its highly personal implications, poetry needs particularly close attention to every clue within it.

Poetry is probably most often inspired by an emotional urge on the part of the writer. A man's emotions are closely tied up with his philosophy of life, his set of values about himself and the people with whom he associates, and the things with which he is surrounded. It is, therefore, helpful to know as much about a poet as possible if one is to understand what he considers worth saying. Information about the poet does not mean knowing mere biographical facts. It means, rather, realizing what effect the time in which he lived and the circumstances of his life had on his attitude and interests.

A poet's attitude is discovered first of all by careful attention to all the details of the poem being studied. It is also helpful to read a number of other things he has written and to find out as much as possible about what interested him and why. Some poets have expressed their theories in essays and books of criticism. Others have been more reticent and left only their poems to speak for them. In the case of those who have achieved a degree of fame, however, there will have been friends and acquaintances to publish what they knew or thought they knew about the poets and their ways of life, or biographers and scholars to reconstruct the stories of their lives and interpret their thoughts. Contemporary poets, most of whom do not insist upon an ivory tower but take part in the world around them, are frequently quite articulate about their intentions and attitudes. Despite all the things the interpreter can find out "about" the poem, however, his most valuable source of information is the poem itself.

One of the clearest indications of attitude is often to be found in the title. For example, the irony of the entire poem is foreshadowed in the title "The Love Song of J. Alfred Prufrock." The combination of "Love Song" with the somewhat pretentious "J. Alfred Prufrock" clearly indicates that this is not a love song in the usual sense. One signs a legal document or formal social note "J. Alfred Prufrock"—not a love song! Another equally effective title is "To His Coy Mistress." "Coy" is a very important word; she is not, obviously, merely reluctant or unalterably opposed. She is being "coy." Poets choose their titles with great care to give us invaluable help in deciding what the poem is about as well as the way we are to take it.

Admittedly, many poets do not use titles. Then we must look at all the matters of style within the poem itself. Choice of words and the use of figures of speech will be of primary importance. The way these are combined into phrases, line units, sentences, and stanzas must be carefully considered. Method of organization and the resultant balance and proportion will give us valuable clues to the weight attached to the various phases of thought development. The sound pattern which supports the content will often indicate the degree of seriousness and dignity inherent in the attitude. We will give this aspect more attention in the next chapter, but a look at the last three lines of each stanza of John Donne's "Go and Catch a Falling Star" (page 433) will convince any reader that this is not a poem of tragic love. The opening lines with their abrupt and impossible commands will indicate this as well.

Exaggeration or hyperbole characterizes the poetry of satire and wit, numerous examples of which are to be found in sixteenth and seventeenth century poems. It is also a useful device for the contemporary poet, who is often primarily interested in reflecting a complex and highly subjective set of psychological associations.

It is extremely important that the interpreter be willing to let the poet have his way. He must examine every word of the poem in its relationship to every other word and let them operate as they *must* within the whole—not as he wishes they did. If there is a line or phrase which will not fit into his concept of the poem, he must reconsider his analysis. He must share with the audience the poet's attitude toward love, death, childhood, or the passing years, not his own. If he does not like the philosophy being expressed, he should find another selection. He is responsible for the totality of the poem as the poet put it down.

FIGURATIVE LANGUAGE

Poetry is, as we have said, a highly condensed form of expression. The poet has neither the time within the poem nor the inclination for literal explanations and logical expositions. Although he may seem to communicate less directly than the prose writer, he is actually making a more direct appeal, for he is not talking *about* something but attempting to present the essence of that something. He does this by reaching the reader at as many points of contact as possible—striking at him through his senses, his emotions, his intellect, his imagination, and calling forth a blended response that gives new insight into experience. Hence he must find the exact word which will carry with it not only the precise denotation but, perhaps more important, the right connotation as well.

The word the poet uses does not *define* his concept so much as it *expands* it in the reader's consciousness, just as a pebble tossed into a pool sends ever-widening circles rippling out from the point of surface contact. The implications of the word take the reader beyond the narrow confines of exact definition into the area of suggested meaning, into the complex realm of the experiences out of which the poet is writing and the reader perceiving. In examining a poet's choice of words, then, the interpreter must remember that just as a poem not only *means* something but *is* something beyond meaning, so the words that make it up go beyond fact and information. To accomplish this, they must be in complete harmony with tone and mood of the poem, and must make their contribution to the sound pattern as well as to logical and emotive meaning. In spite of good intentions, many people never learn to read poetry so that it has meaning for them or for others. This failure often stems from the reader's inability to untangle certain traditional complexities which are present in all but the most direct poetic expression. One of the most common of these complexities is the use of figurative language.

A poet often achieves condensation and emotional impact by the use of references or allusions that embody a wealth of implication. These allusions may contribute materially to the logical meaning of the poem, but they are likely to be most valuable for the associations which they set up by implied comparison. Very often they are references to mythical or historical persons or places; and although, with the passing of the classical tradition, their associational value may be lessened for the modern reader, he readily recognizes them as allusions and knows that he can clarify them by consulting an encyclopedia or other appropriate reference book.

In some modern poetry, however, the connotative literary allusion may prove more difficult, since it involves the deliberate echo of a phrase or line from the work of another poet in order to reinforce mood or emotion by inviting comparison or ironic contrast. When Archibald MacLeish, for example, in his poem, "You, Andrew Marvell" (page 388), expresses his sense of the crowding and closing in of time,

> . . . the always coming on
> The always rising of the night,

he suggests through his title that the reader hold simultaneously in mind the seventeenth-century poet's lines on the same subject; and the reader who takes the allusion finds that his immediate response to MacLeish's poem is intensified by his remembered or re-evoked response to Marvell's "Coy Mistress," and particularly, no doubt, to the famous lines,

> But at my back I always hear
> Time's wingèd chariot hurrying near . . .

And yet MacLeish's poem has meaning and emotion quite independent of Marvell's poem, and conveys that meaning and emotion even to one who has never heard of Andrew Marvell or of the "Coy Mistress." For a literary allusion says something directly, in its context, even though it passes undetected as an illusion. Hearing literary echoes brings an added level of understanding and delight, and a more complex response — it strengthens the impact of the poem — but it is always the poem itself that speaks, not the source of the allusion.

How does all this affect the interpreter? Obviously, he is not going to explain the references to the audience, to stand between poem and audience as a sort of *Bulfinch's Mythology* or *Bartlett's Quotations.* He is, however, concerned with the quality of his own understanding and response, for he cannot give the poem out to his hearers if he has not first assimilated it himself. The more thoroughly he understands the allusions, the more fully he will appreciate the purpose for which the poet has used them — and the more intelligently he himself can use them in communicating the whole intent of the poem to others. He must, therefore, make himself sufficiently familiar with the allusions to understand the *type of response* they are intended to arouse or reinforce; and by integrating them into the poem as it stands, as a self-contained whole, use them as means of drawing the proper empathic response from the audience.

Three of the most common figures of speech — the *simile,* the *metaphor,* and the *analogy* — are all based on comparison of one thing to another. These comparisons appeal to our senses and our motor responses. Therefore, they depend upon sense imagery, which we discussed at some length in Chapter 6.

A *simile* is easily recognized because it makes an explicit comparison, generally using the word "like." It is a simple comparison of two objects of common nature, or a comparison of the particular qualities of one thing to the general qualities of another, as when Keats compares Autumn's activity to that of a gleaner:

> And sometimes like a gleaner thou dost keep
> Steady thy laden head across a brook . . .

A quite different effect is achieved in "The Love Song of J. Alfred Prufrock" by the simile

> When the evening is spread out against the sky
> Like a patient etherized upon a table. . . .

A *metaphor* states that something *is* something else, based on some related but not identical factor. It establishes a relationship between two elements which may be dissimilar in their basic components and yet have attributes in common. Sometimes a metaphor expresses a synthesis of thought and feeling so subtle and complex that it becomes organic or structural in the whole poem. Indeed, contemporary critics often use the term "metaphor" or "metaphorical" to describe any writing which goes beyond fact and obvious relationships.

An *analogy* is an extended metaphor and may serve to implement an entire poem. In Francis Thompson's "The Hound of Heaven," for example, God's pursuit of man is compared to a hound's pursuit in the hunt, and the poem ends with the final triumph of the pursuer over the pursued. This particular poem, as it happens, is also especially rich in similes and metaphors within the analogy.

These three types of figurative language, all means of making comparisons, are important to the oral interpreter for several reasons. First, of course, he must understand what they are and how they function if he is to find the real meaning of the poem. More particularly, however, he needs to be aware not only of the objects being compared but of the attributes of those objects which make their comparison acceptable. Finally, he must use his knowledge of sense imagery and empathy to make the comparisons work effectively for his audience.

Two other figures of speech — *metonymy* and *synecdoche* — carry associational values, which, however, differ somewhat from those of the three "comparison" figures mentioned above. *Metonymy* is the use of one word for another which it suggests, such as "a good table" for "good food." *Synecdoche* is the use of a part for a whole, such as "sail" for "boat." The technical difference between these two figures is unimportant, and in any case they are not likely to present the interpreter with any very real difficulties once he has been made aware of their function. They are useful to him whenever they suggest certain characteristics which are emphasized by the part chosen for the whole. For example, "sail" is a more picturesque word than "boat" and could be used to imply majesty, in which case the interpreter would wish to make some use of the visual and kinesthetic imagery that might be less vivid without the synecdoche.

But the interpreter's concern, as always, is not with putting a name to what the poet did, not with classifying a figure of speech, but with understanding why that figure was used, what it is intended to convey, and what it demands of him when he presents the material to an audience. The poet achieves concreteness and vividness of suggestion by using figures which indicate or imply a comparison or an association. They must be understood for what they are, and for the purpose they serve, before the interpreter can proceed with his job of doing justice to the poetry.

In addition to the five figures of speech already mentioned, there are two others which directly affect the interpreter's communication. They are *personification* and *apostrophe.*

Personification is the attributing of human qualities to an abstract or inanimate object. This figure of speech is closely related to the "comparison" figures discussed above, because the poet treats some inanimate object or an abstraction as if it were a person, and thus gives it definite human characteristics. Keats, for example, uses personification throughout "To Autumn" (page 377), from the second line, in which he calls Autumn the "close bosom-friend of the maturing sun," to the final stanza. The personification reaches maximum vividness in the second stanza where Autumn is visualized as "sitting careless on a granary floor," or "on a half-reaped furrow sound asleep," or "by a cider-press" watching "the last oozings hours by hours."

The interpreter will find the author's use of personification a great aid in visualizing. It is easier to re-create a person than an abstraction. Moreover, this device allows for more kinetic and kinesthetic imagery than if the abstraction were dealt with in some other way. The interpreter must not overlook the animate quality which this figure of speech provides.

Frequently, personification is combined with the figure of speech known as *apostrophe* — direct address to an abstraction or to an absent or inanimate object. "To Autumn" makes consistent use of this combination of personification and apostrophe. The opening line,

> Season of mists and mellow fruitfulness,

might be taken merely as a reflective thought about the season, if considered by itself. On close examination, however, it is evident that the poet becomes more direct in his approach to the season as the poem progresses, and there can be no doubt as to the directness of address in the opening lines of the final stanza,

> Where are the songs of Spring? Ay, where are they?
> Think not of them, thou hast thy music too . . .

An awareness of apostrophe will give the interpreter some help in keeping the unity, as well as in bringing out variety, by adding vitality to the words and enhancing the effect of the imagery. It should be remembered, however, that apostrophe is not so direct as address to an actual person from whom a reply is expected. Even so, the complex train of imagery that develops out of the personification and apostrophe in the two lines just quoted is worth noting.

Thus, figurative language enables a writer to express an abstract idea in concrete terms, to make it more vivid and more readily grasped by comparing it or relating it to a concrete object or a specific quality. Again, through use of a figure of speech the poet may bring together things which are not ordinarily seen in relation to one another, and by thus relating separate areas of experience, open the way to new insights.

Clearly then, sensory imagery and figurative language, sometimes called literary imagery, are interdependent, and the motor responses to literary and sensory imagery are inseparably tied up with emotional response and empathy. Sensory imagery in poetry is usually much more complex than in prose, and there is more of it. For where the prose writer explains or elaborates or describes, the poet suggests. He sends the image vibrating along the reader's consciousness to touch off all sorts of emotive, imaginative, and intellectual associations.

The complexity and urgency of poetic imagery results partly from the condensation of content in poetry, partly from the central importance of the poet's own emotion and attitude, and partly from the poet's use of figures of speech. Because the image comes in through the door of the senses, the poet is likely to select objects or qualities that seem to him particularly rich in sensory suggestion in order to express most completely the experience he is attempting to share. Hence the interpreter, both in preparing his material and in presenting it to an audience, makes the most of the empathic response set up by these appeals to the senses in order to reinforce the emotional and intellectual content of the poem.

Imagery was discussed previously in terms of the primary and secondary strength of the appeals. The primary appeal was fairly easy to isolate in the excerpts used as examples of descriptive prose. In poetry, however, the appeals are often so blended and so many-sided that this separation is not always possible. Even when the primary appeal in individual units is immediately identifiable, the secondary appeals assume an almost equal importance in the total effect. Frequently a type of imagery, such as kinesthetic, or a combination of types, will be used in secondary position throughout the poem and will provide an important clue to unity.

Many poems depend almost completely on sensory appeals for their final achievement. When this is so, the interpreter must accept and make use of all the clues the writer has given him. Such a poem is Keats' "To Autumn." One of the characteristics of Keats' writing is its strong sensory quality, and his skill in blending and even combining words to intensify the appeal to the senses makes this poem one of his most famous.

The chief purpose of "To Autumn" is to record the sights, sounds, smells, and rich texture of the season. This poem makes no significant comment about life, except perhaps to imply the satisfaction to be found in inevitable change, in

> Where are the songs of Spring? Ay, where are they?
> Think not of them, thou hast thy music too . . .

The poet devotes his entire attention to a series of descriptions of autumn, and the poem lays claim to emotional response through the pleasure which this season gives to the senses.

To Autumn

Season of mists and mellow fruitfulness,
  Close bosom-friend of the maturing sun;
Conspiring with him how to load and bless
  With fruit the vines that round the thatch-eaves run;
To bend with apples the mossed cottage-trees,
  And fill all fruit with ripeness to the core;
    To swell the gourd, and plump the hazel shells
  With a sweet kernel; to set budding more,
And still more, later flowers for the bees,
Until they think warm days will never cease,
    For Summer has o'er-brimmed their clammy cells.

Who hath not seen thee oft amid thy store?
  Sometimes whoever seeks abroad may find
Thee sitting careless on a granary floor,
  Thy hair soft-lifted by the winnowing wind;
Or on a half-reaped furrow sound asleep,
  Drowsed with the fume of poppies, while thy hook
    Spares the next swath and all its twinèd flowers:
And sometime like a gleaner thou dost keep
  Steady thy laden head across a brook;
  Or by a cider-press, with patient look,
    Thou watchest the last oozings hours by hours.

Where are the songs of Spring? Ay, where are they?
  Think not of them, thou hast thy music too, —
While barred clouds bloom the soft-dying day,
  And touch the stubble-plains with rosy hue;
Then in a wailful choir the small gnats mourn
  Among the river sallows, borne aloft
    Or sinking as the light wind lives or dies;
And full-grown lambs loud bleat from hilly bourn;
  Hedge-crickets sing; and now with treble soft
  The red-breast whistles from a garden-croft;
    And gathering swallows twitter in the skies.

JOHN KEATS

The opening lines have a characteristic complexity of appeals. Since the title is "To Autumn," the "season of mists" has a strong thermal appeal which combines at once the warmth of the sun and the coolness of the mists. "Mellow fruitfulness" carries with it olfactory, gustatory, visual, and kinesthetic appeal, as well as a continuation of thermal and a possibility of tactual. The second line brings in a still stronger thermal appeal. The effect is one of warmth, and it enhances the feeling of drowsiness and almost static heaviness which recurs in each stanza. The next three lines contain all these previous appeals to sensory perception, but with kinetic appeals added — in fact, with special appeal to kinetic and kinesthetic response — "load with fruit," "vines that run," "to bend with apples."

Because the appeals are so complex and so closely interwoven, it is almost impossible, and probably unnecessary, to decide which is primary within a unit of thought. The strength of the appeals shifts from one type to another almost within a single word. Indeed, the first five lines include every type of imagery except auditory, and even that is suggested later in the stanza by the mention of "the bees."

As the poem progresses, the visual and auditory appeals become increasingly important. The second stanza indicates the poet's concern with the visual by its opening question, "Who hath not seen thee. . . ." The third stanza is strongly auditory with its references to "songs" and "music." Within this framework, the sensory appeals remain complex. The interpreter will find that the imagery not only guides him in making the descriptions vivid, but also contributes significantly to the unity, harmony, and variety of the poem. Attention to the kinesthetic imagery and the kinetic imagery, both of which are made more vivid through personification, will help keep this poem from becoming merely a lush combination of beautiful sounds. Awareness of the shift to visual and then to auditory imagery in the second and third stanzas will help to unravel the complicated sentences and keep the poem moving.

THE STANZAS

In our study of the organization of prose writing (Chapter 5), we noted that paragraphs are the major signposts in the progress of the thought. A stanza often serves the same purpose in a poem. In blank verse and free verse, the stanzas or unit divisions (if they exist) are often of irregular length, dictated by the amount of attention the author wished to devote to each unit of content; hence they may be considered in the same light as prose paragraphs as far as progression of content is concerned. The stanza divisions in "The Love Song of J. Alfred Prufrock" are interesting in this regard, for although the unifying principle of the whole poem may be said to be Prufrock's stream of consciousness, each stanza develops or negates an already considered question or admission. In other types of poetry, however, the poet limits himself to stanzas of a specific length, and condenses or expands each unit of thought to coincide with this structural restriction. Nevertheless, even in the most tightly structured poetry, a stanza usually operates as a major thought unit, and this entity is intensified when there is a formal rhyme scheme.

Stanley Kunitz' poem "Open the Gates" (page 403) progresses chronologically and in giant steps from one four-line stanza to the next. MacLeish is meticulous in his use of four-line units in "You, Andrew Marvell" until he reaches the last four lines, where he changes the pattern. It must not be assumed that he just forgot what he started out to do — or that he could not make those last four lines work as a stanza! His setting off the single line gives it increased importance, adds strength to the next one, a near-repetition of the opening line, and brings the poem full circle to its conclusion.

The interpreter will find considerable help in achieving variety as well as rhythm of content in a careful consideration of stanzaic divisions. He must be careful, of course, not to let these separate units of thought break off from each other, and to keep the transitions from stanza to stanza clear in his mind so that the audience receives a unified experience. Transitions in poetry are often abrupt and implied rather than explicitly stated. They may be transitions of time or place of course, but often, as in "To Autumn," they simply move us into another aspect of the same subject or provide a subtle shift in mood. In any case, the order of the stanzas is not an accident, and the stanza "breaks" must be in reality "links."

In "Soliloquy of the Spanish Cloister," for example, some of the stanzas are linked by the monk's observations of some action by Brother Lawrence as he moves about in his garden; others are connected only by the monk's stream of consciousness as he muses on his "heart's abhorrence" and their daily contacts. Sometimes, as in "Poem in October" (page 391), a single word or phrase will provide the link to the next stanza, as in the use of "still sleeping town" at the end of the first stanza and the progression to "the town awoke" in the second. Also, the establishing of the bird motif and "set forth" and "walked abroad" early in the poem prepare us for the larks and blackbirds in the "roadside bushes" so that we move easily with the poet as he climbs the hill. The third and fourth stanzas are clearly linked by "rain wringing," "Pale rain," "sea-wet" and "mist." The warmth of the sun "On the hill's shoulder" has already been introduced in contrast to the dampness and cold wind "faraway under me" so that we move with no surprise to spring and summer and the "fond climates." The fifth and sixth stanzas are not separated by terminal punctuation and are closely connected by "and" as well as by similar references in "legends" and "twice told fields." The final stanza is introduced by "And" followed by a repetition. Thus the continuity is remarkably clear and carries us smoothly along up to the "high hill" and back into time until we are brought once more to the present by the repeated line — and then turned at once to the future with the final

O may my heart's truth
Still be sung
On this high hill in a year's turning.

SYNTAX AND LINE LENGTH

The stanzas of a poem provide the main divisions of organization and of content, and within these stanzas are sentences which are minor units of thought progression. The length and grammatical structure of the sentences play an important part in the organization of the content, just as they do in prose style. There is in poetry, moreover, the added consideration of the way the sentences are related to the line lengths.

In some forms of poetry both the stanza pattern and the length of the lines, as measured in metrical feet, are prescribed by tradition. Further, although the point should not be too rigidly insisted on, it may be said in a general way that some patterns, like the ballad stanza or the heroic couplet, more commonly lend themselves to sentences that make partial or full stops at the line-ends; other patterns, such as blank verse, to sentences whose pauses and stops occur variously within the lines as well as at the line-ends. The presence and the prominence of rhyme, the simplicity or complexity of the stanza pattern, the relation of the line length to the natural speech phrase, and the tone and purpose of the poem are all factors that enter into an explanation of why this is so, and will be dealt with more explicitly in the next chapter. For the moment, we shall limit our consideration to some aspects of sentence structure and to the relationship between sentences and line lengths as units of content.

In Chapter 5 attention was given to the associative function of syntax in prose style. These considerations operate in poetry as well, and are complicated by the condensation and weight of suggestion in poetry, and by the poet's own heightened subjectivity. Poets often achieve condensation, in part, by using long, involved sentences in which there are numerous dependent clauses and descriptive phrases. These clauses and phrases are not always adjacent to the words they modify, with the result that some care in analysis and in performance may be required to keep the thread of thought from becoming hopelessly entangled and the poem from seeming to consist merely of unrelated sets of words "signifying nothing." The interpreter will need to give some detailed attention to this aspect of content in order to make the necessary relationships clear to his audience when reading the poem aloud.

Perhaps the best approach to an involved sentence is simply to recast it in normal order, identifying the subject, the verb, and the object, if any, and arranging the clauses and phrases to modify the appropriate parts of the sentence. One must not, however, insist that poetry display the same clarity and syntactical precision as factual prose. Often parts of speech are omitted and references implied rather than stated. Normal word order is frequently changed for emotional effect or heightening of sound qualities, or both.

The opening sentence of Hopkins' "The Windhover" is an excellent example of this ellipsis or omission of words.

> I CAUGHT this morning morning's minion, king-
> dom of daylight's dauphin, dapple-dawn-drawn Falcon, in
> his riding
> Of the rolling level underneath him steady air, and striding
> High there, how he rung upon the rein of a wimpling wing
> In his ecstasy! then off, off forth on swing,
> As a skate's heel sweeps smooth on a bow-bend: the hurl
> and gliding
> Rebuffed the big wind. . . .

The sentence begins reasonably enough with the simple "I caught" (meaning of course "caught sight of" rather than "captured"), and the adverbial phrase "this morning" tells us when the event took place. After this comes the object of the sentence, the windhover, which the poet calls "minion," "dauphin," and "Falcon," and we are told what he was doing. He was riding . . . and striding, and he rung upon the rein of a wimpling wing — that is, he flew upward in spirals by folding or "pleating" or tipping one wing. And then he was off as smoothly as an ice skate cuts a curve, and the hurl and gliding rebuffed, snubbed, refused to consider the big wind. This, then, is the syntactical skeleton of the sentence. The next step is to attempt to find the proper relationship of every word which fleshes out this skeleton by eliminating the elliptical quality. In the process we will destroy much of the beauty of the sound, obviously, but that too may help to prove our point. The sentence might now read: This morning I caught [sight of] morning's minion [in his] kingdom of [which he is] daylight's dauphin [and] dapple-dawn-drawn Falcon, in his riding of the rolling level [which was] underneath him [and which was] steady air and [when he was] striding high there [you should have seen] how he rung upon the rein of a wimpling wing in his ecstasy [and] then [he was] off, off forth on a swing as [smoothly as] a skate's heel sweeps on a bow-bend [and] the hurl and gliding rebuffed the big wind.

Admittedly, this is an extremely awkward sentence, which seems to plod heavily from one detail to the next. We have lost all the "hurl and gliding," as well as the sense of lift and freedom, and much of the beauty of the sound combinations. Harmony has almost completely disappeared. The insertion of "and" after the exclamation point defeats the poet's own ecstasy at the sight. The substitution of "and" for the colon before the last clause robs it of its conclusive value by making it just one more item rather than a culmination of several. The interpreter must, of course, fully understand the grammatical relationships, but he then must go back to the sentence as the poet wrote it. If his response is full, his audience will have no difficulty in catching the essential images and the totality of the experience.

Dylan Thomas uses characteristically complex syntax in the opening stanza of "Poem in October," where "woke" operates on several levels. His "thirtieth year" woke to his hearing and the hearing woke him, and he himself woke to "set foot" and "set forth." Another effective use of syntax is to be found in "The Love Song of J. Alfred Prufrock," where Eliot uses the simple, direct statement, "No! I am not Prince Hamlet, . . ." followed by the balancing "nor was meant to be," in which the "I" is not repeated. Omitting it very subtly negates the importance of Prufrock as an individual. The effect is forcefully underscored in the next line, "Am an attendant lord, one that will do." Inserting the personal pronoun each time produces a noticeably different effect. Poetry is full of innumerable instances of this sort of thing, and the interpreter must watch carefully for clues to attitude as well as to suggestion and the intrinsic factors. The way a poet puts his words together into sentences is a highly specialized discipline.

A still more subtle relationship of words can be discovered by attention to the line as a unit of thought within the larger unit of the sentence. Dylan Thomas is particularly skillful in his use of this aspect of writing. The second stanza of "Poem in October," for instance, begins

My birthday began with the water-
Birds and the birds of the winged trees flying my name

The separation of the hyphenated word "water-birds" is not an accident. His birthday, as he has told us in the opening stanza, began with the water and the water-birds. If the lines are read

My birthday began with the water-birds
And the birds of the winged trees flying my name

we get two separate kinds of birds instead of a synthesis of water and water-birds and birds of the winged trees. This last phrase, incidentally, is an interesting transfer of the characteristic of the birds to the trees in which they settle and is continued as the birds "fly" his name. Appreciating the contribution of the line as a closely related unit of thought requires sophistication and experience, as well as a trained ear and a willingness to allow the poet to have his own way with his poem. It cannot always be explained logically, but it operates effectively as one of the many complexities which make poetry a challenge to the interpreter.

TONE COLOR

In addition to connotative values and sensory appeals, there is another very important factor in the choice and arrangement of the words which make a poem. A poet strives for the perfect union of sense and sound and is acutely aware of the contribution each makes to the other. This attention to the sounds of words separately and in combination is that aspect of literary art which we shall call *tone color*.

Tone color is the manipulation of vowels and consonants to help achieve a particular effect. Clearly, poets do not simply scramble together assorted vowels and consonants. They must, of course, use words. But the choice of a word and its position in relation to other words is partially dictated by the way the sounds go together. Cummings' poem "Spring is like a perhaps hand" owes part of its effectiveness to tone color. The two words "perhaps hand" are characteristic of his remarkable freedom with syntax, using "perhaps" as an adjective to modify "hand." The connotation is helped, however, by juxtaposing "haps" and "hand," both of which must be said carefully to pronounce the aspirate *h* and the vowel *a*. The *p* and *s* of "haps" slow the rate, and a slight pause is necessary before the *h* of "hand." This is a subtle effect, but to be aware of its importance one need only consider what a difference it would make if the line read

Spring is perhaps like a hand

in which both meaning and sound values are quite changed.

Tone color is another of the elements which make poetry so satisfying to, and in turn so dependent on, the artist-interpreter. Obviously, there is no way to appreciate tone color, or to permit it to achieve its purpose, except to give the words their sounds. To make full use of tone color, the interpreter must be sure that he is enunciating clearly and that he is forming all his sounds properly. The poet had a purpose in combining the sounds as he did, and the interpreter must accept the responsibility for reproducing them accurately.

The general term *tone color* embraces *onomatopoeia* and *alliteration, assonance* and *consonance.*

Onomatopoeia is the use of words whose sounds suggest or reinforce their meaning, such as "hiss," "thud," "crack," and "bubble."

Alliteration is the close repetition of identical or nearly identical sounds, usually consonants, at the beginning of adjacent words. The phrase "*m*orning *m*orning's *m*inion" in "The Windhover" is a classic example, as are many other combinations in the poem. Prufrock's question "*D*o I *d*are/*D*isturb . . ." and Thomas' "That *s*econd/In the *s*till *s*leeping town and *s*et forth" are other examples. Modern writers are likely to use alliteration even more widely spaced and operating throughout a large unit or indeed an entire brief poem.

The use of identical or closely approximated vowels within words is usually called *assonance,* while the repetition of identical or approximate consonants within or at the ends of words is called *consonance.* These two techniques are also found in the above quotations, with assonance in the repeated "o's," consonance very strong in the *n* sounds of "morning morning's minion," and both assonance and consonance in "minion," "dauphin," and "Falcon" in the long first line. The lines from Thomas contain a repetition of "n's," "l's," and "t's" which figures prominently in the sound pattern.

Tone color performs several functions in poetry. The amount and richness of it will vary with the purpose of the writing. The more marked the aesthetic and emotional effect desired, the richer and more complex the tone color is likely to be. One of the most important uses of tone color is to enrich the emotional content. Most authorities agree that it is nearly impossible to divorce the connotation of a word from the sound of it. Even in everyday conversation, words are colored and their meanings intensified or depreciated by the elongation or shortening of the vowel sounds and by the softening or sharpening of the consonants. This coloring or intensification through sound is even more marked in poetry, when a word is used in relation to others which strengthen the associational values. Thus it makes an important contribution to suggestion.

Tone color is also important in helping to implement poetic imagery. "To Autumn" offers a particularly good example of this function of tone color. The opening lines, or indeed any lines chosen at random, will provide unmistakable proof of Keats' concern with the sounds he used:

Season of mists and mellow fruitfulness,
Close bosom-friend of the maturing sun;

Within these lines there is a predominance of "s's," "m's," "n's" and of the liquid "l." These are skillfully combined with the "oo" and "u" sounds that add to the richness, while the lighter touch on "mists," "mell," "ness," and "friend" keeps the effect from becoming monotonous. With such a strong hint from the poet in the opening lines, the interpreter will do well to pay particular attention to the combinations of sounds in the entire poem. He will find that they vary as the content varies and that in every case sound, connotation, and imagery reinforce each other.

Another extremely important function of tone color is to provide for change of tempo. Certain combinations of vowels and consonants allow and even encourage the reader to speak more rapidly than other combinations. If the poet is a skilled craftsman, he has been aware of the need for variety of tempo, and the interpreter will find considerable help in the combinations of sounds. These variations, of course, will also depend upon the content, both emotional and logical, and upon the type of imagery which they augment.

In the last stanza of "To Autumn," there is an excellent example of the use of tone color to provide variety of tempo. The short speech phrases in the form of the questions

Where are the songs of Spring? Ay, where are they?

help the interpreter achieve needed variety after the rich, slow sounds of

Thou watchest the last oozings hours by hours.

which closed the preceding stanza. "Think not of them" is likewise light and almost crisp in its sound and its implication of dismissal. Immediately, however, the tempo slows again with "thou hast thy music too," and even more in the next line with "barred clouds bloom." The pace picks up slightly on "touched the stubble-plains," but immediately slows again on "rosy hue." This alternation continues throughout the entire stanza. The contrast between "lambs loud bleat from hilly bourn" and the following "hedge-crickets sing" is particularly effective. Attention to subtle changes indicated by the sounds will allow the interpreter to make the most of the needed variety.

What, then, is the secret of the poem's effectiveness? It is impossible to answer that question satisfactorily. We only know from our own experience that the poet has somehow expressed and lifted out of time the transient moment — the universal moment — that may not, cannot be prolonged. The blending of the logical and the emotional is certainly one of the important factors, but it is not the whole answer. Nor will we find the *whole* answer even after the most careful analysis. An objective study of the component parts will enable the interpreter to make the best possible use of the poet's technique as a guide to interpretation. But the essence of a poem is not quantitative; its whole is more than the sum of its parts. We must accept the fact that at the heart of every good poem there is something beyond objective analysis — just as there is always something "beyond" the laboratory or the scalpel.

SELECTIONS FOR ANALYSIS AND ORAL INTERPRETATION

LET THE FULL richness of the sounds come through to increase the lift and sweep of this poem. The dedication will help you understand the poet's attitude. The two stresses in line eleven were put there by the poet.

The Windhover:

To Christ our Lord

I CAUGHT this morning morning's minion, king-
dom of daylight's dauphin, dapple-dawn-drawn Falcon, in his riding
Of the rolling level underneath him steady air, and striding
High there, how he rung upon the rein of a wimpling wing
In his ecstasy! then off, off forth on swing,
As a skate's heel sweeps smooth on a bow-bend: the hurl and gliding
Rebuffed the big wind. My heart in hiding
Stirred for a bird, — the achieve of, the mastery of the thing!

Brute beauty and valour and act, oh, air, pride, plume, here
Buckle! AND the fire that breaks from thee then, a billion
Times told lovelier, more dangerous, O my chevalier!

No wonder of it: shéer plód makes plough down sillion
Shine, and blue-bleak embers, ah my dear,
Fall, gall themselves, and gash gold-vermilion.

GERARD MANLEY HOPKINS

From *Poems of Gerard Manley Hopkins,* Third Edition, edited by W. H. Gardner. Copyright 1948 by Oxford University Press, Inc. Reprinted by permission.

THIS SEVENTEENTH CENTURY poem, a famous example of the use of hyperbole, served as the springboard for MacLeish's "You, Andrew Marvell." Contrast it with the MacLeish poem in attitude and use of figures of speech. The rhyme reinforces the sophisticated light touch.

To His Coy Mistress

Had we but world enough, and time,
This coyness, lady, were no crime.
We would sit down, and think which way
To walk, and pass our long love's day.
Thou by the Indian Ganges' side
Should'st rubies find: I by the tide
Of Humber would complain. I would
Love you ten years before the Flood,
And you should, if you please, refuse
Till the conversion of the Jews.
My vegetable love should grow
Vaster than empires, and more slow.
An hundred years should go to praise
Thine eyes, and on thy forehead gaze:
Two hundred to adore each breast:
But thirty thousand to the rest;
An age at least to every part,
And the last age should show your heart
For, lady, you deserve this state,
Nor would I love at lower rate.
    But at my back I always hear
Time's wingèd chariot hurrying near:
And yonder all before us lie
Deserts of vast eternity.
Thy beauty shall no more be found;
Nor, in thy marble vault, shall sound
My echoing song: then worms shall try
That long-preserved virginity,
And your quaint honour turn to dust,
And into ashes all my lust.
The grave's a fine and private place,
But none, I think, do there embrace.
    Now, therefore, while the youthful hue
Sits on thy skin like morning dew,
And while thy willing soul transpires
At every pore with instant fires,
Now let us sport us while we may;
And now, like amorous birds of prey,
Rather at once our Time devour,
Than languish in his slow-chapt power.

Let us roll all our strength and all
Our sweetness up into one ball,
And tear our pleasures with rough strife
Thorough the iron gates of life.
Thus, though we cannot make our sun
Stand still, yet we will make him run.

ANDREW MARVELL

THIS POEM, mentioned within the chapter in the discussion of literary allusions, will require some attention to geographical allusions as well. The continuous use of "And" will need careful handling in order to achieve the very subtle effect of the extremely long, complex sentence and the broken final stanza.

You, Andrew Marvell

And here face down beneath the sun
And here upon earth's noonward height
To feel the always coming on
The always rising of the night:

To feel creep up the curving east
The earthly chill of dusk and slow
Upon those under lands the vast
And ever-climbing shadow grow

And strange at Ecbatan the trees
Take leaf by leaf the evening strange
The flooding dark about their knees
The mountains over Persia change

And now at Kermanshah the gate
Dark empty and the withered grass
And through the twilight now the late
Few travellers in the westward pass

And Baghdad darken and the bridge
Across the silent river gone
And through Arabia the edge
Of evening widen and steal on

And deepen on Palmyra's street
The wheel rut in the ruined stone
And Lebanon fade out and Crete
High through the clouds and overblown

From *Collected Poems* by Archibald MacLeish. Copyright 1952 by Archibald MacLeish. Reprinted by permission of Houghton Mifflin Company.

And over Sicily the air
Still flashing with the landward gulls
And loom and slowly disappear
The sails above the shadowy hulls

And Spain go under and the shore
Of Africa the gilded sand,
And evening vanish and no more
The low pale light across the land

Nor now the long light on the sea:

And here face downward in the sun
To feel how swift how secretly
The shadow of the night comes on . . .

ARCHIBALD MACLEISH

KEATS TELLS US clearly in the title that this poem will have at least some of the characteristics of the traditional ode. Remember that the poet is contemplating the urn, and that this is an almost completely static poem. Nevertheless, there are numerous details which give it variety.

Ode on a Grecian Urn

Thou still unravished bride of quietness,
  Thou foster-child of silence and slow Time,
Sylvan historian, who canst thus express
  A flowery tale more sweetly than our rime:
What leaf-fringed legend haunts about thy shape
  Of deities or mortals, or of both,
    In Tempe or the dales of Arcady?
  What men or gods are these? What maidens loath?
What mad pursuit? What struggle to escape?
  What pipes and timbrels? What wild ecstasy?

Heard melodies are sweet, but those unheard
  Are sweeter; therefore, ye soft pipes, play on;
Not to the sensual ear, but, more endeared,
  Pipe to the spirit ditties of no tone:
Fair youth, beneath the trees, thou canst not leave
  Thy song, nor ever can those trees be bare;
    Bold Lover, never, never canst thou kiss,
Though winning near the goal — yet, do not grieve;
    She cannot fade, though thou hast not thy bliss,
  For ever wilt thou love, and she be fair!

Ah, happy, happy boughs! that cannot shed
  Your leaves, nor ever bid the Spring adieu:
And, happy melodist, unweariéd,
  For ever piping songs for ever new;
More happy love! more happy, happy love!
  For ever warm and still to be enjoyed,
    For ever panting, and for ever young;
All breathing human passion far above,
  That leaves a heart high-sorrowful and cloyed,
    A burning forehead, and a parching tongue.

Who are these coming to the sacrifice?
  To what green altar, O mysterious priest,
Lead'st thou that heifer lowing at the skies,
  And all her silken flanks with garlands drest?
What little town by river or sea shore,
  Or mountain-built with peaceful citadel,
    Is emptied of this folk, this pious morn?
And, little town, thy streets for evermore
  Will silent be; and not a soul to tell
    Why thou art desolate, can e'er return.

O Attic shape! Fair attitude! with brede[1]
  Of marble men and maidens overwrought,
With forest branches and the trodden weed;
  Thou, silent form, dost tease us out of thought
As doth eternity: Cold Pastoral!
  When old age shall this generation waste,
    Thou shalt remain, in midst of other woe
  Than ours, a friend to man to whom thou say'st,
"Beauty is truth, truth beauty," — that is all
    Ye know on earth, and all ye need to know.

JOHN KEATS

THE REVERSED ORGANIZATION of content in the second stanza must be carefully coordinated with the opening stanza to allow this "credo" to come full circle. Pay close attention to the kinesthetic imagery, the slight alteration of the repeated lines, and the parallel grammatical structure.

In My Craft or Sullen Art

In my craft or sullen art
Exercised in the still night
When only the moon rages

[1] Braid or garland.

And the lovers lie abed
With all their griefs in their arms,
I labour by singing light
Not for ambition or bread
Or the strut and trade of charms
On the ivory stages
But for the common wages
Of their most secret heart.

Not for the proud man apart
From the raging moon I write
On these spindrift pages
Nor for the towering dead
With their nightingales and psalms
But for the lovers, their arms
Round the griefs of the ages,
Who pay no praise or wages
Nor heed my craft or art.

DYLAN THOMAS

THE LINES AS UNITS of thought make a very important contribution to the progression of this poem. Observe them carefully. Notice the number of "lifting" images.

Poem in October

It was my thirtieth year to heaven
Woke to my hearing from harbour and neighbour wood
And the mussel pooled and the heron
Priested shore
The morning beckon
With water praying and call of seagull and rook
And the knock of sailing boats on the net-webbed wall
Myself to set foot
That second
In the still sleeping town and set forth.

My birthday began with the water-
Birds and the birds of the winged trees flying my name
Above the farms and the white horses

From *The Collected Poems of Dylan Thomas.* Copyright 1953 by Dylan Thomas, © 1957 by New Directions. Reprinted by permission of New Directions, Publishers. Also reprinted by permission of J. M. Dent & Sons, Ltd. and The Dylan Thomas Estate.

And I rose
In rainy autumn
And walked abroad in a shower of all my days.
High tide and the heron dived when I took the road
Over the border
And the gates
Of the town closed as the town awoke.

A springful of larks in a rolling
Cloud and the roadside bushes brimming with whistling
Blackbirds and the sun of October
Summery
On the hill's shoulder,
Here were fond climates and sweet singers suddenly
Come in the morning where I wandered and listened
To the rain wringing
Wind blow cold
In the wood faraway under me.

Pale rain over the dwindling harbour
And over the sea-wet church the size of a snail
With its horns through mist and the castle
Brown as owls,
But all the gardens
Of spring and summer were blooming in the tall tales
Beyond the border and under the lark-full cloud.
There could I marvel
My birthday
Away but the weather turned around.

It turned away from the blithe country,
And down the other air and the blue altered sky
Streamed again a wonder of summer
With apples
Pears and red currants,
And I saw in the turning so clearly a child's
Forgotten mornings when he walked with his mother
Through the parables
Of sunlight
And the legends of the green chapels

And the twice told fields of infancy
That his tears burned my cheeks and his heart moved in mine.
These were the woods the river and sea
Where a boy
In the listening
Summertime of the dead whispered the truth of his joy
To the trees and the stones and the fish in the tide.

And the mystery
Sang alive
Still in the water and singing birds.

And there could I marvel my birthday
Away but the weather turned around. And the true
Joy of the long-dead child sang burning
In the sun.
It was my thirtieth
Year to heaven stood there then in the summer noon
Though the town below lay leaved with October blood.
O may my heart's truth
Still be sung
On this high hill in a year's turning.

DYLAN THOMAS

THIS PSALM ON the glory of God and the dignity of man is a prayer of exaltation. Make careful use of the parallel constructions, which are a basis of rhythm in Hebrew poetry. They function in much the same way in this translation taken from the King James Bible.

Psalm 8

O Lord our Lord,
how excellent is thy name in all the earth!
who hast set thy glory above the heavens.
Out of the mouth of babes and sucklings hast thou ordained
strength because of thine enemies,
that thou mightest still the enemy and the avenger.

When I consider thy heavens, the work of thy fingers,
the moon and the stars, which thou hast ordained;
What is man, that thou art mindful of him?
and the son of man, that thou visitest him?
For thou hast made him a little lower than the angels,
and hast crowned him with glory and honor.
Thou madest him to have dominion over the works of thy hands;
thou hast put all things under his feet:
All sheep and oxen,
yea, and the beasts of the field;
The fowl of the air, and the fish of the sea,
and whatsoever passeth through the paths of the sea.

O Lord our Lord,
how excellent is thy name in all the earth!

This is one of a series of poems by the contemporary Greek poet who won the Nobel Prize for literature in 1963. The title is a combination of "myth" and the Greek word meaning "novel" or "tale." Watch carefully for important clues in the syntax and line units.

Mythistorema X

Our country is a shut-in place, all mountains
And the mountains roofed by a low sky, day and night.
We have no rivers, we have no wells, we have no fountains,
Only some cisterns, empty; they ring and are to us
Objects of worship.
A sound stagnant, hollow, like our solitude,
Like our love and like our bodies.
It seems to us strange that once we were able to build
These houses of ours, these huts, these sheep-folds.
And our marriages, — the dewy garlands, the marriage fingers,
Have become insoluble riddles for our souls.
How were they born
Our children? How then did they grow up?

Our country is a shut-in place. It is enclosed
By the two black Clashing Rocks. And when we go
On Sundays down to the harbour for a breath of air,
We see, lit by the sunset,
The broken timbers of unfinished journeys,
Bodies that know no longer how to love.

George Seferis

Allusions are important here within the context of the ancient city of Byzantium. Some research on its position in the antique world of art and material wealth will help clarify the implied analogy.

Sailing to Byzantium

That is no country for old men. The young
In one another's arms, birds in the trees
— Those dying generations — at their song,
The salmon-falls, the mackerel-crowded seas,
Fish, flesh, or fowl, commend all summer long
Whatever is begotten, born, and dies.
Caught in that sensual music all neglect
Monuments of unaging intellect.

From *Poems: George Seferis* by George Seferis, by permission of Little, Brown and Company-Atlantic Monthly Press. English translation by Rex Warner, copyright © 1960. Also reprinted by permission of The Bodley Head, Ltd.

Reprinted with permission of the publisher from *The Collected Poems of W. B. Yeats* by William Butler Yeats. Copyright 1928 by The Macmillan Company, renewed 1956 by Bertha Georgie Yeats. Also reprinted with permission of Mrs. W. B. Yeats, A. P. Watt & Son, and The Macmillan Company of Canada.

An aged man is but a paltry thing,
A tattered coat upon a stick, unless
Soul clap its hands and sing, and louder sing
For every tatter in its mortal dress,
Nor is there singing school but studying
Monuments of its own magnificence;
And therefore I have sailed the seas and come
To the holy city of Byzantium.

O sages standing in God's holy fire
As in the gold mosaic of a wall,
Come from the holy fire, perne in a gyre,
And be the singing-masters of my soul.
Consume my heart away; sick with desire
And fastened to a dying animal
It knows not what it is; and gather me
Into the artifice of eternity.

Once out of nature I shall never take
My bodily form from any natural thing,
But such a form as Grecian goldsmiths make
Of hammered gold and gold enameling
To keep a drowsy Emperor awake;
Or set upon a golden bough to sing
To lords and ladies of Byzantium
Of what is past, or passing, or to come.

WILLIAM BUTLER YEATS

WE GAVE SOME attention to this poem in the preceding chapter. Make careful use of the sentence structure and length, and of the lines as units. The allusions are immediately identifiable but important. Notice particularly the frequent questions, the use of negatives and of the past subjunctive.

The Love Song of J. Alfred Prufrock

S'io credesse che mia risposta fosse
A persona che mai tornasse al mondo,
Questa fiamma staria senza piu scosse.
Ma perciocche giammai di questo fondo
Non torno vivo alcun, s'i'odo il vero,
Senza tema d'infamia ti rispondo.[1]

[1] "If I thought my answer were to one who could ever return to the world, this flame should shake no more; but since, if what I hear is true, no one ever returned alive from this depth, I answer you without fear of shame." A statement made by a spirit in hell to Dante in the twenty-seventh canto of the *Inferno.*

From *Collected Poems 1909–1962* by T. S. Eliot. Copyright, 1936, by Harcourt, Brace & World, Inc.; © 1963, 1964, by T. S. Eliot. Reprinted by permission of the publishers. Also reprinted by permission of Faber and Faber, Ltd.

Let us go then, you and I,
When the evening is spread out against the sky
Like a patient etherised upon a table;
Let us go, through certain half-deserted streets,
The muttering retreats
Of restless nights in one-night cheap hotels
And sawdust restaurants with oyster-shells:
Streets that follow like a tedious argument
Of insidious intent
To lead you to an overwhelming question . . .
Oh, do not ask, "What is it?"
Let us go and make our visit.

In the room the women come and go
Talking of Michelangelo.

The yellow fog that rubs its back upon the window-panes,
The yellow smoke that rubs its muzzle on the window-panes
Licked its tongue into the corners of the evening,
Lingered upon the pools that stand in drains,
Let fall upon its back the soot that falls from chimneys,
Slipped by the terrace, made a sudden leap,
And seeing that it was a soft October night,
Curled once about the house, and fell asleep.

And indeed there will be time
For the yellow smoke that slides along the street,
Rubbing its back upon the window-panes;
There will be time, there will be time
To prepare a face to meet the faces that you meet;
There will be time to murder and create,
And time for all the works and days of hands
That lift and drop a question on your plate;
Time for you and time for me,
And time yet for a hundred indecisions,
And for a hundred visions and revisions,
Before the taking of a toast and tea.

In the room the women come and go
Talking of Michelangelo.

And indeed there will be time
To wonder, "Do I dare?" and, "Do I dare?"
Time to turn back and descend the stair,
With a bald spot in the middle of my hair —
[They will say: "How his hair is growing thin!"]
My morning coat, my collar mounting firmly to the chin,
My necktie rich and modest, but asserted by a simple pin —
[They will say: "But how his arms and legs are thin!"]

Do I dare
Disturb the universe?
In a minute there is time
For decisions and revisions which a minute will reverse.

For I have known them all already, known them all: —
Have known the evenings, mornings, afternoons,
I have measured out my life with coffee spoons;
I know the voices dying with a dying fall
Beneath the music from a farther room.
So how should I presume?

And I have known the eyes already, known them all —
The eyes that fix you in a formulated phrase,
And when I am formulated, sprawling on a pin,
When I am pinned and wriggling on the wall,
Then how should I begin
To spit out all the butt-ends of my days and ways?
And how should I presume?

And I have known the arms already, known them all —
Arms that are braceleted and white and bare
[But in the lamplight, downed with light brown hair!]
Is it perfume from a dress
That makes me so digress?
Arms that lie along a table, or wrap about a shawl.
And should I then presume?
And how should I begin?

. . . . .

Shall I say, I have gone at dusk through narrow streets
And watched the smoke that rises from the pipes
Of lonely men in shirt-sleeves, leaning out of windows? . . .

I should have been a pair of ragged claws
Scuttling across the floors of silent seas.

. . . . .

And the afternoon, the evening, sleeps so peacefully!
Smoothed by long fingers,
Asleep . . . tired . . . or it malingers,
Stretched on the floor, here beside you and me.
Should I, after tea and cakes and ices,
Have the strength to force the moment to its crisis?
But though I have wept and fasted, wept and prayed,
Though I have seen my head [grown slightly bald] brought in upon a platter,
I am no prophet — and here's no great matter;

I have seen the moment of my greatness flicker,
And I have seen the eternal Footman hold my coat, and snicker,
And in short, I was afraid.

And would it have been worth it, after all,
After the cups, the marmalade, the tea,
Among the porcelain, among some talk of you and me,
Would it have been worth while,
To have bitten off the matter with a smile,
To have squeezed the universe into a ball
To roll it toward some overwhelming question,
To say: "I am Lazarus, come from the dead,
Come back to tell you all, I shall tell you all" —
If one, settling a pillow by her head,
Should say: "That is not what I meant at all.
That is not it, at all."

And would it have been worth it, after all,
Would it have been worth while,
After the sunsets and the dooryards and the sprinkled streets,
After the novels, after the teacups, after the skirts that trail along the floor —
And this, and so much more? —
It is impossible to say just what I mean!
But as if a magic lantern threw the nerves in patterns on a screen:
Would it have been worth while
If one, settling a pillow or throwing off a shawl,
And turning toward the window, should say:
"That is not it at all,
That is not what I meant, at all."

. . . . .

No! I am not Prince Hamlet, nor was meant to be;
Am an attendant lord, one that will do
To swell a progress, start a scene or two,
Advise the prince; no doubt, an easy tool,
Deferential, glad to be of use,
Politic, cautious, and meticulous;
Full of high sentence, but a bit obtuse;
At times, indeed, almost ridiculous —
Almost, at times, the Fool.

I grow old . . . I grow old . . .
I shall wear the bottoms of my trousers rolled.

Shall I part my hair behind? Do I dare to eat a peach?
I shall wear white flannel trousers, and walk upon the beach.
I have heard the mermaids singing, each to each.

I do not think that they will sing to me.

I have seen them riding seaward on the waves
Combing the white hair of the waves blown back
When the wind blows the water white and black.

We have lingered in the chambers of the sea
By sea-girls wreathed with seaweed red and brown
Till human voices wake us, and we drown.

T. S. Eliot

E. E. Cummings uses his own distinctive syntax in this love poem. Let the sounds support the mood by making full use of them. The line entities must be carefully and faithfully observed.

anyone lived in a pretty how town

anyone lived in a pretty how town
(with up so floating many bells down)
spring summer autumn winter
he sang his didn't he danced his did.

Women and men(both little and small)
cared for anyone not at all
they sowed their isn't they reaped their same
sun moon stars rain

children guessed(but only a few
and down they forgot as up they grew
autumn winter spring summer)
that noone loved him more by more

when by now and tree by leaf
she laughed his joy she cried his grief
bird by snow and stir by still
anyone's any was all to her

someones married their everyones
laughed their cryings and did their dance
(sleep wake hope and then)they
said their nevers they slept their dream

Copyright, 1940, by E. E. Cummings. Reprinted from his volume *Poems 1923–1954* by permission of Harcourt, Brace & World, Inc.

stars rain sun moon
(and only the snow can begin to explain
how children are apt to forget to remember
with up so floating many bells down)

one day anyone died i guess
(and noone stooped to kiss his face)
busy folk buried them side by side
little by little and was by was

all by all and deep by deep
and more by more they dream their sleep
noone and anyone earth by april
wish by spirit and if by yes.

Women and men(both dong and ding)
summer autumn winter spring
reaped their sowing and went their came
sun moon stars rain

E. E. Cummings

This love poem of the sixteenth century has a light-hearted quality in the images used, and especially in the lifting, lilting rhythm. The tight rhyme scheme must not be overlooked for its contribution to deliberate naïveté. Some care will be required, however, to keep the prosodic elements from overshadowing the content.

The Passionate Shepherd to His Love

Come live with me and be my love,
And we will all the pleasures prove
That valleys, groves, hills, and fields,
Woods, or steepy mountain yields.

And we will sit upon the rocks,
Seeing the shepherds feed their flocks,
By shallow rivers to whose falls
Melodious birds sing madrigals.

And I will make thee beds of roses
And a thousand fragrant posies,
A cap of flowers, and a kirtle
Embroidered all with leaves of myrtle;

A gown made of the finest wool
Which from our pretty lambs we pull;

Fair-linèd slippers for the cold,
With buckles of the purest gold;

A belt of straw and ivy-buds,
With coral clasps and amber studs:
And if these pictures may thee move,
Come live with me, and be my love.

The shepherds' swains shall dance and sing
For thy delight each May morning:
If these delights thy mind may move,
Then live with me and be my love.

CHRISTOPHER MARLOWE

WALLACE STEVENS BELIEVED that art is the highest product of the imagination because it orders disordered nature. For him imagination and what we call reality were of equal importance in life and were interdependent. You will find that this poem contains overlapping analogies to support this theme. Ramon is probably just a name for his companion rather than an allusion to any historical figure.

The Idea of Order at Key West

She sang beyond the genius of the sea.
The water never formed to mind or voice,
Like a body wholly body, fluttering
Its empty sleeves; and yet its mimic motion
Made constant cry, caused constantly a cry,
That was not ours although we understood,
Inhuman, of the veritable ocean.

The sea was not a mask. No more was she.
The song and water were not medleyed sound
Even if what she sang was what she heard,
Since what she sang was uttered word by word.
It may be that in all her phrases stirred
The grinding water and the gasping wind;
But it was she and not the sea we heard.

For she was the maker of the song she sang.
The ever-hooded, tragic-gestured sea
Was merely a place by which she walked to sing.
Whose spirit is this? we said, because we knew

Copyright, 1936, 1942, by Wallace Stevens. Reprinted from *The Collected Poems of Wallace Stevens,* by permission of Alfred A. Knopf, Inc.

It was the spirit that we sought and knew
That we should ask this often as she sang.
If it was only the dark voice of the sea
That rose, or even colored by many waves;
If it was only the outer voice of sky
And cloud, of the sunken coral water-walled,
However clear, it would have been deep air,
The heaving speech of air, a summer sound
Repeated in a summer without end
And sound alone. But it was more than that,
More even than her voice, and ours, among
The meaningless plungings of water and the wind,
Theatrical distances, bronze shadows heaped
On high horizons, mountainous atmospheres
Of sky and sea.

It was her voice that made
The sky acutest at its vanishing.
She measured to the hour its solitude.
She was the single artificer of the world
In which she sang. And when she sang, the sea,
Whatever self it had, became the self
That was her song, for she was the maker. Then we,
As we beheld her striding there alone,
Knew that there never was a world for her
Except the one she sang and, singing, made.

Ramon Fernandez, tell me, if you know,
Why, when the singing ended and we turned
Toward the town, tell why the glassy lights,
The lights in the fishing boats at anchor there,
As the night descended, tilting in the air,
Mastered the night and portioned out the sea,
Fixing emblazoned zones and fiery poles,
Arranging, deepening, enchanting night.

Oh! Blessed rage for order, pale Ramon,
The maker's rage to order words of the sea,
Words of the fragrant portals, dimly-starred,
And of ourselves and of our origins,
In ghostlier demarcations, keener sounds.

WALLACE STEVENS

BEAUTY FOR STEVENS implied both sense experience and an awareness of form. Thus there is always the mind to consider. Because we are human and of this world, we will find our greatest beauty in something which has an essentially temporal quality.

The Poems of Our Climate

I

Clear water in a brilliant bowl,
Pink and white carnations. The light
In the room more like a snowy air,
Reflecting snow. A newly-fallen snow
At the end of winter when afternoons return.
Pink and white carnations — one desires
So much more than that. The day itself
Is simplified: a bowl of white,
Cold, a cold porcelain, low and round,
With nothing more than the carnations there.

II

Say even that this complete simplicity
Stripped one of all one's torments, concealed
The evilly compounded, vital I
And made it fresh in a world of white,
A world of clear water, brilliant-edged,
Still one would want more, one would need more,
More than a world of white and snowy scents.

III

There would still remain the never-resting mind,
So that one would want to escape, come back
To what had been so long composed.
The imperfect is our paradise.
Note that, in this bitterness, delight,
Since the imperfect is so hot in us,
Lies in flawed words and stubborn sounds.

WALLACE STEVENS

THE STRENGTH OF the words and images, combined with the starkness and near-brutality of syntax, helps keep this brief poem moving fiercely and swiftly to its conclusion.

Open the Gates

Within the city of the burning cloud,
Dragging my life behind me in a sack,
Naked I prowl, scourged by the black
Temptation of the blood grown proud.

Copyright, 1936, 1942, by Wallace Stevens. Reprinted from *The Collected Poems of Wallace Stevens,* by permission of Alfred A. Knopf, Inc.

From *Selected Poems* by Stanley Kunitz by permission of Little, Brown and Company-Atlantic Monthly Press. Copyright © 1958 by Stanley Kunitz.

Here at the monumental door,
Carved with the curious legend of my youth,
I brandish the great bone of my death,
Beat once therewith and beat no more.

The hinges groan: a rush of forms
Shivers my name, wrenched out of me.
I stand on the terrible threshold, and I see
The end and the beginning in each other's arms.

STANLEY KUNITZ

SENTENCE LENGTHS PROVIDE variety within the philosophical attitude of this poem. Keep careful control of the "who" references.

I Think Continually of Those Who Were Truly Great

I think continually of those who were truly great.
Who, from the womb, remembered the soul's history
Through corridors of light where the hours are suns,
Endless and singing. Whose lovely ambition
Was that their lips, still touched with fire,
Should tell of the spirit clothed from head to foot in song.
And who hoarded from the spring branches
The desires falling across their bodies like blossoms.

What is precious is never to forget
The delight of the blood drawn from ageless springs
Breaking through rocks in worlds before our earth;
Never to deny its pleasure in the simple morning light,
Nor its grave evening demand for love;
Never to allow gradually the traffic to smother
With noise and fog the flowering of the spirit.

Near the snow, near the sun, in the highest fields
See how those names are fêted by the wavering grass,
And by the streamers of white cloud,
And whispers of wind in the listening sky;
The names of those who in their lives fought for life,
Who wore at their hearts the fire's centre.
Born of the sun they traveled a short while towards the sun,
And left the vivid air signed with their honour.

STEPHEN SPENDER

Copyright 1934 and renewed 1961 by Stephen Spender. Reprinted from *Collected Poems 1928–1953* by Stephen Spender, by permission of Random House, Inc. Also reprinted by permission of Faber and Faber, Ltd.

THIS ELEGY FOR a little girl contains some interesting problems of balance and proportion. Look carefully at the structure of the three middle stanzas.

Bells for John Whiteside's Daughter

There was such speed in her little body,
And such lightness in her footfall,
It is no wonder her brown study
Astonishes us all.

Her wars were bruited in our high window.
We looked among orchard trees and beyond,
Where she took arms against her shadow,
Or harried unto the pond

The lazy geese, like a snow cloud
Dripping their snow on the green grass,
Tricking and stopping, sleepy and proud,
Who cried in goose, Alas,

For the tireless heart within the little
Lady with rod that made them rise
From their noon apple-dreams, and scuttle
Goose-fashion under the skies!

But now go the bells, and we are ready;
In one house we are sternly stopped
To say we are vexed at her brown study,
Lying so primly propped.

JOHN CROWE RANSOM

THIS POEM PRESENTS a character study not only of the monk who is speaking but of Brother Lawrence as well. Remember that it is a soliloquy, an indication that the speaker is alone. Evidently, however, Brother Lawrence is moving within sight of the speaker, and his actions provide the motivations for the swift changes of thought. Notice the spite which the monk who follows the letter of the law feels for the man who lives by the spirit. The structure of the poem helps to underscore this feeling.

Soliloquy of the Spanish Cloister

Gr-r-r — there go, my heart's abhorrence!
Water your damned flower-pots, do!
If hate killed men, Brother Lawrence,
God's blood, would not mine kill you!

Copyright 1924 by Alfred A. Knopf, Inc. Renewed 1953 by John Crowe Ransom. Reprinted from *Selected Poems,* Revised Edition, by John Crowe Ransom, by permission of Alfred A. Knopf, Inc.

What? Your myrtle-bush wants trimming?
  Oh, that rose has prior claims —
Needs its leaden vase filled brimming?
  Hell dry you up with its flames!

At the meal we sit together:
  Salve tibi![1] I must hear
Wise talk of the kind of weather,
  Sort of season, time of year:
Not a plenteous cork-crop: scarcely
  Dare we hope oak-galls, I doubt:
What's the Latin name for "parsley"?
  What's the Greek name for Swine's Snout?

Whew! We'll have our platter burnished,
  Laid with care on our own shelf!
With a fire-new spoon we're furnished,
  And a goblet for ourself,
Rinsed like something sacrificial
  Ere 'tis fit to touch our chaps —
Marked with L for our initial
  (He-he! There his lily snaps!)

Saint, forsooth! while brown Dolores
  Squats outside the Convent bank
With Sanchicha, telling stories,
  Steeping tresses in the tank,
Blue-black, lustrous, thick like horse-hairs,
  — Can't I see his dead eye glow,
Bright as 'twere a Barbary corsair's?
  (That is, if he'd let it show!)

When he finishes refection,
  Knife and fork he never lays
Cross-wise, to my recollection,
  As do I, in Jesu's praise.
I the Trinity illustrate,
  Drinking watered orange-pulp
In three sips the Arian[2] frustrate;
  While he drains his at one gulp.

Oh, those melons! If he's able
  We're to have a feast! so nice!
One goes to the Abbot's table,

[1] Hail.

[2] The Arian heresy held that Christ was created by God, and was inferior to Him in nature and dignity.

All of us get each a slice.
How go on your flowers? None double?
Not one fruit-sort can you spy?
Strange! — And I, too, at such trouble
Keep them close-nipped on the sly!

There's a great text in Galatians,
Once you trip on it, entails
Twenty-nine distinct damnations,
One sure, if another fails:
If I trip him just a-dying,
Sure of heaven as sure can be,
Spin him round and send him flying
Off to hell, a Manichee![3]

Or, my scrofulous French novel
On gray paper with blunt type!
Simply glance at it, you grovel
Hand and foot in Belial's gripe:
If I double down its pages
At the woeful sixteenth print,
When he waters his greengages,
Ope a sieve and slip it in't?

Or there's Satan! One might venture
Pledge one's soul to him, yet leave
Such a flaw in the indenture
As he'd miss till, past retrieve,
Blasted lay that rose-acacia
We're so proud of! *Hy, Zy, Hine . . .*[4]
'St, there's Vespers! *Plena gratia,*
Ave, Virgo![5] G-r-r-r — you swine!

Robert Browning

[3] A sect that combined Persian and Christian beliefs.

[4] This series of sounds has caused considerable dissension among critics. It may be the beginning of a curse on Brother Lawrence.

[5] Full of grace, Hail, Virgin!

✶ Bibliography

Since, as we noted at the beginning of this chapter, content and structure must ultimately be considered in combination, the bibliography for Chapters 10 and 11 appears at the end of Chapter 11.

11

The Structure of Poetry

The statement was made in the preceding chapter that poetry carries order to its highest degree. This order is apparent in the condensation and organization of the content and in the close interrelationship of content and form. It is even more apparent, however, in the discipline which poetic structure places upon the writer, and consequently upon the interpreter. In good poetry, structure and content are in perfect harmony, and neither may be considered without the other in an evaluation of the whole.

The writer of prose is disciplined by the need to present his materials with clarity and to find the most effective method of organizing them in order to achieve the purpose for which he is writing. The dramatist has the added problem of expressing himself entirely in dialogue, with only the brief and occasional aid of stage directions to keep his plot believable and to make the progression clear and motivated. The poet also accepts the need for clarity and for effective organization. If he is dealing with dramatic elements, as in the dramatic monologue or verse drama, he must also be aware of the restrictions under which the dramatist writes. In addition, his writing must be characterized by certain elements of structure which are inherent in poetry.

These elements influence the poet's choice of stanzaic form, line length, structural rhythm, and rhyme. They are the basis of the sound pattern upon which much of the poem's effectiveness depends. The sound pattern of a poem is made up of the interweaving of sound combinations, which we know as tone color; the combination of light and heavier stresses, which is meter; and the flow of sound units in sentence, line, and the speech phrases within the line, which we call cadence. These component parts of the sound pattern depend in a very special way upon the services of the interpreter, because they can be thoroughly appreciated and allowed to fulfill their function only when the poem is read aloud.

Since the late nineteenth century it has been convenient to make a distinction between conventional poetry and free verse. The structure of *conventional poetry* is based on a clearly discernible pattern of light and heavier stresses which can be grouped into the traditional metrical feet, and on a fixed pattern of stanza and line length. The same pattern, with only slight variation, usually recurs from stanza to stanza, both as to length of lines and arrangement of stresses within those lines. Moreover, the number of lines per stanza is usually consistent. Within this fixed structural framework, however, there may occur numerous variations in stress pattern and in the location of pauses within a line to keep the fall of the words from becoming monotonous. Finally, conventional poetry — with the notable exception of blank verse — has the added element of rhyme, with the corresponding sounds in the line-end positions arranged in an easily perceived pattern called the rhyme scheme.

Blank verse is a special type of conventional poetry. It is unrhymed and has no recurring stanza pattern, for the stanzas divide according to the development of the thought and hence are irregular in length. It has, however, a definitely prescribed line length of five metrical feet, and a prescribed prevailing foot, the iamb. Blank verse is of particular interest to the interpreter because it is so often used in material inherently attractive to an audience. The absence of rhyme and the lack of restriction on stanzaic structure permit the skillful poet to use this form effectively with narrative and dramatic materials. Shakespeare, an acknowledged master of blank verse in poetic drama, used it to wed nobility of utterance to acceptable rhythms of speech; poets as diverse as Robert Browning and Robert Frost, to sustain the dramatic quality of a long poem and to achieve the difficult feat of making poetry sound like conversation, and conversation like poetry.

Free verse is often considered a recent addition to the realm of poetry. At least the term is modern, and the genre has developed during the last hundred years or less, though it is not impossible to find earlier examples. Free verse is a term adopted from the French *vers libre. Vers* in French refers to a *line* of poetry; hence *vers libre* actually means a "free line." Thus it is from the varying lengths of the lines and the arrangement of stresses within them that we get our surest indication that the poem falls within this classification.

Free verse differs in many ways from conventional poetry. If the free verse poem is divided into stanza units at all, they are often irregular in length, although a free verse poem may have quite regular stanzaic division. The free verse line may vary in length from a single syllable to fifty or more — if the author feels that he needs to use so long a line and that he can bring it off successfully. Free verse often makes no use of rhyme, though the poet may choose to introduce it in order to achieve some special effect. It exhibits no significant pattern of metrical feet, and its rhythm is based on cadence rather than on meter.

Successful free verse is not, as the term might suggest, completely lacking in form and discipline. It is a subjective discipline imposed by the poet without strict adherence to regular, traditional forms. There must be, however, a discoverable rhythmic basis. Sometimes it will be found in the number of syllables in the speech phrases within the lines, or in the number of heavier stresses within those speech phrases. Sometimes it will be discovered by careful analysis of the number of heavier stresses per line regardless of their relative positioning with lighter stresses. The important point is to find out what the *poet* has done and then see how it works with the content to produce a successful whole.

The strict dichotomy between conventional verse and free verse is becoming much less important in contemporary poetry. Most poets today work *from* rather than *within* strict metrical patterns so that we often find an interesting combination of the two modes within a single poem. The traditional lines set up an expectation for us which, when it is denied a few lines later by insertion of free verse, helps underscore variety and contrast. Or on the other hand, the strictly regular line may surprise us with its steady beat and help point up a climax. Stanley Kunitz' poem "Open the Gates" has an interesting example of this effect (page 403). William Van O'Connor, speaking of T. S. Eliot's prosody, quotes the poet when he says, "Even in the 'freest' of free verse there should lurk the ghost of some simple meter 'which should advance menacingly as we doze, and withdraw as we arouse.' "[1] And Robert Frost once remarked that writing what some people called free verse was like playing tennis with the net down. Thus contemporary free verse is more accurately "freed verse," but the interpreter must make a careful study to find out how freed it is from traditional patterns, and how this freedom is coordinated with the content to produce the whole.

STANZAIC STRUCTURE

As we saw in the last chapter, a stanza of poetry is comparable to a paragraph in prose, in that it is often a major unit of thought, and as such, is an important factor in the organization. But a stanza may also

[1] William Van O'Connor, *Sense and Sensibility in Modern Poetry* (Chicago: The University of Chicago Press, 1948), p. 58.

be a unit of sound, just as a line of poetry is not only a line of print but also a unit of sound, and a word is not only a symbol for meaning but a sound or combination of sounds as well. That is, the stanzaic structure may contribute significantly to the poem's pattern of sound. The recurrence of the same stanza pattern throughout, together with the poet's skill in making his thought units coincide with the stanzas, may divide the poem into nearly identical units of sound when the poem is read aloud, since the interpreter tends to separate major divisions in thought by appropriate use of pause and to establish terminations both by pause and by vocal inflection.

A stanza in conventional poetry is measured by the number of lines it contains. The normal stanza ranges from units of two lines (couplets) to nine lines or more. Without going into technical details, we may note in passing that the stanza may be named with reference to its line length alone, as a *quatrain* (four-line unit); or with reference not only to the number of lines it contains but also to the measure and rhyme scheme of the lines, as the *heroic quatrain* (four lines of iambic pentameter with the lines rhyming alternately, *abab*); or the *Spenserian stanza* (nine lines in the meter and rhyme scheme of Spencer's stanzas in *The Faerie Queene*).

The contribution of stanzaic length to the sound pattern of the poem varies considerably in importance from one selection to another. In general, the shorter the stanzas and the tighter the rhyme scheme, the more apparent is the sound effect. For example, a poem written entirely in two-line stanzas sets up a very close pattern of sounds and silences, especially if each pair of lines completes a thought division. This would constitute an important aspect of structural unity but might seriously threaten the variety. The interpreter would then be faced with the problem of deciding how successful the poet had been in combining such a strict pattern with the idea he wished to express and with the mood he wished to create. In blank verse, on the other hand, the contribution of stanzaic structure to sound pattern is almost negligible, partly because of the absence of rhyme but primarily because the stanzas are of unequal length and may run to a hundred lines or more.

Sometimes the division of the poem into regular stanzas is emphasized by repetition of the opening or closing line. We are familiar, of course, with this characteristic of the ballad form. The villanelle, which is the form of Theodore Roethke's "The Waking" (page 430), is particularly restrictive in the use of repetition and stanzaic structure. The following poem exhibits the use of refrain within a regular but less traditional framework.

The Dead in Europe

After the planes unloaded, we fell down
Buried together, unmarried men and women;
Not crown of thorns, not iron, not Lombard crown,
Not grilled and spindle spires pointing to heaven
Could save us. Raise us, Mother, we fell down
Here hugger-mugger in the jellied fire:
Our sacred earth in our day was our curse.

Our Mother, shall we rise on Mary's day
In Maryland, wherever corpses married
Under the rubble, bundled together? Pray
For us whom the blockbusters marred and buried;
When Satan scatters us on Rising-day,
O Mother, snatch our bodies from the fire:
Our sacred earth in our day was our curse.

Mother, my bones are trembling and I hear
The earth's reverberations and the trumpet
Bleating into my shambles. Shall I bear,
(O Mary!) unmarried man and powder-puppet,
Witness to the Devil? Mary, hear,
O Mary, marry earth, sea, air and fire;
Our sacred earth in our day was our curse.

ROBERT LOWELL

Here each seven-line stanza presents a new plea built on and growing out of the one before it, yet each is terminated by the same cry:

Our sacred earth in our day was our curse.

Further, the recurrence of the word "fire," immediately preceding the refrain line, serves subtly to intensify the repetition which follows it, and to mark off each stanza as a distinct unit. Since in this poem the thought units are identical with the structural units, the interpreter should take pains to use the stanza and its emphasized termination in such a way as to point up the poem's quality of prayer and lament.

Frequently in modern poetry of regular stanza pattern the thought units are not identical with the stanzas, but run on from one to another. A comma or other mark of punctuation not indicative of a full stop — or, indeed, the absence of any punctuation at all — at the end of the last line of the stanza, as we find in the fifth stanza of "Fern Hill"

From *Lord Weary's Castle,* copyright, 1944, 1946, by Robert Lowell. Reprinted by permission of Harcourt, Brace & World, Inc.

(page 434) and throughout MacLeish's poem "You, Andrew Marvell" (page 388), serves as a warning that the thought is unfinished and that the break imposed by the stanza pattern is a suspended one. The poet has chosen to set himself a discipline but has reserved the right to take liberties within it whenever he feels justified by his over-all purpose.

Thus the interpreter must be aware of whatever contribution the stanza length may make to the sound pattern the poet has adopted. In evaluating its importance, he must take his cue from the poet. When the poet has made a point of adhering to brief, regular stanzas, or has emphasized stanza divisions by repetition, the interpreter must assume that this strict discipline serves a definite purpose. On the other hand, when the stanzas are long or irregular in length, the interpreter may assume that the stanzas function primarily as means of organizing the logical or emotional content.

METER

The structural rhythm of conventional poetry is based upon meter, which is the pattern set up by a reasonably regular recurrence of an identifiable combination of light and heavier stresses within a line. In Chapter 5 we spoke of the contribution of stresses to the rhythm of prose. Poetry, however, is characterized in part by a high degree of regularity in the pattern of structural rhythm which is not found in other forms of writing. This pattern in conventional poetry is discovered through scansion, the division of the poetic line into metrical feet. A metrical foot is a grouping of light and heavier stresses into a unit. The most common feet in English poetry are these:

1. the *iamb* — an unstressed syllable followed by a stressed syllable (˘ ′)[1]

> When I | have fears | that I | may cease | to be

2. the *anapest* — two unstressed syllables followed by a stressed syllable (˘ ˘ ′)

> Of my dar | ling — my dar | ling — my life | and my bride

3. the *trochee* — a stressed syllable followed by an unstressed syllable (′ ˘)

> Tell me | not in | mournful | numbers

[1] (′) indicates a stressed syllable; (˘) an unstressed syllable. A vertical line (|) is used here to mark off the feet.

4. the *dactyl* — a stressed syllable followed by two unstressed syllables (′⌣⌣)

Cánnŏn tŏ | ríght ŏf thĕm

Technically speaking, there are all sorts of combinations of stressed and unstressed syllables in metrical feet, but most of them can be accounted for as variations on the four basic types given above. Of the variants, the two most common are the *spondee* (two heavy stresses) and the *pyrrhic* (two light stresses).

In almost all conventional poetry, one type of metrical foot will prevail. But although certain harmonies are sometimes achieved most successfully by strict consistency in meter, or by approximate consistency (as in the combination of iamb and anapest), most poets make effective use of variations in the prevalent measure, since variety-in-unity is the keystone of all art.

There are two details which may need to be mentioned to clarify the process of scanning a conventional poem. The first of these is the matter of relative stress. Not all stressed syllables receive the same degree or value of stress. Thus, though the following line might be scanned

Nót már | blĕ, nór | thĕ gíld | ĕd món | ŭménts

as a regular iambic pentameter, except for the irregularity of the emphatic opening spondee, in an oral reading the relative values of the stresses would be something like this, where (′) indicates a heavy stress and (ˋ) a lighter one and (⌣) no discernible stress:

Nòt már | blĕ, nòr | thĕ gíld | ĕd món | ŭmènts

The second detail is, on the surface, an obvious one, but it is often used with great effectiveness. As we know, strict scansion often splits syllables and combines the last syllable of one word with the first syllable of another to form a foot, as in the line just quoted. Thus, scansion is a method of dividing verse into metrical units regardless of the sense units formed by words and speech phrases. The point for the interpreter to remember is that he is not concerned with the individual foot, and is not going to be called on to deal with a nonsensical entity like "ble nor" or "ed mon," but with the combination of feet that produce the characteristic rhythm of the whole. Here, once again, it cannot be too strongly emphasized that it is the over-all pattern which is important to the interpreter as he brings content and structure together.

Often, therefore, when a line is read aloud the word as a sense unit *over-rides* the foot division and helps control a too-regular beat. Modern poets frequently use this device to produce a sort of counter-rhythm and increase mood and connotation. Theodore Roethke is a master of this technique as may be seen in these two lines from "The Waking" (page 430), where the over-rides impose a falling rhythm on the strictly iambic lines.

> I wake | to sleep | and take | my *wak* | *ing* slow.
>
> I learn | by *go* | *ing* where | I have | to go.

Without scanning the lines, one would be instinctively aware of this effect, for certainly it reads itself out. But having found it used with such deliberate skill, as a close analysis of the whole poem will reveal, the interpreter can certainly assume it is no accident and use it confidently as a guide to his own technique.

How does one begin to scan a poem? Since stress in poetry, as in prose, is based on sense, one begins by reading for the sense. In conventional poetry a dominant rhythmic pattern soon emerges, though almost always with certain irregularities that please by affording variety.

The student should start his scansion by marking first the words of more than one syllable. Such words, whether they are key words or not, have a familiar combination of stressed and unstressed syllables which carries over to the reading of verse. In the lines above, then, he would begin with "waking" and "going." If he is not sure of syllabification, he should check the dictionary; it is imperative that each syllable be accounted for.

The next step is to mark for sense. It is hardly conceivable that he would read the lines

> I wake to sleep and take my waking slow.

Often, however, the proper stresses will emerge only after attitude and connotation are clearly established. For instance, if Roethke were arguing the best way to "wake to sleep," and contrasting it with another way, the line might be marked "I wake to sleep and take my waking . . . ." This is obviously not the tone of the poem. The interpreter scans a poem the way it must be read to achieve its total effect. He scans to find what the poet has actually done, not to make the lines fit a preconceived pattern.

After these first two steps he may discover that a *fairly* regular pattern of light and heavier stresses, which can be grouped into traditional feet, will begin to emerge. He then completes the pattern by filling in whatever syllables have not yet been assigned a degree of stress to conform as nearly as possible to the predominant type of foot. If no such pattern emerges, he examines further to determine whether or not he is dealing with free verse and must look to line lengths, speech phrases, and the number of stresses within them for his structural unity.

The relative degree of stress is a matter which the interpreter must work out for himself from his understanding of the poem, for no one "right way" of reading a poem can be imposed from without. Not to submerge meaning in meter, not to lose sight of pattern in an attempt to communicate expressively — these are the twin channel markers the interpreter must watch in steering his course. He must let the poet have his way. He must find out what he did with meter and allow him his variations. If the poet can best achieve the rhythmic effect he wants by following a regular meter very closely, he will keep to that meter; if by departing from a regular meter, he will do that. Stanley Kunitz' lyric "Open the Gates," included in the suggested material at the end of Chapter 10, is an excellent example of how scansion works within a contemporary poem. Since it is so brief, we shall repeat it here with the lines numbered for convenient reference and the light and heavier stresses marked, ignoring for the moment the problem of relative strength of stress. The over-rides are italicized.

Open the Gates

Within | the *ci* | *ty* of | the *burn* | *ing* cloud,
Dragging | my life | behind | me in | a sack,
Naked | I prowl, | scourged by | the black
Temp*ta* | *tion* of | the blood | grown proud.

Here at | the *mon* | *ument* | *al* door,
Carved with the | curious | legend of | my youth,
I *brand* | *ish* the great | bone of | my death,
Beat once | therewith | and beat | no more.

The *hing* | *es* groan: | a rush | of forms
Shivers | my name, | wrenched out | of me.

From *Selected Poems* by Stanley Kunitz by permission of Little, Brown and Company-Atlantic Monthly Press. Copyright © 1958 by Stanley Kunitz.

11 I stand | on the *ter* | *rible thresh* | *old,* and | I see

12 The end | and the | beginning | in each *oth* | *er's* arms.

STANLEY KUNITZ

Admittedly, there is more than one way to group the light and heavier stresses into traditional feet, particularly in lines 6, 11, and 12. This is a problem which plagues a prosodist, but our concern is basically with the relative positioning of the stresses within the line. For the interpreter, the grouping of stresses into traditional feet is largely a convenient way of clarifying the pattern.

From our preliminary marking, then, we discover that the first two lines and the last two lines of "Open the Gates" have five feet, the others four. The four pentameter lines all have a pyrrhic foot, however, so that the stresses per line are consistently four, except for lines 8 and 10 where spondees add a fifth stress. Thus, despite the greater length of the opening and closing lines, unity of stress is carefully preserved. It is important to note that line 8 is clearly the fulcrum of the poem, and that line 10 contains the emotional climax.

Some interesting details immediately become apparent. For instance, line 6 contains eleven syllables and yet contains only four heavy stresses, as does the nine-syllable line which follows it. These two lines immediately preceding the fulcrum are the only ones with an uneven number of syllables.

There are two over-rides in the first line, brought about by "city" and "burning," which help to control the force of the opening image. There is also an over-ride in line 4, which closes the stanza, resulting from "temptation." The second stanza opens with a double over-ride, as the result of "monumental," and line 7 has a single over-ride in precisely the same position as the one in line 4 of the first stanza. The opening line of the third stanza again has an over-ride in the same position as lines 4 and 7. There are two almost precisely in the middle of line 11, and the over-ride of "other's" in the last line is in the same position as "burning" in the first line of the poem.

Six of the twelve lines open on a stress, and three of them then revert immediately to a rising meter. Line 3 has a sort of double reversal of rising and falling meter which the poet has divided neatly by his comma. This division of the line into two separate units is right for the heaviness of "Naked . . . prowl . . . scourged . . . black." Although line 4 opens on a light stress, it has a spondee balanced by a pyrrhic to bring the stanza to a pounding conclusion with "blóod grówn próud" and yet retains the four-stress line. In lines 8 and 10 there is no compensating pyrrhic. Line 10 (the third line from the end, incidentally) has a reversal in the first half which is identical to that in line 3, and the line is also divided in the middle by a comma.

An examination of the scansion of this brief poem assures us that there is more to meter than a "da-dá da-dá" alternation of light and heavier stresses. Stanley Kunitz has achieved remarkable variety-within-unity, which has always been a mark of the best English poetry. It must be remembered, however, that meter is only one of the many elements that go to make up a poem and that it can never be divorced from its harmony with content.

Robert Lowell's "The Dead in Europe" is a good modern example of extreme irregularity handled to give variety-in-unity. No one type of metrical foot is dominant, although there are a number of iambics as there usually are in English verse because of the basic rhythm of our syllabic stress. Of far greater interest, however, is the fact that with this slight preponderance of iambs twelve of the twenty-one lines begin with the heavy stress of trochees or spondees. Of the other nine, three are refrain lines. There is considerable irregularity in the opening stanza, with a marked clustering of stresses. The second line affords an interesting combination of iambs and trochees in

> Buried | tog*eth* | *er, un* | *mar*ried | men and | women;

and the center of the line is further altered by the two over-rides of "together" and "unmarried." The second stanza is more regular by far, lines 9 and 12 being clearly iambic except for the extra syllable of the feminine or light-stress "married." Within this regular "rising meter," however, there are important over-rides in

> In *Ma* | *ry*land, | where | *ver corp* | *ses* married

and in

> When *Sa* | *tan scat* | *ters* us | on *Ris* | *ing*-day . . .

Whether we characterize Robert Lowell's poem as conventional poetry, highly patterned free verse, or a combination of both is a matter of debate. In any case it varies widely from a regular pattern, but the complexity of that variation plays against our expectation to produce a high degree of shock and tension.

We have repeatedly stated that classifications are important to the interpreter only in so far as he can use them to understand and communicate his material more effectively. How, then, is he to use meter? He uses meter first to establish the norm or dominant pattern in regular poetry and then to follow the poet's lead in using or breaking away from that norm or pattern for the more effective communication of logical and emotional content. Meter is only one aspect of poetry. It must be blended with every other aspect to achieve a total effect. In short, the interpreter never forgets that his concern is the communication of meaning and emotion in poetry, not of meter: when the poet uses the pattern in order to intensify meaning or emotion, the interpreter will do the same; and when the poet departs from the pattern, the interpreter must understand why and use the irregularities in a way that carries out the poet's intent. Sometimes the break in the established pattern reinforces a particularly strong turn of emotion, a change of thought, of attitude, or of imagery, to bring structure and content into harmony. This the interpreter must recognize and reflect. The important thing, then, is not for him to say, "This is iambic — or trochaic — or anapestic — or dactylic," but rather for him to be aware of the *particular* metrical pattern, with all its variations, of the *particular* poem, and to reflect sensitively the unique mixture of pattern and irregularity which the poet has produced.

LINE LENGTH

Having established the unit, the metrical foot, by which the line of conventional poetry is measured, we are ready to consider the contribution of line length to the poem as a whole. A line of poetry, it must be remembered, is not just a line of print; it is a line of sound, established and constructed in its own particular way because the poet chose to do it that way for its contribution to both meaning and sound. It is important, then, to consider the discipline which the poet has imposed upon himself — and consequently upon the interpreter — by his use of specific line lengths.

A line is classified according to its prevalent foot as iambic, anapestic, trochaic, or dactylic; and according to the number of feet it contains as a monometer (one foot), dimeter (two), trimeter (three), tetrameter (four), pentameter (five), and so on. Thus, a line of five iambic feet is spoken of as an iambic pentameter.

A poet who writes conventional poetry consistently divides his stanzas into lines whose length is prescribed by or appropriate to the form of stanza he is using, and he combines this measure with a more or less regular arrangement of stresses, and perhaps with rhyme, to achieve his pattern of sound. Obviously, then, the line units must not be ignored. After all, the poet has put his content into units of a specific length, and the interpreter may assume that he had some reason for selecting the particular line length, or at least that, having selected it, he made some effort to fit his thought units — which will also become sound units when the poem is read aloud — into that pattern. We mentioned in the previous chapter the two-way effect of "water-Birds" in "Poem in October" in which "water-" is allowed to operate in the line which it ends and then to link into the following line. Often a poet breaks his thought into separate lines to point up either the last word of a line or the opening word of the next line. There are frequent examples of this use of line division in "The Dead in Europe."

Blank verse affords the greatest temptation to ignore the contribution of line length, partly because the line-ends do not have the added reinforcement of rhyme. Yet one of the accepted requisites of the best blank verse is that there be an opportunity to establish the line length when the poem is read aloud. The degree or value of the pause will vary, but the line length must be given special consideration, since it is one of the components of the rhythmic pattern. The extent to which the poet is able to conform to this discipline, while achieving variety within it, is one standard for measuring the excellence of his achievement. On the other hand, the interpreter must remember that verse is written in sentences as well as in lines, and that he should not emphasize lines at the expense of sentences and over-all sense. Not only would a drop of the voice or a distinct pause at the end of every line produce monotony; it would also distort the sense (since we are accustomed to consider a marked pause as signifying the completion of a thought) and cancel out one of the chief advantages of the blank-verse line — its approximation of the rhythms of conversational speech.

A writer of free verse often uses long sentences so that the flow of sound may be technically uninterrupted for an entire unit. One may certainly assume, then, that since a writer of free verse may arrange these sentences in lines as long or as short as he wishes, he had a reason for the line division which he used. Some critics contend that a line of free verse ends where it is convenient to take a breath; in other words, that it is written with the scope of a breath in mind. We may invert this statement and say that for the interpreter's practical purposes it is convenient to take a breath where the free verse line ends. It is logical, too, because the breath comes at a division of the thought, or at a point where the poet wishes to reinforce feeling or establish a relationship or progression.

There is an excellent example of such subtle progression in T. S. Eliot's poem, "Journey of the Magi" (page 431). In the last stanza we find the lines

All this was a long time ago, I remember,
And I would do it again, but set down
This set down
This: . . .

Such a line arrangement gives a far different effect when read aloud than if the words were arranged

All this was a long time ago,
I remember, and I would do it again,
But set down this, set down this:

It must be remembered that pauses vary greatly in duration. The line-end as a line-end (that is, apart from punctuation and sentence construction and over-all meaning) does not require a terminal pause of the kind used to end a sentence. Indeed, if the sentence or speech phrase runs over into the next line — a device technically known as "*enjambment*"[1] — there will be no *obvious* hesitation. Nevertheless, the line length imposes a sense of the boundaries or "shape" of the poem, to be marked by the eye in silent reading and carried over into the voice in oral interpretation, though not to the point where the physical pattern of the poem obtrudes into the listener's consciousness at the expense of meaning, sound, and feeling.

Thus the length, force, and terminal effect of the line-end pauses will vary, from virtually no pause at all or a slight drawing out or suspension of the terminal vowel sound, to a semi-stop or "breath pause," to a full pause at the end of the sentence or thought unit. The interpreter, accordingly, should be alert to make the most of these opportunities for variety in treating line lengths by his use of pauses and voice inflections at the line-ends. In a caution to poets, Ezra Pound once wrote: "Don't make each line stop dead at the end, and then begin every next line with a heave. Let the beginning of the next line catch the rise of the rhythm wave, unless you want a definite longish pause." This is advice which the interpreter, too, can apply to his own art.

Line length, especially in free verse, will be considered further in the following section on cadence. For the moment, however, it is sufficient that its importance be realized in a general way and that the interpreter give the poet credit for being able to fit his thoughts into whatever restrictions of structure he has set for himself. Obviously, the audience

[1] From the French *enjambement,* meaning "straddling."

should not be made aware of each line length, any more than of any other single aspect of the material. Each element makes its contribution to the whole and must be carefully blended with and properly related to all the other elements.

CADENCES

Earlier in this chapter we said that the sound pattern of a poem is made up of the interweaving of sound combinations which we know as tone color; the combination of light and heavier stresses, which is meter; and the flow of sounds in line lengths, in speech phrases within the lines, and in sentences, which we call cadences. A *cadence,* as we shall use the term, is a flow of sound. Pauses of varying duration and prominence break the flow of sound and thus establish a cadence pattern. A complete sentence is called a *primary cadence. Secondary cadences* include both line length and the speech phrases within the lines. Since the syllable is the smallest functional unit of sound, cadences are measured by the number of syllables they contain.

It is of course immediately obvious that the mere counting of syllables will not give us the total picture. Cadences must always be considered in relation to two other elements which exist within them. The first of these is number and arrangement of stresses, especially within lines. This consideration, of course, overlaps scansion in conventional poetry, and it is of considerable importance in free verse even though a clear, consistent metrical pattern cannot be established. The second element is partly a matter of tone color and has to do with the length or duration of the sounds within syllables. For instance, "easy" is clearly a two-syllable word, but within the opening line of "Fern Hill" (page 434), the first syllable is considerably longer than the "y." Thus there will be a duration pattern as well as a stress pattern at work within the syllables in secondary cadences.

There can be no question about the length of the primary cadences in a given poem. A primary cadence is the number of syllables in the sentence, from its beginning to its end as marked by terminal punctuation, which the poet has clearly indicated. The line lengths are also immediately evident. The lengths of the speech phrases, however, are somewhat more subjectively determined, since not all interpreters would pause at precisely the same places. Sometimes there can be little question about the need for a pause, and hence for the establishment of a cadence, as when the poet has inserted appropriate punctuation. Beyond these restrictions, however, the interpreter may make his own decisions about pauses, guided by the requirements of content (both logical and emotive), by the relationship of phrases and clauses to the terms they modify and to the complete sentence, and by opportunities for variety and contrast within unity and for the communication of imagery and tone color. His pauses, however slight, will break the line into speech phrases.

Meter is the basis of the rhythmic structure in traditional poetry, but a consideration of the cadences may open up unsuspected possibilities for variety and for harmony. Frequently a poet will achieve a large part of his rhythm by manipulating the cadences within a strict pattern of scansion. This is one of the important attributes of successful blank verse.

In "Open the Gates," which we have just scanned and found to be an interesting example of carefully controlled variation *from* traditional metrics, the cadences contribute to unity and harmony as well as to variety and contrast. Counting the syllables and major stresses within lines and speech phrases, and noting the sentence lengths, we discover the following pattern:

	Secondary Cadence				*Syllables per Primary Cadence*
LINE NO.	SYLLABLES PER LINE	STRESSES PER LINE	SYLLABLES PER SPEECH PHRASE	STRESSES PER SPEECH PHRASE	
1	10	4	10	4	36
2	10	4	7–3	3–1	
3	8	4	4–1–3	2–1–1	
4	8	4	3–3–2	1–1–2	
5	8	4	1–7	1–3	36
6	11	4	1–7–3	1–2–1	
7	9	4	9	4	
8	8	5	4–4	3–2	FULCRUM
9	8	4	4–4	2–2	16
10	8	5	4–4	2–3	CLIMAX
11	12	4	9–3	3–1	24
12	12	4	2–5–5	1–1–2	

The primary cadences usually tell us less by their specific length than by their relation to each other. Though they are of minor significance in this poem, they are obviously a unifying factor in the first two stanzas. Furthermore, the change from the established thirty-six syllables to sixteen syllables helps set off the climax. Primary cadences of much greater significance are found in Eliot's "Journey of the Magi" (page 431).

Turning to the secondary cadences, we notice that lines of identical length are used in pairs or threes, except for the two center lines. These two are neatly bracketed by eight-syllable lines, which serve as a steadying force throughout the middle of the poem. The stresses per line are a strong unifying force, with the added stress in lines 8 and 10 providing contrast to re-inforce the fulcrum and the climax.

The speech phrases provide needed variety within this unity. They too, however, tend to cluster, with three predominating near the opening, varied by units of seven, four, one, and two. The one and seven combination is apparent in line 5, and one and seven and three in line 6. Of particular interest is the even four and four division in lines 8, 9, and 10. This even division, which was mentioned in relation to scansion, helps reinforce the emotional weight of the content. Again, despite the opening two-syllable phrase, there is an even division in the five and five of the last line.

Further analysis will reveal even more subtle effects in this remarkable poem, but we have perhaps proved sufficiently that the line length and speech phrase cadences, and the stresses and elongated syllables within them, are important in the patterning of a successful poem, and that such analysis is basic in discovering the rhythmic elements of free verse. A careful analysis of the cadences and stresses within a poem will convince the interpreter that conventional poetry need not be read like a nursery rhyme, and that the discipline inherent in free verse will safeguard him from the danger of reading this type of poetry as if it were prose. Free verse, properly written, is probably the most demanding type of poetry to read aloud, and any interpreter who chooses it must be prepared to analyze its structure painstakingly. Such analysis will greatly increase his own artistic ability and his appreciation of the poet's artistic achievement.

Clearly, no audience could be expected to appreciate the subtlety of this rhythmic pattern for itself when the poem is read aloud. Indeed, it would be most unfortunate if attention were called to the pattern. Nevertheless, the interpreter must understand what the poet has done in order to communicate the total effect.

RHYME

Closely allied to the consideration of line length is another important aspect of poetic structure: the contribution made by rhyme and by other correspondences of sound in the terminal syllables of two or more words. By now it must be abundantly clear that poetry is not "something that rhymes"; that rhyme, unlike rhythm and cadence, is not an essential element of poetry, and that when it is used it is important because it reinforces rhythm, cadence, and pattern rather than because it is itself the stuff of poetry.

Although correspondences of sound strike the mind's ear in silent reading, they emerge for complete appreciation only when poetry is read aloud, and consequently, like so many other factors in poetry, are peculiarly dependent upon the interpreter for their effectiveness. Rhyme satisfies the ear because it is like a chime of music, and it pleases the mind by affording the delights of repetition and anticipation. But the purpose of rhyme is not to decorate but rather to bind the poem more closely together. For one thing, it unifies the pattern of sound. It reinforces the stanza pattern by establishing a recurring rhyme scheme. For another thing, it emphasizes the line lengths by creating an expectation of repeated sounds at regular intervals; thus rhyme reinforces content and rhythm by helping to establish cadences and thought divisions. On the other hand, skillful poets and interpreters know that rhyme, unwisely used, can shatter rather than intensify the unity of a poem, and they therefore exhibit great care and variety in handling it. An interpreter who bears down hard on every rhyme will make the physical shape of the poem block out everything else. He will give his audience the sensation of being taken for a ride on a rocking-horse instead of on a Pegasus.

Rhyme is the exact correspondence of both vowel and final consonant sounds; *assonance* is the correspondence of vowel sounds only, regardless of the final consonant sounds (*place-brave*). There are many kinds of rhyme. There are half-rhymes like *pavement-gravely* and *river-weather,* in which only half of a two-syllabled word rhymes; double rhymes in which the two final syllables correspond (*crying-flying, arrayed-afraid*); and even triple rhymes (*din afore-pinafore*), though these are usually too jingling and ingenious for anything but humorous verse. And there is approximate rhyme or rhyme by *consonance,* when the final consonant sounds are identical but the vowel sounds are not (*rock-luck*).

A rhyme scheme is indicated in prosodic analysis by letters standing for the terminal rhyme sounds, with *a* representing that of the first line and of every line corresponding to it, *b* the next terminal sound and its corresponding lines, and so on; thus, in this stanza from Shelley's "Adonais":

> Most musical of mourners, weep anew! *a*
> Not all to that bright station dared to climb; *b*
> And happier they their happiness who knew, *a*
> Whose tapers yet burn through that night of time *b*
> In which suns perished; others more sublime, *b*

Struck by the envious wrath of man or God, *c*
Have sunk, extinct in their refulgent prime; *b*
And some yet live, treading the thorny road, *c*
Which leads, through toil and hate, to Fame's serene abode. *c*

This gives a rhyme scheme designated by *ababbcbcc,* which is the characteristic pattern of the Spenserian stanza.

Rhyme is an essential part of all conventional poetry except, of course, blank verse. The rhyme of a poem has several important functions to fulfill. It can be a strong factor in the harmony between what is being said and the way it is expressed. It is of vital importance both in unifying the poem and in providing appropriate variety and contrast, while at the same time it enriches and intensifies tone color. It invariably tends to emphasize the line-ends and make the harmony between structure and content more apparent.

Rhyme can also cause an interpreter some trouble, however, if the poet has not used it skillfully. Even the best poets are sometimes unable to cope with too strict a pattern, and then the rhyme begins to manage the poet instead of the other way around. Sometimes the form the poet has adopted becomes too rigid for effective oral reading. When this is true, and the poem is nonetheless worthy of presentation on other counts, the interpreter must attempt to compensate for the weakness. He will be able to do this by close attention to every opportunity for variety in his use of pauses and inflection at the line-ends. Particular attention to tone color within the line can bring some of the interior words to a prominence which will challenge that of the rhyming words, and emphasis on imagery will add variety.

The interpreter ought first to be very sure, however, that the poem really does have structural imperfections for which he must compensate. It is always wise to give the poet the benefit of the doubt. He should be very certain that the repeated sounds do not serve an important purpose. If a poem is good on other counts, it is safer to assume, until a careful objective analysis disproves the assumption, that the poet was at least competent in his handling of the problem of rhyme.

The problem of rhyme does not, as we have said, arise in blank verse. But the very absence of it affects the interpreter: on the one hand, he is released from one of the disciplines which he often must consider in interpreting poetry; on the other, he is deprived of a significant means of communicating structural unity. For these reasons, the interpreter of blank verse should pay particular attention to other elements in the sound pattern, alliterations, harsh or liquid vowel and consonant combinations, the echoing of mood or sense in sound. He will find his surest guide to structural unity, however, in the prevalence of the iambic meter and in the consistent line length.

The writer of free verse may or may not use rhyme, as he sees fit. He may use it more or less consistently throughout an entire poem, although such a technique is not common. Ordinarily rhyme will appear, if at all, only within brief units of the poem. When the interpreter finds such units, he should examine carefully their contribution to the whole, for the poet will have used rhyme consciously, not as part of a conventional pattern to which he has committed himself, but out of a subjective decision on the need for rhyme at that point. The sounds of the rhymes and the length of the lines which contain them are of considerable importance in intensifying certain aspects of the content. T. S. Eliot makes very skillful use of rhyme in "The Love Song of J. Alfred Prufrock."

To draw upon another example with which we have become familiar, Robert Lowell uses an intricate and effective combination of rhymes in "The Dead in Europe." We mentioned earlier his use of feminine line-endings. A line-end is said to be *feminine* when the last syllable carries a light stress, as do the second and fourth rhymes of each stanza in this poem ("wómĕn" and "héavĕn," "márrĭed" and "búrĭed," and "trúmpĕt" and "púppĕt"). The other lines have *masculine* endings — that is, they end on a stress. Sometimes feminine endings are used to weaken the line-end, especially when they are combined with enjambment. Modern poets frequently use them, however, to reinforce a feeling of instability. They are effective psychologically because the added light stress denies our expectation. Certainly they help build tension as they work against the masculine endings in "The Dead in Europe."

In the first stanza, the first, third, and fifth lines correspond in terminal sounds and are masculine. The second and fourth lines have feminine endings, and only the unstressed syllables really agree, since the first syllable of "women" only approximates the first syllable of "heaven." Here the intentionally minor rhyme keeps the poem from becoming ponderous in its sound pattern. It is interesting to notice, though, that all the lines end in "n" until the last two. The last two lines do not rhyme at all, though "fire" and the entire last line are repeated at the end of every stanza and thus set up a pattern of their own. Moreover, the "r" is common to both "fire" and "curse." The numerous repetitions of the rhyme words within adjacent lines and the use of "buried" with "married" and "unmarried," as well as the near identity with "Mary," deserve attention.

Modern writers are most sophisticated in their use of rhymes and near-rhymes. Again, Stanley Kunitz provides us with an excellent example in "Open the Gates." On reading it aloud, we find rhyme sounds woven intricately throughout all the lines of the poem. (Although it is not technically a rhyme, we cannot resist pointing out the pun of "grown" and "groan.") The terminal rhymes are identical and therefore satisfying, except for the paradoxical rhyme of "youth" and "death" immediately preceding the fulcrum, and the slight variance between "forms" and "arms" in the last stanza. Moreover, their identity is emphasized because all but three of the lines are wholly or partially end-stopped by punctuation. Of the three enjambment lines the first is the inescapable, harsh rhyme of "black" and "sack." The other two are found in the last stanza, one softening "forms," the other softening "see."

Another extremely subtle manipulation of rhyme sounds, which will probably escape an audience but delight an interpreter, may or may not have been accidental, although in a poem so meticulously constructed we can take nothing for granted. This is re-patterning of the same sounds in successive rhymes, as in *"proud"* and *"door"* and *"more"* and *"forms."* Also, the "d" of "cloud" and "proud" introduces "door" and "death" in the second stanza; the "m" of "more" carries over into "forms," "me," and "arms"; and the "s" introduces the fourth rhyme word "see."

Careful and detailed analysis of the structure of a poem will provide the interpreter with a very sure basis for the use of his own techniques. Poetry is an art, but it is also a kind of science, and the intricacies of a successful poem are amazing.

Having discovered the aspects of structure which the poet has used, and so far as possible his purpose in using them, the interpreter must carefully relate them to content. He must then evaluate both content and structure in the light of those factors which serve as touchstones for the worth of a piece of literature: the extrinsic factors of universality, individuality, and suggestion; the intrinsic factors of unity and harmony, variety and contrast, balance and proportion, and rhythm. Finally, in oral presentation the interpreter must remember that no single aspect of structure is to be exhibited for its own sake, but must be skillfully blended with every other aspect to communicate the total effect which the poet intended.

SELECTIONS FOR ANALYSIS AND ORAL INTERPRETATION

THIS VILLANELLE WAS referred to frequently within the chapter. Examine it carefully for the patterning of the over-rides. Let the stanzaic structure help keep the cadences from becoming abrupt. Make full use of the remarkable tone color, especially assonance.

For Roethke all of life was a waking toward the sleep of death. He reminds one of Thomas in his affirmation of life.

"The Waking," copyright 1953 by Theodore Roethke, from *Words for the Wind* by Theodore Roethke. Reprinted by permission of Doubleday & Company, Inc.

The Waking

I wake to sleep, and take my waking slow.
I feel my fate in what I cannot fear.
I learn by going where I have to go.

We think by feeling. What is there to know?
I hear my being dance from ear to ear.
I wake to sleep, and take my waking slow.

Of those so close beside me, which are you?
God bless the Ground! I shall walk softly there,
And learn by going where I have to go.

Light takes the Tree; but who can tell us how?
The lowly worm climbs up a winding stair;
I wake to sleep, and take my waking slow.

Great Nature has another thing to do
To you and me; so take the lively air,
And, lovely, learn by going where to go.

This shaking keeps me steady. I should know.
What falls away is always. And is near.
I wake to sleep, and take my waking slow.
I learn by going where I have to go.

THEODORE ROETHKE

THE STANZAIC STRUCTURE is interesting here. There is also a good deal of ellipsis. Be sure you understand the seemingly simple allusions as they are used to reflect attitude. The line lengths as units of thought are particularly important.

As I Would Wish You Birds

Today — because I must not lie to you —
there are no birds but such as I wish
for. There is only my wish to wish you
birds. Catbirds with spatula tails up
jaunty. Jays, gawky as dressed-up toughs.
Humming birds, their toy engines going.
Turkeys with Savonarola heads. Bitchy
Peacocks. The rabble of Hens in their
stinking harems — these three (and

From *In Fact* by John Ciardi. Reprinted by permission of the Rutgers University Press.

Ostriches and Dodos) a sadness to think
about. But then Gulls — ultimate bird
everywhere everything pure wing and wind
are, there over every strut, flutter, cheep,
coo. At Dover over the pigeon-cliffs.
At Boston over the sparrows. Off tropics
where the lyre-tails and the green-
iridescent heads flash. And gone again.

You never see Gulls in aviaries. Gulls are
distance. Who can put distance in a cage?

Today — and I could never lie to you —
there is no distance equal to what I wish
for. There is only my wish to wish you
a distance full of birds, a thronged air
lifting above us far, lifting us, the sun
bursting in cloud chambers, a choir there
pouring light years of song, its wings
flashing. See this with me. Close your eyes
and see what air can do with more birds in it
than anything but imagination can put there.
There are not enough birds in the eyes we
open. There are too many hens, turkeys, and
that peacock seen always on someone else's
lawn, the air above it wasted unused, songless.
Birds cannot be seen in fact. Not enough
of them at once, not now nor any day. But think
with me what might be, but close your eyes and see.

JOHN CIARDI

IN THIS POEM the line length cadences are not only important for structural rhythm, but provide clues to emotional content and connotations. The first five lines are quoted from a famous sermon. Notice how skillfully Eliot moves into his own comment. The quote must not be set off too obviously from the rest of the stanza. Eliot uses capital letters for spiritual birth and death as opposed to physical birth and death.

Journey of the Magi

"A cold coming we had of it,
Just the worst time of the year
For a journey, and such a long journey:
The ways deep and the weather sharp,

From *Collected Poems 1909–1962* by T. S. Eliot. Copyright, 1936, by Harcourt, Brace & World, Inc.; © 1963, 1964, by T. S. Eliot. Reprinted by permission of the publishers. Also reprinted by permission of Faber and Faber, Ltd.

The very dead of winter."
And the camels galled, sore-footed, refractory,
Lying down in the melting snow.
There were times we regretted
The summer palaces on slopes, the terraces,
And the silken girls bringing sherbet.
Then the camel men cursing and grumbling
And running away, and wanting their liquor and women,
And the night-fires going out, and the lack of shelters,
And the cities hostile and the towns unfriendly
And the villages dirty and charging high prices:
A hard time we had of it.
At the end we preferred to travel all night,
Sleeping in snatches,
With the voices singing in our ears, saying
That this was all folly.

Then at dawn we came down to a temperate valley,
Wet, below the snow line, smelling of vegetation;
With a running stream and a water-mill beating the darkness,
And three trees on a low sky,
And an old white horse galloped away in the meadow.
Then we came to a tavern with vine-leaves over the lintel,
Six hands at an open door dicing for pieces of silver,
And feet kicking the empty wine-skins.
But there was no information, and so we continued
And arrived at evening, not a moment too soon
Finding the place; it was (you may say) satisfactory.

All this was a long time ago, I remember,
And I would do it again, but set down
This set down
This: were we led all that way for
Birth or Death? There was a Birth, certainly,
We had evidence and no doubt. I had seen birth and death,
But had thought they were different; this Birth was
Hard and bitter agony for us, like Death, our death.
We returned to our places, these Kingdoms,
But no longer at ease here, in the old dispensation,
With an alien people clutching their gods.
I should be glad of another death.

T. S. Eliot

Much of the wit in this poem is underscored by the rhymes and feminine line-ends. Use the structure confidently.

Go and Catch a Falling Star

Go and catch a falling star,
  Get with child a mandrake root,
Tell me where all past years are,
  Or who cleft the devil's foot,
Teach me to hear mermaids singing,
Or to keep off envy's stinging,
    And find
    What wind
Serves to advance an honest mind.

If thou beest born to strange sights,
  Things invisible to see,
Ride ten thousand days and nights,
  Till age snow white hairs on thee,
Thou, when thou return'st, wilt tell me
All strange wonders that befell thee,
    And swear
    No where
Lives a woman true, and fair.

If thou find'st one, let me know,
  Such a pilgrimage were sweet;
Yet do not, I would not go,
  Though at next door we might meet;
Though she were true when you met her,
And last till you write your letter,
    Yet she
    Will be
False, ere I come, to two or three.

John Donne

Dylan Thomas was a native of Wales, and the melody and flavor of his country are in his poems. This example of memories of rural childhood demands a great deal of the interpreter. "Fern Hill" must be approached first of all from the standpoint of sheer pleasure of sound and connotation. You must allow this poem to work on you before you begin to work on it. Careful attention must be given to the intricacies of structure and word order and to the unexpected combinations of words. Make full use of the rich tone color and imagery. Observe the line lengths meticulously.

"Fern Hill," beginning on p. 434, is from *The Collected Poems of Dylan Thomas*. Copyright 1953 by Dylan Thomas, © 1957 by New Directions. Reprinted by permission of New Directions, Publishers. Also reprinted by permission of J. M. Dent & Sons, Ltd. and The Dylan Thomas Estate.

Fern Hill

Now as I was young and easy under the apple boughs
About the lilting house and happy as the grass was green,
    The night above the dingle starry,
        Time let me hail and climb
    Golden in the heydays of his eyes,
And honoured among wagons I was prince of the apple towns
And once below a time I lordly had the trees and leaves
        Trail with daisies and barley
    Down the rivers of the windfall light.

And as I was green and carefree, famous among the barns
About the happy yard and singing as the farm was home,
    In the sun that is young once only,
        Time let me play and be
    Golden in the mercy of his means,
And green and golden I was huntsman and herdsman, the calves
Sang to my horn, the foxes on the hills barked clear and cold,
        And the sabbath rang slowly
    In the pebbles of the holy streams.

All the sun long it was running, it was lovely, the hay-
Fields high as the house, the tunes from the chimneys, it was air
    And playing, lovely and watery
        And fire green as grass.
    And nightly under the simple stars
As I rode to sleep the owls were bearing the farm away,
All the moon long I heard, blessed among stables, the nightjars
    Flying with the ricks, and the horses
        Flashing into the dark.

And then to awake, and the farm, like a wanderer white
With the dew, come back, the cock on his shoulder: it was all
    Shining, it was Adam and maiden,
        The sky gathered again
    And the sun grew round that very day.
So it must have been after the birth of the simple light
In the first, spinning place, the spellbound horses walking warm
    Out of the whinnying green stable
        On to the fields of praise.

And honoured among foxes and pheasants by the gay house
Under the new made clouds and happy as the heart was long,
    In the sun born over and over,
        I ran my heedless ways,
    My wishes raced through the house-high hay
And nothing I cared, at my sky blue trades, that time allows

In all his tuneful turning so few and such morning songs
Before the children green and golden
Follow him out of grace,

Nothing I cared, in the lamb white days, that time would take me
Up to the swallow thronged loft by the shadow of my hand,
In the moon that is always rising,
Nor that riding to sleep
I should hear him fly with the high fields
And wake to the farm forever fled from the childless land.
Oh as I was young and easy in the mercy of his means,
Time held me green and dying
Though I sang in my chains like the sea.

DYLAN THOMAS

TRUST THIS POET completely and use his line-lengths exactly as he has put them down. He uses capital letters for a shade of emphasis. Make the most of the kinesthetic imagery implied. Keep the thought suspended across the parentheses, which make a sort of "sub poem" in themselves.

III

Spring is like a perhaps hand
(which comes carefully
out of Nowhere)arranging
a window,into which people look(while
people stare
arranging and changing placing
carefully there a strange
thing and a known thing here)and

changing everything carefully

spring is like a perhaps
Hand in a window
(carefully to
and fro moving New and
Old things,while
people stare carefully
moving a perhaps
fraction of flower here placing
an inch of air there)and

without breaking anything.

E. E. CUMMINGS

Copyright, 1925, by E. E. Cummings. Reprinted from his volume *Poems 1923–1954* by permission of Harcourt, Brace & World, Inc.

SPEECH PHRASE CADENCES provide much of the basic rhythm in this selection.

from *Song of Myself*

A child said *What is the grass?* fetching it to me with full hands,
How could I answer the child? I do not know what it is any more than he.

I guess it must be the flag of my disposition, out of hopeful green stuff woven.

Or I guess it is the handkerchief of the Lord,
A scented gift and remembrancer designedly dropt,
Bearing the owner's name some way in the corners, that we may see and remark, and say *Whose?*

Or I guess the grass is itself a child, the produced babe of the vegetation.

Or I guess it is a uniform hieroglyphic,
And it means, Sprouting alike in broad zones and narrow zones,
Growing among black folks as among white,
Kanuck, Tuckahoe, Congressman, Cuff, I give them the same, I receive them the same.

And now it seems to me the beautiful uncut hair of graves.

Tenderly will I use you curling grass,
It may be you transpire from the breasts of young men,
It may be if I had known them I would have loved them,
It may be you are from old people, or from some offspring taken soon out of their mothers' laps,
And here you are the mothers' laps.

This grass is very dark to be from the white heads of old mothers,
Darker than the colorless beards of old men,
Dark to come from under the faint red roofs of mouths.

O I perceive after all so many uttering tongues,
And I perceive that they do not come from the roofs of mouths for nothing.

I wish I could translate the hints about the dead young men and women,
And the hints about old men and mothers, and the offspring taken soon out of their laps.

What do you think has become of the young and old men?
And what do you think has become of the women and children?

They are alive and well somewhere,
The smallest sprout shows there is really no death,
And if ever there was it led forward life, and does not wait at the end to arrest it,
And ceas'd the moment life appear'd.

All goes onward and outward, nothing collapses,
And to die is different from what any one supposed, and luckier.

WALT WHITMAN

PARODIES MUST BE read with almost exaggerated seriousness. The fun lies in the awareness on the part of the interpreter, the poet, and the audience of the characteristic style of the one being parodied.

Jack and Jill

(As Walt Whitman Might Have Written It)

I celebrate the personality of Jack!
I love his dirty hands, his tangled hair, his locomotion blundering.
Each wart upon his hands I sing,
Paeans I chant to his hulking shoulder blades.
Also Jill!
Her I celebrate.
I, Walt, of unbridled thought and tongue,
Whoop her up!
What's the matter with Jill!
Oh, she's all right!
Who's all right?
Jill.
Her golden hair, her sun-struck face, her hard and reddened hands;
So, too, her feet, hefty, shambling.
I see them in the evening, when the sun empurples the horizon, and through the darkening forest aisles are heard the sounds of myriad creatures of the night.
I see them climb the steep ascent in quest of water for their mother.
Oh, speaking of her, I could celebrate the old lady if I had time.
She is simply immense!

But Jack and Jill are walking up the hill.
(I didn't mean that rhyme.)
I must watch them.
I love to watch their walk,
And wonder as I watch;
He, stoop-shouldered, clumsy, hide-bound,
Yet lusty,
Bearing his share of the 1-lb. bucket as though it were a paperweight.

She, erect, standing, her head uplifting,
Holding, but bearing not the bucket.
They have reached the spring.
They have filled the bucket.
Have you heard the "Old Oaken Bucket"?
I will sing it: —

Of what countless patches is the bed-quilt of life composed!
Here is a piece of lace. A babe is born.
The father is happy, the mother is happy.
Next black crêpe. The beldame "shuffles off this mortal coil."
Now brocaded satin with orange blossoms,
Mendelssohn's "Wedding March," an old shoe missile,
A broken carriage window, the bride in the Bellevue sleeping.
Here's a large piece of black cloth!
"Have you any last words to say?"
"No."
"Sheriff, do your work!"
Thus it is: from "grave to gay, from lively to severe."

I mourn the downfall of my Jack and Jill.
I see them descending, obstacles not heeding.
I see them pitching headlong, the water from the pail outpouring, a noise
from the leathern lungs out-belching.
The shadows of the night descend on Jack, recumbent, bellowing, his pate
with gore besmeared.
I love his cowardice, because it is an attribute, just like
Job's patience or Solomon's wisdom, and I love attributes.
Whoop!!!

CHARLES BATTELL LOOMIS

NO MODERN POET has more fun with rhyme than Ogden Nash. Use it fully. His humor is sophisticated and carries best when the interpreter undercuts it, as the poet himself has done.

A Stitch Too Late Is My Fate

There are some people of whom I would certainly like to be one,
Who are the people who get things done.
They never forget to send their evening shirts to the laundry and then
when they need them can't find anything but a lot of shirts without
any starch,
And they always file their income tax return by the fourteenth of March.

From *Verses From 1929 On* by Ogden Nash, by permission of Little, Brown and Company. Copyright 1936 by Ogden Nash.

They balance their checkbooks every month and their figures always
agree with the bank's,
And they are prompt in writing letters of condolence or thanks.
They never leave anything to chance,
But always make reservations in advance.
When they get out of bed they never neglect to don slippers so they never
pick up athlete's foot or a cold or a splinter,
And they hang their clothes up on hangers every night and put their
winter clothes away every summer and their summer clothes away
every winter.
Before spending any money they insist on getting an estimate or a sample,
And if they lose anything from a shoelace to a diamond ring it is covered
by insurance more than ample.
They have budgets and what is more they live inside of them,
Even though it means eating things made by recipes clipped from the
Sunday paper that you'd think they would have died of them.
They serve on committees
And improve their cities.
They are modern knight errants
Who remember their godchildren's birthdays and the anniversaries of
their godchildren's parents,
And in cold weather they remember the birds and supply them with
sunflower seed and suet,
And whatever they decide to do, whether it's to save twenty-five per cent
of their salary or learn Italian or write a musical comedy or touch
their toes a hundred times every morning before breakfast, why they
go ahead and do it.
People who get things done lead contented lives, or at least I guess so,
And I certainly wish that either I were more like them or they were
less so.

OGDEN NASH

THE FOLLOWING TWO sonnets contain some difficulties in the denotation and connotation of words and in the involved sentence structure. Moreover, a sonnet has certain requisites of organization of content. Variety-in-unity is apparent in the structure.

Sonnet XXIX

When, in disgrace with Fortune and men's eyes,
I all alone beweep my outcast state,
And trouble deaf Heaven with my bootless cries,
And look upon myself and curse my fate,
Wishing me like to one more rich in hope,
Featured like him, like him with friends possessed,
Desiring this man's art, and that man's scope,
With what I most enjoy contented least;

Yet in these thoughts myself almost despising,
Haply I think on thee; and then my state,
Like to the lark at break of day arising
From sullen earth, sings hymns at heaven's gate;
  For thy sweet love remembered such wealth brings
  That then I scorn to change my state with kings.

WILLIAM SHAKESPEARE

Sonnet XVIII

Shall I compare thee to a summer's day?
Thou art more lovely and more temperate:
Rough winds do shake the darling buds of May,
And summer's lease hath all too short a date:
Sometime too hot the eye of heaven shines,
And often is his gold complexion dimm'd;
And every fair from fair sometime declines,
By chance, or nature's changing course untrimm'd;
But thy eternal summer shall not fade,
Nor lose possession of that fair thou ow'st,
Nor shall death brag thou wander'st in his shade,
When in eternal lines to time thou grow'st;
  So long as man can breathe, or eyes can see,
  So long lives this, and this gives life to thee.

WILLIAM SHAKESPEARE

THE THREE SECTIONS of this modern elegy vary in their structure rather markedly. Use everything the poet has given you to insure the proper changes of tone.

In Memory of W. B. Yeats

(d. Jan. 1939)

1

He disappeared in the dead of winter:
The brooks were frozen, the airports almost deserted,
And snow disfigured the public statues;
The mercury sank in the mouth of the dying day.
O all the instruments agree
The day of his death was a dark cold day.

Far from his illness
The wolves ran on through the evergreen forests,

Copyright 1940 by W. H. Auden. Reprinted from *The Collected Poetry of W. H. Auden,* by permission of Random House, Inc. Also reprinted by permission of Faber and Faber, Ltd.

The peasant river was untempted by the fashionable quays;
By mourning tongues
The death of the poet was kept from his poems.

But for him it was his last afternoon as himself,
An afternoon of nurses and rumours;
The provinces of his body revolted,
The squares of his mind were empty,
Silence invaded the suburbs,
The current of his feeling failed: he became his admirers.

Now he is scattered among a hundred cities
And wholly given over to unfamiliar affections;
To find his happiness in another kind of wood
And be punished under a foreign code of conscience.
The words of a dead man
Are modified in the guts of the living.

But in the importance and noise of tomorrow
When the brokers are roaring like beasts on the floor of the Bourse,
And the poor have the sufferings to which they are fairly accustomed,
And each in the cell of himself is almost convinced of his freedom;
A few thousand will think of this day
As one thinks of a day when one did something slightly unusual.
O all the instruments agree
The day of his death was a dark cold day.

2

You were silly like us: your gift survived it all;
The parish of rich women, physical decay,
Yourself; mad Ireland hurt you into poetry.
Now Ireland has her madness and her weather still,
For poetry makes nothing happen: it survives
In the valley of its saying where executives
Would never want to tamper; it flows south
From ranches of isolation and the busy griefs,
Raw towns that we believe and die in; it survives,
A way of happening, a mouth.

3

Earth, receive an honoured guest;
William Yeats is laid to rest:
Let the Irish vessel lie
Emptied of its poetry.

Time that is intolerant
Of the brave and innocent,

And indifferent in a week
To a beautiful physique,

Worships language and forgives
Everyone by whom it lives;
Pardons cowardice, conceit,
Lays its honours at their feet.

Time that with this strange excuse
Pardoned Kipling and his views,
And will pardon Paul Claudel,
Pardons him for writing well.

In the nightmare of the dark
All the dogs of Europe bark,
And the living nations wait,
Each sequestered in its hate;

Intellectual disgrace
Stares from every human face,
And the seas of pity lie
Locked and frozen in each eye.

Follow, poet, follow right
To the bottom of the night,
With your unconstraining voice
Still persuade us to rejoice;

With the farming of a verse
Make a vineyard of the curse,
Sing of human unsuccess
In a rapture of distress;

In the deserts of the heart
Let the healing fountain start,
In the prison of his days
Teach the free man how to praise.

W. H. Auden

Hyperbole in the selection of allusions sets the cavalier tone of this love poem. The rhymes will help as well, especially in the closing couplet.

Since There's No Help

Since there's no help, come let us kiss and part.
Nay, I have done; you get no more of me,
And I am glad, yea, glad with all my heart,
That thus so cleanly I myself can free;

Shake hands for ever, cancel all our vows,
And when we meet at any time again,
Be it not seen in either of our brows
That we one jot of former love retain.
Now at the last gasp of Love's latest breath,
When, his pulse failing, Passion speechless lies,
When Faith is kneeling by his bed of death,
And Innocence is closing up his eyes,
Now if thou wouldst, when all have given him over,
From death to life thou mightst him yet recover.

MICHAEL DRAYTON

YOU WILL NEED to know the story of Orestes to understand this poem fully. The speech phrases and the primary cadences are very important in suggesting and controlling pace and emotional impact. The kinetic and kinesthetic imagery is basic.

XVI

The name — Orestes

Again, again into the track, once more into the track!
How many turns, how many laps of blood, how many black
Circles of faces watching: the people watching me
Who watched me when, upright in the chariot,
I raised my hand, brilliant, and they roared applause.

The froth of horses beats upon my flesh. When will the horses
Weary? The axle shrieks, the axle glows. When will the axle
Seize up in flame? When will the rein break?
When will the whole hooves tread
Full on the ground, on the soft grass, among
The poppies where in spring you picked a daisy?

They were lovely, your eyes. You did not know where to look with them
Nor did I know where to look, I, without a country,
I who struggle on this spot — how many turns and laps! —
And I feel my knees failing me above the axle,
Above the wheels, above the savage track.
The knees fail easily when the gods will have it so.
No one is able to escape; no strength will do it, you cannot
Escape the sea which cradled you, for which you turn and search
In this moment of contest, among the breathing of horses,

From *Poems: George Seferis* by George Seferis, by permission of Little, Brown and Company-Atlantic Monthly Press. English translation by Rex Warner, copyright © 1960. Also reprinted by permission of The Bodley Head, Ltd.

With the reeds that used to sing in autumn to a Lydian mode,
The sea that you cannot find again, run as you may,
Turn as you may, lap after lap, in front of the black
Eumenides who are bored and cannot forgive.

GEORGE SEFERIS

✱ Bibliography

Bateson, F. W. *English Poetry and the English Language.* New York: Russell and Russell, 1961.

A careful examination of a wide variety of poetic devices.

Bloom, Edward A., Charles H. Philbrick, and Elmer M. Blistein. *The Order of Poetry: An Introduction.* New York: The Odyssey Press, Inc., 1961.

A clear and direct approach to the critical analysis of poetry with representative selections used for illustrations. Contains a chapter on versification and a glossary of critical terms.

Bodkin, Maud. *Archetypal Patterns in Poetry.* New York: Oxford University Press, 1963.

Poetry analyzed in terms of Jung's theory of the collective unconscious. Psychological studies in imagination.

Brooks, Cleanth. *The Well Wrought Urn.* New York: Harcourt, Brace and World, Inc., 1947.

Based on the theory of poetry as dramatic discourse and on the organic relationship of art and meaning in poetry. Essays on specific poems.

Brooks, Cleanth, and Robert Penn Warren. *Understanding Poetry.* New York: Holt, Rinehart and Winston, Inc., 1950.

A good introductory book. An anthology with critical discussions and commentaries on representative poems.

Cane, Melville. *Making a Poem: An Inquiry into the Creative Process.* New York: Harcourt, Brace and World, Inc., 1962. Harvest Book edition, HB44.

An informal, readable book on how a poem is written.

Ciardi, John. *How Does a Poem Mean?* Boston: Houghton Mifflin Company, 1959.

An excellent discussion of reading poetry, with particularly good examples. Covers many aspects of content and structure.

Ciardi, John (ed.). *Mid-Century American Poets.* New York: Twayne Publishers, 1950.

A collection of poems and essays by fifteen contemporary American poets expressing their attitudes toward writing poetry. Particular attention to the need to read poetry orally.

Crane, R. S. *The Languages of Criticism and the Structure of Poetry.* Toronto: University of Toronto Press, 1953. Alexander Lecture Series.

A highly scholarly discussion of the complexities of poetic criticism.

Daiches, David. *Poetry and the Modern World: A Study of Poetry in English Between 1900 and 1939.* Chicago: The University of Chicago Press, 1940.

Specific poets examined with emphasis on the phenomenon of culture and the effect on their poetry. The range is from the Victorians to Spender and Auden.

Davie, Donald. *Articulate Energy: An Enquiry into the Syntax of English Poetry.* London: Routledge and Kegan Paul, 1955.

A somewhat specialized but stimulating examination of syntactical manipulations in a variety of poems.

Deutsch, Babette. *Poetry Handbook: A Dictionary of Terms.* New York: Funk and Wagnalls, 1957.

A complete, concise sourcebook of poetic terminology.

Dolman, John, Jr. *The Art of Reading Aloud.* New York: Harper and Row, 1956.

Devoted exclusively to the problems of reading poetry aloud. Somewhat uneven but of particular interest to the interpreter.

Drew, Elizabeth. *Discovering Poetry.* New York: W. W. Norton and Company, Inc., 1962. The Norton Library Series, N-110.

Readable and sound introductory book. Contains an appendix of terms and a bibliography of principal English and American poets.

Drew, Elizabeth, and George Connor. *Discovering Modern Poetry.* New York: Holt, Rinehart and Winston, Inc., 1961.

A thematic approach to an excellent selection of modern poems. The second section includes additional poems for study. The third section is a compilation of significant comments of poets on the nature and function of poetry.

Eliot, T. S. *On Poetry and Poets.* New Edition. New York: Farrar, Straus and Company, 1957.

Essays on poetry, poetic drama, and poetic criticism with chapters on specific poets from Virgil to Yeats.

Empson, William. *Seven Types of Ambiguity.* Third Edition. London: Chatto and Windus, Ltd., 1956.

A scholarly consideration of imaginative language as it functions to convey several meanings simultaneously.

Frye, Northrop. *The Well-Tempered Critic.* Bloomington, Indiana: Indiana University Press, 1963.

A refreshing re-evaluation of some traditional and contemporary modes of criticism.

Hemphill, George (ed.). *Discussions of Poetry: Rhythm and Sound.* Boston: D. C. Heath and Company, 1961.

A collection of essays on prosody of the last four centuries.

Ostroff, Anthony (ed.). *The Contemporary Poet as Artist and Critic: Eight Symposia.* Boston and Toronto: Little, Brown and Company, 1964.

A collection of twenty-four essays on eight contemporary poems and the responses of the poets themselves. The poets include Richard Wilbur, Theodore Roethke, Stanley Kunitz, Robert Lowell, John Crowe Ransom, Richard Eberhart, W. H. Auden, and Karl Shapiro.

Sanders, Gerald. *A Poetry Primer.* New York: Farrar, Straus and Company, 1935.

Brief, explicit definitions and examples of the nature and forms of poetry and the elements of poetic structure.

Sebeok, Thomas A. (ed.). *Style in Language.* New York: John Wiley and Sons, Inc., 1960.

Numerous essays dealing with linguistic and psychological approaches to literature with special attention to modern theories of prosody.

Shapiro, Karl. *A Bibliography of Modern Prosody.* Baltimore: The Johns Hopkins Press, 1948.

A valuable sourcebook for detailed study of critical and practical discussions of poetic techniques.

Spender, Stephen. *The Making of a Poem.* New York: W. W. Norton and Company, Inc., 1962.

A collection of readable and penetrating essays on various aspects of the contemporary literary situation with a comparative look at the Romantics. Also includes discussions of novels and autobiographies.

Stauffer, Donald A. *The Nature of Poetry.* New York: W. W. Norton and Company, Inc., 1962. The Norton Library Series, N-167.

Sound introductory study of poetry and poetic language.

Thompson, John. *The Founding of English Metre.* New York: Columbia University Press, 1961.

An historical survey of the basic meters and variations in English poetry.

Wimsatt, W. K., Jr. *The Verbal Icon: Studies in the Meaning of Poetry.* New York: Farrar, Straus and Company, 1954. Noonday Press edition, N-123, 1958.

One of the classics of modern criticism with particular attention to some of the fallacies of poetic criticism.

Wright, George T. *The Poet in the Poem: The Personae of Eliot, Yeats and Pound.* Berkeley and Los Angeles: University of California Press, 1960.

Excellent discussion of Eliot, Yeats, and Pound, plus a sound, provocative analysis of poetry in general.

In addition to the books listed above, you will find much to interest you in the letters, notebooks, and critical essays of a large number of poets both pre-modern and contemporary.

APPENDIX

A Brief History of Theories of Interpretation

From earliest times the spoken word has attracted audiences and influenced their thinking. The history of public speaking has been traced by numerous authorities, who have shown that its thread is unbroken from the fourth century B.C. down to the present. The theater enjoys a similarly clear history. Oral interpretation, too, even though its genesis and growth as a distinct art may be less easy to define, has a long lineage of its own.

The art of interpretation probably had its beginnings with the rhapsodies of ancient Greece, when poets gathered to read their works in public competition. However, the emergence of interpretation as a field of study in its own right was delayed because it was long confused with oratory and rhetoric. Some of the works dealing in detail with the history of interpretation are listed in the general bibliography at the end of this appendix. It will be sufficient here to sketch the outlines very lightly, in order to note the development of certain theories and to see where we now stand in relation to those theories.

The colleges of America were already giving some attention to the oral interpretation of literature by the beginning of the nineteenth century. As early as 1806, when John Quincy Adams assumed the chair of Rhetoric and Oratory, Harvard, which from its founding had carried on the medieval tradition of "declamations" and "disputations," was offering a few courses that included the interpretative approach to literary materials. As the century progressed, more and more colleges offered specific courses in spoken English — courses that carried such titles as "Declamation and Composition," "Declamation," "Elements of Orthoëpy and Elocution," or simply "Elocution."

The word *elocutio* (Latin, *eloqui, elocutus* = speak out) originally referred to effective literary or oratorical style. Between 1650 and 1750, however, a shift in connotation took place, and the term *elocution* began to be applied to the manner of oral delivery rather than to the written style of a composition. *Pronuntiatio,* which had meant primarily the management of voice and body, gradually took on our modern meaning of pronunciation as the correct phonation of individual words. By 1750 then, these shifts in meaning had taken place, and the term *elocution* had come to connote a considerable degree of emphasis on delivery. By this time, also, a renewed interest in reading aloud and in oratory had developed, especially in England where an important group of writer-speakers known as the English Elocutionists had come into being. Outstanding among them were Thomas Sheridan (1719–1788) and John Walker (1732–1807), whose books and lectures had great bearing on the development in America of what we now call interpretation.

Thomas Sheridan, father of the famous dramatist Richard Brinsley Sheridan and himself an actor, published his *Course of Lectures on Elocution* in 1763. This book came out strongly against artificialities and laid much stress on the method of natural conversation in the oral presentation of literature. Sheridan thus became known as the leader of the "natural school." His thesis was that elocution should follow the laws of nature. He held that body and voice were natural phenomena and were thus subject to the laws of nature. He pointed out that nature gave to the passions and emotions certain tones, looks, and gestures which are perceived through the ear and the eye. Therefore, he contended, the elocutionist should reproduce these tones, looks, and gestures as nearly as possible in presenting literature orally to an audience. Basically, this theory was sound.

As often happens in the application of a theory, however, Sheridan became caught up in his efforts to be specific, and he began to evolve a system of markings and cues for the discovery and reproduction of these "natural" tones and gestures. Hence, by the end of his career he had become the exponent of a method which, judged by modern standards, was much more mechanical than natural. Nevertheless, the term "natural school" has persisted to the present day.

The other famous English Elocutionist, John Walker, published his *Elements of Elocution* almost twenty years later, in 1781. He, too, professed to take his cues from nature. However, he could not (or at least did not) resist the urge to set down specific rules and markings for the slightest variations of vocal tempo, inflection, and force, and for the various aspects of gesture. These markings caught the public fancy because they were more concrete than anything that had been offered before. (It is always so much easier to be told exactly how to do a thing than to put one's own intelligence to work to solve each individual problem as it arises!) Walker must be given credit for stating clearly that these markings were intended as helps toward the satisfactory projection of the material at hand; and perhaps he is not to be held wholly responsible for the fact that future generations were to place more emphasis on the markings and other mechanical devices than on the projection of material. Walker and his imitators, then, established what has been called the "mechanical school" in seeming opposition to Sheridan's "natural school." Thus began a schism which is only now disappearing.

Two other names must be mentioned in connection with the English Elocutionists of the eighteenth century. Although they were less prolific and influential than Sheridan and Walker, John Mason (1706–1763) and James Burgh (1714–1775) both wrote books which enjoyed considerable popularity. Mason's *An Essay on Elocution, or Pronunciation* (1748), the first book to include the word "Elocution" in its title, put heavy emphasis on the "right" management of the voice.

James Burgh was primarily a political philosopher whose interest in speech probably grew out of his political activities. In his book *The Art of Speaking* (1762), he discussed with some vehemence the rules for expressing "the principal Passions and Humors." This volume, which contained an anthology of readings, with the passions and humors carefully documented, was based on the theory that nature had given every passion its proper physical expression and that only by careful attention to the physical features, such as the eye, could the proper passion be projected.

To sum up, the closing years of the eighteenth century saw an increased interest in the use of voice and body in the oral presentation of literature. Sheridan had set up a "natural school," purportedly based on the "laws of nature"; while Walker had established a "mechanical school," based in fact on the same premises but more preoccupied with markings and charts. It is understandable that the followers of these men would tend to emphasize their differences rather than their similarities, and that some degree of confusion and dissension would result.

In the nineteenth century two names stand out above all others in the history of interpretation. The first is that of an American doctor, James Rush (1786–1869), a medical man turned speech teacher and lecturer. Dr. Rush confined himself almost entirely to the study of vocal projection. He believed that the management of the voice was in reality not an art but a science, and he went to great lengths to develop an appropriate vocabulary for that science. Indeed, much of his terminology has become standard among modern teachers of speech. He also went to great lengths in the title of his book, published in 1827: *The Philosophy of the Human Voice: Embracing Its Physiological History: Together with a System of Principles by Which Criticism in the Art of Elocution May Be Rendered Intelligible, and Instruction, Definite and Comprehensive, to Which Is Added a Brief Analysis of Song and Recitative.*

Dr. Rush developed elaborate charts and markings for pitch, force, abruptness, quality, and time. He was convinced that rules could be developed to govern the analysis of vocal technique, although he was careful to point out that the practice of these rules must be accompanied by concentration on the literature being read. This last bit of advice, however, was often forgotten by his more zealous and less discriminating followers; as a result, attention was focused even more sharply on markings and symbols. Nevertheless, Dr. Rush's use of appropriate scientific method and vocabulary and his studies of the mechanism of the human voice were valuable contributions to the field of speech.

The second significant name in nineteenth-century interpretation is François Delsarte (1811–1871). About the same time Dr. Rush's method was making its way in America, Delsarte was delivering lectures in France on elocution and calisthenics. He left no writings, but so strong was his influence that many of his students recorded his philosophy and system in great detail. The Delsarte system concerned itself entirely with bodily action, and it became an accepted complement to Dr. Rush's treatises on vocal management. Delsarte based his system on a philosophy of the interrelation of man's soul, mind, and body, and on a complicated and highly mystical concept of a corresponding triune relationship throughout the entire universe. Despite this philosophical premise, the system became mechanical in the extreme. The writings which reflect and interpret it are filled with elaborate charts and diagrams.

Delsarte, like Walker and Rush, suffered somewhat at the hands of his followers. One example of the perversion of a basically sound but inadequately expressed theory — that gestures must spring from the heart — was the notion that all gestures must start from the breastbone and sweep out in a graceful curve. This misconception persisted for generations. Although Delsarte's system in practice took on mechanical aspects that had some unfortunate results, modern teachers of speech have been greatly influenced by his concept of mind, soul (heart or emotions), and body working together.

Thus, almost simultaneously, Rush in America was setting up a scientific approach to vocal technique and Delsarte in France was teaching a philosophical approach to bodily action. Although both men were originally concerned with the artistic projection of materials, those whom they influenced tended often to concentrate on the techniques rather than on the reasons for the techniques. In this way the mechanical school, well established under the aegis of Walker's disciples, became even more firmly entrenched.

Near the close of the nineteenth century, the natural school received new impetus under the leadership of Samuel Silas Curry (1847–1921).

His first book, *The Province of Expression,* published in Boston in 1891, was based on the major premise that the mind, in order to express an idea, must actively hold that idea and thus dictate the appropriate means of expression. This theory he summed up in the admonition, "Think the thought!" It is understandable that such a phrase would catch the fancy of those who read his books and heard of his teachings — and equally understandable that it would lead to oversimplification, to the extent that Curry's fundamentally sound theory came to be popularized as "Think the thought and all things else will be added unto you." As a result, many teachers began to assert that the training of voice and body consisted of wholly artificial and mechanical procedures, and that comprehension of thought and active concentration on that thought would insure adequate projection of any material to an audience.

Admittedly, this idea came as a relief to those who had become weary of the exhibitionism that prevailed among the second- and third-generation advocates of the mechanical method. In an attempt to break more completely with the earlier artificialities, teachers even began to shy away from the term "elocution," with all its connotations, and to adopt instead Curry's term "expression." Thus, lessons in "elocution" became lessons in "expression."

One of the most interesting and influential teachers in America at the close of the century was Charles Wesley Emerson (1837–1908), founder of the Emerson College of Oratory, now Emerson College in Boston. His *Evolution of Expression* (1913) stressed vocal technique and gymnastics for their therapeutic value as well as for their contribution to the techniques of communicating literature.

By the end of the nineteenth century, then, three distinct groups had emerged: one which militantly carried on the traditions of the mechanical school; another which distrusted mechanics, relied upon the natural method, and developed in the direction of "think-the-thought"; and a third which was composed of a few independents who found some values in each camp and who attempted to blend the two approaches.

By the turn of the twentieth century, a number of colleges were offering courses in elocution or expression, but the average student did not usually include speech in his program of studies unless he was preparing himself for the ministry, politics, or law. Most of those who wished to do "platform work" as "readers" enrolled in private schools or studios. There they worked under teachers often three or four times removed from the originators of basically sound theories, and received instruction which, having filtered through several personalities, was strongly flavored by the individual teacher's own taste and understanding.

The first decade or so of the twentieth century was the era of the private, highly specialized school or studio of speech. Each had its own staff of teachers, most of whom had been trained by the head of that particular school. Each had its own course of study and its own special emphasis. And each prided itself on its independence and its difference from the others. Consequently, there was no common philosophy or methodology. Each school tended to emphasize its individuality rather than to work with the others toward solidarity and a unity of purpose among all teachers in the field.

Many who studied at these schools returned to their homes, framed their certificates, hung them on their walls, and opened their own studios, where they taught to the best of their ability what they had learned. Their students, in turn, acquired certificates and went out to spread the gospel as they understood it. Thus, of the thousands of teachers who were conducting classes and giving private lessons, very few had had an opportunity to receive sound training under the great leaders. As a result, the original principles and practices were continually watered down. Not only were teachers often imperfectly prepared, but they worked in comparative isolation, without professional associations and strong university departments of speech to serve as centers for the exchange of ideas. The better informed and more progressive teachers who studied under Curry and his contemporaries grew with the entire educational system, to become the outstanding men and women in the field of speech as a whole and in the more specialized area of interpretation. Others, however, continued to teach specific gesture, highly obtrusive vocal technique, and the use of materials of questionable literary merit, thus perpetuating to our own day not only the more regrettable excesses and misconceptions in vogue in the early years of the century, but also a confusion in terminology and in standards of performance.

An important link between the theorists and teachers of the nineteenth century and the present is *Principles of Vocal Expression* (1897), by William B. Chamberlain (1847–1903) and Solomon H. Clark (1861–1927). This book, acknowledging a deep indebtedness to Curry, stressed the interaction of mind and body and the control of "instincts" by reason. Clark was to make a more important contribution in his *Interpretation of the Printed Page* (1913), which helped to turn the attention of teachers and students from the mechanical techniques to the appreciation and analysis of the literature itself. His concept of "impression" as distinct from and prerequisite to "expression" was to become the basis of *The Art of Interpretative Speech* by Charles H. Woolbert and Severina E. Nelson, published in 1929.

Another book of the early twentieth century which enjoyed great popularity was *Natural Drills in Expression with Selections* (1909). The author, Arthur Edward Phillips (1867–1932), reflects much of Chamberlain's interest in paraphrase and tone drills, and the book was used extensively for many years in schools and colleges.

With the advance of the twentieth century, departments of speech grew in stature in the colleges and universities and became fully accepted members of the academic family. Many private schools also moved with the times, some of them burgeoning into degree-granting colleges. Speech training, freed from the cultist studio, flourished under the stimulating cross-winds of professional associations and the spur of more homogeneous standards. Ideas were pooled, theories argued, heritages re-evaluated. The student was nurtured not in one tenuous tradition but in a synthesis of many. Interpretation, which had long been inextricably bound up with public speaking, emerged from the strait jacket of the "reading" (which was not a reading at all, but a virtuoso exhibition of memory and technique) and re-oriented itself to the printed page.

It should by no means be assumed that the earlier teachers of elocution and expression had nothing of value to hand on to the latter-day student of oral interpretation. Most teachers today, when questioned about their approach to interpretation, are quick to say that they are "eclectic" in their method — that they select what seems sound from the theories of the past, balance these ingredients against one another, and blend them into a modern philosophy. This selectivity of approach is an indication of strength and maturity.

The modern interpreter believes in training both voice and body. He knows that his voice must be flexible and strong, and his articulation clear, if he is to do full justice to the material he has chosen. He knows, too, that his body must be trained to respond in harmony with his voice if both are to work together effectively.

He also believes in careful analysis of his material and in active concentration on that material when it is presented to an audience. In a sense, he reverts to the classical tradition of rhetoric in his insistence on the importance of understanding the elements of literary craftsmanship in the selection to be interpreted. He is concerned with the author's art — how he shapes the whole out of its parts.

This, then, is what we mean by saying that the modern concept of oral interpretation is eclectic. It is concerned with training the voice and body *in order that the material may be communicated effectively.* It borrows from the natural conversational method *in order that the material may be communicated unobtrusively.* It borrows from the "think-the-thought" school *in order that the material may be handled with intelligence and directness.* It is concerned with literary art *in order that the material may achieve its artistic purpose.* The modern interpreter makes use of his twofold instrument of voice and body, governed by an informed and disciplined mind, *in order that the material may call forth the desired intellectual, emotional, and aesthetic response from the audience.* In a word, he is concerned above all else with the material—with what the author has to say and how he says it.

✱ Bibliography

Aggertt, Otis J., and Elbert R. Bowen. *Communicative Reading.* Second Edition. New York: The Macmillan Company, 1963.

Bacon, Wallace A., and Robert S. Breen. *Literature as Experience.* New York: McGraw-Hill Book Co., 1959.

Chaytor, H. J. *From Script to Print: An Introduction to Medieval Vernacular Literature.* Second Impression. Cambridge: W. Heffer and Sons, Ltd., 1950.

Clark, Solomon Henry, and Maud May Babcock. *Interpretation of the Printed Page.* New York: Prentice-Hall, Inc., 1940.

Cobin, Martin. *Theory and Technique of Interpretation.* Englewood Cliffs, New Jersey: Prentice-Hall, Inc., 1959.

Cunningham, Cornelius Carman. *Literature as a Fine Art.* New York: The Ronald Press Company, 1941.

Curry, Samuel Silas. *Foundations of Expression, Studies and Problems for Developing the Voice, Body, and Mind in Reading and Speaking.* Boston: Expression Co., 1907.

Emerson, Charles Wesley. *Evolution of Expression. A Compilation of Selections Illustrating the Four Stages of Development in Art as Applied to Oratory.* 4 vols. Boston: Emerson College of Oratory, Publishing Department, 1905.

Geiger, Don. *Oral Interpretation and Literary Study.* San Francisco: Peter Van Vloten, 1958.

Geiger, Don. *The Sound, Sense, and Performance of Literature.* Chicago: Scott, Foresman and Company, 1963.

Grimes, Wilma H., and Alethea Smith Mattingly. *Interpretation: Writer-Reader-Audience.* San Francisco: Wadsworth Publishing Company, Inc., 1961.

Joseph, B. L. *Elizabethan Acting.* London: Oxford University Press, 1951.

Kenyon, Frederic G. *Books and Readers in Ancient Greece and Rome.* Second Edition. Oxford: The Clarendon Press, 1951.

Lowrey, Sara, and Gertrude E. Johnson. *Interpretative Reading.* Revised Edition. New York: Appleton-Century-Crofts, Inc., 1953.

Lynch, Gladys E., and Harold C. Crain. *Projects in Oral Interpretation.* New York: Henry Holt, 1959.

Mouat, Lawrence H. *Reading Literature Aloud.* New York: Oxford University Press, 1962.

Parrish, Wayland Maxwell. *Reading Aloud.* Third Edition. New York: The Ronald Press Company, 1953.

Phillips, Arthur Edward. *Natural Drills in Expression, with Selections, a Series of Exercises Colloquial and Classical, Based Upon the Principles of Reference to Experience and Comparison, and Chosen for their Practical Worth in Developing Power and Naturalness in Reading and Speaking. With Illustrative Selections for Practice.* Chicago: The Newton Company, 1920.

Robb, Mary Margaret. *Oral Interpretation of Literature in American Colleges and Universities.* New York: H. W. Wilson Company, 1941.

Smith, Joseph F., and James R. Linn. *Skill in Reading Aloud.* New York: Harper and Brothers, 1960.

Wallace, Karl R. (ed.). *History of Speech Education in America: Background Studies.* New York: Appleton-Century-Crofts, Inc., 1954.

Woolbert, Charles H., and Severina E. Nelson. *The Art of Interpretative Speech: Principles and Practices of Effective Reading.* Fourth Edition. New York: Appleton-Century-Crofts, Inc., 1956.

Unpublished Dissertations

Burns, Kenneth. "A Survey of the Contemporary Outlook Relative to the Basic Aspects of Oral Interpretation as Evidenced in Selected Writings in the Field." Northwestern University, Evanston, Illinois, 1952.

Coger, Leslie Irene. "A Comparison for the Oral Interpreter of the Teaching Methods of Curry and Stanislavsky." Northwestern University, Evanston, Illinois, 1952.

Laird, Dugan. "American and English Theories in the Natural Tradition of Oral Reading, 1880–1915." Northwestern University, Evanston, Illinois, 1952.

Mattingly, Alethea Smith. "The Mechanical School of Oral Reading in England, 1761–1821." Northwestern University, Evanston, Illinois, 1954.

Vandraegen, Daniel E. "The Natural School of Oral Reading in England, 1748–1828." Northwestern University, Evanston, Illinois, 1949.

INDEX OF TOPICS

INDEX OF QUOTED MATERIAL

ABCDEFGHIJ-BP-743210/698765